The Joan Palevsky  Imprint in Classical Literature

In honor of beloved Virgil—

"O degli altri poeti onore e lume . . ."

—Dante, *Inferno*

The publisher gratefully acknowledges the generous support of the Classical Literature Endowment Fund of the University of California Press Foundation, which was established by a major gift from Joan Palevsky.

A State of Mixture

TRANSFORMATION OF THE CLASSICAL HERITAGE
Peter Brown, General Editor

I. *Art and Ceremony in Late Antiquity,* by Sabine G. MacCormack

II. *Synesius of Cyrene: Philosopher-Bishop,* by Jay Alan Bregman

III. *Theodosian Empresses: Women and Imperial Dominion in Late Antiquity,* by Kenneth G. Holum

IV. *John Chrysostom and the Jews: Rhetoric and Reality in the Late Fourth Century,* by Robert L. Wilken

V. *Biography in Late Antiquity: The Quest for the Holy Man,* by Patricia Cox

VI. *Pachomius: The Making of a Community in Fourth-Century Egypt,* by Philip Rousseau

VII. *Change in Byzantine Culture in the Eleventh and Twelfth Centuries,* by A. P. Kazhdan and Ann Wharton Epstein

VIII. *Leadership and Community in Late Antique Gaul,* by Raymond Van Dam

IX. *Homer the Theologian: Neoplatonist Allegorical Reading and the Growth of the Epic Tradition,* by Robert Lamberton

X. *Procopius and the Sixth Century,* by Averil Cameron

XI. *Guardians of Language: The Grammarian and Society in Late Antiquity,* by Robert A. Kaster

XII. *Civic Coins and Civic Politics in the Roman East, A.D. 180–275,* by Kenneth Harl

XIII. *Holy Women of the Syrian Orient,* introduced and translated by Sebastian P. Brock and Susan Ashbrook Harvey

XIV. *Gregory the Great: Perfection in Imperfection,* by Carole Straw

XV. *"Apex Omnium": Religion in the "Res gestae" of Ammianus,* by R. L. Rike

XVI. *Dioscorus of Aphrodito: His Work and His World,* by Leslie S. B. MacCoull

XVII. *On Roman Time: The Codex-Calendar of 354 and the Rhythms of Urban Life in Late Antiquity,* by Michele Renee Salzman

XVIII. *Asceticism and Society in Crisis: John of Ephesus and "The Lives of the Eastern Saints,"* by Susan Ashbrook Harvey

XIX. *Barbarians and Politics at the Court of Arcadius,* by Alan Cameron and Jacqueline Long, with a contribution by Lee Sherry

XX. *Basil of Caesarea,* by Philip Rousseau

XXI. *In Praise of Later Roman Emperors: The Panegyrici Latini,* introduction, translation, and historical commentary by C. E. V. Nixon and Barbara Saylor Rodgers

XXII. *Ambrose of Milan: Church and Court in a Christian Capital,* by Neil B. McLynn

XXIII. *Public Disputation, Power, and Social Order in Late Antiquity,* by Richard Lim

XXIV. *The Making of a Heretic: Gender, Authority, and the Priscillianist Controversy,* by Virginia Burrus

XXV. *Symeon the Holy Fool: Leontius's "Life" and the Late Antique City,* by Derek Krueger

XXVI. *The Shadows of Poetry: Vergil in the Mind of Augustine*, by Sabine MacCormack
XXVII. *Paulinus of Nola: Life, Letters, and Poems*, by Dennis E. Trout
XXVIII. *The Barbarian Plain: Saint Sergius between Rome and Iran*, by Elizabeth Key Fowden
XXIX. *The Private Orations of Themistius*, translated, annotated, and introduced by Robert J. Penella
XXX. *The Memory of the Eyes: Pilgrims to Living Saints in Christian Late Antiquity*, by Georgia Frank
XXXI. *Greek Biography and Panegyric in Late Antiquity*, edited by Tomas Hägg and Philip Rousseau
XXXII. *Subtle Bodies: Representing Angels in Byzantium*, by Glenn Peers
XXXIII. *Wandering, Begging Monks: Spiritual Authority and the Promotion of Monasticism in Late Antiquity*, by Daniel Caner
XXXIV. *Failure of Empire: Valens and the Roman State in the Fourth Century* A.D., by Noel Lenski
XXXV. *Merovingian Mortuary Archaeology and the Making of the Early Middle Ages*, by Bonnie Effros
XXXVI. *Quṣayr 'Amra: Art and the Umayyad Elite in Late Antique Syria*, by Garth Fowden
XXXVII. *Holy Bishops in Late Antiquity: The Nature of Christian Leadership in an Age of Transition*, by Claudia Rapp
XXXVIII. *Encountering the Sacred: The Debate on Christian Pilgrimage in Late Antiquity*, by Brouria Bitton-Ashkelony
XXXIX. *There Is No Crime for Those Who Have Christ: Religious Violence in the Christian Roman Empire*, by Michael Gaddis
XL. *The Legend of Mar Qardagh: Narrative and Christian Heroism in Late Antique Iraq*, by Joel Thomas Walker
XLI. *City and School in Late Antique Athens and Alexandria*, by Edward J. Watts
XLII. *Scenting Salvation: Ancient Christianity and the Olfactory Imagination*, by Susan Ashbrook Harvey
XLIII. *Man and the Word: The Orations of* Himerius, edited by Robert J. Penella
XLIV. *The Matter of the Gods*, by Clifford Ando
XLV. *The Two Eyes of the Earth: Art and Ritual of Kingship between Rome and Sasanian Iran*, by Matthew P. Canepa
XLVI. *Riot in Alexandria: Tradition and Group Dynamics in Late Antique Pagan and Christian Communities*, by Edward J. Watts
XLVII. *Peasant and Empire in Christian North Africa*, by Leslie Dossey
XLVIII. *Theodoret's People: Social Networks and Religious Conflict in Late Roman Syria*, by Adam M. Schor
XLIX. *Sons of Hellenism, Fathers of the Church: Emperor Julian, Gregory of Nazianzus, and the Vision of Rome*, by Susanna Elm

L. *Shenoute of Atripe and the Uses of Poverty: Rural Patronage, Religious Conflict, and Monasticism in Late Antique Egypt,* by Ariel G. López

LI. *Doctrine and Power: Theological Controversy and Christian Leadership in the Later Roman Empire,* by Carlos R. Galvão-Sobrinho

LII. *Crisis of Empire: Doctrine and Dissent at the End of Late Antiquity,* by Phil Booth

LIII. *The Final Pagan Generation,* by Edward J. Watts

LIV. *The Mirage of the Saracen: Christians and Nomads in the Sinai Peninsula in Late Antiquity,* by Walter D. Ward

LV. *Missionary Stories and the Formation of the Syriac Churches,* by Jeanne-Nicole Mellon Saint-Laurent

LVI. *A State of Mixture: Christians, Zoroastrians, and Iranian Political Culture in Late Antiquity,* by Richard E. Payne

A State of Mixture

Christians, Zoroastrians, and Iranian Political Culture in Late Antiquity

Richard E. Payne

UNIVERSITY OF CALIFORNIA PRESS

University of California Press, one of the most distinguished university presses in the United States, enriches lives around the world by advancing scholarship in the humanities, social sciences, and natural sciences. Its activities are supported by the UC Press Foundation and by philanthropic contributions from individuals and institutions. For more information, visit www.ucpress.edu.

University of California Press
Oakland, California

© 2015 by The Regents of the University of California

First paperback printing 2016

Library of Congress Cataloging-in-Publication Data

Payne, Richard E., author.
    A state of mixture : Christians, Zoroastrians, and Iranian political culture in late Antiquity / Richard E. Payne.
    p. cm. — (Transformation of the classical heritage ; LVI)
    Includes bibliographical references and index.
    ISBN 978-0-520-28619-1 (cloth: alk. paper)
    ISBN 978-0-520-29245-1 (pbk.: alk. paper)
    ISBN 978-0-520-96153-1 (electronic)
    1. Christianity and other religions—Zoroastrianism. 2. Christianity and politics—Iran—History—To 1500. 3. Zoroastrianism—Relations—Christianity. 4. Christians—Iran—Social conditions—To 1500. 5. Iran—Civilization—To 640. I. Title. II. Series: Transformation of the classical heritage ; 56.
BR128.Z6P39 2015
275.5'03—dc23   2015003679

24 23 22 21 20 19 18 17 16
10 9 8 7 6 5 4 3 2 1

Till Michael, Nicholas, och Maria

*Människor, samlen icke skatter
som göra er till tiggare;
samlen rikedomar
som giva er konungamakt.
Skänken edra barn en skönhet
den människoögon ej sett,
skänken edra barn en kraft
att bryta himlens portar upp.*
—EDITH SÖDERGRAN, "SAMLEN ICKE
 GULD OCH ÄDELSTENAR," 1918

CONTENTS

A Note on Names, Translations, and Transliterations   xi
Acknowledgments   xiii

    Introduction   1

1. The Myth of Zoroastrian Intolerance: Violence and the Terms of Christian Inclusion   23

2. Belonging to a Land: Christians and Zoroastrians in the Iranian Highlands   59

3. Christian Law Making and Iranian Political Practice: The Reforms of Mar Aba   93

4. Creating a Christian Aristocracy: Hagiography and Empire in Northern Mesopotamia   127

5. The Christian Symbolics of Power in a Zoroastrian Empire   164

    Conclusion   199

Notes   205
Bibliography   237
Index   293

A NOTE ON NAMES, TRANSLATIONS,
AND TRANSLITERATIONS

Wherever possible, the names of persons, places, and sources have been given in the Anglicized form that has gained the widest currency in scholarly literature. Middle Persian names, however, have been rendered in a simplified version of the original instead of the commonly used Greek or New Persian forms: Husraw rather than Chosroes (after the Greek) or Khosrow (after the New Persian), and Shapur rather than the strictly transliterated Šāhpuhr. The same principle applies to Syriac names. The goal has been to make the names as accessible as possible to an audience unfamiliar with these languages. In keeping with the conventions of Islamic history, Arabic and New Persian sources have been given in transliterated versions of the original titles, and the names of their authors have been transliterated.

All translations are the author's, unless reference to an English translation has been indicated with a foreword slash following the page number(s) of the source. Some forward slashes, however, direct the reader to a translation in another language, which has been taken into account in the formulation of the English version. Editions and translations of sources are to be found in the bibliography. All Bible quotes are from the New International Version.

For the transliteration of Middle Persian, the system of D. N. MacKenzie, *A Concise Pahlavi Dictionary* (London: Oxford University Press, 1971) has been followed. For the transliteration of Syriac, the simplified schema of the online journal *Hugoye* has been adopted, with two modifications: the use of ḥ and š to transliterate the letters heth and shin, respectively. Importantly, Middle Persian words in the plural appear in the singular form—without the grammatically optional plural ending -ān—to emphasize species rather than multiplicity.

ACKNOWLEDGMENTS

A State of Mixture is the product of generous mentoring. At Red Rocks Community College, Kerry Edwards introduced me to the philosophical stance that distracted me from climbing and cars and led me to the study of history. Only later would I learn its name: historical materialism. My teachers at the University of Colorado–Boulder not only encouraged me to pursue an academic career but also gave me the tools with which to do so. Susan Prince fostered my interest in ancient languages and set a standard for philological rigor that I have tried, haltingly, to achieve. Scott Bruce unveiled the world of late antiquity in all its dynamism and tutored me in the arts of historiography. He showed me how history, like literature, could serve as a vehicle for exploring our collective condition, potential, and limits. His words and work continue to animate my own. Noel Lenski gave me an appreciation of ancient politics, administration, and law that has only grown over time. In the Department of History at Princeton University, I was fortunate to have had four mentors who contributed to my formation in distinct, if complementary, ways. Peter Brown tested the empirical, analytical, and imaginative limits of my writing at every stage, with his characteristic sagacity and generosity. John Haldon provided models for the writing of social history on the basis of recalcitrant sources. Bill Jordan not only exemplified the practice of historiography but also reminded me what was at stake in the discipline when my will flagged. Patricia Crone of the Institute for Advanced Study enthusiastically accepted me as a student when I departed from the more comfortable confines of the Mediterranean for the Iranian world. Her critical support has been unfailingly generous. Maria Macuch welcomed me for a semester at the Institut für Iranistik at the Freie Universität in Berlin and provided an indispensable introduction to Iranian philology.

Finally, Peter Sarris of Trinity College, Cambridge University, guided the development of my dissertation into a more expansive study. Each of these individuals played a determinative role in the shaping of this book.

Institutional support for research and writing came from Princeton University, Dumbarton Oaks / The Trustees of Harvard University, Phi Beta Kappa, the Deutscher Akademischer Austausch Dienst, Universität Konstanz, Trinity College, the University of Cambridge, Mount Holyoke College, the Institute for the Study of the Ancient World at New York University, the University of Chicago, the Oriental Institute, and the Neubauer Family Foundation. Trinity College extended me a research fellowship that allowed me to embark on new research and to expand the project beyond the limits of my dissertation. Mount Holyoke offered me not only a research leave but also one of the most stimulating environments I have encountered. Its faculty and students constituted the ideal incubator for this book. The writing of the manuscript was largely completed at the Institute for the Study of the Ancient World during my tenure of a Visiting Research Scholarship in 2012–13, and I benefited greatly from ISAW's expansion of the confines—methodological as well as geographical—of the ancient world. From the summer of 2013, the University of Chicago, its Oriental Institute, and the Neubauer Family Foundation have supported my research within an uncommonly committed and critical community of scholars. It has been a privilege to revise the manuscript in their company.

This book has evolved as much from the conversations I have had in classes, conferences, cafés, and bars as from my solitary labors. My cohort in Princeton included a group of scholars working in late antiquity who taught me a great deal: Damián Fernández, Nancy Khalek, Daniel Schwartz, Uriel Simonsohn, and Jack Tannous. In Cambridge and London, I found a similarly enthusiastic community: Phil Booth, Beci Dobbin, Matthew Dal Santo, Myles Lavan, Michael Ledger-Lomas, Sarah Savant, David Todd, and Philip Wood. Thanks to the invitations of Walter Pohl and Helmut Reimitz, scholars in Vienna took me in directions I could not have foreseen, especially Gerda Heydemann and Roland Steinacher. Samra Azarnouche guided me on Middle Persian matters and corrected many missteps. Particularly influential and helpful has been the friendship of John Weisweiler, who has read, discussed, and refined nearly every argument to be found within the following pages. Elizabeth Campbell joined me on a sometimes quixotic search for Sasanian sites in northern Iraq, and Narmen Ali Amen shared her ongoing fieldwork in the region. Senior scholars in various fields provided guidance and opportunities to present my work at critical stages: Cliff Ando, Adam Becker, Matthew Canepa, Michael Cook, James Howard-Johnston, Walter Kaegi, Hubert Kaufhold, Hugh Kennedy, Bruce Lincoln, Michael Maas, Arietta Papaconstantinou, Michael Penn, Walter Pohl, Parvaneh Pourshariati, Helmut Reimitz, Chase Robinson, Sebastian Schmidt-Hofner, Shaul Shaked, Nicholas Sims-Williams, Matt Stolper, Joel Walker, and Dorothea Weltecke. Conversations with Joan Cocks, Kavita Datla, and Monica Ringer shaped my thinking on fundamental questions of political theory and comparative history. Phil Booth, Jamie Kreiner, Sergei Minov, Seth Richardson, Alexander Schilling, and Kyle Smith have shared works in advance of publication that have had a substantial impact on my thinking. Emily Hammer carefully produced the maps. Rich Heffron assisted in the preparation of the bibliography. I extend special thanks to Samra Azarnouche, Scott Bruce, Damián Fernández, Bruce Lincoln, Michael Maas, and John Weisweiler for reading penultimate drafts of chapters. Their comments resulted in significant changes. Lesha Shah provided the assistance and, not least, the affection that brought the project to completion.

The two guiding lights in my life flickered out during the writing of this book. My grandmother Theresa Ferrell (née Pronovost) not only inspired me to take books seriously but also taught me to view past and present from the vantage point of her home, the Flathead Indian Reservation in Montana, to one side of history's victors. My father, Richard Payne, encouraged my work at every stage and insisted that hustle, not luck, was the key to success. Their legacies are omnipresent in the following pages. The Liljeström family too played a fundamental role in the development of the project. Mikael patiently explained the nuances of Eastern Christian thought and practice to me when I first developed an interest in late antiquity. Helena endured—and even enjoyed—a half-dozen transcontinental and transatlantic moves and shared a delight in the art, architecture, and landscapes of the Middle East, from Binbirkilise in 2002 to Svaneti in 2009. Without her support, this book would never have been written. I have learned the most from my children: from Michael that Sinai is just another mountain, from Nicholas that the Bosporus is best for brunch, and from Maria that even the most grandiose temples (the Temple of Heaven!) are dull in comparison with the kids who play in their courtyards. Above all, they bring me hope and wonder, essential instruments in the historian's tool kit. I dedicate *A State of Mixture* to them.

Vänge
August 2014

Introduction

A BISHOP AT THE IMPERIAL PALACE

In late antiquity, Iranian political culture developed a distinctive approach to the problem of religious difference characteristic of the era. Throughout the Mediterranean and the Near East, monotheist faiths sought to create social and political communities united around their respective truths from the second century onward. In ancient cultures accustomed more to diversity than uniformity, these communities were novel not merely for their claims of exclusively possessing true religion but also for their ambitions to bring all of humanity within their folds. Adversarial toward unbelievers, they had enormous potential for social and political disruption. Christianity was the most successful of such faiths, at least until the rise of Islam. The marriage of Christianity and Roman imperialism after the conversion of Constantine the Great increasingly transformed the Roman Empire into a community of orthodox believers, in which the positions of polytheists, Jews, and heretics became precarious. The triumph of Christianity over paganism in the Roman world provides the prevailing image of monotheist success: the repression of unbelievers in a zero-sum contest for the truth. In Iran, the plot lines of Christian success converge to tell a strikingly different story. The Christians of the Iranian world, known as East Syrians, neither appropriated the imperial apparatus nor supplanted the imperial religion, Zoroastrianism, a set of beliefs and rituals practiced in Iran and Central Asia from circa 1000 BCE. They instead cooperated with a Zoroastrian ruling elite and participated in Zoroastrian institutions. Rather than seek to exclude religious others from their political communities, East Syrian Christians negotiated the terms of their own inclusion in a Zoroastrian political community. At the same time, Zoroastrian rulers and religious authorities established legitimate positions for Christians in the Iranian political order as well as boundaries between the two religions that facilitated their coexistence and cooperation. Zoroastrian and Christian elites, institutions, and symbols came to commingle in a political culture that the present book calls "a state of mixture," employing a metaphor current in contemporaneous Iranian political thought. The politics of mixture emerged and evolved in the course of sustained encounters between Zoroastrians and Christians in a variety of spaces, ranging from provincial landscapes and cities to the imperial court. It depended as much on Zoroastrian innovation to include a previously unknown religious other as on Christian adaptation to an empire that could not be converted. To begin a history of this political culture, a particularly vivid episode of mixture—that of a Christian bishop in the palace of a Zoroastrian ruler—offers an example of the encounters in which Zoroastrians and Christians innovated and adapted to maintain the relations that allowed Christian communities to flourish in a Zoroastrian empire.

In 596, the Church of the East, a network of Christian communities that extended across the Iranian Empire from South Arabia to Afghanistan, obtained a new leader. A monk named Sabrisho, famed for receiving visions and performing miracles in the wilderness of the Zagros Mountains, was made bishop at the royal court, in the imperial cities of Seleucia-Ctesiphon, along the Tigris River to the south of modern Baghdad.[1] The selection of a monk as the leader of the East Syrian Christian community was, according to contemporaries, the initiative of the king of kings Husraw II, the ruler of Iran from 590 to 628.[2] Like the other members of the Sasanian dynasty, who ruled Iran from the beginning of the empire in 226 until its collapse in the face of conquering Arab Muslims in 636, Husraw II was an avowed Zoroastrian, an adherent of the ancient religion that provided the ideological and infrastructural foundations of Iranian imperialism in late antiquity. The Zoroastrian king of kings nevertheless cultivated a particularly intimate relationship with a wonder-working monk and personally raised him to the most powerful bishopric in Iran. For their part, East Syrian religious leaders such as Sabrisho regarded Zoroastrianism as a deviant polytheism that their faith would ultimately transcend and, in the process, eradicate. They were, in this respect, heirs to the legacy of the triumphalist Christianity of the Roman Empire. East Syrian Christian representations of Zoroastrian antagonism toward Christians and vice versa have colored modern studies of the Iranian Empire, which have largely presumed that religious conflict pervaded its diverse society. It was, however, Zoroastrian rulers who established the political foundations of Christian communities in Iran. Sasanian kings of kings recognized and sanctioned the authority of ecclesiastical leaders in their empire almost as soon as Christian institutions became visible in their territories, raising bishops to positions of prestige at court from 410. Under their rule, Christian and Zoroastrian institutions evolved in tandem rather than in conflict, as ruling Zoroastrians and East Syrian elites developed parameters of interaction that permitted the institutions of both religions—as well as Judaism—to flourish without eroding the boundaries and foundations of the imperial cult. The dynamic processes that integrated Christians into a Zoroastrian political system form the subject of this book. As an apex of East Syrian fortunes in Iran, the elevation of Sabrisho reveals not simply the exalted political status that the Church of the East had attained but also the ongoing negotiation of institutional relationships and boundaries that attended the rise of Christianity in a Zoroastrian empire.

The arrival of the new bishop in the capital was an occasion of celebration for the churches, the court, and an urban populace that included Christians, Jews, and Zoroastrians. For the varied audiences of Seleucia-Ctesiphon, the ceremonies attending the elevation of the monk-bishop displayed the interdependence of the Church of the East and the Iranian Empire. Sabrisho was enthroned, with the express permission of the king of kings, in the patriarchal church of Weh-Ardashir, known in Syriac as Kokhe, one of the constituent cities of the capital and the center of thriving Christian and Jewish communities as well as the East Syrian ecclesiastical leadership. After the liturgical consecration of the bishop, the soldiers of the king of kings led a procession through crowds of the admiring and the curious across the Tigris River to the royal palace at Ctesiphon.[3] At this late Sasanian palace, known as the Ayvan-e Kisra, the king of kings received Sabrisho amid the glittering lamps, silk tapestries, and exotic incense in the throne room, as if the bishop were on par with the greatest aristocratic warriors of the empire or an envoy of the Roman emperor.[4] From Husraw II, Sabrisho obtained the sanction needed to wield authority over the communities of the Church of the East, whose boundaries were coterminus with those of the empire. The authority of the patriarchs of Seleucia-Ctesiphon depended on the support of the Zoroastrian kings of kings no less than the authority of the patriarchs of Rome, Alexandria, Antioch, Jerusalem, and Constantinople depended on the support of the Christian Roman emperors.

The newly consecrated patriarch arrived at court in an entirely unconventional way: on foot. Husraw II had dispatched royal cavalrymen to deliver him to the palace on horseback, in the manner appropriate to an elite male representative of Iran. To ride upon a horse, even in the streets of the capital, was to display one's membership in the aristocratic order. For Sabrisho's journey across the Tigris, the king of kings had lent his own horse, a high honor in a culture in which elite male identities were often intertwined with those of their personal steeds. The patriarch refused the favor: "Long live the king! But I am not mounting the beast. It is not permitted for me to see him, let alone to mount him, and I am also no good at horsemanship [al-farūsiyya]."[5] The king of kings insisted, ordering the cavalrymen forcibly to install the patriarch on the mount. The holy man nevertheless commanded the beast to remain still in the name of Christ, and "the most agile of horses" refused to budge.[6] Sabrisho made his way to court on foot, a painstaking journey of three hours through swarming crowds that even the royal cavalrymen could scarcely beat into submission. He exchanged the style of an aristocrat for the humble manner of a monk. Represented and recalled as a miracle, the episode showcased the ability of the ascetic to draw on supernatural powers, while clearly distinguishing the spiritual authority of the bishop from the worldly authority of the king of kings. Even if the successful patriarch depended on the court in mundane affairs, the spiritual source of his authority resided beyond its remit, in the Christian God. Such a distinction permitted Sabrisho, as well as other East Syrian bishops, to recognize the authority of the Zoroastrian ruler and to cooperate intimately with the court without diminishing the authority they attained through prayer and ascetic practice. In arriving barefoot at the Ayvan-e Kisra, the patriarch simultaneously acknowledged the sovereignty of the king of kings and represented the transcendent nature of a religious community that retained spiritual autonomy even in its subordination to imperial rule in the world.

The consecration of the patriarch in 596 embodied the political theology of the architects of Christian communities in the Iranian Empire. The early seventh-century authors of this account, preserved in the early medieval *Chronicle of Seert*, were ecclesiastical leaders in Weh-Ardashir, at the heart of Iran, and they expressed in narrative a vision of community that sustained churches throughout the Iranian world in late antiquity. They stood at the culmination of an East Syrian tradition of political thought that had come to recognize the legitimacy of the kings of kings as secular rulers devoid of religious significance except as instruments of the Christian God, on the model of the Achaemenians in the Hebrew Bible.[7] Husraw I (r. 525–76), for example, was designated a new Cyrus. The rise of Christianity in the first millennium has typically been viewed from the perspective of empires and kingdoms whose rulers converted to the faith, such as Constantine, Ezana, Trdat, or Clovis, and facilitated the diffusion of its institutions within these realms. The case of the Church of the East in Iran provides an opportunity to consider how Christian institutions took shape, expanded, and accumulated social, cultural, and economic capital in a non-Christian political system. Receiving the highest honors of the empire, in the company of Christian elites with exalted positions at court, Sabrisho exemplified the success with which the Syrians integrated themselves into Iranian political networks and institutions. It is the worldly attainments of East Syrian communities that the following chapters seek to explain. The account of Sabrisho suggests that a negotiation of boundaries and roles accompanied every such attainment. In distancing himself from the empire while embracing its power, the monk-bishop drew a boundary that defined a role as a leader of the Christian community acting in concert with the Zoroastrian ruler. Husraw II, for his part, allowed the patriarch to demonstrate his religious powers publicly and to demarcate his spiritual authority, as long as he ultimately arrived at the palace in recognition of imperial sovereignty. According to the authors of the account, patriarch and king of kings made plain that relations between Christians and Zoroastrians were continually being redefined and recalibrated, through the symbolic actions of their respective leaders.

The virtuoso performance of Sabrisho offers an ideal point of departure for a study of how Zoroastrian authorities located Christians within their social and political order and how Christians created places for themselves in a political culture not of their own making. Myriad negotiations attended the construction of churches, shrines, and monasteries, the elevation of bishops, and, most important, the entry of Christian elites into the ranks of the imperial aristocracy. The account of Sabrisho recalls only one such encounter, from a frankly sectarian perspective, obscuring as well as revealing the circumstances that allowed Christians to become so powerful at the court of Husraw II. Framed melodramatically as an encounter between saint and sovereign, it gives worldly Christian aristocrats a sideline role and ignores the Zoroastrian aristocrats known to have been predominant at court. Husraw II himself appears only as an admirer of the holy man, playing the role of the secular king of kings that East Syrian political theology ascribed to him. From this perspective, the account is entirely characteristic of East Syrian literature as a whole, which ecclesiastical authors produced largely for their own use as supports for their claims to leadership and their respective visions of community. They presented events in binary terms, either of Christianity in conflict with Zoroastrianism or of Christianity in cooperation with a secularized, sanitized Sasanian dynasty.

This book aims to escape, insofar as the sources allow, the witting and unwitting deceptions of ecclesiastical authors, with a view to recovering the social and political circumstances of worldly Christians and the perspectives of the Zoroastrian elites whose positions were always supreme in Iranian political culture. It substitutes a triangular relationship among ecclesiastical leaders, Christian secular elites, and Zoroastrian authorities in place of the binaries that East Syrian texts rhetorically constructed. The goal is not to unmask the agendas of East Syrian authors and leaders but rather to demonstrate the interplay of their literary constructions with the shifting social and political structures and relationships in their communities. Chapters 2, 3, and 4 show how East Syrian Christians articulated their social and political status in Iran through the selective appropriation of Iranian ideas, institutions, and practices, in implicit or explicit conversation with their Zoroastrian counterparts. At the same time, the approach of Zoroastrian elites toward the Christians in their empire requires reconstruction. Chapters 1 and 5 show how Zoroastrians drew upon their conceptual resources to establish and innovate the terms of Christian inclusion. Whether landed aristocrats or ascetics, East Syrian Christians collectively and individually defined and claimed positions for themselves within the room for maneuver that the Zoroastrian elite afforded them, with as much adaptive improvisation as the monk-bishop Sabrisho exhibited.

ĒRĀNŠAHR: A ZOROASTRIAN EMPIRE

The empire over which Husraw II ruled was known in Middle Persian as Ērānšahr, "the Iranian Empire," the most enduring and territorially extensive imperial system in the ancient Near East (see map 1). It had its origins in the Parthian kingdom of Fars, in southwestern Iran. In the first two decades of the third century CE, the ruler of the region, one of the constituent kingdoms of the Parthian Empire, eschewed Parthian overlordship and subordinated Fars, Khuzestan, and Mesopotamia. With the subjugation of the Parthian king of kings in 224, the eastern Iranian kingdoms also recognized the suzerainty of the ruler of Fars, Ardashir I, who was crowned the king of kings of an empire, designated Ērānšahr, that extended from Northeast Arabia to Bactria.[8] The extent and nature of Iranian control over its Central Asian, Caucasian, and Arabian frontiers fluctuated in the following centuries. What is remarkable to the historian of ancient empires, nevertheless, is the integrity of Iran over four centuries, until the beginning of the Islamic conquests. The geographical, social, and cultural diversity of the territories that Ardashir I and his successors placed under the authority of a single ruling house, the Sasanian dynasty, was dizzying. The Zagros Mountains bifurcated the empire into the highlands of the Iranian Plateau and the lowlands of Mesopotamia, and the absence of a central sea like the Mediterranean made sluggish overland routes the primary means of transportation and communication along its roughly twenty-five-hundred-kilometer (sixteen-hundred-mile) axis.[9] The various Parthian sub-kingdoms that Iran now encompassed possessed their own distinct political traditions and aristocracies whose symbolic and material resources could rival those of the ruling house.[10] The inhabitants of the empire, including elites, spoke a variety of languages ranging from Armenian to Bactrian, which developed their own literary and scribal traditions. The Middle Persian language and scripts that the ruling house employed never displaced provincial languages, even if the courtly tongue had a significant impact on their vocabularies, as we will see in chapter 2. Moreover, even as the Iranian court promoted the Zoroastrian religion, the cults of its inhabitants remained as varied as their languages and indeed seem only to have grown more disparate with the emergence of Christianity, Rabbinic Judaism, Manichaeism, and Mandaeism, the religions characteristic of late antiquity.

Zoroastrianism, known to its ancient adherents as the Good Religion, was the primary means through which the Sasanians institutionally unified their diverse, geographically disconnected territories. If scholars have long sought anachronistically to distinguish between a Zoroastrian "church" and a secular Sasanian state, Iranian religious and political institutions appear everywhere entwined.[11] The very name of the empire, Ērānšahr, announced the inextricability of the court from the religion. It refers to the homeland of Zoroaster in the Avesta, the orally recited traditions of Zoroastrian ritual, ethics, cosmology, and myth that evolved from

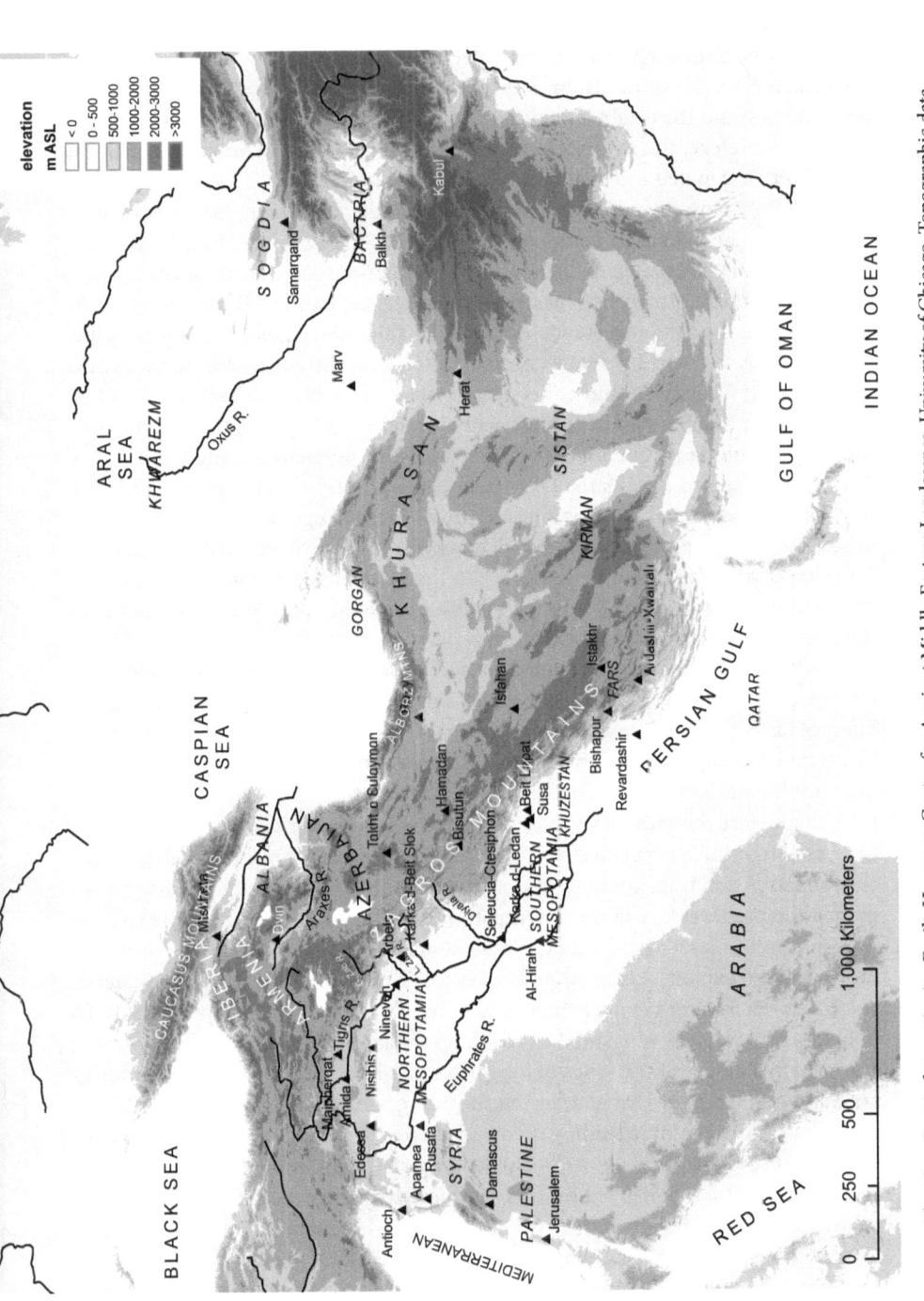

MAP 1. The Near East in late antiquity. Emily Hammer, Center for Ancient Middle Eastern Landscapes, University of Chicago. Topographic data from GTOPO30, available from the U.S. Geological Survey.

circa 1000 BCE through the Parthian period.[12] The land of Ayriana Vaējah, the mythical forerunner of Ērānšahr, was the central region of a world that comprised seven climes, and the origin of legitimate political power and civilization.[13] Its rulers were, therefore, the sovereigns of the earth. In the third century, the term for Iranian, ēr, designated a genealogical connection with the mythical rulers of Ayriana Vaējah / Ērānšahr, and this book uses the adjective in the same mythical-historical rather than ethnonationalist sense. In claiming to rule Ērānšahr, Ardashir I, with the assistance of the Zoroastrian religious specialists in his retinue, revived a mythical history as a model for the emergent empire. The Sasanians considered themselves the successors not of the Parthians but rather of the primordial sovereigns of the world, who, according to the Zoroastrian tradition, had ruled from Ayriana Vaējah. As such, they were instruments of the suzerain deity Ohrmazd and the ancillary gods through whom the restoration of the material world, including its human population, to a state of cosmic perfection could be achieved. The early Sasanians articulated their cosmological roles in inscriptions and rock reliefs that represented them as allies of the Zoroastrian gods, in what was recognizable to contemporaries as a sharp break from the hybrid Partho-Hellenistic tradition of kingship then predominant in the Near East.[14] In the self-conception of its ruling elites, the Iranian Empire was a cosmological project, whose institutions were rooted in a mythical-historical past.

The ideology of Ērānšahr entailed a set of social, political, and economic institutions in addition to Zoroastrian kingship that permitted the authority of the kings of kings to penetrate their vast territories to an extent previously unimaginable. A new, rapidly evolving and expanding class of religious specialists tended the fire temples and judicial courts through which a distinctively Zoroastrian society took shape. Fire temples served as sites not only for the performance of a normative version of the Yasna ritual, the central rite of Zoroastrianism, but also for the consolidation and transmission of aristocratic landholdings through pious endowments, the predecessors of the waqf institutions that have played crucial roles in Muslim economies.[15] As the economic possibilities of such endowments were ever more widely exploited, the aristocracies of the empire found their material resources increasingly intertwined with the Zoroastrian priestly elite, which upheld cosmological kingship. Zoroastrian religious specialists served as the authoritative judges of the kings of kings, developing a complex system of inheritance and marriage law that guaranteed the intergenerational transfer of wealth for aristocratic households, a leading theme of chapter 3. Whether to criminal offenders or to disputants, the *mowbed*—the leading ritual and judicial authorities in a region—and other priestly officials administered justice believed ultimately to derive from the authority of the royal house, as well as from their religious expertise. A calendar of Zoroastrian feasts offered occasions for the convening—for purposes of political communication—of the aristocracies of the empire whom geography generally kept at a distance from one another. Zoroastrian priestly elites, moreover, developed a body of literature, especially mythical historiography and *andarz*, "political guidance," that provided the court with a potent discourse for discussing and debating the nature of just political power, as well as media through which to communicate imperial claims. The practice of Iranian imperialism was inconceivable without the institutions of the Good Religion.

Yet the progressive development of Zoroastrian institutions of empire in no way hindered the contemporaneous diffusion of the institutions of other religions, particularly Christianity, in Iranian territories. In the course of Sasanian history, Christian churches were established in every region and in seemingly every major settlement. In some regions where the religion became predominant, the Christianization of the leading aristocratic houses took place before their incorporation into Iran. The Caucasian kingdoms of Armenia and Iberia were converted at the hands of their respective monarchs—Trdat and Mirian, notionally subordinate to the kings of kings—in the early fourth century, upward of a century before their direct inclusion in the empire.[16] In these regions, the installation of fire temples and a Zoroastrian ruling elite in the 450s posed few obstacles to the expansion of the Caucasian churches, whose ranks and ecclesiastical structures continued to grow into the late Sasanian period and beyond. In the central regions of the empire, Mesopotamia, the Iranian highlands, and the Iranian Plateau, however, the leaders of nascent Christian communities never enjoyed the patronage of a converted monarch. Although some sixth- and seventh-century Christian authors imagined that the Sasanians had clandestinely converted to Christianity while outwardly promoting Zoroastrianism, no king of kings ever espoused Christianity, and only very few members of leading aristocratic houses converted.[17] However, the rise of Christianity in Iran took place under the authority and even the direct patronage of Zoroastrian elites. Historians have struggled to explain how these two religions could develop institutionally in tandem, at the same time and often in the very same places. The following chapters resolve this paradox through a reconstruction of the ways in which Zoroastrian elites integrated Christians into their institutions and Christians in turn positioned themselves within Iranian structures.

The title of the book evokes the argument in two ways. On the one hand, "a state of mixture" refers to the Zoroastrian concept of *gumēzišn*, the present condition of humanity in an intermediate and mixed state in a multimillennial cosmological schema. In the *gumēzišn*, the forces of Ahreman, the evil deity, have intermingled with the good creation of the benevolent Ohrmazd, leaving the world in a state of conflict and contamination. The Iranian Empire was conceived as a cosmological project to organize beneficent humans to accelerate the restoration of the world to the primordial state of perfection that would mark the end of the state of mixture. But in the meantime, the world, even Ērānšahr and its inhabitants, remained mixed. The commingling of good and evil characterized the climate, the environment, and the inner states of humans, including the ruling Zoroastrian Iranians. This understanding of mixture as natural to human political communities in their intermediate state, chapter 1 contends, provided an ideological framework for including religious others in Iran. On the other hand, "a state of mixture" refers to the contemporary usage of the terms *state* and *mixture*. Zoroastrian cosmological thinking gave rise to a culturally specific understanding of the state as a universalist empire, and a study of this understanding's interaction with Christians reveals one aspect of its state-making potential, namely its capacity to create networks and to shape imaginaries in the empire's constituent provinces. Christian communities are the best-documented subjects of the court, whether at the center or at the peripheries of Iran. Their sources offer the only means of gauging the penetration of imperial institutions at social levels beneath the highest strata of the Zoroastrian aristocracy. The East Syrian perspective on Iranian imperialism is the most important view for ascertaining the means by which imperial structures were established and perpetuated, made and remade, in the provinces. *Mixture*, moreover, adventitiously recalls a body of anthropological literature that shows how an analytical focus on cultural hybrids and *métissages* can reveal the most profound effects of imperial systems and provide clues to how they endured.[18] It is through the study of mixture as idea and mixture as practice that this book accounts for the making of the Iranian Empire.

THE CHURCH OF THE EAST: AN IMPERIAL CHURCH AND ITS INSTITUTIONS

The institutions of the Church of the East expanded in scope and scale throughout the Iranian Empire in the fifth, sixth, and early seventh centuries. At the first empire-wide ecclesiastical synod, in 410, thirty-eight bishops from Mesopotamia, Khuzestan, and the Persian Gulf convened at Seleucia-Ctesiphon.[19] By the time Sabrisho arrived at Husraw II's palace, there were upward of sixty bishops in each of Iran's major provinces, including Fars, Azerbaijan, Khurasan, Gorgan, and Bactria.[20] Their churches became salient features of the political landscape. Although archaeological research in the Near East has tended to neglect the Sasanian period, a remarkable number of churches, monasteries, and Christian objects have been revealed in the course of the handful of excavations that have focused on Iranian sites.[21] As Stefan Hauser has observed, "over half of all excavations in strata or surveys of buildings of the Sasanian period have yielded Christian evidence."[22] The churches uncovered in southern Mesopotamia, the Persian Gulf, and most recently the northern Mesopotamian sites of Nineveh and Bazyan (near Kirkuk) are particularly impressive testimonies to Christian communities with the economic capital to invest in richly ornamented buildings and the political capital to locate them in highly symbolic points in the landscape.[23] Situated in proximity to centers of imperial power, churches at Weh-Ardashir, al-Ḥīra, and elsewhere had stucco decorations that were executed in the style of Iranian elite residences, albeit with crosses adorned with pearls rather than scenes of the hunt (see figure 1).[24] The architecture mimicked the *ayvāns* (vaulted halls) of the palaces, with multiple niches along the walls, characteristic of churches in Iran.[25] The East Syrian tradition of construction in the style of Iranian elites continued into the first Islamic century, when the monastic complexes, recently excavated, on the islands of Kharg and Sir Bani Yas in the Persian Gulf, off the coasts of Bushehr and Abu Dhabi respectively, each came to house upward of one hundred monks in finely stuccoed cells.[26] Future excavations will undoubtedly enrich our understanding of East Syrian signatures on the Iranian political landscape.

Such an institutional efflorescence indicates neither the swelling of Christian ranks nor widespread, successful proselytism in the late Sasanian period. The Jains of late Mughal India, for example, established communities throughout the subcontinent and constructed some of the most impressive monuments of Delhi while constituting no more than 1 percent of the population.[27] What the diffusion of bishoprics and churches reveals is the success of East Syrian secular and ecclesiastical leaders at acquiring wealth, forming relationships with imperial authorities, and establishing religious institutions that transmitted their sources of economic and political capital across generations. Christianity gained its adherents among the largely invisible, middling inhabitants of the villages, towns, and cities in Mesopotamia and Khuzestan and along the transregional mercantile routes that extended into Central Asia through Khurasan and into the Indian Ocean through the Persian Gulf.[28] The Aramaic-speaking networks that crisscrossed the Fertile Crescent in late antiquity facilitated the spread of Christian ideas and institutions, and from the early third century at the latest a recognizably Christian set of doctrines was one option among others in the Mesopotamia in which the prophet Mani came to intellectual maturity.[29] Iran's campaigns into Roman territory in the third and fourth centuries also inadvertently enlarged the Christian population of the empire. Deportees brought from the rapidly Christianizing Roman Near East to Mesopotamia, Khuzestan, and the Iranian Plateau formed the foundations of communities that continued to grow into the seventh century.[30] If estimating the number of Christians or the rate of Christianization is hazardous even in the best documented of Roman regions, the enterprise would be foolhardy in an Iran entirely devoid of either the corpora of documentary texts or the systematic archaeological analyses on which such estimates have been based.[31] The notion that Christianity expanded at the expense of Zoroastrianism is, on this account, unsubstantiated, as well as implausible in the context of Iranian political culture. It is therefore the evolution of East Syrian institutions—and their associated texts— that is of greatest interest for the social and political history of Iran in late antiquity, not their implicit or explicit threat to the Good Religion. Regardless of the

FIGURE 1. Decorative stucco of a figure—perhaps a saint—from a late Sasanian church excavated in Weh-Ardashir. It is an example of the rich ornamentation, on par with the stucco uncovered in Sasanian palaces, that adorned even comparatively modest ecclesiastical buildings. Museum für Islamische Kunst, Staatliche Museen zu Berlin, Preußischer Kulturbesitz.

question of Christian numbers, the institutionalization of the Church of the East and the political integration of its believers offer revealing vantage points from which to consider the dynamics of both ecclesiastical expansion and Iranian imperialism in late antiquity.

A major impetus for East Syrian institutional growth came from the Iranian court. In the face of the catastrophic invasions of the Huns in the late fourth and early fifth centuries, the ruling elite sought to reorganize its networks to maximize its fiscal and martial resources. Like the Christian Roman emperors, the kings of kings found willing agents of empire in the bishops. In 410, Yazdgird I formally recognized the bishop of Seleucia-Ctesiphon as the leader—known as the catholicos until the adoption of the title *patriarch* in the middle of the sixth century—of an ecclesiastical organization that extended throughout the empire with a structure homologous to what bishops and emperors had constructed in neighboring Rome. Peace with the Roman Empire had precipitated an exchange of envoys, including the Roman bishop of Maipherqat, Maruta, who persuaded the king of kings to establish an imperial church of his own.[32] This community, designated "the Church of the East," rendered itself distinct from Roman Christianity through its loyalty to the king of kings, whom its bishops honored as "the victorious," as if he were himself a Constantine.[33] Its constituent elements—a pyramidal hierarchy of bishops culminating in the catholicos-patriarch of the imperial capital, a shared set of canons regulating communal life, and a common orthodox profession of faith—came together gradually over the next two centuries of Sasanian history.[34] But the Church of the East, in an aspirational form, was brought into being at the behest of the ruler of Iran in 410.

In establishing an imperial church on the model of his Roman counterparts, Yazdgird I resolved a problem that his fourth-century predecessor Shapur II (r. 309–79) had been the first to encounter, as chapter 1 emphasizes: how to enlist the bishops who were gaining in social prominence in some of the empires key cities in the service of the court. If Shapur II used violence to discipline ecclesiastical leaders, the Roman envoy gave Yazdgird I a more sophisticated means of subordinating bishops to himself—namely, the creation of political dependency on a worldly ruler whom, as we have seen, East Syrian leaders were prepared to accept. From the early fifth century, bishops served as diplomatic envoys on behalf of the political and economic interests of the court, as intermediaries with the Christian subjects of the kings of kings, and even as companions of the Sasanians on military campaigns in Christian Roman territories. Unlike their fellow bishops in the Roman Empire, East Syrian leaders rarely drew on their religious authority to call into question the actions of the kings of kings, at least publicly.[35] They were content to demonize kings of kings in a reassuringly distant past rather than in the present, such as the highly mythologized Shapur II in Christian works of the fifth, sixth, and seventh centuries, and to locate imperial Zoroastrianism in the religious authorities rather than in the rulers. If anything, the demarcation of secular and spiritual spheres in East Syrian thought caused the leaders of the Church of the East to become more docile servants of empire than the bishops of the Christian Roman Empire.

What remains largely unexamined are the social and political changes that the creation of an imperial church provoked in Christian communities and in Iranian society as a whole. Scholarship on East Syrian Christians has considered their communities as discrete, even insular within the empire and autonomous with regard to its social and political relations. Their exclusive social and political imaginaries and institutions have been thought effectively to demarcate Christians from Zoroastrians. Christians are supposed to have formed a "nation, or people, of God" who organized themselves separately from Zoroastrians, constituting their own ethnoreligious group.[36] Iranian political ideology and institutions played no role in shaping East Syrian thinking about the self in relation to society, and Christians and Zoroastrians shared no common, horizontal terms of belonging apart from personal, vertical loyalty to the king of kings. Even if the East Syrians are no longer characterized as Nestorians, a heresiographical label, they continue to be represented primarily in terms of their doctrinal identities.[37] The structures of Christian community, moreover, have been taken to reinforce this conceptual autonomy. A distinctive system of East Syrian law is supposed to have provided justice and judicial services independent of Zoroastrian courts. The argument of Eduard Sachau that ecclesiastical leaders possessed formal judicial authority (*Verfügungsrecht*) over the members of their communities has remained the scholarly consensus, despite the criticism of Walter Selb.[38] In the most influential formulation of this interpretive model, Michael Morony argued that the development of "autonomous systems of religious law" in the late Sasanian period underpinned a society of religious communities in which religious identities took precedence over social and political relationships.[39] Other scholars have gone so far as to suggest that separate Christian and Zoroastrian communal judges and laws foreshadowed, or were even the genetic forerunners of, the Ottoman millet system.[40] As we will see in chapter 3, there is no evidentiary basis for such claims of East Syrian legal autonomy. More important, the model of insular communities sits uneasily with the shared practices, discourses, and networks that are increasingly known to have characterized the relations of Christian, Jewish, and Zoroastrian elites.

Two subdisciplines have demonstrated the extent to which non-Zoroastrians participated in Iranian political culture in late antiquity. Scholars of the ancient Caucasus have long been attentive to the historical links of Armenia, Iberia, and Albania with the Iranian Empire but traditionally emphasized the cultural and ethnic distinctiveness of their inhabitants, especially after their Christianization in the fourth century. Nina Garsoïan has, however, pioneered a revisionist historiography of Armenia in late antiquity that emphasizes its integration into the culture, society, and political structures of Iran. The Armenian Christianity that gained the adherence of the elite—albeit more gradually and irregularly than once thought—spoke the language of the Iranian aristocracy, employing Zoroastrian concepts such as *xwarrah* (Armenian *p'ark'*), "supernatural glory," and representing Armenian *nakharar*s, the landowning aristocrats at the apex of society, as men as valiant as the greatest Iranian aristocrats at court.[41] The *nakharar*s, moreover, held powerful positions of leadership alongside bishops in their communities. Indeed, the bishoprics were often rooted in aristocratic houses rather than in cities.[42] Armenian aristocrats were genealogically intertwined with Iranian houses, were important military officeholders on behalf of the court, and even in their tendency toward rebellion acted as regular *wuzurg*, "great nobles," not unlike their peers from Parthia or Fars. The case of the Iberian elite was similar.[43] For the aristocrats of the Caucasus, Christianity presented no obstacles to political integration.

There has been a corresponding revival of the study of the Babylonian Talmud in its Iranian context. Yaakov Elman and Isaiah Gafni have led a vanguard of scholars who have documented the extent of the engagement of Jewish religious leaders—the rabbis and the exilarch, respectively—with Zoroastrian thought and law and with the Iranian court. Rabbis generally adapted Iranian legal institutions such as temporary marriage and substitute successorship to their own purposes, while the exilarch, the representative of Jewish communities at court, and certain rabbis fully adopted Iranian aristocratic customs of dress and dining.[44] The Talmud has been shown to have been in dialogue with Zoroastrians on questions of cosmology, purity, and mythical history.[45] Scholarship on Caucasian Christian and Jewish communities thus destabilizes the boundaries thought to separate Zoroastrians from religious others and invites a rethinking of the models and metaphors that historians have used to understand and to represent interreligious interactions in the Iranian Empire.

The following chapters undermine the foundations of the model of an Iranian society composed of separate, bounded religious communities in favor of a model of mixture that focuses on the institutions through which East Syrian communities were realized. The approach arises from the nature of the evidence. Two institutions have yielded the great bulk of the source material available for the study of Christian communities in Iran in the Sasanian period: the shrines of martyrs and the episcopal court. East Syrian ecclesiastical leaders introduced cults and canons from the Roman world, together with the associated technologies of communication, to instantiate their communities in time and space. Chapters 2, 3, and 4 offer case studies of how the organizers of cults of the saints and courts operated in terrain that they shared with their Zoroastrian counterparts. Their social and political imaginaries corresponded with what imperial authorities articulated, and their legal principles were often those of Zoroastrian judges. Rather than acting as bulwarks that effectively segregated Christians from Zoroastrians, East Syrian institutions sought to manage interactions between these groups and to provide communal narratives that facilitated Christian integration into the empire without compromising what ecclesiastical leaders regarded as the essential components of religious identity.

The use of the term *institution* is central to this study, as a means of placing hagiographical and judicial texts in temporal and spatial contexts and attributing to them a role in the development of social and political relations while remaining skeptical of their normative value. *Institutions*, in the sense intended here, refers to reproducible structures that have recognized roles for individuals and are granted the authority to communicate norms, symbols, and narratives to participants.[46] In the case of cults and courts, ecclesiastical leaders enjoyed the authority to speak, specifically to recount a narrative of the martyrs and to bring justice, on the basis of Christian norms. What needs to be emphasized is the institutional complexity of Iranian society. Shrines of martyrs were far from omnipresent in the landscape, and the ritual performances that rendered them institutions took place only annually. Bishops were only one judicial authority in a pluralist legal culture, and East Syrian laws presumed that Zoroastrian judges always wielded superior authority. To make sense of the East Syrian sources, the variety of institutions in which Christians participated, or could have participated, must be kept in mind: the audience halls of Iranian aristocrats and kings of kings, imperial administrative offices, the courts of Zoroastrian judges. The evocation of such fora in the scripts read at the cults of the saints and at the courts of bishops reminds us that Christians were involved in a number of institutions, which collectively structured their experience of Iranian society. The contemporaneous development of Christian and Zoroastrian institutions under the Sasanians precipitated the mixing of cultures rather than their insulation from one another. It is against the backdrop of such institutional complexity that the sometimes strident voices of Christian and Zoroastrian authors insisting on the superiority of their respective religious identities should be heard.

CHRISTIAN AND ZOROASTRIAN TEXTS AND THEIR CONTEXTS

The study of Iranian society in late antiquity requires engagement with literatures of a highly sectarian nature. The vast corpora of religious texts that the various literary specialists of the Iranian world produced, ranging from the sometimes jocular reflections of the rabbis to the shrill polemics of Christians, present enormous interpretive difficulties to the historian. The major literary traditions that emerged in the Sasanian period—Zoroastrian Middle Persian, Armenian and Georgian, East Syrian Syriac, Babylonian Jewish Aramaic, and Mandaean—all require highly specialized training. As a consequence, few studies have systematically integrated evidence from more than one. Even a scholar trained in the relevant languages finds the writing of social or political history on the basis of such sectarian literatures a daunting task. The most productive lines of research in the past four decades have circumvented the challenges of the literary evidence by privileging inscriptions, seals, coins, and other materials considered documentary.[47] The studies of Rika Gyselen in Sasanian sigillography, which reappear throughout the following chapters, have transformed our understanding of the imperial administration. Nevertheless, avoiding the religious literatures that have been preserved in Sasanian or post-Sasanian forms not only downplays the literary and ideological aspects of seemingly documentary texts but also misses an opportunity to explore the relationship between religious ideas and social and political structures. This book examines Christian and Zoroastrian religious texts within their respective institutional contexts as interventions in the surrounding society and political culture, with a view to demonstrating how stories of saints, miracles, and myths and speculative theological and cosmological theories played fundamental roles in the making of the Iranian Empire in late antiquity.

The East Syrian hagiographical tradition constitutes the most voluminous body of evidence for the history of Christianity in Iran and for the experience of empire in the provinces. The increasing profusion of lives of saints—written primarily to establish and propagate cults, most often of martyrs—charts the growth of their corresponding institutions.[48] The 1890s Paris publications of Paul Bedjan have more than fifty individual texts that were written under Sasanian rule, ranging from rudimentary works of a single folio to sophisticated compositions filling dozens of printed pages. Bedjan based his editions on the important early medieval manuscripts Vaticanus Syrus 160 and Vaticanus Syrus 161 and consulted medieval and modern manuscripts in Diyarbakir, London, and Berlin.[49] Scholars introduced a number of additional manuscripts to the study of East Syrian hagiography during the twentieth century, on the basis of which new works were published and known ones were revised. Greek, Armenian, and Sogdian translations of many of these works have further enriched our knowledge of their dates of composition and cross-cultural, even transimperial transmission. These were products of multilingual Christian communities with ample expertise in the arts of translation.[50] They likely produced works in the imperial language, although the surviving examples of Christian Middle Persian literature are entirely liturgical in nature.[51] The discovery of East Syrian hagiographical texts in Sogdian in the manuscript collection of the monastery excavated in the Turfan Oasis of western China provided evidence for their remarkably wide circulation in the sixth through eighth centuries.[52] The lives of saints that East Syrian authors produced in the Sasanian era were so fundamental to the institutions of Christianity that its proponents exported them, together with scriptures and liturgical texts, to the embryonic communities of Central and East Asia. The functions of texts within the projects of the Christian religious professionals who composed, copied, read, and recited them need to be kept at the forefront of any analysis of East Syrian hagiography. The bulk of scholarship on these texts has endeavored to establish their dates of composition as the basis for evaluating the historicity of the events they describe. While incorporating the insights of these studies, this book joins the company of recent works that move beyond the question of whether or not certain events occurred to ask what hagiographers and their texts accomplished in a given historical moment.[53] The reception of East Syrian hagiography in the Turfan Oasis suggests that the stories of saints did more than merely document the specific circumstances of their production.

These lives of saints were, after all, works whose authors were directly involved in brokering the relations of Christians with the social structures, economies, and political cultures in which their communities were embedded.[54] It is not accidental that hagiographical writing began to flourish in the fifth century, just as the Church of the East began to expand institutionally.[55] If scholars once considered the surviving corpora to have been mere martyrologies, compendia of names and known details of historical martyrs, Paul Peeters, Gernot Wiessner, and others have introduced the problem of authorship to the study of East Syrian literature. First, they built on the work of other early twentieth-century scholars to emphasize the regional nature of accounts of the so-called Great Persecution. Rather than a single collection compiled by Maruta of Maipherqat, as the eighteenth-century ecclesiastical historian Joseph Assemani had influentially argued, these were distinct collections from the northern Mesopotamian cities of Arbela and Karka d-Beit Slok, Khuzestan, Seleucia-Ctesiphon, and the Iranian highlands.[56] Second, these historians disaggregated these collections into individual works that display their own particular priorities. Peeters demonstrated that the texts that constitute the so-called martyrology of Adiabene are discrete compositions. Wiessner more ambitiously identified the authors of accounts of the martyrdom of Simeon, the bishop of Seleucia-Ctesiphon, as distinct individuals with sharply divergent views on the relationship between Christianity and the empire. The author of the *History of Simeon*, for example, insisted on the necessity of Christian loyalty to the kings of kings and the court.[57] In Wiessner's study, hagiographical writings came not merely to represent a community but also to reshape its perspective on particular social and political dilemmas. East Syrian lives of saints were thus original compositions of ascetics, priests, and bishops trained in the hagiographical arts. When their backgrounds become discernible, East Syrian hagiographers were invariably ascetics and ascetic bishops actively involved in the construction of socially and politically viable Christian communities. Hagiographers whose names went unrecorded were similarly engaged in the conflicts that attended the emergence of Christian institutions.[58] If Peeters, Wiessner, and others intended to recover historical facts from hagiographical texts, in doing so they laid the groundwork for exploring the historical implications of the literary creativity of East Syrian authors.

Hagiographers were the anonymous architects of Christian communities in Iran. To speak of authors as undertaking constructive work is to evoke a generation of scholarship on religion and society in late antiquity. The argument that holy men played crucial roles in the transformation of late Roman society helped to rejuvenate the field. But the emphasis now tends be placed on the transformative capacities of the texts themselves.[59] Scholars have turned from extracting historical details from hagiographical texts toward analyzing their narrative structures, signs, symbols, and, in a word, discourses, with the goal of uncovering the shifting self-understandings and self-representations of Christian communities. The best of such studies have linked Christian discourses with social and political practice, especially in the domain of interreligious interaction. Saints were manifestations of Christ, and hagiographically mediated accounts of their lives established parameters for legitimate action within Christian communities.[60] Stories of saintly action were therefore efficacious ways of establishing and maintaining boundaries between Christians and Jews, Muslims, and Zoroastrians.[61] The importance of hagiography for defining the limits of Christian communities in culturally diverse environments recurs in the following chapters. This approach toward the lives of saints, however, is in itself inadequate. The authors of hagiographical works understood their task to be an ascetic practice, and they sought through writing to strengthen communities that a variety of social, economic, and political challenges beset.[62] The creation of a vision of community that could withstand, or indeed gain strength from, the particular material circumstances in which Christians found themselves was also a basis for the authority to lead. Rather than mere propaganda, hagiographical works would more productively be interpreted as "propositions pitched to a heterogeneous elite culture."[63] The most revealing line of inquiry into hagiographical sources for the historian is to uncover the intersections between ascetic writing and the social economic, and political structures to which hagiographers often addressed themselves. This requires critical attention to the historical details that literary studies tend to downplay.[64] Accounts of religious identity should not be extricated from the social location, economic resources, and political institutions and ideologies of their authors and audiences. In studying the act of writing the life of a saint, we will repeatedly find in this book the fusing of otherworldly asceticism and worldly authority that was so characteristic of Christian leadership in late antiquity.

The writing of lives of saints was not, from this perspective, as readily distinguishable from the making of Christian canons or laws as the traditional disciplinary segregation of these genres implies. The Church of the East produced laws, regulations, and canons precociously at a remarkable rate, culminating in the comprehensive legal compendia of the early Islamic period. The most important collection of canons was the so-called *Synodicon Orientale*, edited in the eleventh century, whose earliest manuscripts date to the thirteenth or fourteenth century. Although its language was sometimes revised to reflect the priorities of its editors, the *Synodicon Orientale* preserved the substance of the canons issued at the dozen synods that convened during the Sasanian era, as well as related materials. These canons regulated the beliefs, rituals, and social and economic activities of Christians, especially ascetics, priests, and bishops. In addition, Eduard Sachau, Walter Selb, and Hubert Kaufhold have edited East Syrian legal texts whose manuscript transmissions were independent of the *Synodicon Orientale*.[65] Ranging from the *Regulations of Marriage* of the fifth-century Mar Aba to an eleventh-century treatise on inheritance and marriage, these jurisprudential works concentrate on the social and economic dilemmas of lay men and women. Scholarship in East Syrian canons and laws has regarded them as reflective of broadly accepted norms that bishops, in their capacity as judges, enforced consistently in Christian communities. "It cannot be," however, "that schematic legal texts exactly encapsulated the range of social practice anywhere, or that they could even begin to reflect the huge micro-regional differences in that practice that will have existed everywhere."[66] Chapter 4 discusses approaches to these sources in greater detail and suggests that, like East Syrian hagiographies, laws and canons served to outline models of community to be created rather than existing juridical communities. These texts nevertheless foreground, more explicitly than hagiographical works, the social and economic challenges in the context in which communal imaginaries were constructed. If hagiographers presented Christians as unified, laws and canons revealed the dissonance, often grounded in material exigencies, at the heart of constructions of Christian community. The study in chapter 4 of East Syrian jurisprudence in the Sasanian period, in particular Mar Aba's *Regulations of Marriage*, emphasizes the comparative weakness of the religious authorities who composed Christian texts.

Zoroastrians, by contrast, produced their literature in positions of political predominance. Religious authorities held some of the most powerful offices at court and in the provincial administration, ranging from local judges through the mowbed of entire provinces to the *mowbedān mowbed*, the chief Zoroastrian official of the empire, whose judgments were considered infallible. Only one work, the *Hazār Dādestān* (Thousand judgments), emerged directly from the judicial administrative activities of the Zoroastrian religious authorities in the late Sasanian period, specifically the early seventh century. Nevertheless, there are significant methodological and legalistic parallels between this collection of late Sasanian case law and the corpora of Zoroastrian scholarly literature edited in the ninth century. These works, most famously the definitive collection of Zoroastrian thought known as the *Dēnkard*, preserved the myths, speculations, arguments, and rulings of Sasanian scholars in the manner of medieval florilegia. Like their medieval Christian counterparts, the editors organized earlier materials to suit the circumstances of their communities in the Abbasid era. But the names of the quoted scholars consistently correspond with known religious authorities of the fifth and sixth centuries, such as Abarag and Sōšāns, two jurists who feature in the *Hazār Dādestān*.[67] What the appearance of the same scholars in late Sasanian case law and in the ninth-century compendia suggests is not only that the Abbasid collections consisted of Sasanian materials but also that juridical and cosmological texts were components of the same discourse. The religious authority of the mowbed and other Zoroastrian officials resided in their mastery of the Yasna ritual, the Avesta recited in the course of its performance, and the interpretation of both. Such expertise was acquired in the formal institution of the priestly school, the *hērbedestān*, a topic of chapter 2. Whether acting as judges, advisers to kings of kings or aristocrats, or speculative intellectuals, religious authorities shared a discourse whose framework included Zoroastrian mythical history, law, and, in a word, cosmology. The works of Zoroastrian literature surviving in Middle Persian are manifestations of a polyphonic discourse that structured the thought and action of the religion's authorities and, to a certain extent, of the kings of kings and aristocrats who recognized their authority. These works have little to yield in the way of historical detail but much to reveal of the history of the development of Zoroastrian ideology and institutions.

The situation is similar with the Iranian historiographical tradition. From the middle of the sixth century at the latest, the court was producing written accounts of its activities that circulated in the provinces.[68] No such composition has survived. But the wide range of authors who made use of courtly accounts in different settings and centuries attests to the dissemination and normative status of a work known as the *Xwadāy-nāmag*, the *Book of Kings*, among communities as disparate as the Mandaeans and Sogdians. If contemporary histories in Greek, Armenian, and Syriac constitute the earliest texts that refer to such a work, the great bulk of the Iranian historiographical tradition has been preserved in Arabic and New Persian, in particular the epic of Firdawsī and the works of al-Ṭabarī, al-Dīnawarī, and other Abbasid historiographers.[69] Their accounts of the Iranian court and its relations with outside powers are the main sources available, alongside the Roman and Armenian historiographical traditions, for the reconstruction of the political history of the Sasanian period. Research has therefore centered on untangling the various strands of narrative with which the authors of the early Islamic period constructed their accounts, in pursuit of the original *Xwadāy-nāmag*. The scholarship of Zeev Rubin in particular has demonstrated the possibility of reconstructing aspects of Iranian political history on the basis of a critical examination of the different recensions of this work.[70] But the contradictions of accounts purporting to have been drawn from the *Xwadāy-nāmag* should not be discounted as mere interpolations. As Timothy Greenwood has observed, historians might more productively "envision that an unknown number of parallel, arguably contradictory, accounts of Sasanian origin survived in written form long after the collapse of the Sasanian Empire, and were translated, reworked, and developed to a greater or lesser extent over time."[71] The *Xwadāy-nāmag* possessed a shape-shifting nature. While retaining value as sources of historical detail, the works of the courtly historiographers participated in the Zoroastrian discourse that also contained Middle Persian juridical and cosmological literature. Surviving examples of the *Xwadāy-nāmag* traditions interweave mythical accounts of the Kayanian dynasty of the Avesta with historical accounts of the Sasanian dynasty. Literary specialists trained in the Zoroastrian scholarly tradition designed the *Xwadāy-nāmag* to demonstrate that the Sasanians acted in accordance with the mythical models of cosmologically efficacious kingship. The narration of events in the language of myth continually remade the claim of realizing Ērānšahr, especially in the increasingly complex politics—in terms of both interreligious and interstate relations—of the sixth and early seventh centuries. This aspect of the historiographical traditions—as sources of political self-representation and legitimacy—is of greatest interest for this book's study of the court's negotiation of religious difference.

The religious literatures produced in the Iranian Empire should therefore be interpreted in the context of their corresponding institutions. Hagiographers composed accounts of martyrs primarily as transcripts to be narrated in the course of the annual commemorations that gathered Christians at sacred sites. Bishops composed canons and regulations as guidelines for their decisions as judges and pastors of their communities. Saints' shrines and episcopal courts were sufficiently consequential to the social and political development of East Syrian communities to have yielded the great bulk of the surviving evidence for their history. The cosmological literature of Zoroastrian scholars reflects the intellectual milieu of the interpretive schools where the priestly officeholders were educated. The hērbedestān were the sites not only of the reproduction of the Zoroastrian religious elite but also of discussion and debate of the various problems that the banal realities of empire posed to an evolving tradition of religious knowledge. The literary specialists who composed the *Xwadāy-nāmag*, themselves products of the hērbedestān, were similarly addressing the concerns of a Zoroastrian court that was accepting increasing numbers of Christian aristocrats and religious professionals into its networks. Conceived as a package of Zoroastrian institutions operating in concert with the court, the empire came to depend on ancillary Christian institutions in its provinces, and even at its center, to articulate its authority and to mobilize the military and fiscal resources constitutive of its power. Through the texts they composed, Christian and Zoroastrian religious leaders established and continually retooled the boundaries and terms of interaction of their religions in light of the shifting political landscapes of Iran, from the creation of an imperial Christian church in 410 until the beginning of the Islamic conquests in 636. It is at the nexus of texts and institutions—cults of martyrs, bishoprics, Zoroastrian schools, and the Iranian court—that we can capture the cooperation of Christians and Zoroastrians in the making of the Iranian Empire.

1

The Myth of Zoroastrian Intolerance

Violence and the Terms of Christian Inclusion

THE LEGACY OF KERDIR

A single religious authority has shaped our understanding of how Zoroastrians regarded the adherents and institutions of other religions. The mowbed Kerdir who served three successive kings of kings in the third century—Shapur I (r. 241–70), Ohrmazd I (r. 270–71), and Wahram I (r. 271–74)—was the only priest in the Sasanian period prolifically to have produced inscriptions.[1] On the stone walls of the so-called Kaaba of Zoroaster, alongside an inscription of Shapur I and beneath relief sculptures of early Sasanian rulers, he recounted his career as the supervisor of the institutionalization of Zoroastrianism throughout the nascent empire. This inscription was duplicated on the neighboring reliefs of Naqsh-e Rustam and on the image of Wahram I at Sar Mashad, where Kerdir appears alongside the king of kings as a partner in rule. According to the mowbed's account of his own activities, he erected fire temples everywhere from the heart of Iran in Babylonia to its limits in Peshawar. He organized the performance of the Yasna and instructed believers in the principles of the Good Religion. He also claimed to have suppressed the other religions in Iranian territory: "The Zoroastrian religion [*dēn mazdēsn*] and the priests held great authority in the empire [*šahr*]. The gods, water, fire, and domestic animals received satisfaction, and Ahreman and the demons received blows and suffering. The doctrine [*kēš*] of Ahreman and the demons was expelled from the empire and became unbelief. The Jews, Buddhists, Brahmins, Nazarenes, Christians, Baptizers, and Manichaeans were struck in the empire. Idols were destroyed, and the residences of demons were eliminated and became the place and seat of the gods."[2] On the basis of this account, historians have argued that Kerdir oversaw a persecution of the named groups, inaugurating a project whose aim was the elimination of religious others, toward which subsequent Zoroastrian religious authorities worked until the end of the empire.[3] If such was the goal, the flourishing of Jewish and Christian communities from the third century through the seventh suggests that they made little headway against these groups.[4] The prophet Mani was slain at the behest of the court for rivaling the ritual power and cosmological knowledge of Zoroastrians, but there is no persuasive evidence for action against Christians or Jews during the era of his tenure.[5] Nevertheless, histories of Zoroastrian interactions with Christians, Jews, and others in the Sasanian period often begin with, and rely on, Kerdir's self-representation as a paradigmatic example of how his fellow religious authorities, whether in the third century or the sixth, treated or wished to treat rival religious groups. He has provided the archetype of the persecutory Zoroastrian.

What follows questions whether Zoroastrian religious authorities were inherently persecutory, beginning with the most articulate member of their ranks. At first glance, Kerdir's inscription seems to lump together "the doctrine of Ahreman," idolatry, and the deviant religions as equivalently evil institutions that Zoroastrians should work to eliminate. Closer inspection, however, suggests important distinctions among these institutions that could have provided a basis for preserving certain religious groups within a Zoroastrian empire. Ahreman's kēš, a term that could designate a doctrine or a sectarian group, was to be expelled.[6] Idols and idolatrous places of worship were to be destroyed. The deviant religions were, by contrast, simply to be "struck" (*zadan*). This verb has been interpreted as implying destructive actions with a view to elimination. But a struck object is neither destroyed nor eliminated. It is, rather, subdued. Blows are instruments of discipline and subordination instead of destruction. Regardless of whether the mowbed realized the claims he pronounced in his inscriptions, he envisioned the suppression of religious others rather than their elimination, their subordination to the institutions of the Good Religion, which was to reign supreme in an Ērānšahr embodying its cosmological ambitions. Christians, Jews, and others were to be disciplined, where supposed demon worshipers and idolaters were to be destroyed. It was this task of subordination that the mowbed set for himself. His primary goal was to place the Good Religion on solid institutional foundations in an era when the ideology of Iran was merely an idea, without fire temples, ritual performances, or laws as its anchors in space and society. He thus not only established such institutions but also propagated the superiority of the religion as the foundation of the new empire in inscriptions and rock reliefs. The reference to religious others in the inscriptions rhetorically defined the superior position of the Good Religion in relation to its known rivals at the same time as fire temples, a class of religious professionals, and laws were being created. The undertaking of actions physical or symbolic, such as violence against Christians, Jews, or others, was not necessarily an essential feature of the project of Kerdir and his successors.

The fine distinctions in Kerdir's verbs prefigure the views of later Zoroastrian religious authorities who allowed for the inclusion of subordinated religions in the empire. The third-century mowbed has too often been seen in isolation, largely on account of his industrious self-promotion. Scholars have generally privileged his voice as representative of Zoroastrian religious professionals since his inscriptions are the only extensive contemporary literary sources for their thought. But, for the reasons we have considered in the introduction, the views of Zoroastrian exegetes, scholars, and jurists that have been preserved in the ninth-century collections of Middle Persian literature should not be dismissed. They include voluminous discussions of the problem of the place of religious others in a Zoroastrian empire, with which Kerdir was perhaps the first to wrestle in writing. In her study of "tolerance and intolerance in Zoroastrianism," Mary Boyce juxtaposed the mowbed's claim of having struck Christians and others to the statements of Sasanian kings of kings and scholars hostile toward non-Zoroastrian groups, providing a catalog of intolerant views which argued that the supposedly destructive fantasies of Kerdir proliferated in the following centuries.[7] What such studies of Zoroastrian thought and practice have overlooked are statements in the selfsame texts expressing a positive regard for the *agdēn*, "those of bad religion," within the empire. Zoroastrian discussions of bad religions as social and political problems were grounded in the concerns of late Sasanian scholars over the capacities of humans to contribute to the cosmological struggle that the kings of kings superintended in league with Ohrmazd. These scholars were not inclined to the simplistic, binary thinking and inveterate antipathy toward religious others that the label *intolerant*, often applied to them, evokes. The third-century mowbed's differentiation of bad religions into separate categories meriting distinct actions and approaches finds resonance in these later texts that evaluated religious others in terms of a hierarchy of better and worse rather than a binary of good versus evil. Their novel perspective on the religious landscape of late antiquity merits exploration.

Alongside the inscription of Kerdir and the more militant voices among the Zoroastrian scholars, historians have placed another, more voluminous corpus of sources: East Syrian histories of martyrs. As we saw in the introduction, there are nearly sixty accounts composed in the Sasanian era of Christians killed at the hands of Zoroastrian religious authorities in the fourth through early seventh centuries. These describe periods of persecution, *radupye* in Syriac, both before and after the recognition of the Church of the East in 410. Shapur II was believed to have persecuted Christians relentlessly from 340 to 379, the so-called Great Persecution that was paradigmatic for the framing of subsequent outbreaks of violence as time-bound, systematic radupaye. The reigns of Yazdgird I, Wahram V, Yazdgird II, Peroz, Husraw I, and Husraw II were each reported to have contained periods of persecution against the Church of the East, even though its rapidly developing institutions continued to expand unabated. The catalyst for violence was, in the hagiographical representations, the unwavering hostility of Zoroastrian religious authorities toward Christians. In the accounts of persecution, mowbed torment and kill Christians with bloodthirsty glee, devising ever more elaborate modes of torture and execution to inflict as much pain as possible on the persecuted. If their willingness to slay Christians and destroy churches was constant, their influence at the court of the king of kings was supposed to have fluctuated. Kings of kings who heeded the religious authorities persecuted Christians, while those with the will to ignore their demands did not. This framework for understanding and representing interactions between Zoroastrian religious authorities and Christian communities, ultimately derived from East Syrian self-representations, remains the historiographical consensus.[8]

Periods of persecution, fluctuating relations between kings of kings and mowbed, and intolerant Zoroastrians are stock themes of historical writing on the Sasanian period that have been perpetuated in the absence of critical studies on the East Syrian and Armenian hagiographical sources on which these accounts are based.[9] The Christian representation of Zoroastrians, in other words, has triumphed in the modern imagination of the past, regardless of whether East Syrian authors achieved the social and political ambitions they set for themselves in late antiquity. The introduction has highlighted the consistency of the Sasanian commitment to Zoroastrianism anchored in the idea of Iran. This chapter seeks to replace the commonplace of Zoroastrian intolerance around which historians have so frequently organized their analyses of Iranian society in late antiquity with a model of the differentiated, hierarchical inclusion of religious others rooted in Zoroastrian cosmological thought. It lays the foundations for the subsequent chapters, which examine the particular contexts in which Christians and Zoroastrians negotiated the terms of the former's inclusion in the empire. Concepts of tolerance and intolerance, redolent with notions of liberal political virtue, are unhelpful instruments for the analysis of ancient societies, not least because they fail to capture ancient understandings of religious difference and their corresponding practices.[10] The image of the intolerant mowbed has obscured Zoroastrian concepts and practices of inclusion and exclusion that evolved in tandem with the empire. Dispensing with the language of tolerance allows for the analysis of the culturally and historically specific ways in which hierarchically organized groups, themselves shape-shifting entities, regulated their interactions with one another in theory and practice. Symbolic and physical acts of violence were instruments of organization and regulation in ancient political cultures, and decoding their significance can as often reveal the dynamics of cooperation as of conflict.[11]

To reconstruct the institutions, including norms and practices, through which Zoroastrians structured their interactions with religious others, this chapter pursues two distinct objectives. First, we recover the cosmological perspective of Zoroastrian religious authorities on the culturally diverse population of Iran, which gave rise to a range of accounts of the place of bad religions in the social and political order. Rather than seek, or even imagine, the systematic exclusion of religious others, priestly scholars developed techniques for their regulation and disciplining, with the goal of ensuring that they did not jeopardize the operation of the institutions of the Good Religion. If ancient Zoroastrians are best known for their dualism, their concepts of mixture, intermingling, and hierarchical order will emerge as equally salient in Iranian political culture. Second, a strong correlation between such theoretical discussions and the political practice of the Iranian court will be demonstrated on the basis of a comprehensive and critical reexamination of the East Syrian hagiographical sources. East Syrian authors composed their works for polemical purposes, to construct communities defined through their experience of violence at the hands of their religious adversaries—Jews, Manichaeans, and especially Zoroastrians. They also drew from Roman martyrologies to compose the representations of Zoroastrian religious authorities and kings of kings as persecutors. Their accounts of how Zoroastrian authorities thought or behaved cannot be accepted as historical. The following sections, therefore, look beyond the stereotyped and polemical passages of the East Syrian hagiographical works to context-specific details concerning the actions of imperial authorities, such as names, dates, precise locations, and historically verifiable or plausible acts of mowbed or kings of kings. This reading of the corpus of East Syrian hagiography reveals the consistent, rather than fluctuating, use of violence against religious others by the Iranian court in particular circumstances as a means of establishing norms of interaction between Christian and Zoroastrian elites. These lines of research converge to show how the Zoroastrian institutions of the empire facilitated the expansion of Christian and Jewish communities throughout its history. Zoroastrians in late antiquity should be known for having practiced differentiated, hierarchical inclusion rather than intolerance.

A STATE OF MIXTURE

To understand how Zoroastrian elites regarded the human populations of their empire, we need to begin with the primordial creation, accounts of which established models for political action.[12] Ohrmazd brought the physical world into being as a vehicle with which to defeat Ahreman.[13] His creation was to pass through three successive three-thousand-year stages, according to the most prevalent schema, in order for the cosmological triumph to be achieved.[14] This beneficent deity initially created the heavens, water, earth, and fire as well as the primordial plant, animal, and human as wholly good material elements that would serve him in the impending struggle with his evil counterpart.[15] After three thousand years, Ahreman created material elements of his own—darkness and *xrafstar*, wicked animals—and penetrated the good creation with demonic powers, precipitating an era of confrontation between good and evil supernatural forces acting through their respective good and evil creations.[16] This age of struggle constituted the three-thousand-year period of human history in which Zoroastrians found themselves in late antiquity.[17] The arrival of a savior figure, the Sōšyāns, was to mark the end of the age, indeed the end of history, and the beginning of a world restored to its state of primordial perfection, the *frašgird*. The intervening period of human political history was known as the "state of mixture" (*gumēzišn*).[18] During the mixed age, Ohrmazd and his supernatural allies waged war against Ahreman by means of good creations, enlisting the stars against demonic planets, crafting mountains to make waters flow into pure, life-giving reservoirs, and revealing religion and its rites to humanity. Every component of the material world of necessity participated in the cosmic struggle. But humans played a special, even determinative, role. As fundamentally good creations, they contributed to Ohrmazd's restorative work by means of their mere existence, like flora and beneficent fauna. The revelation of Zoroastrianism, however, gave humanity a package of rituals and actions through which men and women could not only support the efforts of the good deity but also accelerate the gradual victory of good over evil, tipping the balance in the interim in favor of Ohrmazd even as humans continued to await the frašgird. It was the capacity to choose whether or not to serve the forces of good that distinguished humans from other corporeal creatures in the state of mixture.

The implications of this understanding of the nature of the world and humanity for the politics and society of the Iranian Empire cannot be underestimated. The empire was conceived as a vehicle—akin to Ohrmazd's original creation—for organizing collective actions to maximize the contribution of humanity to the cosmological struggle. Through the erection of fire temples for the performance of the Yasna, the extension of arable lands for the cultivation of plants, and the creation of legal institutions to heighten human fertility, Ērānšahr anchored what was a global restorative project in the territories that the Sasanians ruled. The responsibility for organizing and operating these cosmological institutions rested with a privileged, comparatively narrow group of men: those descended from the first man, Gayōmard, via the primordial kings through the Kayanian dynasty, which accepted and propagated the teachings and rituals of Zoroaster into the present—that is, the Sasanians and allied aristocratic houses that constituted the ēr, the "Iranians."[19] To be Iranian was first and foremost to possess an ethical disposition transmitted via a lineage that positioned one as an ally of Ohrmazd more efficacious in facilitating the cosmological struggle than any other kind of human. This branch of humanity enjoyed such superior ethical qualities as loyalty, righteousness, and nobility that rendered theirs a "lineage of leaders" (*dahibedān tōhmag*).[20]

The ēr were also those who had full knowledge of the religion that Zoroaster had revealed. According to accounts circulating in the Sasanian period, Ohrmazd created his messenger (*paygāmbar*) as a means of communicating the instruments through which humans could act, think, and organize themselves in ways most conducive to assisting him in the cosmic struggle. As the seventh book of the *Dēnkard* summarizes Zoroaster's contribution, "From the all-knowing creator Ohrmazd he received utterly complete—and even oral—knowledge of the theory and practice of the priestly, warrior, agricultural, and artisanal classes. At the command of the creator he also brought the entire Mazda-worshiping religion [*dēn mazdēst*] to the king Kay Wishtasp, ... enlightening with the greatest light the wise men in the clime [*kišwar*] of the most exalted, the gods' ruler, [and] spreading [the religion] in the seven climes."[21] It was the Kayanians of Airyana Vaējah—the successors and allies of the mythical King Wishtasp, who had supported Zoroaster—who received the fullness of religion and directed its distribution to the other six kišwar on earth. The extent to which other lands and peoples gained possession of the Good Religion, whether fully or fragmentarily, depended upon the Iranians to whom Zoroaster had entrusted its principles and practices. The connection between Iranianness (*ērīh*) and Zoroastrianism was basic to the self-understanding of the *wehdēn* (adherents of the Good Religion) in late antiquity Zoroastrian scholars routinely equated the two, using the adjectives *ēr* and *wehdēn* as virtual synonyms.[22] And although ancient scholars emphasized the ethical content of *ērīh*, its foundations always resided in lineage, in genealogical relationships with the *ēr* of Zoroaster's mythical homeland.[23] The flexible nature of Iranian mythical histories, as we will see in chapter 4, allowed for persons of diverse backgrounds to construct such relationships with the Iranians, if not to become *ēr* themselves, although there is no documented case of a convert to Zoroastrianism articulating such an identity. It was unthinkable, on the other hand, for an Iranian to abandon the Good Religion or for an *agdēn* to lay claim to the adjective *ēr*.[24] If the injunction to propagate the religion beyond the kišwar of Iran shows that Zoroastrianism was hardly conceived as exclusive to Iranians, the privileged position of Iranians possessing superior knowledge of religion was unassailable.

Iranians, however, were not without their imperfections. As the efficacy of the Good Religion depended on practice rather than mere belief, the possession of *ērīh* implied certain ethical obligations, which Iranians invariably fell short of fulfilling.[25] The capacity of Iranians for inaction or even wicked action in the service of Ahreman could destabilize the boundaries between the *ēr* and the *anēr* (non-Iranians). As one of the scholars quoted in the sixth book of the *Dēnkard* pointedly stated, "There is no person in whose substance these things are not found: knavery, the condition of a whore, sorcery, and non-Iranian behavior [*anērīh*]."[26] Juxtaposing non-Iranianness to some of the most monstrous sins underlined how dimly scholars, in comparison with their superiors, viewed anēr, while admitting some overlap in their capacities for ethical practice. Cosmologically efficacious practices were, moreover, available even to non-Iranian agdēn. The same text that recounts Zoroaster's revelation of religion to the Kayanians also mentions the activities of earlier *waxšwar*, "spirit-bearers," who brought individual components of religion to humans. These unnamed agents of Ohrmazd introduced various beneficial practices to humanity. In particular, they taught cultivation, husbandry, and craftsmanship to the first couple and ancestors of all humans, Mašyā and Mašyānē.[27] All of this couple's descendants retained these capacities even as they strayed, like their primogenitors, into demon worship or other destructive activities.[28] Thus, according to some scholars, the perfection of the frašgird was the common inheritance of humanity, and Zoroastrians and non-Zoroastrians alike would ultimately enter paradise.[29] Although Zoroastrians developed decidedly hostile views toward non-Iranians and non-Zoroastrians, the notion that waxšwar preceding Zoroaster had granted, in the words of Albert de Jong, "most aspects of human culture and civilization, including the germs of what it means to be pious and righteous, as the inheritance of all humans" provided the ideological foundation for acknowledging the potential contributions of agdēn to the Iranian Empire.[30]

BAD RELIGIONS

If humans found themselves collectively in a state of mixture, there was only one Good Religion that could bring the world to a state of perfection. Every other system of ritual and belief was "bad religion," *agdēnīh*, whose institutions were irredeemably deficient and potentially maleficent. The concept derived from the Avestan *aka-daēnā**, "evil piety" or, in the understanding of Sasanian scholars who took *daēnā* to designate a belief system, "evil religion."[31] The Middle Persian term *agdēn* became common in the discourse of Zoroastrian scholars in the Sasanian period as a blanket designation for non-Zoroastrians, collapsing the distinctions among Christianity, Judaism, and other religions into a single binary opposition between the single Good Religion and the various bad ones. *Agdēn* and *anēr* became as synonymous as *wehdēn* and *ēr*. In part on account of *agdēn*'s seemingly straightforward Avestan etymology, the use of the term has been taken to indicate the vehement antipathy of Zoroastrian authorities toward religious others. The dualism of Zoroastrian cosmology seems, in the categories of wehdēn/ēr and agdēn/anēr, to have provided a blueprint for dividing humanity into two distinct groups, one allied with Ohrmazd, the other with Ahreman.[32] As with other evil creatures, this interpretation implies, Zoroastrians would ideally have violently expunged their empire of bad religions and their adherents if political and economic constraints had not forced them to practice what Christopher MacEvitt has termed "rough tolerance" in describing the conduct of Christian crusaders in the twelfth-century Levant.[33] This representation of Zoroastrian concepts of religious difference ignores the nuanced discussions of agdēn found in the literary sources that priestly and courtly elites produced. The idea of bad religion was the beginning, not the end, of scholarly discourse on the relationship between the wehdēn and the great mass of humans who stood outside the imperial religion yet within Iran. The religions lumped together under the rubric of *agdēnīh* were in fact distinguished into more or less deficient varieties, only a select few of which merited eradication and/or expulsion. Ancient scholars went so far as to suggest that in the state of mixture, adherents of bad religions could make valuable contributions to the cosmological struggle. Zoroastrians did not practice a rough tolerance of non-Zoroastrians in the manner of crusader Christians, who tolerated heretical Christians, Jews, and Muslims in their territories but would have preferred forcibly to convert them. Rather, Zoroastrians possessed ideological, cosmological foundations for enlisting the adherents of some bad religions, such as Christians and Jews, into their imperial project.[34]

The presence of *agdēn* in Iranian territories and societies had the potential to disrupt the Zoroastrian social order in one particularly important domain: purity.[35] The evil forces of Ahreman, in Zoroastrian thought and practice, operated through physical manifestations, such as drought, winter, locusts, corpses, disease, and menstruation.[36] If the material world was in a state of mixture of rival powers and creations, one of the tasks of the wehdēn was to disaggregate these entities, to carve out spaces purged of evil that could provide a platform for combat against the material and spiritual agents of Ahreman. This took the form of rites of purification that protected the good elements—the human body, water, earth, fire, and so forth—from evil forces.[37] The constant maintenance of the purity of the body and the natural environment was the task not only of the priests but of individual believers. Of greatest concern for the social history of Iran was the treatment of bodies, especially after death. As the demon Nasuš was believed to have inflicted corpses, the dead became repositories of evil and had to be kept distant from living bodies, water, and earth. The exposure of corpses, which dogs and vultures both beneficent creatures with special powers against the demon Nasuš, picked clean, was characteristic of Zoroastrian societies from the Achaemenian period onward.[38] The dry bones of the dead were placed in ossuaries, *astōdān*, which have been attested archaeologically throughout Iran and Central Asia.[39]

Neither Christians nor Jews were customarily or theologically inclined to expose their dead or to inter them in ossuaries rather than the ground. Yet there are examples of Christians embracing Zoroastrian practices of interment, if not exposure. A rock-cut astōdān on the Kuh-e Rahmat between Istakhr and Persepolis displays a Christian cross on its entrance, indicating that an agdēn was interred alongside his Zoroastrian counterparts.[40] East Syrian hagiographical texts, moreover, describe Christians waiting until "the flesh had fallen from the bones" before interment and preventing blood and flesh from mixing with the earth.[41] Even so, inhumation was a common practice, archaeologically documented in Mesopotamia and the Persian Gulf, and apparently the norm among Christians and Jews.[42] The treatment of the dead was therefore a possible zone of conflict between wehdēn and agdēn, which Christian and Jewish authors frequently emphasized in their polemical representations of the authorities of the Good Religion.[43] Their reports that Zoroastrians often forcibly exhumed bodies that Christians and Jews had buried have contributed to the image of the persecutory mowbed.[44]

Sasanian scholars, however, debated the problem of agdēn bodies in ways that reveal more complex approaches toward religious others. Although historians have assumed the burials of Christians and Jews to have been a great offense to Zoroastrians, the *Wīdēwdād*, the Avestan treatise on purity and purification, states that the corpses of agdēn pollute the earth no more than those of deceased wicked creatures, that is, not in any measurable way that would be of concern to the religious authorities.[45] A ninth-century text, the *Gizistag Abāliš*, explains that demons afflict the deceased bodies of good, not evil, persons, making the corpses of anēr insignificant as sources of pollution.[46] The idea that Zoroastrian authorities intervened in the practices of religious others to coerce them to adhere to Zoroastrian principles overestimates their interest in communities whose contributions to Iran were more practical than religious. Some Zoroastrian scholars, discussed below, considered agdēn capable of performing cosmologically beneficial work, but no known exegete thought their bodies or spirits could attain the perfection that came with *wehdēnīh* (the Good Religion). The question of which deceased bodies caused pollution was an occasion for debating larger problems concerning the place of agdēn in a Zoroastrian society. The Middle Persian commentators of the *Wīdēwdād* in the Sasanian period elaborated on the passage concerning agdēn corpses to argue that anēr, whether alive or dead, could not pollute ēr.[47] The reasons for this claim varied in remarkable ways. The exegete and jurist Sōšāns, well known for strident views, considered non-Zoroastrians ontologically evil, incapable of pollution because they stood outside the wax and wane of good and evil forces in which wehdēn waged the cosmic struggle.[48] As Yaakov Elman has argued, Sōšāns represented the extreme end of the spectrum of Zoroastrian views concerning religious others. At the other end was the scholar Gōgušnasp, who argued that "we may become polluted by their [corpses], because men of any religious law [*dād*] may become righteous [*ahlaw*]."[49] According to Gōgušnasp, agdēn could act righteously, and their good deeds exposed them to demonic forces. Ironically, the arguments of the scholar with the most sympathetic views logically required non-Zoroastrians to adhere to Zoroastrian practices of purity, and the most antagonistic scholar regarded the burial of agdēn as entirely unproblematic. The significance of these views resides less in their implications for the treatment of the dead than in their explicit unveiling of a spectrum of approaches toward religious others among the authoritative scholars of the late Sasanian period.

If the bodies of agdēn were not as threatening to the social order as has been assumed, the institutions of the different religions present in Iranian territory were evaluated on their own terms. Not all religions were equally bad. The treatment of idolatry under the Sasanians shows how Zoroastrian authorities distinguished among agdēn.[50] At the outset of this chapter, we encountered a crucial distinction in the inscriptions of Kerdir. Christians, Jews, and other monotheistic religious groups were only to be "struck," while the institutions of idolaters and demon worshipers were to be eliminated to make way for Zoroastrian shrines. Their idols (*uzdēs*) were to be broken, their temples destroyed. Regardless of whether the mowbed undertook these actions in the third century, the twofold program he announced of subordinating monotheists and eradicating the institutions of idolatry well captured the approach of Zoroastrian religious authorities toward bad religions throughout the Sasanian era. Literary and legal sources attest to attempts to destroy supposed sites of idol worship from the reign of Ardashir I onward. Idols, their temples, and their worshipers had, in Zoroastrian thought, the capacity directly to unleash the powers of Ahreman in the world, making their destruction a characteristic of legitimate kingship.[51] Iranian and Armenian historiographical traditions recall the first king of kings, whose history was paradigmatic for subsequent rulers, as having uprooted idolatrous temples together with their priests.[52] The *Hazār Dādestān*, an early seventh-century collection of Zoroastrian judicial decisions, explicitly describes the process of destroying a temple of idols and establishing a fire temple in its place. A certain Pusanweh "tore down" a "house of idols" (*uzdēs kadag*) in a case concerned with legal authority over fire temples.[53] The incidental nature of the reference suggests that such destruction of idolatrous shrines was entirely unremarkable and so obviously legally justified that this aspect of the case was unworthy of comment. This legal sanction might even have provided support for Christians who uprooted idolatrous temples, a phenomenon documented in northern Mesopotamia.[54] If magic bowls and other sources reveal the continued veneration of a great many gods and demons in domestic contexts, the institutionalized worship of Mesopotamian and Hellenistic deities ceased in the early Sasanian centuries, whether on account of active destruction of their temples or the gradual draining of their treasuries.[55] The worship of the Assyrian gods at Karka d-Beit Slok in the sixth century took place privately, even clandestinely.[56] The antagonism of imperial authorities toward idolatry, moreover, helps to explain the absence of Buddhist communities in northeastern Iran even though they flourished just beyond the frontiers.[57] The identification of Buddhists as idolaters—indeed, *but-parast*, or "Buddha worshiper," became a standard term for *idolater* in New Persian—prevented them from earning the recognition that Christian and Jewish communities enjoyed.[58] There were, in sum, not merely bad religions but also worse religions, whose institutions Iranian authorities endeavored to eliminate from their empire.

The contrast with the experience of the Church of the East is striking. Not only were churches, saint's shrines, and monasteries constructed without attracting the intervention of Zoroastrian authorities throughout the territories of the empire, but the kings of kings often contributed funds to Christian infrastructural projects. East Syrian hagiographers frequently claimed in formulaic terms that Zoroastrians dismantled their churches and shrines, without specifying the sites and dates at which such acts were supposed to have occurred. The one concrete example, which appears in the *Martyrdom of Peroz*, describes the destruction, at a moment of renewed warfare with Rome, of a church that a Roman emperor had had built at Seleucia-Ctesiphon.[59] If other churches were assailed in the course of the tumultuous political relations of East Syrian bishops with the Iranian court, such actions had little impact on the ongoing proliferation of Christian buildings in the cities and regions of Iran, even at highly visible, politically potent sites, such as Weh-Ardashir or the tells of Arbela and Karka d-Beit Slok. Had Zoroastrian authorities wished to keep the construction of churches in check, there would have been more instances in the East Syrian sources of constraints imposed and fewer, or at least more modestly sited, Christian structures. In the entire corpus of Zoroastrian literature, there is not a single injunction to destroy the institutions of Christians, Jews, or other monotheists along the lines of the cases of the eradication of idol worship. As we will see, Christian churches that displaced fire temples were an altogether different matter, requiring Zoroastrian authorities to realign the proper spatial relationship between the two religions. In keeping with the distinction of Kerdir, Christians and other groups with the capacity for beneficent action were to be suppressed, in the literal sense of "subdued," while idolaters were to be expunged on account of their irredeemable propensity for maleficence.

Idolaters were not the only category of human without a place in Iran. The voices of Zoroastrian authorities became markedly shrill when treating deviance within their ranks. Labeled *ahlamōg* or *zandīg*, those who practiced rituals and/or interpreted the Zand—hence *zandīg*—in ways that the authorities deemed transgressive of established norms excluded themselves not only from the institutions of the Good Religion but from the empire.[60] If religious deviance and bad religion were sometimes juxtaposed as equivalent evils, approaches to the latter were considerably more violent.[61] Deviance in ritual and doctrine surpassed apostasy as a social and political evil in undermining the foundations of the imperial religion. In the *Sīrat Ānūširwān*, an autobiographical work establishing paradigms for his successors to follow, Husraw I wrote of having a group of aristocratic deviants at Rayy executed as soon as he learned of their existence.[62] Another group of deviants, whom the editor of the text argues were Manichaeans, were expelled from Iranian territory.[63] Royal anxieties about the possibility of religious deviants disrupting the political order were hardly baseless. In the early sixth century, the zandīg Mazdak developed the teachings of a third-century scholar known as Zardusht into a platform for thoroughgoing rebellion against the Sasanians. In Husraw I's forcible repression of the movement, thousands of its followers were reportedly executed.[64] Although idolaters and deviants seem to have been at opposite ends of the spectrum, the latter regarded as wayward Zoroastrians, the former as adherents of Ahreman, there was an underlying similarity in Zoroastrian understandings of the two categories. Both compromised the Good Religion from the inside. Whether for real or imagined reasons, Zoroastrian religious authorities feared that wehdēn would be drawn to worship demons, as we will see in the next chapter. At the foundation of the empire, Ardashir I was believed to have destroyed not only centers of idol worship but also fire temples that the Parthians had established, on account of the divergence of their rituals and customs from the new Sasanian norms.[65] From the third century, demon worship, idolatry, and deviance were potential rivals to the priestly authorities of the Good Religion. In spite of East Syrian representations of mowbed seeking the destruction of their communities, the Christian threat to Zoroastrian institutions never attained the same immediacy in the eyes of the imperial religious authorities, in either the third century or the sixth.

Zoroastrian religious authorities thus made important distinctions among different varieties of agdēn. Some were inherently allied with evil forces and therefore impermissible in a Zoroastrian society, namely idolatry and deviance. Others were composite entities, neither wholly good nor wholly evil, capable of contributing materially or spiritually to an Iranian Empire, namely Christianity and Judaism. In place of the binary division of humanity into good and evil populations that has hitherto prevailed in historical discussions of Zoroastrian interactions with religious others, a concept drawn from the writings of Sasanian scholars is more helpful for understanding their approaches toward Christians, Jews, and others: hierarchy.[66] As the previous section has shown, the idea of Iran implied not a binary but a hierarchical conception of humanity. The *Mēnōg ī Xrad* says that humans are to be measured according to a certain scale: "How many kinds [*sardag*] of human are there? There are three kinds of human. One is human [*mardōm*], the other half human [*nēm mardōm*], and another half demon [*nēm dēw*]." The fully fledged human was, predictably, a believer in the Good Religion, without any tendency toward deviance (*jud ristagīh*). The demonic human pursued only self-interested evil. The half human, however, was a curiously amalgamated creature who could not be neatly categorized as either good or evil: "The half human is one who performs material and spiritual things according to his own thinking, arrogantly and disobediently [*xwad-dōšagīhā*]. Actions and deeds [*kār u kirbag*] proceed from him in accordance with both the will of Ohrmazd and the will of Ahreman."[67] Half humans, in other words, undertook good and evil work, on account of their ignorance of the perfect knowledge of the Good Religion, which would have rendered their thoughts, words, and actions entirely beneficent. The terms *kār* and *kirbag* evoke the entire edifice of Zoroastrian ethics, which was predicated on the notion that humans could help to restore the cosmos to a primordial state of perfection through their work, their *xwēškārīh*. The empire organized the collective efforts of wehdēn to maximize beneficent cosmological labor, a project that, in the interim mixed state of the world, required them to cooperate with agdēn. In this process, the so-called half humans could make potentially positive contributions, unlike their half demon counterparts.

Internal Zoroastrian debates concerning the extent to which the half humans who constituted the great bulk of the population of the empire performed good work on its behalf have been left largely undocumented. There are, however, clear signs that such discussions frequently took place. The imagined scholarly interlocutor of the *Mēnōg ī Xrad* asks, "Which sects [*kēš*], laws [*dād*], and beliefs [*wurrōyišnīh*] are harmful to the well-being of the gods and are not good?"[68] *Kēš* designates, in the inscriptions of Kerdir and elsewhere, agdēn religions. The presupposition of the scholar asking the question is thus that some kēš possessed laws and beliefs that were more damaging (*wizendgar*) to the Good Religion than those of others. The *Pursišnīhā*, a question-and-answer text that was redacted in the early Islamic period and considers queries relevant to Sasanian society, tackles similar issues. Its interrogator asks, "[If] an agdēn is allied with the wehdēn in goodness . . . and helps the wehdēn in matters of prosperity . . . , does he join in the righteousness of good work and deeds [*kār u kirbag*]?" The following question makes explicit what the *kār u kirbag*, which we have so far seen in ambiguous contexts, entailed: "[If] anēr warriors kill other anēr together with the Turks and ourselves and keep destruction from us, do good deeds [*kirbag*] reach their souls for bravery and strength or not?"[69] These passages make plain that non-Zoroastrians were routinely thought capable of performing meritorious deeds, *kirbag,* through military service or economic activities that enhanced the prosperity of Iran. But the scholars who answered these questions rejected their presumption that agdēn could achieve righteousness or even enter the spiritual realm after death.[70] Nevertheless, they regarded these queries as sufficiently urgent to write, to compile, and to preserve the questions and responses, providing insights into the range of views that circulated among imperial religious authorities in late antiquity. They are rare examples of Zoroastrian scholars conscious of their dependence on agdēn for the realization of Ērānšahr.

The scholar Gōgušnasp explicitly articulated a conception of the position of religious others in a Zoroastrian society, which underpinned the questions that the editors of the *Mēnōg ī Xrad* and *Pursišnīhā* addressed: "In every law [*dād*] there are righteous people."[71] Agdēn could, like their wehdēn counterparts, attain righteousness through the performance of good work. They could, by extension, contribute to the empire, in essence a congeries of institutions designed to coordinate the cosmologically beneficent efforts of individuals. Rather than a liability, they were an asset to Iran. We have no way to gauge the prevalence of such a view in relation to others, such as the opinion of Sōšāns that agdēn were incapable of righteousness. For the reconstruction of the actions and approaches of Zoroastrian religious authorities, moreover, a mowbed apparently antagonistic toward religious others—or a more sympathetic counterpart—cannot be isolated as representative of the class. Neither Sōšāns nor Gōgušnasp encapsulated the range of thought of scholars across four centuries on such a cosmologically complex religious and political problem. There were some who considered agdēn capable of good work, others who considered them capable only of evil. The great majority of Zoroastrian authorities likely creatively combined cosmological paradigms to make judgments of their own that fell somewhere along the spectrum between Sōšāns and Gōgušnasp. Zoroastrian cosmological thought, as the introduction notes, was predicated on myths and rituals that predisposed their interpreters to polyphonic discourse rather than the definition of normative orthodoxies. There were voices within this discourse that agitated for the recognition of the contributions that agdēn could make to the cosmological struggle, others that strenuously contested such claims. Absent were voices requiring the exclusion of bad religions in general from the empire or their segregation within its confines. Particular agdēn and agdēnīh were to be evaluated on their own terms for their respective ethical merits. As sources from both within and without the scholarly discourse show, these processes of judgment favored monotheisms that did not outwardly exhibit features of Ahremanic cults as imagined in the Avesta over polytheisms or deviant movements that openly challenged the Good Religion. The body of thought and ritual that the early Sasanians institutionalized and rendered normative predisposed them as much to include as to exclude particular religious others with respect to their political system.

Yet violence against Christians occurred with the sanction of Zoroastrian religious authorities at court. Recently, Richard Kalmin reinterpreted passages of the Babylonian Talmud previously believed to indicate the persecution of Jewish communities at various points in the history of the Sasanians. The Jews, he shows, were never subject to the persecutory violence that scholars claimed Zoroastrians sometimes exercised against them.[72] What follows similarly reviews the East Syrian sources in their respective literary contexts to deconstruct narratives of persecution. The hagiographical works, nevertheless, describe specific episodes of violence whose historicity cannot be discounted. Hagiographers creatively adapted their narratives in the pursuit of theological and political agendas, subordinating the events they recorded to the shaping of Christian communities in accordance with the interests of ecclesiastical leaders. But in writing for audiences of East Syrian elites increasingly integrated into courtly and aristocratic circles, they did not invent the basic facts of their accounts, often including details that are seemingly at variance with their overarching representations and thus allow for alternative interpretations. Rather than deny episodes of martyrdom their historicity, the following three sections seek to understand acts of violence by the Iranian court—insofar as the sources permit historical analysis—in light of the Zoroastrian cosmological discourse of religious difference, with a view to showing how they served to order hierarchically, and thereby to integrate, Christian elites indispensable to the functioning of the empire. In extreme cases, the sword was used to place limits on Christians who challenged the supremacy of the Good Religion through disobedience to the king of kings, the destruction of fire temples, or proselytism among wehdēn. To characterize such violence as persecution is to overlook its ultimately inclusive intentions and effects.

THE "GREAT PERSECUTION"

According to East Syrian hagiographical and historiographical traditions, the Christian populations of the Iranian Empire were subject to systematic persecution from 340 until the death of Shapur II in 379. Upward of forty works describe Zoroastrian religious authorities relentlessly tormenting Christian men and women at every possible opportunity on account of their religious identities.[73] Zoroastrian mowbed reportedly aimed to eliminate "the Christian people," who were a threat to the religion, society, and political structures of Iran, for example in the *Martyrdom of Aqebshma*:

> The Christians are destroying our teaching. They are teaching people to serve only one God, not to worship the sun, not to honor fire, to defile the waters with despicable ablutions, not to marry women, not to produce sons or daughters, not to enter battle with the kings, not to kill, to slaughter and eat animals without murmuring [the ritual prayers], and to bury and to conceal the dead in the earth. They say that God created serpents and scorpions together with vermin, not Satan. They impair many of the servants of the king and teach them the sorcery that they call books.[74]

For their evil beliefs and practices, the Christians were to be expunged from the empire. This passage is characteristic of East Syrian hagiographical literature in emphasizing the mowbed rather than the king of kings or the aristocracy as the instigators of persecution.[75] Nevertheless, the outpouring of Zoroastrian hostility toward Christians takes place, in these accounts, at the command of a king of kings, who often directly supervises the torture and execution of the martyrs. These accounts were, after all, generally composed at a comfortable distance from the purportedly persecutory ruler, during the fifth, sixth, and seventh centuries, when East Syrian leaders had come to enjoy the patronage of the kings of kings. Despite this gap in both chronology and political context, historians have typically interpreted accounts of violence during the reign of Shapur II as reliably documenting the activities of a Zoroastrian ruler and/or religious authorities hostile toward other religions.[76] This section questions whether a persecution in fact occurred. To do so, we must define the concept of *persecution* at the outset. According to the *Oxford English Dictionary*, the term designates "systematic violent oppression, directed against members . . . of a particular religious group."[77] If East

Syrian authors claimed that events fitting such a description happened, the recent historical reconstructions of Karin Mosig-Walburg and Kyle Smith, based on comprehensive surveys of the evidence, suggest otherwise.

Shapur II, in the traditional narrative, initiated a persecution of Christians in response to the conversion of Constantine the Great and the Christianization of the Roman Empire. It was not until the Romans became Christian, Jérôme Labourt and most subsequent historians have asserted, that the Iranian court targeted Christian communities as latent extensions of the Roman state in Iranian territory.[78] The sources for this claim are twofold: the letter that Eusebius of Caesarea reported Constantine to have sent to the king of kings, and East Syrian hagiographical works in which persecuted Christians are accused of supporting the Romans. According to the *Life of Constantine*, the first Christian emperor appealed to Shapur II circa 324–37 to respect the Christians of Iran, who came under Constantine's purview as the universal sovereign of all Christians.[79] If the letter reached the Iranian court, a highly uncertain proposition, Shapur II would have perceived its claim as an infringement on his own pretension to universal sovereignty. But the view that the letter inspired the king of kings to take action against the Christians of his empire as agents of Constantine relies on a bishop's rewriting of a Roman imperial epistle to reconstruct the decision-making processes of an Iranian court. It was not until the middle of the fifth century, moreover, that East Syrian authors began to report that Shapur II had accused Christians of harboring Roman loyalties.[80] These allegations appeared in a specific literary context. Hagiographers who argued that Christians could be loyal servants of the Iranian court as long as their obedience was compatible with their Christianity were the same authors who reported accusations of divided loyalties. The literary topos of a king of kings denouncing a Christian for serving the Romans provided a foil for hagiographers who insisted on the undivided allegiance of East Syrian communities to Iran. These representations also gained plausibility from the fifth-century circumstances in which they were written. As Christians became courtly elites serving as diplomatic intermediaries between the two empires, the question of their loyalty and disloyalty became acute. Only a Christian performing a service on behalf of the king of kings, such as the catholicos Baboi (d. 484), could be seriously accused of treason.[81] In the fourth century, however, Christians could not be identified as agents of Rome. Even if Shapur II received and read a letter from Constantine, the argument that the Iranian court perceived Christianity as a Roman phenomenon overestimates the extent to which the Roman state presented itself in Christian terms.[82]

The cause of the violence that Christians encountered was a matter of internal politics only indirectly related to the Roman wars. To reconstruct the historical events that were reworked into a narrative of a "Great Persecution," we have to rely on critical studies of the hagiographical accounts that constitute our only substantive sources, however tendentious. The most detailed, extensive, and influential of these are the *History of Simeon* and the *Martyrdom of Simeon*, both narratives of the bishop of Seleucia-Ctesiphon whose martyrdom marked the beginning of the violence. Although historians have tended to use these texts interchangeably as reliable accounts of the events, Gernot Wiessner long ago established that they represent distinct hagiographical traditions compiled in the course of the fifth century, which in turn shaped the great bulk of the other surviving East Syrian narratives of martyrs from the reign of Shapur II.[83] The demonstration that the accounts of Simeon were fifth-century productions paved the way for scholarly investigation of their literary importance and their role in Iranian political culture. Wiessner nevertheless also established a foundation for their reliability as historical sources, with the demonstration that the *History of Simeon* and the *Martyrdom of Simeon* share a common source, likely composed in the immediate aftermath of the martyr's death. Details that these two texts share therefore can be accepted as historical.[84]

The *History of Simeon* and the *Martyrdom of Simeon* agree on one essential feature of the violence: its cause. According to the authors of both works, Shapur II had Simeon and his associates executed for refusing to collect taxes on behalf of the court.[85] From his summer palace in Khuzestan, the king of kings issued a decree to the authorities in Seleucia-Ctesiphon, including the bishop, in the *History of Simeon*: "As soon as you see this command of ours ... arrest Simeon, the head of the *naṣraye*, and do not release him until he signs a document and takes it upon himself to collect and give to us a double poll tax and double tribute from all the people of the *naṣraye* who are in our land ... and who inhabit the land of our authority.... They dwell in our land, yet they are of one mind with Caesar, our enemy. And while we fight, they rest."[86] This edict, the hagiographers insisted, was the stimulus of the Great Persecution. Although they elaborated on the events to present the king of kings as requiring Simeon and the other martyrs to worship the sun and the Jews as instigators, these were secondary developments epiphenomenal to an attempt to coerce the bishop of the imperial capital to contribute to the fisc. Just as Antiochus IV had plundered the Jews to replenish his treasury during the era of the Maccabean revolt, the *Martyrdom of Simeon* asserted, Shapur II had endeavored to despoil the Christians, whose leader steadfastly resisted.[87] The account of a king of kings seeking the collaboration of religious authorities in the levying of taxes in preparation for military campaigns is eminently plausible. When the edict was pronounced, Shapur II was in the middle of organizing imperial resources in a bid to reconquer the city of Nisibis, which had been lost to Rome in a humiliating concession in 299.[88] In the absence of financial instruments that would allow for the large-scale accumulation of capital through state debt, the successful practice of war required substantial cash reserves for the provisioning of men and materials.

Early Sasanian infrastructures of taxation, however, appear to have been underdeveloped. There is, at this stage, little documentation concerning the levying of taxes during the first two centuries of the empire, even if the regular minting of silver drachms throughout its territories shows that the court enjoyed a reliable influx of precious metals.[89] Early Sasanian efforts to intensify and control the production of high-value commodities in Khuzestan nevertheless suggest that the court sought to transcend the limitations of its fiscal system.[90] Navigable rivers debouching into the Persian Gulf—an avenue of both interregional and transcontinental trade over which Shapur II asserted Sasanian control—punctuated the fertile plains of the region, making its cities ideal sites for the production of commodities specifically for long-distance exchange.[91] Shapur I and Shapur II constructed new cities in Khuzestan, in particular Beit Lapat / Jundishapur (Middle Persian Weh-Antiyōk-Šāpūr) and Karka d-Ledan (Middle Persian Ērānšahr-Šāpūr) respectively, for the resettlement of artisans from the Roman world who specialized in the production of highly trafficked textile and precious metal commodities.[92] So central was commercial production at Karka d-Ledan to the treasury of Shapur II's court that he established his winter palace in the city, alongside a structure built to house the administration of its artisans.[93] In addition to concerted efforts to profit from long-distance trade, East Syrian hagiographers reported that the king of kings attempted to enlist bishops in the fiscal system. The turn to religious authorities as intermediaries with provincial populations or, even more directly, as supervisors of taxation was in keeping with what is known of courtly practice in later periods. Husraw I depended on Zoroastrian religious authorities to enact and enforce his reforms of the fiscal system in the sixth century.[94] In cities with substantial Christian populations, bishops would have been indispensable ancillary authorities for organizing the levying of taxes. In requesting that Simeon and his episcopal partners contribute to the collection of taxes among their Christian constituencies, Shapur II aimed to draw upon their organizational powers in the two regions economically most important to the court, Mesopotamia and Khuzestan, to maximize royal revenues in anticipation of war with Rome. The royal edict requiring Simeon to collect taxes was an invitation to participate in the extension of imperial fiscal structures rather than an act of persecution.

The refusal of the empire's leading bishop to contribute to the renewal of the fisc, however, constituted an act of contumacy meriting punishment. Simeon reportedly regarded the collection of taxes as outside the scope of his authority as a bishop, in a passage of the *History of Simeon* that communicates his unfailing loyalty to the Sasanian: "I bow to the king of kings, and I honor his commands with all my power, however, concerning that which is required of me in the edict, I believe even you know that it is not my business to demand taxes from the people of Christ, my Lord. Indeed, our authority over them is not in the things which are seen but in those things which are unseen."[95] The author of the *History of Simeon* drew a distinction between the worldly authority of the ruler and the spiritual authority of the bishop, which provided an intellectual foundation for Christians in both ecclesiastical and secular offices who served the king of kings in imperial institutions.[96] The refusal of Simeon to collect taxes created a separate, secular space for the Sasanian state, in which the ecclesiastical leaders of the Christian community could only assume roles if their service complemented their spiritual responsibilities. The importance of this distinction between the secular and the ecclesiastical that the fifth-century author articulated recurs throughout the following chapters. Simeon, in this view, could not collect taxes, because such service impinged on the welfare of Christian communities. But if the separateness of worldly and spiritual spheres became common language in the writings of East Syrian leaders, there was no consensus on the permissibility of participating in the fiscal system. The only bishop of Seleucia-Ctesiphon to have left behind letters on the mundane affairs of the office presumed facilitating the organization of taxation to have been a fundamental episcopal responsibility. Ishoyahb III, in the middle of the seventh century, even sought to arrogate to himself the privilege of levying the land and poll taxes—precisely the combination rejected in the accounts of Simeon—on the Christians of Iran.[97] The views of the intervening bishops of Seleucia-Ctesiphon and other cities have not survived. There is, however, an intimation in the *Martyrdom of Simeon* that not all bishops rejected the opportunity to collaborate in the collection of taxes as readily and definitively as Simeon did. Although almost all of the bishops of the other major cities of Khuzestan were executed together with the bishop of Seleucia-Ctesiphon, the bishop of Karka d-Ledan, the site of Shapur II's palace, was spared.[98] He was perhaps among the dissenting East Syrian leaders against whom the authors of the *Martyrdom of Simeon* and the *History of Simeon* composed their elaborate, theologically informed expositions of the view that taxation was incompatible with the episcopal office. An alternative conception of the relationship between the worldly and the spiritual need not have been an innovation of Ishoyahb III.

Simeon and allied ecclesiastical leaders perished in the 340s for failing to cooperate in the extension of the fiscal system, not simply for being Christians. Execution was the consequence for disobeying a king of kings, whether the offender was Christian or Zoroastrian, an aristocrat or a commoner. Unlike their Roman peers, Iranian elites regardless of their status or background enjoyed no exemption from corporeal punishment. The violence that followed Simeon's disobedience targeted ecclesiastical leaders associated with the bishop and his circle, with only a handful of documented secular Christian men and women finding themselves accountable for the actions of their leaders. Among the Christians executed in the outskirts of Karka d-Ledan in 344 were the bishops of Beit Lapat and Ohrmazd-Ardashir in Khuzestan and Prat d-Maishan and Karka d-Maishan in Mesopotamia, ninety-seven priests and deacons, two secular elites who associated themselves with the recalcitrant bishops, and an ascetic woman, a *ba(r)t qyama*.[99] More or less reliable accounts describe the execution during the following three decades of bishops, priests, and ascetics in Seleucia-Ctesiphon and Kashkar in southern Mesopotamia; Arbela, Karka d-Beit Slox, and their hinterlands in northern Mesopotamia; and Khuzestan.[100] In the absence of source-critical studies of these martyrologies of the kind that Wiessner and more recent scholars have performed for the Simeon accounts, the historicity of these martyrdoms after 344 remains uncertain.[101] Even a highly optimistic reading of the evidence, however, shows the violence to have been limited and largely restricted to ecclesiastical leaders.[102] Significant in this context is the prominence of *banat qyama*, female ascetics, whose sufferings hagiographers often emphasized as illustrating the vulnerabilities of Christian communities. Although their activities were gradually suppressed in the course of the institutionalization of the Church of the East in the fifth and sixth centuries, ascetic women were organizers of Christian ritual, prayer, and charity in the fourth century.[103] To Iranian officials, they were representatives of Christian communities as important as the male bishops and priests whose ranks they joined as martyrs. The court of Shapur II might have identified Christianity as a potentially centrifugal force within the empire. But the violence that Iranian elites inflicted on Christians was restricted to its religious leaders who had failed adequately to fulfill the obligations that the court imposed on them. Shapur II punished ecclesiastical leaders for disobedience. Neither he nor his court persecuted Christians as a collective.

The "Great Persecution" was thus a myth. Christians were not systematically persecuted as a recognizable group on account of their religious identity, but rather ecclesiastical leaders were executed for disobedience in their capacity as potential intermediaries of particular provincial populations vis-à-vis the court. Iranian elites identified a generation of ecclesiastical leaders—bishops, priests, and bnai qyama—as complicit in the contumacy of the bishop of Seleucia-Ctesiphon, leading to episodes of violence that might have seemed indiscriminate to contemporary observers and, especially, to later hagiographers. The underlying logic was nevertheless consistent. The killing of Christians under Shapur II was the result of a refused invitation that the court had extended to ecclesiastical leaders to participate more actively in the administration of the empire. It was not the result of the ineluctable hostility of Zoroastrians at court toward religious others. This reinterpretation of the violence of the fourth century allows for a new perspective on the court's elevation—or indeed creation—of the Church of the East in the early fifth century. The measures of Shapur II and Yazdgird I were of a piece, equally intended to integrate Christians into imperial networks and to discipline Christian communities into a subject position dependent on the king of kings and his court. Accounts of violence against Christians in the fourth century suggest that Christian ecclesiastical leaders, secular elites, and their subordinate communities were becoming visible to a court eager to make sense of the populations and resources under its control with a view to maximizing their exploitation. If the court had to learn how to negotiate with Christian communal leaders during the decades between 379 and 410, East Syrian leaders had to come to terms with Iranian power within their own framework. The *History of Simeon* outlines the foundations of a rapprochement between bishops and kings of kings with its insistence on the compatibility of worldly and spiritual authorities as long as their distinction remained secure. The execution of ecclesiastical leaders for disobeying Shapur II counterintuitively points to the intimate collaboration of their successors with the Iranian rulers of the fifth, sixth, and early seventh centuries.

PATRONS OR PERSECUTORS?

There was greater continuity in the attitudes of fourth- and fifth-century kings of kings than has been appreciated.[104] The reign of Yazdgird I nevertheless remains a turning point. After his recognition of the Church of the East in 410, churches, martyr's shrines, and eventually monasteries were constructed in prominent places in the Iranian political landscape, notably in the vicinity of the court at Seleucia–Ctesiphon. Yazdgird I openly sanctioned such constructions and even contributed funds to churches whose principal patrons were East Syrian leaders or Roman envoys. The participation of Christians—both secular and ecclesiastical elites—in the administration only intensified, a trend that continued until the end of the empire. The potential pitfalls of holding imperial offices, or simply serving as a humble scribe, were major themes of accounts of fifth-century martyrs. But the transformation of ecclesiastical leaders' roles in imperial politics was more dramatic. Bishops began to serve the kings of kings in a variety of capacities, not least as envoys pursuing Iranian political and economic interests within and especially without the empire[105] Where Simeon and allied ecclesiastical leaders had strenuously objected to Shapur II's invitation to participate in the imperial administration, fifth-century bishops—and their sixth- and early seventh-century successors—acted as representatives of Iran even while distancing themselves, through hagiographical literature and its attendant institutions, from its religion. It was precisely at a time of convergence of the interests of the Church of the East and the Sasanian dynasty that hagiographers recounting fourth- and fifth-century martyrdoms debated the nature of the relationship between East Syrian leaders and their rulers and produced the first extensive, sometimes even substantive, polemics against Zoroastrianism.[106]

Episodes of violence nevertheless punctuated the history of fifth-century political integration. During the final years of the reign of Yazdgird I and the reigns of his successors Wahram V and Yazdgird II, Iranian officials interrogated, imprisoned, and executed Christians at the behest of kings of kings and destroyed some recently erected churches. In contrast with the narratives of the Great Persecution, these were frequently cases of martyred lay persons, officials in the administration whose Christianity seemed to present an obstacle to their imperial loyalty. Recent studies have characterized these episodes as periods of persecution that kings of kings undertook to appease Zoroastrian religious authorities or to respond to the incursions of Christian Romans.[107] However, as with the circle of Simeon and related martyrs, the specific cases of the individuals killed and their political contexts reveal more of the historical significance of the violence than do the descriptions of general persecution that prevail in historiographies ancient and modern. The number of documented fifth-century martyrs is modest, the reasons for their execution more complex than mere anti-Christian sentiment. The relations of individual Christian elites with the court depended, this section argues, on their political positions and actions rather than the supposedly shifting religious policies of their rulers. However militantly anti-Zoroastrian Roman rhetoric became during the course of Rome's fourth- and fifth-century wars against Iran, internal Iranian developments determined the fate of these martyrs.[108] Instability on the northeastern frontiers played, in any case, a more important role than relations with Rome in shaping the policies of the fifth-century kings of kings vis-à-vis their constituencies. There were two kinds of violence in the fifth century that have been lumped together under the carapace of persecution: the purging of elites in political crises, and the execution of individuals for particular misdeeds that communicated norms for interaction between Christians and Zoroastrians. The former phenomenon was restricted to the middle decades of the fifth century, while the latter shaped the social and political history of Christians throughout the late Sasanian period.

Throughout the fifth century, the Hun kingdoms of the Kidarites (ca. 360–457) and Hephthalites (ca. 457–560) forced Iran to engage in nearly continuous warfare on its northern and northeastern frontiers.[109] The reigns of Wahram V and Yazdgird II, in particular, were dedicated to campaigns to regain control of Bactria that succeeded only in retaining Khurasan. The Central Asian wars provoked an institutional and ideological crisis that eventually resulted in the robust, confident empire of the late Sasanians, but in the middle of the fifth century the very survival of Iran was uncertain. One symptom of the crisis was the unprecedentedly unpredictable violence of the court against elites whose loyalties became suspect. In an unparalleled episode, Wahram V had sixteen scribes apprehended and, according to the *Martyrdom of Jacob the Notary*, required to renounce Christianity on pain of death.[110] These were scribes in royal service with access to sensitive information. Although the hagiographer presented the episode as an example of persecution, the execution of scribes and messengers in possession of state secrets was a banal fact of courtly life, not an indication of an imperial anti-Christian policy. That Christians could now become scribes, envoys, and informants exposed them to the risks that accompanied the offices of the court. Accounts of the violence that Christians experienced under Yazdgird II emphasize that the supposed persecution was part of a package of measures intended to discipline imperial aristocracies more generally rather than specifically to target Christians. The *History of Karka d-Beit*

Slok and Its Martyrs recounts the execution of Christians in this northern Mesopotamian city in the 450s. Unlike the ascetics and clerics who perished there in the fourth century, the fifth-century martyrs were uniformly aristocratic landowners, members of the middling ranks of nobility who provided cavalry for Iranian campaigns in the East.[111] These northern Mesopotamian nobles might have shared the anxieties of their Armenian counterparts about campaigning in the distant, unfamiliar steppe.[112] What is clear is that their execution was connected with Yazdgird II's treatment of both Zoroastrian and Christian aristocrats in military and courtly contexts. He revoked privileges of access to the court and castrated men in his field armies to create eunuchs more loyal to the king of kings than to their own houses.[113] The *History of Karka* has preserved an example of Christians experiencing the selective application of violence to uncooperative nobles that was a basic instrument of ensuring aristocratic discipline. As Nina Garsoïan has observed, the violence that Armenians experienced in the aftermath of their rebellion of 451 served to bring the *nakharar*s (Armenian nobles) to obedience rather than to convert Armenia to Zoroastrianism.[114] The execution of Christian elites, from this perspective, differed little from the savagery that Zoroastrian aristocrats were accustomed to expect from the court. Such violence was effective in disciplining the northern Mesopotamian and Armenian houses, which remained among the most loyal agents of the empire in the following century. These episodes were nevertheless isolated, at least in our hagiographical documentation.

The other recorded cases of exceptional violence in the fifth century established modalities of interaction between Christian and Zoroastrian elites that defined their relations in the following centuries. The recognition of the Church of the East as a royally sanctioned institution of the Iranian Empire raised questions about the relationship between the two religions to which violence, and its literary representation, provided answers. The first question concerned the relationship between their physical infrastructures. To what extent did churches emerge at the expense of fire temples? The presence of churches within the lines of sight of observers of Iranian landscapes could pose, in the eyes of Christians and Zoroastrians alike, a symbolic challenge to the supremacy of the Good Religion, a theme that recurs in chapters 2 and 4. Of greater concern to Iranian authorities, however, were Christians who attempted directly to destabilize Zoroastrian infrastructures, particularly through the destruction of fire temples. The second question concerned conversion. Did the newfound political legitimacy of Christianity permit Zoroastrian elites to participate in its rites and institutions or even to apostatize in its favor? When Yazdgird I gave his sanction to the Church of the East, he appears not to have known much of Christian doctrine or practice, particularly the religion's propensity for proselytism and polemics. Focused like his forerunner Shapur II on the capacity of the episcopal network to contribute to the court's political and economic resources, he was seemingly unaware of the ideological challenges that

Christians could pose to Zoroastrian preeminence. Although militant ascetics disabused him of the illusion of Christian passivity, the problem of how to constrain Christians antagonistic toward Zoroastrianism remained even after he safeguarded the fire temples of the empire from Christian assailants. The imperial religion, in the view of its authorities, could be diminished not only through the outright destruction of its temples but also, more subtly, through attrition. Zoroastrian authorities therefore developed principles and procedures for prosecuting and executing apostates. The problem of conversion—the topic of the next section—remained of acute concern to the court until the end of the dynasty.

The phenomenon of Christians assaulting fire temples first appeared toward the end of Yazdgird I's reign, circa 419–20. The bishop of Ohrmazd-Ardashir in Khuzestan, Abda, in league with a group of Christian clerics and laymen, destroyed a fire temple, and the court accordingly called them to account.[115] The king of kings reportedly demanded of the bishop, "Since you are the chief and leader of these men, why do you allow them to despise our kingdom, to transgress against our command, and to act in accordance with their own will? Do you demolish and destroy our houses of worship and the foundations of our fire temples, which we have received from the fathers of our fathers to honor?" The ruler who had elevated bishops to positions as imperial agents now turned to one of their ranks to discipline Christians who had undermined an institution of the state. Abda temporized, but a priest in his retinue took responsibility for the act and justified the destruction of a fire temple as a pious demonstration of the falsehood of Zoroastrianism: "I demolished the foundation and extinguished the fire because it is not a house of God, nor is the fire the daughter of God."[116] Destroying a fire temple, the author of the *Martyrdom of Mar Abda* contended, was a means of communicating the triumph of Christianity. Although the conclusion of this East Syrian account has not survived, the nearly contemporaneous work of Theodoret of Cyrrhus (ca. 393–457) reports that the bishop refused to rebuild the shrine and was executed, together with his companions, for destroying a Zoroastrian shrine without making reparations.[117] The case of the martyr Narsai was similar.[118] After discovering that an aristocrat who had temporarily embraced Christianity and constructed a church had converted it into a fire temple, the ascetic forcefully entered the shrine, extinguished its fire, and removed the accoutrements of Zoroastrian rites.[119] Imperial authorities intervened, and the chief mowbed gave Narsai the opportunity to repair the damage: "Promise that you will go and build the hearth as it was and bring in and set up a fire within it. Good will be accomplished through you, and your life will be given to you."[120] The leading Zoroastrian authority was willing to pardon the ascetic for dismantling a fire temple. Narsai, however, remained uncooperative. Following a brief imprisonment, he was beheaded for the damage done to a fire temple and, symbolically, to the position of the Good Religion as a whole.

These zealous Christians were killed not for failing to contribute to the organization of the empire but for intentionally—and unapologetically—dismantling its infrastructure. In addition to being sites of ritual functions, foundational of imperial authority, fire temples were an indispensable basis for the economic and social power of the aristocratic houses.[121] It was through isolated acts of temple destruction that certain Christians openly challenged Iran's social and political structures, with or without knowledge of how they were embedded in fire temples and their rituals. In so doing, Abda and Narsai imitated the actions of Christian zealots in the Roman world, known to them through reports transmitted either orally or textually, who in the fourth and fifth centuries rendered the destruction of polytheist, Jewish, and other non-Christian places and objects of worship an ascetic practice.[122] In the hagiographical literature of the era, violence against temples, idols, synagogues, and their respective believers became a mark of ascetic distinction. This vision of Christian holiness resulted in countless hostile acts that have left their imprint on both literary sources and numerous remaining, or archaeologically excavated, polytheist statues and temples.[123] Significantly, such religious militance often flourished without the involvement or sanction of Roman officials.[124] East Syrian martyrs, like the bulk of their Roman counterparts, assailed temples without the support of a state and in the face of significant opposition from their fellow Christians. A number of prominent Roman Christian bishops preached against such violence, and Theodoret of Cyrrhus condemned the actions of Abda on the grounds that the apostle Paul had not destroyed the altars of Athens, even if a Christian contributing to the reconstruction of a fire temple was, for this Roman bishop, unimaginable.[125] The martyrdoms of Abda and Narsai were written to rebut similar arguments among East Syrian ecclesiastical leaders who found their actions an unwelcome attack on the authority of a king of kings otherwise so favorable to them. This view, not that of the hagiographers, became normative among East Syrians, who henceforth largely abstained from celebrating acts of violence against Zoroastrians or their fire temples.[126] Their rejection of the paradigms of ascetic violence, at least until after the Islamic conquests, stands in contrast to the Roman world, where they only became more prevalent. If the court of Yazdgird I aimed clearly to communicate to Christians that attacks on Zoroastrian fire temples would be investigated, prosecuted, and punished, the executions of Abda and his retinue and Narsai were effective. East Syrian temple smashing was a short-lived phenomenon. Proselytism, however, was a Christian practice that East Syrian leaders could restrict only with difficulty.

THE LIMITS OF THE GOOD RELIGION: PROSECUTING APOSTASY

Accounts of Zoroastrians who converted to Christianity and were martyred for apostasy proliferated in the fifth, sixth, and early seventh centuries. Indeed, histories of converts martyred under the Sasanians continued to be produced long after the empire had collapsed, an indication of the importance of such stories for the social and political imaginaries of East Syrian communities. The first apostate martyrs reportedly perished during the reign of Shapur II, but the pursuit and prosecution of apostates appears to have gathered pace under Yazdgird I.[127] A certain Shapur was perhaps executed for apostasy as early as 417 at royal command, and the so-called ten martyrs of Beit Garmai, who had been adherents of the "religion of the Magians" (*deḥlta d-mguše*), were punished at the hands of the mowbed Mihrshapur and the king of kings in 420.[128] Yazdgird I's successors Wahram V and Yazdgird II continued to prosecute elite converts, whose stories East Syrian hagiographers chose to propagate as examples of martyrdom. In the sixth century, Husraw I and Husraw II presided over the prosecution and execution of nine particularly well-documented converts. The Sasanians were apparently consistent in their treatment of apostates whose cases were brought to their attention throughout the fifth and sixth centuries.[129] The regular use of the sword to punish converts has given rise to the widespread assumption that a so-called law of apostasy, according to which apostates were to be killed, governed interactions between Zoroastrians and Christians throughout the empire, at all social levels and in all periods.[130] The prosecution of apostasy has therefore been taken as an example of the persecutory tendencies of Zoroastrian religious authorities. Although the view that apostates merited death was indeed normative, the application of the principle in practice depended on political circumstances and the development of Zoroastrian jurisprudence. The "law of apostasy" repays a closer examination in light of Zoroastrian theoretical discussions of the treatment of apostates and Christian accounts of particular historical episodes of martyred converts. The execution of apostates served to establish mutually recognizable limits on interreligious encounters that facilitated social and political interaction.

As the martyr acts attest, the problem of conversion first attracted the attention of Zoroastrian authorities in the era of Christian institutional ascendancy. There is no reason to believe, however, that Zoroastrians abandoned their religion in any significant numbers at any point in Sasanian history. The following chapters consider cases of conversion in greater detail. What bears consideration at this stage are the circumstances that compelled leading mowbed to intervene in matters of religious identity in the fifth century. The only episodes of conversion for which fifth-century hagiographers have provided detailed accounts reveal the fluidity of religious boundaries, especially in elite circles. Two martyrs were Christian elites with imperial offices—Peroz and Jacob, both from wealthy, noble houses in Beit Lapat—who had converted to Zoroastrianism from Christianity, only to return to their natal faith.[131] These cases suggest that some Christians adopted Zoroastrian practices, which, in the eyes of the authorities, indicated their membership in the ranks of the wehdēn, while retaining Christian loyalties. Vacillation rather than straightforward conversion was characteristic of fifth-century encounters of Christianity with Zoroastrianism and vice versa. Zoroastrians in Christian accounts took an interest in a new source of supernatural power, particularly for healing, without undergoing the baptism and catechesis that constitute Christian conversion.[132]

This was the case of Adurfarrobag, the Zoroastrian aristocrat who built the church later transformed into the fire temple that Narsai destroyed.[133] In pursuit of healing for an illness, he discovered a Christian priest, Shapur, who cured him in exchange for a disavowal of the Good Religion. Adurfarrobag built a church out of gratitude, only to remodel the building as a fire temple as soon as the imperial authorities demanded. For the Christian hagiographer, this represented a clear case of apostasy, but from the bare facts of the narrative the Zoroastrian appears not to have regarded the acceptance of healing or the patronage of a church as incompatible with adherence to the Good Religion. Such cases of mutual incomprehension of the nature of the other's religious identity, which facilitated symbiotic relations, were likely legion. The most important aspect of the episode is that the court intervened forcibly to provide clarity, indeed to enforce a boundary between the two religions, which individual Zoroastrians and Christians were inclined to combine in their own religious practice. Chapter 2 further develops these themes from the perspective of a Christian hagiographer working to disentangle specifically Christian and Zoroastrian beliefs while preserving a domain of shared culture, and chapter 3 considers the problem at the level of social practice. The present goal is to examine how imperial authorities endeavored to establish limits on interaction between Christians and Zoroastrians, specifically on the latter's embrace of the former's beliefs and rituals. If cases of outright apostasy were few, the court prosecuted those that came to its attention, in the manner of attacks on temples, as assaults on the imperial religion, whose superior position was to be maintained.

Zoroastrian legal, literary, and political treatises were unanimous in describing apostates who, unlike Adurfarrobag, refused to recant as *margarzān*, "worthy of death." The principle that the rejection of the Good Religion was an offense meriting capital punishment appears to have been ancient, although the fifth-century hagiographical works are the earliest evidence for its application. According to the *Mēnōg ī Xrad*, a work of late Sasanian political advice literature, disciplining apostates was among the basic responsibilities of "good rulership" (*hupādixšāyīh*): "If there is someone who separates from the path of the gods [*rāh ī yazadān*], then [the good ruler] should command his restoration to it, seize him, and bring him back to the path of the gods. He should distribute from his wealth shares for the gods, worthy men, good deeds, and the poor and forfeit the body for the soul [*ud tan ruwān rāy be abespārēd*]."[134] The apostate, in short, was to be expropriated and executed. If the principle is well attested, the treatment of apostates in practice varied according to political and social circumstances, even in cases where Zoroastrian authorities were directly involved. There are converts to Christianity in East Syrian hagiography who went unpunished.[135] Even if one takes a minimalist view of rates of conversion, there were likely many more apostates than the paltry number of documented martyrs. Zoroastrian legal texts, moreover, refer to apostates who were known to the authorities but not prosecuted. The *Hērbedestān*, as we will see in the next chapter, discusses the case of an apostate whose son was permitted to participate in the advanced study of the Yasna, while the *Hazār Dādestān*, the sole collection of Iranian case law, considers the question of whether an apostate son could inherit from his father without mention of further investigation into the son's religious identity.[136] There is, we will see, confirmation in East Syrian sources that such situations could arise. Individual apostates were not prosecuted on a regular or consistent basis but rather only in particular circumstances, which require further investigation on the basis of hagiographical accounts of particular cases.

The victims of the "law of apostasy" were uniformly members of aristocratic houses. In the more detailed hagiographical literature of the sixth and early seventh centuries, Zoroastrian authorities initiate proceedings against apostates at the instigation of patrilineal relatives.[137] There were cases of converts deliberately exposing their apostasy, and one of an apostate who fell victim to a Christian political rival.[138] But kinsmen most frequently took the initiative to prosecute. Zoroastrian institutions provided the material and symbolic foundations of the aristocratic houses, as chapters 3 and 4 show, and apostasy jeopardized the transmission of their patrilineages and patrimonies. We therefore find East Syrian authors consistently recounting stories of fathers, brothers, and paternal uncles seeking the prosecution and execution of relatives who rejected the Good Religion. Two of these martyrs were from the great house of Mihran, politically the most powerful aristocratic family in the empire in the late Sasanian period. One of their ranks, known as Rabban Mar Saba, converted to Christianity in his youth under the influence of his wet nurse, according to an early seventh-century account of fifth-century events.[139] Because his father had perished while on campaign on the northeastern frontiers, one of the myriad aristocrats who dedicated his life to military service during the fifth-century crisis, the act of apostasy went unnoticed until the youth was invited to a feast of the Mihranid house. When a paternal uncle discovered that his nephew had apostatized, he threatened to appropriate the patrimony that the convert had inherited, without raising the specter of violence.[140] Gregory the Commander, who was from among "the inhabitants of Rayy, from the lineage of the house of Mihran," was not so fortunate.[141] The commander of Iranian field armies in the sixth-century Caucasus, which was a zone of contestation between Iran and Rome, managed to find favor with Husraw I in 534 even after ostentatiously renouncing the imperial religion before other soldiers assembled at a feast in 518.[142] Voices at court, however, appealed to the king of kings to take action against an apostate from such an important house: "It is a great dishonor for the religion of the Magians that such a great man from the lineage of the house of Mihran, who have always been servants of Ohrmazd, now becomes a servant of Christ."[143] In response, Husraw I had Gregory dispossessed and imprisoned, but the Mihranids considered such measures inadequate. Mihran, the son of Gregory's paternal uncle, requested that the king of kings punish his cousin for bringing dishonor to "our lineage."[144] Having returned from a victorious campaign against the Hephthalite Huns, Mihran was in a strong position to demand such a favor, and Gregory was executed to vindicate the honor of the house of Mihran.

More modest aristocratic houses also pursued apostates among their ranks for undermining their material and symbolic foundations. Two known cases emerged in northern Mesopotamian milieux where interaristocratic relations between Christians and Zoroastrians were commonplace, making the demarcation of religious boundaries between noble houses of great urgency. In these episodes, intimate relations between the Zoroastrians and Christians gave rise to conversions that threatened the boundaries on which such amiable interactions depended. Shirin (d. 559) was from a Persian-speaking aristocratic house in Karka d-Beit Slok and gained knowledge of Christianity from a Christian wet nurse.[145] She kept her conversion secret for some time, but the manifestation of her apostasy before the household caused her father to invite the Zoroastrian authorities to return her to the Good Religion or to punish her for her offense.[146] Another martyr from Karka d-Beit Slok, Christina, was also from an aristocratic house, that of a *marzbān*, a regional military commander, although the circumstances of her prosecution are unclear in the fragmentary *Martyrdom of Christina*.[147] In the neighboring region of Arbela, a third northern Mesopotamian aristocrat, Mahanosh, apostatized, becoming Ishosabran after marrying a woman who had converted to Christianity.[148] He was not molested until he publicly declared his conversion. His brother then petitioned the Zoroastrian authorities to prosecute the apostate, reportedly to expropriate the estate of his patrilineal relative.[149]

Similar in nature were cases of Zoroastrian religious authorities converting, such as Adurohrmazd in the following chapter. These were offenses that compromised the positions not only of the aristocratic houses to which they belonged but also the simultaneously religious and political offices that they occupied. Even in the hagiographical literature, however, there are cases of apostate aristocrats who went unprosecuted, nobles whose conversions became known to Zoroastrian authorities but who escaped punishment.[150] The abovementioned converts, moreover, often continued to flourish in Iranian society and even attained imperial offices and social status while practicing their Christianity in the open for years before encountering the forces that precipitated their punishment.[151] Apostates were executed only in precise political circumstances, a theme to which we will return when considering the early seventh century in chapter 5. The 'law of apostasy" was applied only in cases of aristocratic conversion, and the martyrdoms of converts in the sixth and early seventh centuries are further examples of the Iranian court upholding the power of the aristocratic houses that formed the backbone of the empire.

While East Syrian authors were composing these accounts, Zoroastrian jurists at court were debating the use of violence against apostates and developing procedural norms for their treatment. The problem of aristocrats converting to other religions recurs in the political advice literature that emanated from the late Sasanian court. Husraw I claimed to have banished nobles who had embraced and propagated a religion other than Zoroastrianism in the autobiographical account of his rule, the *Sīrat Ānūširwān*.[152] Other texts, like the aforementioned *Mēnōg ī Xrad*, concentrate on punitive measures against the bodies of apostates, and the *Letter of Tansar* describes the introduction and innovation of formal procedures for prosecuting cases of apostasy. Composed in the name of a mowbed from the reign of Ardashir I, the *Letter of Tansar* aimed to legitimate the actions of the sixth-century court with recourse to a normative, early Sasanian past.[153] Among the aspects of the court that certain aristocrats had criticized was its excessive use of violence: "There is much talk about the blood shed by the king, and the people are dismayed."[154] The *Letter of Tansar* insists that any blood the ruler shed was justifiable within the framework of Iranian cosmology and takes execution for apostasy as an example of the cautious, considered use of the sword:

> The king of kings has established a law far better than that of the ancients. For in former days any man who turned from the faith [*dīn*] was swiftly and speedily put to death and punished. The king of kings has ordered that such a man should be imprisoned and that for the space of a year learned men should summon him at frequent intervals and advise him and lay arguments before him and destroy his doubts. If he become penitent and contrite and seek pardon of God, he is set free. If obstinacy and pride hold him back, then he is put to death.[155]

According to the *Letter of Tansar*, norms had been established for handling cases of apostasy through a three-stage procedure: the apostate was to be imprisoned, interrogated for one year concerning his beliefs, and executed only if he remained loyal to the new religion. East Syrian accounts confirm that such procedures became normative during the sixth century. Although there are traces of such a process in fifth-century martyrology, these procedures became consistent only in accounts from the sixth and early seventh centuries. What the *Letter of Tansar* indicates is that such norms were introduced in courtly milieux where state violence was subject to debate and criticism. The killing of apostates often represented as indiscriminate, had to be defended and regulated, and its functions had to be defined carefully.

East Syrian ecclesiastical leaders appear generally to have respected the limit on Zoroastrian relations with Christians that the court established. In works from the latter half of the fifth through the early seventh century, the priest or bishop reluctant to baptize an elite Zoroastrian eager to gain membership in the church is an omnipresent topos. Even the authors who commemorated acts of conversion abstained from composing narratives that celebrated or enjoined proselytizing activities. The principal exception, the *History of Rabban Mar Saba,* was produced at a time of heightened Christian expectations during the reign of Husraw II, which we will consider in chapter 5. Otherwise, the martyrological literature suggests that the avoidance of high-profile cases of apostasy was normative in the very clerical and ascetic circles most dedicated to the propagation of the faith. When the elite Zoroastrian youth Yazdin wished to convert, his Christian foster father— who had introduced him to the church—appealed to him to refrain from seeking baptism. Yazdin fled to the comparatively distant city of Karka d-Beit Slok, where priests ignorant of his background baptized him in the faith and instructed him in its rites and texts.[156] Gregory the Commander had to seek out an ecclesiastical community that was unaware of his status as a martial, Mihranid leader in order to obtain baptism.[157] The bishop of Karka d-Beit Slok, for his part, refused to baptize Shirin.[158] Ishosabran was similarly forced to travel to a monastery far from his village in the region of Arbela to find clerics who would not recognize him as a member of a Zoroastrian aristocratic house. Even at this distant monastery, however, the abbot interrogated him concerning his origins and hesitated to baptize him on discovering his identity. It was only after having a vision of an angel that the abbot agreed to introduce him to the community of believers.[159] The author of the *History of Ishosabran,* Ishoyahb III, intended to justify active proselytism among Zoroastrians circa 640, an indication that East Syrians still regarded the baptism of Zoroastrian elites as exceptional and even impermissible in the years of the empire's fall.[160] These accounts share the presumption that East Syrian leaders considered the conversion of imperial elites ideal in theory but impossible in practice. Even if they harbored the universalist aspirations common to late antique Christianity, East Syrians accepted the restriction on conversion as a means of accommodating their institutions to the realities of Iranian political culture.

If we combine the East Syrian and Zoroastrian evidence, the "law of apostasy" emerges as an instrument for regulating interaction rather than an example of the persecutory tendencies of the Good Religion. On the one hand, Zoroastrian jurists insisted that converts be prosecuted in a systematic way in line with procedures established as normative during the sixth century. In theory, every convert to Christianity was to be returned to the ranks of the wehdēn or to perish for the offense of apostasy. On the other hand, the hagiographical descriptions of historical prosecutions demonstrate that the "law of apostasy" was invoked only in cases of elite conversions. Converts were pursued only when their acts of apostasy openly challenged a social order whose foundations were formed by Zoroastrian institutions. This occurred when apostates were members of aristocratic houses or when their actions were made public within the confines of an imperial institution. There was no systematic enforcement of a law of apostasy within the general population. The regulation of conversion will not, therefore, have restricted the spread of Christianity among the subordinate populations of the empire that were—and continue to be—largely invisible. Because Christian communities restrained their proselytizing activities among elites in accordance with the commands of the kings of kings, the "law of apostasy" served to create a mutually recognized boundary between the two religions that allowed Christians and Zoroastrians to share social and political spaces, practices, and ideas without the risk of one universalizing religion constraining the viability of the other. The execution of a select few apostates established norms that fostered the increasingly intimate interaction of Christians and Zoroastrians that we know characterized fifth- and sixth-century Iranian political culture.

The violence that Christian communities in Iran experienced in the fifth century signaled their integration into imperial politics. As Christians came to occupy strategic positions, whether as scribes for the court or as provincial aristocrats contributing men and material to Sasanian field armies like the nobles of Armenia or northern Mesopotamia, they found themselves subject to the coercive powers of a state that depended upon the shedding of blood to communicate its authority over elites, particularly the great aristocratic houses that—though consistently loyal to the house of Sasan as a lineage—routinely contested royal authority by force, for example through the deposition of kings of kings. Purges, assassinations, and other extrajudicial killings were basic instruments of rule for the Sasanians throughout their history.[161] Unlike those of their Roman peers, the bodies of Iranian elites were in no way regarded as inviolable.[162] Zoroastrians were if anything more likely to fall victim to violence than adherents of other religions, simply because the more power they accrued, the more likely they were to threaten royal authority. The difference between Christian and Zoroastrian victims was the former's access to literary specialists well versed in the arts of martyrology, who could transform executed nobles into valiant aristocratic martyrs, such as those of Karka and Arbela, who are the topic of chapter 4. We therefore possess accounts of Christian aristocrats who perished during the reign of Yazdgird II, while the non-Christians killed, castrated, or imprisoned remained nameless. Although anti-Christian language doubtless colored these executions, they should not be extracted from the political context in which the hagiographers placed them

Whether in the fourth century or the fifth, Iranian authorities acting within the framework of Zoroastrian cosmology killed neither senselessly nor needlessly but in order to define and communicate the terms of political relations between Christians and Zoroastrians and between elites and the court. Beyond disciplining elites, violence served to place Christian communities in a subordinate—yet viable—position in relation to the imperial religion, whose supremacy some Christians openly and ostentatiously challenged. The hagiographical works highlight two domains that the state apparatus policed with force: the souls and shrines of Zoroastrians. As long as Christians did not seek to expand their institutions or ranks at the expense of the Good Religion, their ecclesiastical leaders could establish churches, shrines, and bishoprics and secular elites could gain office in the imperial administration and attain aristocratic status. The sources for the ideals and actions of East Syrians in the late Sasanian period suggest that ecclesiastical leaders accepted these limitations as the terms of integration. That secular elites would continue to experience some violence was unavoidable, given its structural position within political relations. And public acts of apostasy in favor of Christianity, however rare, would continue to precipitate conflicts. But within these boundaries, Christian communities consistently grew in the fifth century, in their institutional structures and the social, economic, and political power of their members, a trajectory that did not slow until long after the Islamic conquests. Far from representing an inescapable antagonism between Christianity and Zoroastrianism, acts of violence constituted the foundation for their cooperation and coexistence.

CONCLUSION

The Sasanian dynasty, the leading Iranian aristocratic houses, and the Zoroastrian religious hierarchy worked to create a cosmologically conceived, hierarchically organized social order in the territories of their empire that could incorporate religious others. The anchors of this order were the institutions of the Good Religion—the fire temples, rituals, and corpora of cosmological thought that Kerdir and his successors established. The supremacy of the Good Religion was therefore to be maintained, with violence if necessary, but religious others were to be included in positions subordinate to wehdēn and ēr. The East Syrian hagiographical tradition, through the lens of a literary genre dedicated to the commemoration of conflict with religious rivals, counterintuitively attests to the creation of an inclusive empire conceived in the terms of another religion. The most momentous outbreak of violence in the East Syrian literary tradition was the result of an attempt by a king of kings to enlist bishops and other Christian religious authorities in the fiscal system. In the fifth century, the successful integration of Christian bishops and secular elites into imperial structures caused them to encounter the dangers that came with power, as they began to experience the violence that the Iranian court used to discipline its elites. These were episodes that marked the ongoing incorporation of Christians into the networks of the court. Their advance into the ranks of officeholders and aristocrats took place within the framework of

Zoroastrian ideology rather than in spite of a supposed antipathy toward agdēn. There were cosmological reasons that Zoroastrians, whether kings of kings, aristocrats, or mowbed, could invoke to justify the participation of agdēn in the institutions of the military, the fiscal administration, or the court, as well as of aristocratic sociability. They contributed good work, *kirbag*, on account of their access to the civilizational goods available as the common inheritance of humanity or their attainment of ethical righteousness, possibly even through the laws of their respective religions. The concept of intolerance as a heuristic device is therefore not only of dubious value in itself but also inaccurate in its general sense of a propensity toward violence against religious others. Christians were not killed, in any historically verifiable episode, in general persecutions because of their religious identities. They were killed for disobeying the court or for violating mutually recognized norms in particular acts. The absence of persecutory violence, moreover, suggests the importance and influence of Zoroastrian views of the potential merits of agdēn, despite Christian representation to the contrary. Zoroastrian authorities, in theory and practice, recognized the place of Christians and Jews in Iran and regarded their institutions as ancillary to the empire. Their capacity to recognize and emplace religious others distinguished Zoroastrians from their Christian contemporaries in the Roman world.

Christians could flourish within the Zoroastrian ideological and infrastructural framework of the Iranian Empire only as long as they refrained from challenging the superiority of the Good Religion. A proselytizing religion with ambitions to propagate universal truths globally posed significant threats to Zoroastrianism that never entirely disappeared. The court, however, quickly arrested Christian attempts in the fifth century to attack Zoroastrian institutions physically in imitation of their Roman counterparts and to proselytize in elite circles, establishing norms for interreligious interaction that structured relations between Zoroastrians and Christians in the late Sasanian period. Neither the destruction of fire temples nor the conversion of prominent wehdēn to agdēnīh was acceptable under the Sasanians. These were the terms of inclusion, and Christian ecclesiastical and secular elites overwhelmingly accepted them, precipitating the efflorescence of Christian institutions characteristic of the era. From the East Syrian perspective, the problem of the relationship between the two religions abided. If at the level of practice Christians abstained from eroding the foundations of Zoroastrian institutions, in theory they continued to insist on the superiority of their faith. Christians developed no parallel to the Zoroastrian idea of a hierarchy of religions. There was one true religion and many false ones. Their de facto accommodation of Iranian categories and structures therefore required East Syrian leaders continually to underline for their constituencies the incommensurable superiority of Christianity vis-à-vis the religion to which they were politically subject. This was the polemical project in which every single hagiographical and juridical text that the East Syrians produced was involved. The following three chapters show how East Syrian religious authorities used texts as instruments for redefining the relationships of their communities with Iranian structures of power while reasserting the distinction between Christianity and Zoroastrianism on which their authority rested. The disentangling of secular and religious spaces within imperial structures that the *History of Simeon* and related texts accomplished was the most important legacy of the "Great Persecution." The myth of Zoroastrian intolerance was ultimately an instrument of Christian institution building.

2

Belonging to a Land

Christians and Zoroastrians in the Iranian Highlands

A SACRED MOUNTAIN

In the Zagros Mountains, between the plains of Mesopotamia and the Iranian Plateau, stands an icon of antique Iranian imperialism: Mount Bisutun. Ancient travelers, including the Sasanian kings of kings on pilgrimage to the imperial shrine of Adur Gushnasp, encountered the mountain as a sheer precipice looming over the so-called royal road that linked Seleucia-Ctesiphon with Azerbaijan, northeastern Iran, and Central Asia (see figure 2).[1] As the tenth-century geographer al-Muqaddasī observed, the peak captured the attention of its viewers: "Here are towering mountains, such as Bisutun, forbidding, smooth, unclimbable."[2] Its grandeur was, to ancient Iranian cultures, distinctly numinous. The name of the mountain in Middle Persian, *baystūn*, derives from the Old Persian **baga-stāna-*, "the place of the gods." Achaemenian, Parthian, and Sasanian rulers thus chose the site to broadcast their intimate relationship with the gods in rock reliefs.[3] The Achaemenian Darius I selected the peak's steepest, southeastern flank for his famous Bisutun inscription, under which several Parthian kings placed reliefs of their own. Although the early Sasanians concentrated their rock reliefs in Fars, in the fourth century Bisutun became the premier location for the propagation of imperial ideology in stone. At the western end of the landmass, at Taq-e Bustan, the kings of kings Shapur II (r. 309–79), Shapur III (r. 383–88), and Husraw II (r. 590–628) represented the gods Mithra, Anahid, and Ohrmazd investing them as rulers.[4] The mountain formed the centerpiece of an interconnected set of sacred sites in the region, such as the shrine to Anahid at Kangavar, and fire-centered cults—of which the Zoroastrian Yasna was an example—were performed on the crags of

FIGURE 2. View from the Dinawar Valley of Mount Bisutun, the site of the shrine of Pethion, Adurohrmazd, and Anahid, in the region known in the Sasanian period as Walashfarr. The Royal Road from Seleucia-Ctesiphon to northeastern Iran and Central Asia passed beneath its flanks. The Ernst Herzfeld Papers, Freer Gallery of Art and Arthur M. Sackler Gallery Archives, Smithsonian Institution, Washington DC.

Bisutun.[5] Zoroastrian rituals were frequently conducted, whether in fire temples or in the open air, on mountains, within view of the natural environments and human populations that they were intended to sustain.[6] Mountains, after all, possessed their own variety of *xwarrah*, or manifestation of divine power, the "xwarrah of the mountain and hill" (*xwarrah ī gar ud kōf*).[7]

The most sacred of xwarrah-suffused mountains had become, by the early sixth century, the abode not merely of Zoroastrian gods but also of Christian saints. A hagiographical work known as the *Martyrdom of Pethion, Adurohrmazd, and Anahid* relates the history of the conversion of four Zoroastrian aristocrats—Yazdin, Pethion, Adurohrmazd, and Anahid—to Christianity and the martyrdom of the three saints after whom the text is titled during the reign of Yazdgird II (r. 438–57). The narrative centers on a mountain where the saints practiced the ascetic life and ultimately died, of natural causes in the case of Yazdin and at the hands of Zoroastrian persecutors in the case of the others. It was upon the mountain that the holy relics of the saints were interred. Remarkably detailed descriptions allow us to identify the mountain omnipresent in the text as Bisutun. The peak of the saints was composed of smooth cliffs and crags, too steep for soil to adhere to, according to the hagiographer whose descriptive language is reminiscent of al-Muqaddasi's account. There are other, similarly craggy peaks in the region, but none of them are so near to the royal road. The site of the martyrdom of the saints and their shrine was identified precisely beneath the precipice that overhung "the great road of the king, which passes the foot of the mountain of the coronation of the saint and continues to many lands, as far as the outside lands of the kingdom," namely the kingdoms of Central Asia.[8] The direct reference to the royal road places the site in the area of the southeastern flank where the Achaemenian and Parthian reliefs congregate.[9] This aspect of the mountain faces the juncture of two rivers, both of which the text mentions, and forms the western entrance to the Dinawar Valley, which was the original home of Yazdin and Pethion.

The martyrs transformed a mountain that was among the most potent symbols of the traditions of the Zoroastrian religion into a symbol of the Christian faith, the basis for a novel vision of religious community. In the process, the mountain retained its sacrality in a Christian guise. This is a striking example of the Christian construction of holy places through narrative, ritual, and cultic buildings that took place throughout the Near East and the Mediterranean from the late fourth century. If Christians often established entirely new sites, such as those associated with the life of Christ, their holy places commonly appropriated the temples, shrines, and landscapes of the religions that they claimed to supersede.[10] The reuse of sacred spaces and places by new religions is a phenomenon so commonly encountered in the history of religions as to be banal. The particular ways in which Christians neutralized the preexisting meanings and powers of a site or placed them in the service of their own religiopolitical projects can, nevertheless, reveal the extent of ecclesiastical leaders' engagement with cultures and social structures that they pretended to have transcended.

This chapter examines the refashioning of Bisutun as a Christian site in order to contribute to the history of the encounter in the Iranian highlands in the fifth and sixth centuries of East Syrian Christians with Zoroastrian rituals, beliefs, and landscapes as well as the political structures they underpinned. The study of Christianity in the Iranian world has concentrated on the regions of Mesopotamia and Khuzestan, where the great bulk of our literary evidence was produced. The *Martyrdom of Pethion* has been overlooked as a source for East Syrians in the mountains and valleys of Fars and what has traditionally been called Media, the highlands of the Zagros between Mesopotamia and the Iranian Plateau. The text refers to the region of Media where its events took place as Walashfarr, a name that appears on Middle Persian Sasanian seals and in East Syrian synodal acts (see map 2).[11] Historic Media seems to have been divided into various regions, of which Walashfarr was of paramount political importance as a way station of the royal road and the sometime summer residence of the late Sasanian kings of kings Kawad I and Husraw II.[12] The highlands and the plateau were the native lands, if not the residences, of the great Iranian aristocratic houses and the sites of the great Zoroastrian fire temples as well as myriad minor shrines, often positioned at prominent points in the landscape.[13] If Zoroastrianism tended to be the religion of the highest elite strata in Khuzestan and Mesopotamia, its beliefs predominated at all levels of society in the highlands, and its rites were omnipresent. In chapter 4, we will consider how Christian communities in northern Mesopotamia constructed a political imaginary centered on the city of Karka d-Beit Slok that foregrounded the cultural distinctiveness of a community with Assyrian, Hellenistic, and Iranian pasts. The situation in Walashfarr differed sharply. Christians arrived in the region as outsiders, captives from Roman territory deported to Iran. The indigenous elites were Iranian and Zoroastrian, and there was no pre-Sasanian past available to Christians seeking to define their place in the region. If Christian outsiders were to be incorporated into regional elite networks, they would have to work with the inhabitants of the land and within the prevailing Iranian discourse to establish an identity. Christians who adopted the Iranian language of political belonging would have to assert their difference from Zoroastrians at the same time, to prevent the potential contradictions between Christian and Iranian discourses of identity from coming into view. This was the task that East Syrian ecclesiastical leaders undertook around the beginning of the sixth century.

The *Martyrdom of Pethion* sat astride cultures that we conventionally distinguish as Christian and Iranian. Composed in the late fifth or the sixth century, the text has survived not only in Syriac but also in a fragmentary Sogdian manuscript from the Turfan Oasis in western China that attests to its wide circulation in the Iranian world.[14] Its unknown author was an important innovator in East Syrian literature.[15] The work creatively fuses theological polemics with hagiography. As a hagiographer, the author developed a narrative structure unparalleled in East Syrian saints' lives: the collective biography relating accounts of conversion, each of which serves as a literary instrument for treating particular religious and political concerns. The author was well versed in the hagiographical arts, had perhaps studied in the city of Karka d-Beit Slok, whose monastery appears in the text.[16] As an anti-Zoroastrian polemicist, he drew on a Greek source and on his own knowledge of the Good Religion as a complex of rituals and cosmological ideas widespread in the region of Walashfarr. The *Martyrdom of Pethion* includes the most sophisticated polemics against Zoroastrianism known in East Syrian literature. Its hagiographer was the only East Syrian author who routinely deployed Iranian terminology, most often religious in nature. The appearance of terms such as *ahlamōg* (heretic), *šnūman* (invocation), *nask* (a section of the Avesta), and even *Avesta* itself suggests his familiarity with Zoroastrian discourse and practice. His use of the phrase "as is clear from the Avesta," a standard opening for an argument in

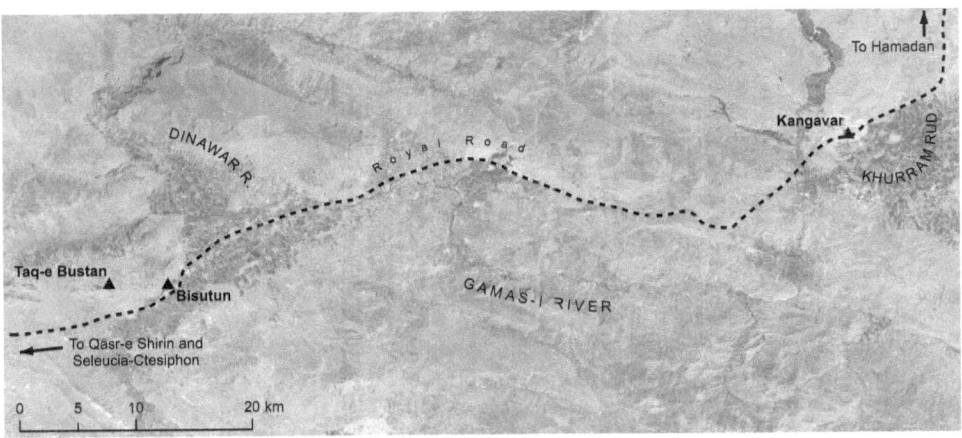

MAP 2. Walashfarr and the royal road. Emily Hammer, Center for Ancient Middle Eastern Landscapes, University of Chicago. Satellite imagery from Google Earth.

Zoroastrian exegetical scholarship, indicates that he was acquainted with the dialectics and debates of the Good Religion's scholars.[17] As we will see, the work repeatedly evokes the environment of the Zoroastrian school for the study of the Avesta and the Yasna, the hērbedestān. In addition to religious language, the author used political terms that rarely occurred in Syriac, such as *marz* (frontier) and *dahigān* (local landowner).[18] He evidently knew Middle Persian, and the milieu in which he worked was bilingual.[19] On account of its author's knowledge of both Christian and Iranian cultures, the *Martyrdom of Pethion* offers rare insight into the world of the Christian diaspora in the Iranian highlands, communities distinct from the indigenous population and the ruling classes in language, origins, religion, and social organization. The hagiographer will emerge from this chapter acting as a broker between these cultures even as he sought to distance Christians from Zoroastrian practices and beliefs. Through writing, he took on the role of the holy man, "thought to be able to embrace and validate a wider range of potentially exclusive explanatory systems."[20] With the goal of containing the indiscriminate mixing of cultures, he identified an aspect of Iranian culture compatible with Christianity around which he could construct a hybrid communal imaginary, religiously distinct yet rooted in Iranian political structures: the idea of a land with ritualized, sacred landscapes as the container of a human community that formed a constituent part of the empire as a whole. His polemics were part of this project. It was to the dynamics of interaction between Christian outsiders and Zoroastrian indigenes that the *Martyrdom of Pethion,* and the associated cult of the saints on the flank of Bisutun, contributed.

CAPTIVES AND CONVERTS

The Christian communities of the Iranian highlands and plateau had their origins in the main in the populations that the Sasanians brought captive to Iranian territory during the third- and fourth-century Roman wars.[21] Although there are indications of a Christian presence at major entrepôts of transregional trade as early as the third century, substantial communities do not become discernible in the sources until the end of the fourth. Beginning with Shapur I's campaigns against Rome, which deported entire Syrian and Anatolian cities to Iran, the Sasanians took the populations of conquered territories as sources of manpower and artistic and artisanal expertise.[22] Deported Romans helped to construct cities, produced commodities of precious metal or textile, and contributed to the labor force behind massive irrigation projects. According to the *Chronicle of Seert*, Shapur I's deportations caused Christianity to expand in Iran, as the Sasanian unwittingly dispersed its adherents throughout his territories.[23] This account, however, presumes that the inhabitants of the Roman Near East, from which Shapur I's took his captives, were already predominately Christian in the third century.[24] A century later, Roman captives still could not have been uniformly Christian, and the processes of Christianization already under way in the Roman Empire would have had to continue within the captive populations for the religion to become dominant among them.[25] Even modest numbers of Christians, however, could have precipitated the growth of the religion among the captives. Deported groups of Romans included priests and bishops—perhaps even the bishop of Antioch Demetrianos—who continued to propagate the faith with no less zeal than their counterparts in Roman territory.[26] Christian religious specialists brought with them a package of institutions—rituals, textual traditions, ecclesiastical buildings, and the clergy—which will have given exiled communities ideological and infrastructural coherence that they could not have obtained elsewhere.

The collection of East Syrian canons known as the *Synodicon Orientale* documents the eastward expansion of Christian institutions, if not populations, in the fifth century. By the Synod of 420, the Church of the East's second council, bishoprics at least notionally subordinate to the catholicos of Seleucia-Ctesiphon, known as the patriarch from the middle of the sixth century, had been established in the principal cities of Fars and the highland regions of Media, according to the list of signatories affixed to synodal records.[27] In the early sixth century we find episcopal signatories from as far afield as Merv, Herat, and southeastern Iran.[28] The bishops who made their way to the imperial capital for the first time represented long-standing communities or, in some cases, embryonic communities sufficiently robust to merit an episcopate. Despite a scholarly tendency to regard the appearance of previously undocumented communities in the synodal registers as a sign of ecclesiastical expansion, the antipathy of eastern Iranian bishops toward the patriarchate's pretensions to suzerainty delayed their appearance at synods.²⁹ Some East Syrian circles celebrated a legendary bishop of Rayy, south of modern Tehran, for violently opposing an ambitious bishop of Seleucia-Ctesiphon in the fourth century.³⁰ The absence of the catholicos-patriarch from the *Martyrdom of Pethion*, in contrast to his appearance in the hagiographical texts produced contemporaneously in Khuzestan, is telling. As the influence of the office grew over the course of the fifth and sixth centuries, more and more ecclesiastical leaders came to acknowledge the authority of its holder at the synods. The increase in the number of eastern Iranian cities that dispatched a bishop to the capital indicates the extension of patriarchal authority more than the swelling of Christian ranks through conversion or diffusion. The bishoprics suggest, nevertheless that captive Christians formed communities and institutionalized themselves in rural and urban spaces.

Roman deportees, or at least the Christians among them, remained distinct from the indigenous populations of Iran. The absence of assimilation among the deportees is all the more striking for documented efforts by Iranian elites to uproot them from their native cultures as well as their lands. The *Martyrdom of Pusai*, composed in the late fifth or early sixth century, provides the most extensive historical account of the deportation, settlement, and attempted assimilation of Romans.³¹ Pusai was the son of a Roman man whom Shapur II had resettled in the city of Bishapur and a "Persian" woman. The king of kings had, according to the hagiographer, compelled the deportee to marry a native of Bishapur to accelerate his assimilation. But the reverse occurred when the woman converted to the Roman's religion, Christianity. In addition to coerced intermarriage, Shapur II reportedly adopted another strategy to detach captives from their Roman roots: the dislocation and subsequent reassembling of populations of disparate origins in new settlements. For this purpose, he had the new urban foundation of Karka d-Ledan constructed as a vehicle for the mixing of peoples: "From all the peoples in the cities of the lands of his jurisdiction he brought more or less thirty families and settled them among one another, so that through the mixture of peoples the captives would be bound by their families and their affection, and it would not be easy for them to depart in flight gradually to the lands from which they were seized."³² Instead of intermarrying captives and indigenes, the king of kings interspersed entire families from various places among one another in a royal foundation, known as Ērān-xwarrah-Šāpūr, "Shapur [increases] the xwarrah of the Iranians." Their origin, destiny, and sense of place were thus irreversibly intertwined with the empire. Their dislocation and transfer also forcefully communicated the position of the inhabitants of Ērān-xwarrah-Šāpūr as subjects of the king of kings wholly dependent on his authority. Because of their resettlement in an emblem of the empire, their everyday experience of space and place reinforced their newly given identities as subjects. What Shapur II could not have intended was that the captives, however disparate their backgrounds, shared Christian institutions, which gave some of the resettled communities structures for organizing themselves. The recombining of populations in urban centers, to which Christian institutions were best adapted, will only have stimulated the growth of churches, as the author of the *Martyrdom of Pusai* suggested.[33] Karka d-Ledan remained a major Christian center throughout the Sasanian era.

If deported Romans became Iranian subjects and inhabitants of places such as Ērān-xwarrah-Šāpūr, an important subset of deportees developed distinctive identities as Christians and captives. To signal their difference from indigenous populations, these deportees came to designate themselves "captives," *bnai šebya*, a potentially derogatory status rendered a point of pride in East Syrian hagiographical texts from Khuzestan, Fars, and Media.[34] These accounts preserve histories of deportation that gave particular shared origins to captive communities. The *Martyrdom of Pusai*, as we have seen, records the successive transfers of a man from Rome to Bishapur and thence, with his family, to Karka d-Ledan. Similarly, the *Martyrdom of the Captives*, an account of a martyrs' cult in the highlands northwest of Khuzestan, narrates the deportation of a Christian community, including its bishop, from a Roman castrum in northern Mesopotamia to the Zagros Mountains.[35] These texts frequently elide the distinction between Christian and captive, a pairing that is evident throughout the *Martyrdom of Pethion*. Its author uses the terms interchangeably, as if captives were Christians and Christians captives. It was the aim of East Syrian hagiographers writing in the eastern half of the empire to insist on the separateness of Christian communities as captives even while describing, and contributing to, their negotiation of the Iranian social and political landscape. But the term *captive* became prevalent only in the fifth century, when, as we saw in the preceding chapter, Christian elites involved themselves to an ever greater degree in Iranian institutions and East Syrian authors placed Christian support for the Sasanians on a solid theological footing. The emphasis on the status of Christians as captives in the hagiographical literature is a manifestation of the heightened concern about the place of Christians in Iranian social and political categories that followed the establishment of a Church of the East identified with the empire.

The idea of Iran posed an obstacle to Christians seeking to occupy a legitimate place in territories that belonged to the "Iranians," the ēr. Since ēr corresponded with wehdēn and anēr with agdēn, the territories of the empire were the possessions of Zoroastrians, and the position of Christians and other non-Zoroastrians in these lands was ambiguous.[36] Their presence was not formally excluded but would have required the negotiation of terms of belonging acceptable to both indigenes and captives. Christian authors—and other non-Zoroastrians—avoided the language of Iran, in recognition of its religious significance, which they could not embrace. Christians writing in Syriac referred to the empire as the "land of the

Persians" (*beit parsaye*), while Manichaeans writing in Parthian described the state as the "Persian kingdom" (*pārs šahrdārīft*).³⁷ Both continued to use pre-Sasanian terms in place of *Ērānšahr*. Eschewing the idea of Iran served to minimize occasions for conflict concerning the place of non-Zoroastrians and even to foreclose the possibility of Christians becoming Iranian. It was only after the collapse of the empire that a Christian traveling to Constantinople referred to himself as *ēr* in a Middle Persian inscription.³⁸ But avoiding the question of Iranianness did not provide Christians with the means to define their membership in imperial society, a necessary prerequisite for joining elite networks. If Christians were captives, complete outsiders, on what basis could they cooperate with Zoroastrian elites in imperial institutions? This chapter and the next consider how Christian communities came to define themselves within the framework of the empire's spatial articulations, in Walashfarr in terms of a regional landscape and in Karka d-Beit Slok in terms of an urban cityscape (see chapter 4). For Christians to transcend their status as outsiders in the late Sasanian period, a new language of belonging that did not compromise their religious identities was needed. The region of Walashfarr, described plainly as "the land," offered a collective referent for both its Christian and its Zoroastrian inhabitants—much as the city of Karka d-Beit Slok acts as a shared locus of belonging in the *History of Karka*, the topic of chapter 4. But to become members of the land, Christians had directly to address the relationship between the Good Religion and Walashfarr, both as an idea and as a ritualized landscape. The efforts of the *Martyrdom of Pethion* hagiographer to polemicize against Zoroastrianism and to claim a Christian place in the region were, the following sections show, intertwined.

The Christians of the *Martyrdom of Pethion*'s Walashfarr occupied a liminal position. They were still captives, and their ecclesiastical leadership was the "clergy of the captives" (*qliros d-bnai šebya*). Yet they had also contracted ties with the region's aristocratic houses. Although Christians held elite offices in fifth-century hagiographical works, the incorporation of Christian secular elites into Iranian aristocratic networks that the author described was unprecedented. The practice used to bring Christians into aristocratic communities was fosterage. The noble Mihryar, "who was great and very distinguished in the land of Walashfarr, ... distinguished more than all the other Magians before the king," entrusted his son Yazdin to a Christian foster father.³⁹ Fosterage was an essential instrument for the construction of networks formed through genealogy in the Iranian world.⁴⁰ Because only patrilineal, not matrilineal, relatives counted as members of one's kin group, fosterage enabled elites to establish close alliances between genealogically distinct aristocratic houses. The captive Christian had become sufficiently important in the region to be integrated into an aristocratic community, via the house of Mihryar. Even if it exaggerates Mihryar's status as the greatest aristocrat in the land, the account of a captive Christian forging an unbreakable tie with a noble house indicates that such acts of integration into elite networks were common enough for the Christian audience of the *Martyrdom of Pethion* to recognize their significance. Its hagiographer did not disclose the basis for the comparatively high status of the foster father or his counterparts, but sources for the captives of nearby regions suggest that incipient processes of elite formation were under way.[41] The *Martyrdom of the Captives* has recorded the development of captives to the south on the route to Khuzestan, in the highlands of Masabadan, into landowners in the story of a Christian who took possession of lands and then restored them to fertility.[42] If the captives of Khuzestan, such as the aforementioned Pusai, had held offices in the service of the king of kings, the landowner of Masabadan was the first explicitly attested Christian entrant into the politics of property east of Mesopotamia. With the creation of patrimonies, Christians could begin to construct themselves as aristocrats on the model of the traditional ruling houses.

Together with increased social interaction between Zoroastrian and Christian elites came the problem of religious boundaries, which the *Martyrdom of Pethion* hagiographer represented as the problem of conversion. If in chapter 1 we saw how Zoroastrian authorities responded to assaults on their institutions, including apostasy, in the *Martyrdom of Pethion* we find more complex patterns of encounter between adherents of the two religions. The narrative centers on conversion from Zoroastrianism to Christianity, detailing the circumstances in which Zoroastrian elites encountered Christians. These are historically plausible, if not historical, scenarios that presume intimate interactions to have been routine. Yazdin, the son of Mihryar, learned of Christianity from his foster father, who brought him to a church and "holy places" before he departed at the behest of his father to attend a Zoroastrian school.[43] Christian sons sent to reside in Zoroastrian houses will similarly have become familiar with the religion of their foster fathers. Yazdin then returned to his native land, where he converted his brother's son, christened Pethion, not only to the faith but also to the ascetic life. Ensconced in their mountainside cell, the ascetic kinsmen propagated the faith throughout the Iranian highlands through teaching and the working of wonders. Their reputation for healing attracted the attention even of eminent Zoroastrians, a commonly recurring theme in East Syrian hagiography. Zoroastrians did indeed view Christians as sources of medical expertise.[44] To liberate his daughter Anahid from a demonic possession, Adurohrmazd, a mowbed in the region, brought her to Pethion. In time, the ascetic persuaded both father and daughter of the truth of Christianity through wonders and words. Between Adurohrmazd's and Anahid's ensuing martyrdoms for apostasy, numerous leading Zoroastrians in the region were also reported to have been inspired to convert, notably Tahmin the *āyēnbed* (literally "master of customs," a provincial representative of the court) together with eighty of his cavalrymen and Nihormizd the *rad* (provincial judge) with sixty-two of the Zoroastrian religious specialists in his service.[45] As a mowbed observing the martyrdom of Pethion observed, "If this man remains alive any longer, know and beware that the Zoroastrian religion [*deḥlta d-mguše*] will depart from the entire kingdom."[46] Such was the view of the hagiographer and his fellow East Syrian authors. The great majority of modern scholars have supported and sometimes directly reproduced their accounts of Christianity's inevitable diffusion at the expense of the Good Religion.[47] Even if we were to accept the historicity of the conversions that the *Martyrdom of Pethion* recounts, its representation of a natural propensity of unbelievers to acknowledge Christian truth should be regarded not merely as triumphalist but as a deliberately distorting narrative that repressed realities which the author aimed to write out of existence. The emphasis on conversion in East Syrian hagiography and in our own historiography has downplayed religious encounters that did not lead to the clear crossing of religious boundaries. Confusion regarding the nature of religious identities, boundaries, and differences was, the Zoroastrian sources suggest, more prevalent than conversion.

In Zoroastrian discussions of interactions between wehdēn and Christians, known as *kilīsyāg* in the exegetical literature, rather different patterns emerge.[48] Within this corpus, it is chiefly in the Zand, the Middle Persian exegesis of the Avesta, that Christians appear, and the peculiarities of the genre discussed in the introduction present both possibilities and problems for historical analysis. The practical concerns of the exegetes who endeavored to resolve concrete dilemmas through consultation of the Avesta exposed complex circumstances, in contrast with the simplifying tendencies of the hagiographers. They wrote, moreover, on behalf of their fellow scholars, not for a wider audience for whom they needed to produce polemics. Their explorations of particular cases are therefore eminently more reliable testimonies than the accounts of East Syrian hagiographers, especially in the domain of interreligious encounters. Significantly, the scholars described cases not only of Zoroastrian apostasy but also of conversions to the Good Religion.[49] One case expressly refers to the previous religion as Christianity and reveals the complexities involved in such a transition. The wife of the convert remained Christian, a situation that forced the scholars to confront the challenges of a mixed household, specifically the question of whether Zoroastrians should provide her with the sustenance (*rōzgar*) to which members of the religious community were entitled: "He is obliged to provide sustenance [for his agdēn wife], and he may not leave this to the church [*kilīsyā*]; thus her sustenance is our responsibility."[50] What the scholars envisioned and sought to prevent was a household that drew upon the services of the religious specialists of both religions. This is a rare glimpse of a situation that would have been common in overlapping communities, even if Zoroastrian and Christian authors alike avoided divulging such disturbingly complex scenarios. Not all Christians who found the Good Religion appealing, however, necessarily converted. The commentators of the *Hērbedestān* also considered situations in which Christians and others sought to participate in

Zoroastrian rituals, even to learn their contents, while remaining recognizably agdēn.

Although the primary function of the hērbedestān was to provide instruction in the Yasna and the Avesta, the scholars described the presence of unbelievers in the schools as routine, if not unproblematic. "How may a man teach a disciple," one scholar asked in an updated interpretation of an Avestan passage, "who belongs to the demon worshipers, that is, *anērān,* or to the *tanāpuhl*-sinners?"[51] A *hērbed* (priestly teacher) could do so, we learn, as long as he received proper remuneration. The scholar added *anērān* in apposition to the demon worshipers of the Avestan text to signal clearly that the potentially problematic students were the Christians, Jews, or other non-Zoroastrians whom a Sasanian teacher would have encountered. Regardless of their agdēnīh, a hērbed in good standing with the authoritative redactors of the *Hērbedestān* could accept religious others as students and instruct them in Zoroastrian traditions.[52] When the background of a student of questionable status was specified, his father was known to have been, and perhaps to have remained, a Christian, according to the most recent editors of the treatise. The details of this case capture the blurred boundaries that could prevail in Zoroastrian schools. Furthermore, the well-known exegete Abarag addressed the problem of whether a student whose father's religious identity was ambiguous could advance to a higher stage of learning, the so-called wisdom of the righteous (*xrad ī ahlawān*).[53] Significantly, the question of the father's religion arose only when the student proceeded to the xrad ī ahlawān, while no similar objections were raised in the preceding discussion of the normal course of studies. Abarag ruled that "when the father has not reaffirmed his conversion to Christianity [*tarsāgīh*], then one should allow his son to come [to resume religious studies]."[54] The son could continue to study as long as the father had not reaffirmed, or more literally renewed, his Christianity. Unlike in the cases of conversion that East Syrian hagiographers represented as normative, the religious identity of the student's father could not be clearly ascertained. He had once converted to Christianity but had either reestablished or retained relations with Zoroastrians in such a way that some could regard him as having returned to the Good Religion. The ambivalence of the father, in any case, was not to prevent the son from advancement within the hērbedestān. What would have foreclosed such a possibility was a definitive break from Zoroastrianism. Abarag, among the most influential Zoroastrian scholars, considered religious ambivalence tolerable but the outright rejection of religion in favor of an alternative an unmistakable disavowal of membership in the community for an individual and his house.

A startling aspect of the *Hērbedestān* is the participation of Christians in the study of the Avesta, the centerpiece of the curriculum of the Zoroastrian school that the youthful Yazdin abandoned in favor of baptism. The contrast that the hagiographer made between the learning of the Zoroastrian school and the learning gained from holy men in preparation for baptism, between the learning of Satan and divine learning, was directed toward Christians who confused the two or who considered study in a hērbedestān beneficial. The advantages of learning from hērbed appeared not only in Zoroastrian accounts but in the East Syrian biography of George of Merv. Preserved in a ninth-century compilation of earlier monastic hagiographies, in this case most likely a life of the saint composed at his monastery in Merv, the account describes the education of a Christian youth from the province of Fars born to a wealthy house, the only biography of an East Syrian whose background resembled the circumstances of the assimilating captives of Walashfarr. His parents intended to send George to study "Persian learning . . . like the worldly rulers." But the would-be saint, like Yazdin, fled from the prospect of being schooled in Zoroastrian doctrine to the Christian school that the bishop of Merv, Bar Shabba, had established, reportedly declaring, "All learning that does not teach the religion of God is the folly of Satan."[55] The narrative recounts circumstances remarkably similar to those of late Sasanian Walashfarr. The case of a Christian household having gained wealth and seeking to achieve status through a son's education suggests a social context for the *Martyrdom of Pethion*'s assault on Zoroastrian learning. A Middle Persian treatise from the mid-sixth century, *Husraw and the Youth*, emphasizes the practical importance for ambitious elites of an education under the direction of hērbed. To impress an audience at court, a young aristocrat boasted of his training in literacy (*frahang*) and scribal ability (*dibīrīh*), which evidently entailed a concomitant education in the Avesta and its interpretation: "I memorized the *Yašt*, the *Hādōxt*, the *Bagān*, and the *Vīdēvdāt* like a hērbed and passage by passage heard the Zand."[56] The ideal aristocratic youth of the late Sasanian era was both literate and learned in the orally transmitted Zoroastrian tradition, skills sometimes inculcated in the same venues if not under the direction of the same teachers.

The manner in which the *Martyrdom of Pethion* hagiographer targeted the hērbedestān in his polemics implies that some Christian houses, like the house of George in Fars, sought to gain such knowledge for themselves, necessitating the development of specifically Christian schools and a systematic deconstruction of Zoroastrian doctrine. If the Zoroastrian school instilled some of the practices of the aristocratic habitus, the religious content of its curriculum was unambiguous. Christian participation in the hērbedestān offers an example of how the pursuit of social status exposed elite captives to Zoroastrian beliefs and rituals to an ever greater degree. Some of these Christians converted to the Good Religion, finding its rituals a more persuasive system of belief in the context of its political dominance. Others admired or even acknowledged the efficacy of its rites without openly converting. As the story of Yazdin's education suggests, Zoroastrian youths could also be exposed to Christianity, for instance if their parents entrusted them to Christian foster fathers. The scholar Sōšāns considered this possibility alarming enough to equate entrusting one's son to a non-Zoroastrian for education with the murder of the child.⁵⁷ The *Martyrdom of Pethion*, interpreted against the backdrop of the Zoroastrian exegetical literature, lays bare the intimacies and ambiguities that characterized interactions between Christians and Zoroastrians. Its author aimed to constrain the room for maneuver that the Christians of the region enjoyed and to eliminate the possibility for them to view belief in the power of the Yasna, for example, as a legitimate option within their faith. He did so, however, through the construction of an identity that Zoroastrians and Christians with irresolvable religious differences could share. The beginning and the end of this spatial and literary project was the mountain that embodied the linkage of religion, society, and politics in the region.

BELONGING TO WALASHFARR

Throughout the accounts of Pethion, Anahid, and Adurohrmazd, Bisutun stands present. Yazdin and Pethion established their cells, Anahid and Adurohrmazd converted to Christianity, and Pethion and Anahid were executed upon its slopes. It was the site of Yazdin's initial propagation of Christianity in the region and of the martyrs' ultimate interment, as well as of so many of the events that transpired in the interim. The *Martyrdom of Pethion* similarly specifies sites of episodes that took place elsewhere, such as the execution of Adurohrmazd or the ordeals of Pethion, creating a larger, regional imagined landscape with Bisutun at the center. The hagiographer inserted the mountain into the narrative wherever possible, often describing its features in richly detailed language. It was also the focus of the ceremonial commemorations associated with the cult of the martyrs. The *Martyrdom of Pethion* and the mountain are inextricable, much as Roman hagiographical works draw rhetorical strength from their urban contexts. Accounts of martyrs in the Roman world emphasize the space of the city in the course of their performance, adopting the symbolics of the spectacle to subvert traditional understandings of urban political belonging in ways that rooted Christian identities in the context of the Greco-Roman city.⁵⁸ The following sections examine the *Martyrdom of Pethion* as a deconstruction of Zoroastrianism, as its focus on natural features points to a related role for the author as the constructor of a Christian landscape. Through the reinterpretation of a Zoroastrian site in terms of a Christian cult, the text offered a solution to the dilemma of captive communities in Iran in the fifth and early sixth centuries: how to articulate their belonging within Zoroastrian politicogeographical categories. The close attention that the author paid to the most prominent, most symbolically resonant site in the northwestern Iranian highlands signaled his efforts to resolve the contradictions of captive life. The mountain was to become the symbol for a new kind of Christian community rooted in a landscape that the saints had made their own.

Land had long been a locus for thinking about the self in relation to larger social and political entities in the Iranian world. Although studies of political identity in Iran have centered on the question of Iranianness, the language of locality and especially of region was at least as potent in social relations.[59] The Avesta provides models for identifying oneself through one's place of origin. It is evident from the Manichaean adaptation of the Avestan categories of house (*māna-*), village (*vīs-*), tribe (*zantu-*), and land (*dahyu-*) that they continued to influence Sasanian thinking about society.[60] House and tribe were questions of blood, village and land questions of place. The genealogical thinking characteristic of Iranian elites frequently conflated land and lineage. In inscriptions, for instance, aristocratic individuals included the land to which they belonged immediately after their patronymic.[61] Identifying with a land was, moreover, sometimes required in legal contexts. The testimony of "a member of a land" (*ādehīg*) was considered more reliable than the words of an outsider.[62] The courts of Zoroastrian judges thus reinforced the cultural tendency to think of oneself in terms of one's land. Landlessness or exile was among the worst fates an individual could imagine. When a religious authority sought to inspire apocalyptic sentiments in the nobility, he raised the specter of *uzdehīgīh*, "the state of being without a land [*deh*]."[63] To be from "outside the land," *anšahrīg*, was straightforwardly to be a slave, a status that was likely ascribed to Christian deportees.[64]

Belonging to a land was evidently indispensable. But what did such membership entail? The only surviving treatise on the qualities of a region reveals what made a land worthy of boasting. The *Wonders and Magnificence of Sistan* presents the land of Sistan as a sacred landscape, that is, an assemblage of mountains, rivers, and seas that were suffused with the stories of Zoroastrian myth.[65] Although such a package of myths and natural monuments has not been recorded for Walashfarr, its very name provides some clues. The compound refers to the "glory of Wālaxš."[66] As the Parthian king Walash, known in Greek as Vologases, was associated with the region, Walashfarr was likely considered the home of the eponymous ancestor of his aristocratic house.[67] Walash II (r. 128/29–47 CE) had himself depicted on a carved stone at the southeast flank of Bisutun making a sacrifice.[68] Like the historical king, the mythical Walash was believed to have possessed or increased xwarrah, hence giving his name to the region in the Sasanian period. The name *Walashfarr* contains the outlines of the interweaving of landscape and sacred history familiar from the *Wonders and Magnificence of Sistan* and other mythical historical accounts from the Iranian world in late antiquity.

The question of whether Christians could claim to belong to a land and to transcend their status as *anšahrīg* recurs at several points in the *Martyrdom of Pethion*. The chief mowbed of the region, who was, like Adurohrmazd, from Bishapur in Fars, equated the espousal of Christianity with the betrayal of one's land. This "fellow landsman" (*bar 'atreh*) appealed to the apostate Adurohrmazd to remain loyal to his land, especially because these fellow sons of Bishapur found themselves in the distant territory of Walashfarr: "You know well that I have no one who is honored as you are in this foreign land in which we dwell. So do not shame our land."[69] The conversion of Adurohrmazd compromised the reputation not merely of the Zoroastrian priestly elite as a class or of the aristocracy more generally but of the inhabitants of Bishapur, who might have thought of themselves as Persians—in the sense of belonging to the land of Fars—like their counterparts in northern Mesopotamia.[70] Natives of Fars, the native region of the Sasanian dynasty, residing elsewhere in the empire constituted the highest strata of the elite, occupying offices such as those of the mowbed Adurohrmazd and his interrogator, a fellow mowbed. Interestingly, this passage indicates that the Persian aristocratic diaspora represented themselves as members of a distinctive land and of distinctive lineages, even describing the territory where they found themselves as a "foreign land." The notion that Christianity was incompatible with belonging to a land—and, in particular, incompatible with belonging to Walashfarr—appears in the interrogation of Anahid. The saint was given the opportunity to avoid punishment by departing from Walashfarr. One of her relatives promised to remove her to a land where Christianity had a place: "Just say, 'I am not a Christian.' I will redeem you and transfer you to one of the lands of the Christians [*nasraye*]." Anahid responded that she would remain in the land: "What land or place is not full of him [Christ]?"[71] Against those who claimed that the region was the exclusive property of Zoroastrians, the hagiographer argued that Christians could adopt Walashfarr for themselves and even take pride in its name as their place of origin.

If Christ was present in every land, as Anahid insisted, his presence manifested itself differently in each, adapting to the culture of its human population and its natural environment. The statement of the martyr preserved the peculiarities of lands within its assertion of Christian universalism. The author intended to produce a Christian Walashfarr rather than to dissolve the peculiarities of lands in a universal Christian community. He did so through the creation of an alternative imaginary for the land that would complement, not replace, preexisting ideas of what defined Walashfarr. The sacred site of the martyrdoms of Anahid and Pethion was the linchpin for this new view. By the beginning of the fifth century, specifically Christian instruments for making a place holy had become commonly available among East Syrian leaders. The prerequisite for transforming mundane places into sacred sites was holy contagion.[72] Objects or places that came into contact with the body of a saint could become sacred themselves. Knowledge of such contagion had necessarily to be transmitted both to the wider Christian community and across generations. Holy places thus required at least two of three institutions: a ceremonial commemoration, or feast; a physical structure for the veneration of the saints, or shrine; and a textual record of the events that brought holiness to the site, or work of hagiography.[73] It is only with the third institution, however, that the holiness of a site can be communicated to persons distant both spatially and chronologically, who will never encounter the place. The author of the *Martyrdom of Pethion* depended on each of these institutions to transform the slopes and crags of Bisutun into sacred sites. He referred to a tomb of the martyrs that suggests a modest shrine, and the procession of clergy described in the course of Anahid's martyrdom prefigures subsequent commemorations. The author turned to the art of hagiography to put the sacred site that his work helped to create in the service of the reimagining of Walashfarr as a Christian land.

The accounts of the executions of Anahid and Pethion transformed the mountain into a contact relic. When the interrogators had failed to persuade Anahid to reject her newfound faith, she was brought to the peak for punishment before an audience of the entire region: "[The mowbed Adurfrazgard] commanded that they transfer her to the mountain where she had resided, smear her body with honey, and stretch her out with four stakes in the middle of the mountain, where all who saw her would be terrified and would abandon her religion." She was affixed, the hagiographer specified, "on a level place at the foot of the cliff."[74] The significance of the honey will become clear momentarily. What is important here is that the saint's body was displayed prominently on the mountain, for the express purpose of attracting an audience, at a specified site. Pethion's execution was conducted with a similar theatricality, and the site is recorded with the same attention to detail. Over the course of six days he was systematically dismembered, beginning with his ears and nose and culminating with his head, on a level place beneath the cliff of the "desolate mountain."[75] He was slain in the very same place as Anahid. His body parts were, moreover, displayed on the mountainside. His limbs were hung from the cliff above him. His upper arms dangled from trees. His head was ultimately affixed to the cliff, so as to hang over the site of his execution.[76] The precise description of the site of the two martyrdoms indicates that the place was an object of veneration, likely the primary site of the cultic commemoration of the martyrs. The portrayal of their executions allowed Christian participants in the cult to imagine the martyrs in the landscape, to identify the slopes, cliffs, and trees that had come into contact with their sacred bodies.

A miracle that followed the binding of Anahid rendered the mountain an object of wonder. Once she was affixed to the peak, naked and smeared with honey, her persecutors expected wild beasts to devour her. But animals came rather to her assistance and, in the process, transformed the mountain: "A great, endless troop of bees gathered, so that the entire mountain was thus covered on all sides.... They did not approach her pure body ... [but rather] formed a kind of tent over her body."[77] The insects prevented both humans and animals from approaching the mountain for seven days. On the seventh day, the clergy from a nearby settlement of Christian captives approached the saint, who was on the brink of death, with the Gospel, candles, incense, and the accoutrements of a proper burial. When they neared the saint, the bees parted and gathered in formation "like a great house" over them while they performed burial rites and installed her body in the tomb of Yazdin. After ensuring that the clergy could seize her body without interference from the authorities, the bees returned to the site of her execution to perform a curious miracle: "All the insects ... piled up in the place where the martyr had been spread out. They devoured all the earth there until [they reached] rock, and they stayed on the mountain for seven more days."[78] The miracle served two seemingly contradictory but possibly complementary functions. On the one hand, the bees prevented earth made sacred through contact with a martyr, known in Syriac as *ḥnana*, from falling into impious hands.[79] On the other, they removed potentially contaminated earth from the site of the interment of the martyrs, suggesting that the saints' bones were placed in an astōdān, in keeping with Zoroastrian practices, similar to the Christian ossuary at Istakhr that we encountered in the previous chapter. In addition, the insects also remade the southeastern flank of Bisutun, the location of the martyrdoms. The mountain's sheer face rises several hundred meters from the Dinawar Valley, and the Achaemenian and Parthian reliefs and inscriptions are congregated at its most vertical, southeastern buttress. It was this signature peak that the bees were reported miraculously to have reworked, leaving the stone precipice visible. The mountain recognizable to late Sasanian observers was, according to the *Martyrdom of Pethion*, the product of a miracle performed at the behest of the Christian martyr Anahid. To recall the original meaning of *Bisutun*, the "place of the gods" became the place of the martyrs, sacred to both Zoroastrians and Christians, albeit on different terms.

The account of the miracle of the bees evokes the relationship among cosmology, ritual, and landscape. Insects were of great importance in Zoroastrian cosmological thought. Together with serpents, scorpions, amphibians, and other noxious creatures, they were manifestations of Ahreman.[80] In selecting bees as the agents of the miraculous power of the Christian God and his saints, the hagiographer introduced cosmological doctrine into the account of the martyr's execution to compose a story that encapsulates the various components of his polemics in a straightforward narrative: because the one Christian God was responsible for creating the world, every creature, even a seemingly harmful animal, is in his service. That insects were under the authority of the Christian saints might have been reassuring to the inhabitants of the Iranian highlands, where agricultural life was notoriously fragile.[81] One of the basic promises of the Yasna was prosperity, in particular agricultural prosperity, since the cultivation of crops was deemed cosmologically beneficial. In insects, the hagiographer identified a bugbear of agriculturalists that Zoroastrian priests could address only indirectly. The saints have direct control not merely over insects but over the entirety of the material creation. They could therefore guarantee prosperity for the land, which the Yasna, discredited by the author, could no longer provide. Immediately preceding her execution, Anahid made an appeal to God, intervening on behalf of the inhabitants of Walashfarr: "Grant, Lord, even unto this place, where we are now, prosperity, all the days of the world."[82] Pethion, in one of his entreaties to God, elaborated on the nature of the prosperity that the petitioners of the saints are promised: "May you receive the request and appeal of all those who call upon you in the name of my weakness, as you are a Savior and Redeemer for them from all the evils in which they are ensnared, whether from evil men, from hunger, wars, or robbers, from corrupting animals and noxious insects, from corrupting demons and evil spirits.... Preserve for them, Lord, their seeds and plants, stop the noxious insects, drive away the noxious winds and destructive hail."[83] The martyrs took on a role as intercessors on behalf of the land of Walashfarr, on whom its inhabitants could rely to safeguard their persons and possessions, especially their fields. These saints were patrons of the land as cultivable earth as well as social and political symbol.

This pattern recurred elsewhere on the Iranian Plateau. Indeed, there are only two other well-documented martyrs' cults in the region, both of which fulfilled prophylactic or regenerative functions. The *Martyrdom of Miles*, a late fourth- or early fifth-century work, recounts how the shrine of the namesake martyr and his companions protected a village in the district of Rayy, known in Syriac as Beit Raziqaye, from thieves, probably from the nearby Alburz Mountains. The relics of the martyrs prevented the marauders from entering the confines of the village: "The thieves were continually coming against the land [*'atra*] at all times in order to pillage and destroy. Whenever they reached the limits of the village, they were hindered and did not accomplish any destruction there. Its inhabitants believe that they are not permitted to enter because of the blessing of the bones of the just ones that are placed inside [the village]."[84] In the second case, in the mountains of Masabadan, a highland region between Walashfarr and Khuzestan, martyred Christian deportees from Beit Zabdai were believed to have determined the fertility of the district. After they were executed, waters vanished from the land as recompense: "The Lord provoked the reeds in the river of that village.... They took root and filled [the river] with soil. Then the inhabitants of the village came together and removed the soil. But the reeds took root and filled [the river] with soil again.... The village became parched and its plants withered. It was desolate for twenty-two years. This happened as if to curse the entire land."[85] But if the Christian God could ruin a land, he could also restore its fertility, and martyrs' bones were his instruments for doing so. When such relics are uncovered in the *Martyrdom of the Captives*, an annual commemoration is instituted, a martyrs' shrine (*beit sahde*) is constructed, and prosperity returns to a land that had previously been cursed.

Although apotropaic functions are commonly encountered in saints' cults across the Mediterranean and the Near East, in East Syrian literature these cases of martyrs bringing material benefits are unique. Their common origin in different regions of the Iranian Plateau suggests that they responded to Zoroastrian ritualized landscapes, where the Yasna was believed to bring prosperity and security.[86] The author of the *Martyrdom of Pethion* took the model of the apotropaic cult that implicitly rivaled Zoroastrian ritual from already existing shrines and embedded his anti-Zoroastrian polemics within the structure of a martyrs' cult, one that explicitly contested the capacity of the Yasna to safeguard a land. In response to those who insisted that Christians were necessarily outsiders, deracinated and deterritorialized captives, the hagiographer fashioned, by means of the narrative of the martyrs and their cult, a vision of a Walashfarr to which Christians could belong. To do so, he had to surmount the preexisting understanding of the land as an inherently Zoroastrian entity.

A DISTORTED COSMOGONY: ZURWANISM

The *Martyrdom of Pethion* articulates a polemic against Zoroastrianism that addresses the Good Religion as a nexus of beliefs, rituals, and landscapes, unlike other East Syrian works, which assail a disembodied, decontextualized body of doctrines that bear little resemblance to actually existing Zoroastrianism. Its hagiographer rightly regarded cosmological doctrines as the cornerstones of the religion. In recognizing that cosmology, and in particular cosmogony, was its most important aspect, the author betrayed an understanding of the religion far deeper than that of his counterparts, who tended to rely on hagiographical models of Greco-Roman paganism. Even hagiographers who wrote extensively against Zoroastrianism, such as the author of the *History of Mar Qardagh*, seem to have possessed only the most superficial knowledge of Zoroastrian thought and practice.[87] The author of the *Martyrdom of Pethion*, on the other hand, could produce cosmogonical accounts that drew on myths, stories, and arguments in circulation among contemporary Zoroastrian scholars.[88] So persuasively did he portray the concerns of Zoroastrian cosmological thought that generations of historians have studied his hagiography as a veritable transcription of Sasanian scholarly discourse, indeed as a more accurate reflection of fifth-century intellectual trends than the Middle Persian sources redacted in the early Islamic period.[89] The foregoing sections have provided a social context for the author's knowledge and shown how he rooted his polemics spatially in a Zoroastrian sacred landscape. The purpose of his learned exposé, however, remains to be considered. Historians have tended to extract seemingly informative sections from it without regard for their position in the work as a whole. An examination of these expositions has implications not only for their reliability as sources of Sasanian-era doctrine but also for the extent of Christian engagement with Zoroastrianism in the domains of both thought and practice.

The cosmogonical accounts appear, in a manner typical of hagiography, in the course of disputations between persecutor and persecuted over the reasons for the latter's conversion. The literary model of the debate in question-and-answer format gave the hagiographer an opportunity to showcase his knowledge of Zoroastrian doctrine, only to undermine its foundations. When the mowbed, the rad, and their companions interrogate the converts, Adurohrmazd and Anahid both give accounts of the essentials of the belief system that they rejected. From the outset, their accounts are intended to upend the teachings that they describe. They speak, moreover, with an authority predicated on their attainment of knowledge and status within the Good Religion. The hagiographer continually underlines their mastery of Zoroastrian texts and rituals prior to their conversion. Adurohrmazd the mowbed is expert in "the learning of the Magians" (*b-yulphana d-mguše*).[90] Anahid is not simply his daughter but the matrilineal granddaughter of a particularly renowned scholar, a certain Mahadurfarrah, "from whom flows all the light of the Avesta."[91] Their very names signal their literary roles as representatives of the Good Religion. Anahid was a deity of water especially prominent during the Sasanian period, while Adurohrmazd's name means literally "the fire of Ohrmazd" or "fire and Ohrmazd."[92] Anahid is even given the appellation of her namesake goddess, *bānūg* (lady).[93] There were now Christianized incarnations of Ohrmazd, fire, and Anahid who condemned rather than accepted veneration through traditional rituals. But if the text emphasizes their backgrounds to ground their polemics in accurate, reliable knowledge of Zoroastrian cosmology, the accounts they give are intended to justify their apostasy, to distort their previous beliefs to demonstrate the truth of Christianity.

The Zoroastrianism that the hagiographer portrayed by means of the literary figures Adurohrmazd and Anahid diverges sharply from the cosmogonical narratives that the Middle Persian tradition has preserved. Unlike the various Zoroastrian accounts, most importantly in the *Bundahišn*, that present Ohrmazd as the author of creation, the *Martyrdom of Pethion* makes a deity who played only a peripheral role in the normative tradition the primary creator: Zurwan, the god of time. The hagiographer has the converts make reference to a cosmogonical account in which Zurwan, not Ohrmazd, creates the world through the performance of a ritual resembling the Yasna, without explaining the details of this alternative view of creation. As Adurohrmazd declares to his interrogators, "What learning do you have that brings benefit? Should we consider Ashoqar, Frashoqar, Zaroqar, and Zurwan gods? Or Ohrmazd . . . ? Ashoqar, Frashoqar, and Zaroqar have emerged as empty names and stones without sense. Thus Zurwan too has been found to be far from any divinity, since indeed he was not even aware of that which was created in his womb. It seems, then, according to your account, that perhaps there was another god, to whom, according to your account, Zurwan made an offering."[94] Anahid too refers to a myth of Zurwan during her demonstration of the falsehood of her previous beliefs: "If Ohrmazd on his own conceived in his own belly and gave birth to children, like his father Zurwan, then he is androgynous, as the Manichaeans say.

But if he fathered them from his mother, daughter, and sister, as your crazy and senseless teaching maintains, how is it he does not resemble us in everything?"[95] In the views of the two apostates, Zurwan is the father of Ohrmazd and therefore preexisted the once supreme god, who is now no more dominant than other deities. These higher deities are specifically compared with the ancillary deity Wahram (or Verethragna), known in Yašt 14 of the Avesta as *aršōkara-*, *maršōkara-*, and *frašōkara-*, of which Ashoqar, Frashoqar, and Zaroqar are distorted versions.[96] The auditors of these polemics were given to understand that Zoroastrian deities great and small—and ultimately good and evil—were indistinguishable and bore a closer resemblance to material than to immaterial beings. These gods were themselves creations, whether of a higher god or of the human imagination, unlike the one God of the Christians, whom the converts had elected to worship.

This representation of Zoroastrianism is predicated upon a variant cosmogony that is attested, at least in antiquity, exclusively in Christian sources.[97] According to Roman, East Syrian, and Armenian authors, Zoroastrians believed that the god of time created Ohrmazd, who then proceeded to create the material world. After performing the Yasna for a thousand years—just as Ohrmazd would later bring the world into being—Zurwan bore two sons, Ohrmazd and Ahreman. The latter was conceived because Zurwan had entertained doubts concerning the efficacy of the Yasna during the course of the rite. The two brothers—one benevolent, the other malevolent—produced their own respective material creations, which formed the terrain on which they vied for control. This is, in brief, what has become known as the Zurwanite cosmogony or Zurwanism.[98] Historians of Zoroastrianism have interpreted these accounts as reliable witnesses to an alternative understanding of the creation of the world that the normative Zoroastrian tradition successfully repressed. For some, the Zurwanite cosmogony was the basis for a distinct religion, a western Iranian belief system that resisted the propagation of Zoroastrianism under the Sasanians.[99] For others, belief in Zurwan as the primary creator constituted a heresy that the Sasanians themselves propagated, an aberrant school of thought that attained ascendancy only in late antiquity.[100] These elaborate histories of Zurwanism have, however, been based on Christian accounts such as the *Martyrdom of Pethion*. Because the supposed Zurwanites were deviants, the scholarly proponents of Zurwanism argue, their beliefs were systematically expunged from Zoroastrian literature, leaving only outsiders as witnesses. The reconstruction of the alternative cosmogony and associated religious phenomena—for example, fatalism—on the basis of the Christian sources and supposed traces in the surviving Zoroastrian tradition was a major concern of twentieth-century scholarship in Iranian studies.[101] Recently, however, several specialists have begun to dismantle the scholarly edifice of Zurwanism. Shaul Shaked has argued that "Zurvanism as an organized religious system is a scholarly invention," based on misconceptions of the nature of Zoroastrianism as a religion.[102] The story of Zurwan, in his view, was one pedagogical account of creation among others, and previous scholars elevated the god of time to the figurehead of an entire alternative cosmological system only because they presumed a uniform, normative account of creation to have been the linchpin of a Zoroastrian "orthodoxy."[103] It was the preconception of the Good Religion as a credal faith, in implicitly or explicitly Christian terms, that caused scholars to transform a story into a sect. Shaked, by contrast, allows for stories potentially in tension with one another to coexist within Zoroastrian communities: "It seems to have been an accepted variant within the range of Zoroastrian thinking that the dualism of Ohrmazd and Ahreman was preceded by undifferentiated time," Zurwan. Within Zoroastrianism, scholars could consider a variety of seemingly contradictory accounts in the same milieux, much as the amoraim recorded alternative, sometimes contradictory accounts in the Babylonian Talmud.[104]

What has remained unexamined in the critique of Zurwanism is the Christian polemical context of its sources. The narrative of Zurwan's creation recurs in three texts produced in the late Sasanian period: the *Treatise on God* of Eznik of Kołb, the *Regulations for Marriage* of the East Syrian patriarch Mar Aba, and the *Martyrdom of Pethion*.[105] Although their accounts have frequently been juxtaposed as independent attestations of Zurwanite doctrine, these authors relied on a common source, composed in the late fourth century by an author scarcely familiar with Zoroastrianism as a living tradition: *On Magianism in Persia* by Theodore of Mopsuestia.[106] Likely drawing on Hellenistic sources, Theodore, according to a ninth-century summary of the lost work, described the teaching "of Zourouam . . . the origin of all . . . who performed libations in order to give birth to Ohrmazd. He bore him as well as Satan."[107] Whether Armenian and East Syrian authors had direct or mediated access to the Greek text, they recapitulated the fundamentals of Theodore's account in their own works, each with distinctive literary structures and objectives. Theodore's treatise, together with a great deal of his oeuvre, would have been widely available in East Syrian circles, and the *Martyrdom of Pethion* hagiographer could have read the text.[108] Mar Aba, an expert in his theology, almost certainly did. But the gist of Theodore's polemic also appears in works whose authors were only vaguely aware of his account, suggesting that its representation of the Good Religion as Zurwan worship became part of the polemical common sense of Christian writers working within what Lucas van Rompay has described as the theological patrimony of Edessa.[109] The *Martyrdom of Pethion* is thus one example of the broader trend among Armenian- and Syriac-writing Christians of polemicizing against Zoroastrianism as a belief system centered on Zurwan rather than Ohrmazd. The cosmogonical accounts that its hagiographer produced derive not from his own knowledge of the Good Religion but from his training in the arts of Christian polemic. They are hardly trustworthy descriptions of historical Zoroastrian beliefs.

This author, however, did not simply reproduce an already well-worn polemic. The position of the Zurwanite cosmogony in his overarching narrative merits closer attention. Despite their dependence on Theodore's treatise, Eznik of Kołb, Mar Aba, and the *Martyrdom of Pethion* hagiographer were intimately familiar with Zoroastrianism and wrote in environments saturated with its ideas, myths, and rituals. Why did the best-informed Christian authors choose Zurwan as the figure around whom to design their polemics? Their representations of Zoroastrian doctrine not only were based on already available Christian polemics but were also intended to evoke tensions in contemporary Zoroastrian thought. Even if the myth of Zurwan was neither normative nor aberrant, speculation concerning the relationship between time and creation appears to have been widespread in the Sasanian hērbedestān. As Shaked has argued, Zurwan was generally considered the "undifferentiated time" that preceded creation, which could have been discussed in terms that approximated those of Christian authors.[110] The importance of time in Zoroastrian thought will have made the eponymous god of time a major topic of scholarly discussion, and Sasanian scholars may have disputed whether time pre-existed the creation of Ohrmazd and, if so, how.[111] The Manichaeans manipulated this problematic in Zoroastrian cosmogony, naming their chief deity Zurwan in Middle Persian. As the Manichaeans carefully adapted Zoroastrian concepts, deities, and terms to present their faith as transcending the Good Religion, the use of Zurwan rather than Ohrmazd was a deliberate step which presumed that wehdēn could recognize the former as a potentially superior god.[112] The ambiguous place of Zurwan in the Zoroastrian cosmogony rendered the deity an ideal candidate for the polemical attentions of Christians and Manichaeans seeking to undermine the religion. If the treatise of a Roman theologian provided the materials, the *Martyrdom of Pethion* hagiographer's expertise enabled him to deploy the Zurwanite cosmogony as the basis for his deconstruction of the Good Religion as a socially and politically embedded, territorialized complex of ideas and rituals.

The accounts of Zoroastrianism as Zurwanism portray the religion as essentially homologous with Christianity. Zoroastrians too are purported to have possessed a creed, a unified and uniform set of doctrines whose profession secured one's membership within the community. The Good Religion, according to the hagiographer, was a "doctrine" or "learning," a *yulphana*, just as Christianity was a doctrine. The difference resided in its content: Christian teachings were true, Zoroastrianism a "doctrine of Satan."[113] Here is an example of a Christian applying what Jan Assmann has called the Mosaic distinction between true and false doctrines to a religion that understood its beliefs to possess ambiguities and uncertainties and preferred myths to rational dialectics as a means of exploring and communicating those beliefs.[114] Represented in the framework of Christian orthodoxy, the speculative discussions that Zoroastrian scholars cultivated could be made to appear incoherent. If Zurwan preceded Ohrmazd how could the latter be the supreme god? In this respect, the *Martyrdom of Pethion* differs from contemporaneous polemics only in its scope and its use of specialist terminology. But the story of Zurwan is only the beginning of the author's polemical project. Even while describing the religion as an evil, irrational doctrine, the hagiographer acknowledged that cosmological thought was inextricable from the Yasna ritual and the natural environments in which it was performed. Unlike his peers, he proceeded to target this ritual, the linchpin of the Good Religion. In recognizing the Yasna as the essence of Zoroastrianism and not of a set of disembodied doctrines, the hagiographer most clearly exhibited his familiarity with its principles and practices.

THE SUBVERSION OF THE YASNA

As a reenactment of the rites that Ohrmazd undertook to bring the created world into existence, the Yasna was the primary means by which humanity contributed to the cosmic struggle.[115] Performed by priests on behalf of the population, the ritual was believed to have supported the beneficent deities, creations, and humans, and the service of Ohrmazd, both physically and spiritually. It also had pedagogical functions for priestly scholars, as the institutional space in which the Avesta was recited. For modern audiences, the Avesta is a text to read. In the ancient world, it was transmitted and recited primarily orally, even after the compilation of a written version in the late Sasanian period.[116] And the oral performance of the Avesta took place in the course of the Yasna. Any speculative thinking based on the Avestan corpus thus began and ended with the ritual. The Yasna is an underlying theme of the *Martyrdom of Pethion*, from Yazdin's abandonment of Zoroastrian learning through the martyrdom of Pethion and the apostates. Anahid and Adurohrmazd rejected not simply Zoroastrian doctrine but the Yasna itself. At the outset of the interrogation of Adurohrmazd, the rad of Walashfarr entreats the convert not to leave behind "the good fortune of the barsom and of Magianism."[117] *Good fortune* refers to xwarrah, which Zoroastrian rites were intended to augment.[118] The barsom, moreover, was the bundle of sacred pomegranate twigs that the priest held during the performance of the Yasna. Through the words of a rad, the hagiographer defined the essence of the religion in terms that Zoroastrians could have embraced. What the Good Religion promised at the most fundamental level was xwarrah achieved through its rites, even if the cosmogonies used to comprehend or explain their efficacy varied. It was this promise that the hagiographer endeavored to discredit.

The Zurwanite cosmogony was deployed to undermine perceptions of the Yasna as a ritual with the potential to influence natural and supernatural forces. The cosmogony, in both Christian and Zoroastrian versions, is all about ritual.

Whether Zurwan or Ohrmazd, the creator brought the world into being by reciting the Ahunwar, the opening of the Avesta, while wielding the barsom. The figure of Zurwan served to call the ritual into question in two ways. First, the deity whom performers of the Yasna were supposed to imitate was unclear. If both Zurwan and Ohrmazd had performed the ritual primordially, whose creative act were the priests to replicate? Second, Ohrmazd and Ahreman became brothers, even twins, potential allies instead of primordial antagonists. Born in the same womb to the supreme Zurwan, the deities whose separateness was the basic principle of the religion became intimate. Within the Zurwanite framework, one could not easily distinguish the benevolent from the malevolent, because the primary creator had introduced both to the world. The question of whether the priests replicated the rites of Zurwan or Ohrmazd, therefore, had major consequences for the function of the Yasna. If Zurwan's ritual had created good and evil deities, could not Zoroastrian priests also generate evil as well as good? How could the priests worship and channel the power of a good deity "the vows and sacrifices of whose father were not brought to fruition until he unwittingly gave birth to Satan"?[119] The powers of Ohrmazd and Ahreman were, in this misrepresentation, coextensive and complementary, and the beneficence of Zurwan hardly self-evident. In the *Martyrdom of Pethion*, Adurohrmazd underlines the ambivalence of the deities that the polemical cosmogony implied. When a mowbed appeals to him, "Say a nask of the Avesta, and at once you will become a part of Ohrmazd, and Satan will leave you," he replies with a quotation of Isaiah 5:20, "Do not call God Satan, because it is said in our book, 'Woe upon those who call evil good and good evil.'"[120] A nask of the Avesta was not necessarily directed to a good deity as opposed to an evil one, because Zurwan, Ohrmazd, and Ahreman were intertwined.

The relationship among the deities that the Zurwanite cosmogony envisioned had immediate consequences for the material creation. If the creative acts of Ohrmazd and Ahreman were interdependent, the distinction between good and evil creations that underpinned Zoroastrian doctrine was rendered ambiguous. After his speech discrediting the Zoroastrian deities, Adurohrmazd turns to the creation of beneficent elements—light, water, and the stars—and animals, with a view to demonstrating their dependency on evil creatures. In the course of this extension of the Zurwanite polemic, the author recounts, in his typically manipulative fashion, otherwise unknown cosmogonical myths concerning interactions between good and evil material creations. Ohrmazd is supposed to have relied on the "disciples" of Ahreman in order to create light, an allusion to a narrative whose details are left unmentioned. An invented contest between the two deities that attended the creation of water, however, is described at length. As Ahreman strove to eliminate the waters newly introduced to the earth, one of his agents—a fly, a *xrafstar*, a wicked creature like the bees that appeared in the course of Anahid's martyrdom—

enabled Ohrmazd to triumph over the evil deity, allowing water to remain a beneficent creation:

> When the water reached Ahreman, he said to Ohrmazd, "Your possessions may not drink from my water." While he was aware of no means [of resistance] and was fearful, a certain demon from the alliance of Ahreman made a revelation to Ohrmazd and instructed him. And he said to Ahreman, "Take your waters from my earth." Then the frog that Ahreman had made consumed the waters, and Ohrmazd remained once again in fear and sadness.[21] He found assistance from the creatures of Ahreman, namely, that a fly entered the nose [of the frog].... The waters then returned to their place and Ohrmazd rejoiced. To the servant of the allies of Ahreman who had made a revelation to him and informed him, he promised that he would give him a seat in paradise [wahišt] and all of the Magians would recite an invocation [šnūman] to him. As it seems from these events, we should subject ourselves to the wise and powerful Satan, not the foolish and weak Ohrmazd.[122]

The account of one of Ahreman's xrafstar aiding Ohrmazd in their battle for control of water bears a close resemblance to the exegetical parables through which Zoroastrians discussed and disseminated cosmological doctrines.[123] Material creations were brought into being as instruments through which the cosmic struggle could be waged, and the *Bundahišn*, a normative cosmogony, thematizes the "battles [ardīg] of the creations against the evil spirit." In this narrative, waters, winds, mountains, and other objects wage war against evil, in concert with their animating, beneficent spirits.[124] Although a precise parallel for the tale of the frog and the fly has not survived, in its basic outlines the account could plausibly have circulated in Zoroastrian scholarly circles as an elaboration of the battle of the waters against Ahreman. Even if the hagiographer invented the story, he was sufficiently familiar with accounts of material creations in combat to craft an exegetical parable that resonated with existing Zoroastrian literary and cosmological discourse.

The polemical distortion of the combat of the creations represents the dialectical development of good and evil elements and beings as an indication of their fundamental interdependence and thus their indeterminacy. At the level of doctrine, the narrative seeks to demonstrate the truth of the Christian cosmogony, according to which the entirety of creation is the work of the one God. Supernatural power is present only in holy persons and the objects and places with which they have come into contact, not in divinized creations. Cosmogonical accounts have profound implications for the perception of the natural world, to which we will turn in the next section. But the hagiographer placed his polemic against the divinization of natural elements and beings within the framework of an overarching narrative directed against a rival ritual complex. In the preceding lines, Adurohrmazd stresses the inability of the deities to assist petitioners because their beneficence is compromised. In the same vein, Ohrmazd's dependence on a xrafstar communicates the inability of the god—the author of the Yasna—to manipulate creation in humanity's favor. Zoroastrian priests, the author insisted, recited a šnūman to the unspecified disciple of Ahreman who had assisted Ohrmazd. As the šnūman was an invocation of a beneficent deity, such as Ohrmazd, Wahram, or Anahid, in the course of the Yasna, the author expressly highlighted the implications of his account of the creation of the natural world for Zoroastrian ritual. The priestly rites invoked good and evil deities, and the priests' claim of augmenting the good creations that bring prosperity to humans and their lands at the expense of destructive, evil creations was, therefore, illusory.

Anxieties concerning the possibility of rituals unleashing destructive powers were indeed present in Zoroastrian sources. Although a properly performed Yasna brought prosperity, ritual mistakes could permit evil forces to harness the powers of ritual *nērang*. According to Shaked, "The notion that a bad ritual reaches not the divine beings but the demons is recurrent in Pahlavi texts."[125] The spilling of an offering, for example, could transform the Yasna into "demon worship" (*dēwēzagīh*).[126] Apart from those who made straightforward mistakes, there were those who purposefully solicited the assistance of demons because of their capacity to control wicked creations such as the xrafstar. A collection of ethical injunctions (*andarz*) attributed to the mythical king Jamshid includes the admonition "not to sacrifice to the demons for any prosperity."[127] If the ritual powers could so easily be misdirected, to support evil instead of good deities, the very nature of the Yasna and associated rites could be called into question. The *Ardā Wirāz Nāmag,* a late Sasanian text, was composed to refute such skepticism of the benefits of the Yasna. A council of religious specialists was reported to have dispatched a righteous man on a journey into hell to prove the reliability of the rites of religion: "[They desired to send someone to the spiritual realm in order] that the people who are in this age may know whether these acts of worship [*yazišn*], offerings [*drōn*], prayers [*āfrīnagān*], ritual powers [*nērang*], ablutions [*pādyābīh*], and rites of purification [*yōjdahrgarīh*] that we enact reach the gods or the demons, and [whether] they come to the assistance of our souls or not."[128] The questions that Adurohrmazd raised—Did the rites solicit good or evil deities? Who benefited from them?—were present in the discussions of Zoroastrian scholars of the late Sasanian period and were of sufficiently grave concern to stimulate the production of a novel literary genre, the journey through hell.[129] The *Martyrdom of Pethion* hagiographer manipulated debates and doubts concerning the efficacy of Zoroastrian rituals that circulated among the contemporaries of the author of the *Ardā Wirāz Nāmag* in order to deny Ohrmazd and his rituals control over the natural world. Evil forces manifested themselves in natural calamities that the allies of Ohrmazd could not withstand—earthquakes, droughts, and locusts.[130] Protection from these was the prosperity that Anahid and Pethion promised. The landscape where

Christians will have heard the hagiography recited remained in the foreground of its polemics, as two miracles of Pethion underlined.

THE ORDEALS OF PETHION

If Anahid and Adurohrmazd pronounced polemics against the Yasna, the third martyr of their hagiography, Pethion, overcame the forces of another Zoroastrian ritual: the ordeal. Studies of religion and society in the Sasanian period have paid comparatively little attention to the various ordeals that Zoroastrian priests employed, particularly in juridical contexts. But the ordeal was the basic means of determining the truth of testimony when witnesses were unavailable, the corollary of torture in Roman law.[131] The ability of the body to withstand naturally unendurable conditions—whether the binding of feet, the force-feeding of sulfur, immersion, or another technique—indicated that supernatural powers bore witness to the truth of an individual's testimony, in place of human witnesses.[132] From its original juridical function, the ordeal developed into an instrument of determining religious truth. It was a polemical account of an ordeal that was frequently repeated in Zoroastrian literary texts. According to a narrative that several treatises have preserved, Adurbad, the mowbedān mowbed under Shapur II, was celebrated for demonstrating the truth of the Good Religion against miscellaneous religious adversaries.[133] He did so through an ordeal of molten metal: "Many varieties of sect, belief, aberration, doubt, and divisiveness appeared in the world until the blessed, immortal Ādurbād ī Māraspandān was born, who performed the ordeal of religion [*passāxt ī pad dēn*]. Molten copper was poured on [his] chest, and he carried out several cases and judgments with the sectarians [*jud-kēšēn*] and the unbelievers [*jud-wurrōyišnān*]."[134] Religious truth could, this narrative implies, be established through a juridical process, namely an ordeal. To appreciate the importance of such a recurring account, one should compare the story of Adurbad with martyrology. Christians described their triumph in cases of religious conflict in terms of martyrdom, Zoroastrians in terms of the ordeal. Adurbad was only the most famous of a number of priests who publicly effected a triumph for the Good Religion over its rivals during the Sasanian era.[135] Indeed, the first human reciter of the Yasna, Zoroaster, was believed to have instituted the ordeal.[136] The sacred elements—such as fire, water, and metal—served as the privileged tutors of the truth in rituals that were as central to Zoroastrianism, and to the authority of its priests, as the Yasna.

In the main, East Syrian martyrologies adhere to Roman literary models in their descriptions of the contests between persecuted and persecutor. The merciless mowbed were equipped with batons of pomegranate wood rather than the torture racks of Roman governors but otherwise tormented their victims with the same bloodthirsty glee.[137] However, unlike Roman Christian hagiographers, East

Syrian authors generally refrained from putting their rulers' mechanisms for establishing truth in the service of their own ideological agendas. By enduring torture, Roman martyrs passed the test of the state for establishing truth while performing a principal virtue of the Roman elite, endurance (Greek: *hypomone*).[138] But enduring the beatings of the mowbed proved nothing to Zoroastrians and their authorities. The ritual beating of persons was penitential, not truth producing.[139] Within Christian communities, the endurance of physical suffering had meaning as imitation of Christ and his martyrs, and elaborate accounts of torment are an essential feature of martyrology. Some East Syrian authors, however, incorporated ordeals into their narratives to prove the truth of their martyrs' testimony in Iranian as well as Christian terms. Dado endured an ordeal of boiling water and Gubralaha one of fire, both during the reign of Shapur II.[140] In seventh- or eighth-century accounts built on late Sasanian precedents, the monks Mar Awgen and Mar Yonan withstand ordeals of fire. The patriarch Mar Aba was reported to have vindicated Christianity in a fiery ordeal that the mowbedān mowbed orchestrated.[141]

Pethion's is the most extended account of an ordeal in East Syrian literature. Seized from his mountainside cell after the two apostates were executed, the ascetic was imprisoned in a village known as Beit Haripe, in the district of Shulam. The hagiographer explicitly located the sites of the ensuing events. Pethion was subjected to an ordeal by water in a river near the village, with the goal of publicly demonstrating the falsehood of his faith. This rite entailed the immersion of an individual in water. The truth of his testimony depended on his reemergence. Although water is sacred in a number of ancient societies, this aspect of Zoroastrianism gave the rite special significance in the Iranian world. Water itself took on the authority to determine the truth. In the case of Pethion, however, the waters vindicated his testimony of faith. Once the holy man was thrown into the river, they receded from him, leaving him untouched: "The river was divided from its place. The waters that were flowing in coming from above gathered and stood as firm as a wall . . . and those that were descending below went down as far as Nharguzan, which is Sinani. . . . The saint remained dry in the river. . . . Those who were standing there were amazed, were frightened, and stood fast while saying with a loud shout, 'Great is your God, Pethion, great is your God.'"[142] After the failure of the waters to cooperate, the mowbed Adurfrazgard initiated a second ordeal: "The Magian gave the order at once to build an altar on top of a rocky hill to the north of the village, and he gave the order to pile up a great deal of oak wood upon the altar."[143] In a mirroring of the preceding ordeal, another sacred element was to test the saint. But fire too stymied the persecutors. When Pethion was brought to the pyre, "the flame of fire gave out a powerful roar and departed from the furnace . . . and curved itself onto the upper height above the altar like a great dome."[144] The saint vanquished the mowbed and his associates in two ordeals. If Anahid and

Adurohrmazd relied on words and logical argumentation to prove the truth of their faith, Pethion turned to the elements sacred to Zoroastrians as his witnesses.

His miraculous exploits were, nevertheless, of a piece with the doctrinal debates of Anahid and Adurohrmazd. Like the Yasna, the ordeal was an instrument through which Zoroastrian priests channeled beneficent powers. Just as supposed sorcerers and demon worshipers could subvert the Yasna to their own ends, the rites of ordeal could be abused to support demons, because the mechanics of the two rituals were identical. Both the ordeal and the Yasna tapped into and redirected undercurrents of cosmic power, known as *nērang,* to which humans were otherwise unwittingly subject. The term *nērang* designates the forces that shape and animate existence, whether spiritual (*mēnōg*) or physical (*gētīg*). For example, the humors that determine the condition of the human body—a theory incorporated into Zoroastrian thought from Galenic medicine—were regarded as nērang, and environmental and climactic differences between regions were ascribed to the same forces.[145] The Yasna and the ordeal were also nērang, powers that actively ordered and reordered the world. Hence, *nērang* is commonly translated as "ritual" or "incantation."[146] But if the Yasna operated more subtly, or theoretically, to manipulate material creations, the ordeal worked directly through the elements. The capacity of the rite to channel nērang manifested in the behavior of fire, water, or other material. It was not only beneficent creations that acted but also the deities identified with them, namely Ohrmazd in the case of fire and Anahid in the case of water. According to a Middle Persian gloss on an Avestan hymn to fire, Ohrmazd was the "master of the ordeal" (*war sālār*), who could dependably distinguish the just from the wrongdoer. The fire through which he acted evinced joy (*hunsandīh*) when encountering those who practiced justice (*ahlāyīh*) and good deeds (*kirbag*) and, presumably, wrath when encountering the wicked.[147] It is here significant that the deities who testify in Pethion's favor in the course of his ordeals are present throughout the narrative in the names of Anahid and Adurohrmazd. In light of the ritual's cosmological background, the place of the ordeal accounts in the hagiographer's polemical structure is apparent. As an observer of Pethion's triumph, Nihormizd the red reportedly declares, "If these deeds that he [Ohrmazd] performed are of the power of demons and Ahreman, it is very perverse that Ohrmazd be so feeble before the power of Ahreman and the demons that they could move his children, the gods, from their abodes. Do you see in the depth of your knowledge, the religion, and the entire Avesta whether it is possible for Ahreman to do something like this?"[148] Zoroastrians were prepared, as we have noted, to explain failed ordeals as the work of demons. Aware of these nuances in ritual theory, the hagiographer designed a narrative of ordeals of water and fire, elements seemingly impervious to evil influence. Pethion, like his counterparts in the preceding passages of their narrative, serves to undercut the authority of Zoroastrian priests and their rituals, through a demonstration that their divinized elements heed not them but a Christian holy man.

While denying Zoroastrians and their gods authority over the natural world, the narrative endows fire and water with peculiarly Christian significance. Elements sacred within the Zoroastrian tradition become components of the cult of the saints, objects of Christian veneration. The elaborate descriptions of the waters of the river, "like a mighty wall of brass," and the flames that formed a "dome" over the saint highlight their roles as agents of miraculous power.[149] The saint did not simply endure fire and water. These elements acted, at his direction, to safeguard him from danger. The capacity to manipulate natural elements supernaturally resided in the saint and his god rather than in mowbed, Ohrmazd, or Anahid. These were Christianized elements that were merely instruments of the divine will, sacred only through their association with the Christian God and his representatives, not in and of themselves. But the hagiographer envisioned a Christian cult in which natural elements would play an important role. He deliberately described Pethion's ordeals as taking place at identifiable sites in the landscape, giving place-names that, despite their obscurity to a modern reader, would have been familiar to contemporaries. The ordeal of fire transpired on a rocky hill above the village of Beit Haripe in the Dinawar Valley, and the river into which Pethion was thrown flowed just outside the village in the direction of a place known as Nharguzan or Sinani. The river that fits this description flowed southward through Dinawar and joined the river flowing westward from Kangavar, before meandering southward into Khuzestan.[150] This was the principal source of water in Walashfarr, on which the inhabitants of the region depended for their sustenance. The named places were likely known to Zoroastrians in the region, as ordeals were to be performed at designated sacred sites, so-called *mān ī mēnōg*, "spiritual abodes."[151] This attention to local geography indicates that the hagiographer aimed to preserve the sites of Pethion's ordeals in the collective memory of the Christians of the region. Those commemorating the saint were to return to the places where fire and water had borne witness to the truth of his faith and where the extent of his supernatural abilities had been made plain. Since he and his God had worked so dramatic a miracle in the waters that formed the lifeline of the region, the cult of Pethion had the potential to contribute to the creation of a Christian Walashfarr, an interconnected series of points in the landscape around which loyalties regional and religious could meld.

The focus of the *Martyrdom of Pethion* on the nexus of cosmological thought and ritual reveals the extent to which its author engaged with the Good Religion as practiced on the Iranian Plateau around the beginning of the sixth century. He built on arguments concerning cosmology and cosmogony in an attempt to discredit the two most socially and politically important rituals in the empire, the Yasna and the ordeal.[152] He thus accurately identified and aimed to destabilize the intellectual and ritual foundations of the Zoroastrian priestly elite. While distorting the beliefs of Zoroastrians, he demonstrated his familiarity with their rituals, myths, and speculative discussions, as well as the Christian polemical and hagiographical traditions of both the Mediterranean and the Iranian world. The *Martyrdom of Pethion* serves to document a sustained encounter of ritual and thought between adherents of the two religions of a kind that historians had previously presumed, but not been able to prove, had occurred, at least outside Armenia.[153] The question of how such an encounter transpired, or of how the author gained such knowledge, returns us to the social context of the acculturating captives of the region. For the emerging Christian elite in a Walashfarr where interelite sociability was commonplace, there were ample opportunities to become acquainted with Zoroastrian rites as well as their implications and explanations. It is not necessary to presume that the author was a convert, like Mar Aba, although the possibility cannot be excluded. The similarly knowledgeable Eznik of Kołb was not. The *Martyrdom of Pethion* is not merely an intellectual work, however, but a polemical one. Its function was to persuade an audience of Christians attending feasts of the martyrs that the Good Religion was false, its doctrines absurd, its rituals inefficacious. The auditors of the work therefore included Christians who regarded the Zoroastrian rituals as significant, wondrous, authoritative, and even beneficial. Christian admirers of the Yasna could have been converts such as Yazdin, Anahid, and Adurohrmazd. But given the lack of evidence for large-scale conversion, they were more likely to have been elites participating in predominantly Zoroastrian social networks or humbler captives who witnessed the performance of the Yasna or ordeals from a distance. The captives of Iran had experience of Zoroastrian rites, if not of cosmological thought, either directly or indirectly. These rituals were frequently performed, whether within the confines of a fire temple or in the open air, at prominent points in the mountainous landscapes of the Iranian Plateau, within the lines of sight of the inhabitants of their valleys.[154]

CONCLUSION

Through the prism of the *Martyrdom of Pethion* we can see how the inhabitants of an Iranian region believed their land to have been sustained through the Yasna, which worked upon the highly unpredictable natural elements to ensure the welfare of its people. These "sons of the land," to adopt the terminology of the work, conceived of their relationship to the land in terms of Zoroastrian ritual and myth.[155] Although scholars have long questioned the influence of Zoroastrianism on the social life of the empire, the *Martyrdom of Pethion* shows that the package of the Yasna, the Avesta, and the cosmological doctrines that were the normative institutions of the Good Religion under the Sasanians structured social and political relations to the extent that assimilating captives had to come to terms with them. Such Christians could adopt the category Walashfarr, if not Ērānšahr, but the imperial religion was as interlinked with the land as with the empire. The cosmological and ritual polemics of the *Martyrdom of Pethion* hagiographer were therefore prerequisites for a Christian claim of belonging fully to the land. It was necessary not only to discredit Zoroastrian rituals but also to introduce a new, specifically Christian complex of land-sustaining rites. The cult of the martyrs that convened the Christians of the region collectively to petition the saints promised to bring prosperity to the land and enabled ecclesiastical leaders to present themselves, in the role of intermediaries, as the patrons and protectors of Walashfarr. For Christian elites and the aristocratic Iranian communities that they joined, a shared commitment to the land and its prosperity provided a basis for cooperation, regardless of religious difference. One could present oneself as a man of Walashfarr without adopting Zoroastrian language. Christian and Zoroastrian elites had differences in beliefs with potentially profound implications for their understandings of self, society, and political order, but they could share an identity as "sons of the land" or even act as representatives of the land vis-à-vis outsiders. The *Martyrdom of Pethion* reveals a tectonic shift in the thinking of East Syrian ecclesiastical leaders and authors, toward the view that they could strengthen their churches politically through the adoption of Iranian social and political categories, in the very process of defining boundaries between the two religions. This process required the evacuation of the religious content of political language, a continuation of the literary project that the hagiographers of fifth-century Seleucia-Ctesiphon had begun. Polemics could thus become vehicles of assimilation and acculturation precisely because they retained essential markers of difference. The following chapter, a study of the sixth-century bishop Mar Aba, best known for polemicizing against Zoroastrian thought and ritual, continues to explore this phenomenon.

3

Christian Law Making and Iranian Political Practice

The Reforms of Mar Aba

At the court of the king of kings Husraw I (r. 531–79), the leader of the Church of the East, the patriarch Mar Aba, found himself subject to an inquest only a year after his elevation to the bishopric of Seleucia-Ctesiphon in 540. The "great nobles of the Magians," a number of provincial Zoroastrian judicial officials, and the empire's highest judge, the mowbedān mowbed, had detained the bishop for allegedly harming the Good Religion. They brought him to an interrogating council that included Christian and Zoroastrian courtly elites. What had attracted the court's attention were the reforms of East Syrian Christian communities that Mar Aba had sought to enact since his appointment. Historians have generally claimed that the patriarch was prosecuted because of his youthful conversion from Zoroastrianism to Christianity and his encouragement of other wehdēn to follow suit.[1] But although accusations of apostasy and of seeking to convert Zoroastrians were, as we saw in chapter 1, serious charges, the aristocrats' reasons for calling the patriarch to account were more complex.[2] Mar Aba had inspired strenuous opposition for his interventions in the lives of the faithful through the making of new laws regulating the behavior of worldly, or more familiarly "lay," Christians. Zoroastrian judges were concerned that a Christian leader was infringing on their authority, interfering in judicial cases over which they had the privilege of presiding.[3] The incautious talk of peculiarly Christian laws that pervades the patriarch's surviving writings caused some imperial authorities to question the political ambitions of the bishops in their midst. In addition to feeling a general anxiety concerning the episcopal courts, the interrogators were distressed over two restrictions that Mar Aba had placed on the Christian faithful. The first concerned marital practice. The mowbed of southern Mesopotamia demanded that the bishop withdraw his proscription of marriage with the wife of one's father, the wife of one's uncle, or a daughter-in-law, referring to marriages that established substitute successors for men who died without a male heir.[4] The second concerned alimentary practice. A judge in Fars complained that the patriarch had "compelled many Christians in Fars who eat the flesh of murmur with his own restraints not to eat."[5] The flesh in question was meat subject to Zoroastrian rites that was consumed at banquets and festivals. On account of his refusal to compromise on these practices, Mar Aba was exiled to Azerbaijan and spent the remaining days of his life under house arrest.

The reforms of Mar Aba reveal the controversies and conflicts that attended the integration of Christians into Iranian imperial institutions and the ranks of their elites. The practices that the bishop aimed to regulate through laws—substitute successorship and the commensal consumption of meat—were fundamental institutions through which Iranian aristocrats reproduced themselves and constructed social networks.[6] In the attempt to constrain Christians from participating in these institutions, Mar Aba betrayed their importance for East Syrian elites who were forming aristocratic houses and entering imperial networks. His legal writings, together with the hagiographical texts that his circle produced, bring to light the otherwise inaccessible world of East Syrian Christian political practice, the embodied actions through which these elites positioned themselves in the institutions of the empire and forged collaborative relationships with their superiors, subordinates, and peers. In the previous chapter, we saw how religious polemics could create a political imaginary that Christians and Zoroastrians could share. This study of sixth-century East Syrian law making focuses less on the productive capacities of Christian texts than on their ability to unveil the underlying social world that Mar Aba sought to discipline. As we will see, the ambitions of the bishop to reform Christian communities that accepted the legitimacy of practices he deemed deviant remained unrealized until after the Islamic conquests. The Christians to be reformed were officeholders and landowners, dependent on working relations with their Zoroastrian counterparts for their authority and wealth. The practices through which they attained and augmented their positions in Iranian society appear, however refracted, for the first time in the laws of Mar Aba. To examine the social strategies of upwardly mobile East Syrian elites is to contribute not merely to the history of Christianity in Iran but also to the social history of the empire. The introduction notes the overwhelming focus of Iranian political history on the personal interactions of kings of kings and aristocrats, without due regard for the institutions that framed political action or for the provincial elites on whose support imperial rule depended. Historians have, moreover, considered Christians and other non-Zoroastrians institutionally discrete communities whose histories were determined by their religious leaders' personal relations with kings of kings. This chapter and its corollary, chapter 4, seek to transcend these historiographical impasses with studies of the authoritative roles of worldly Christians vis-à-vis their religious leaders within Christian communities and the practices through which they constructed noble families and interaristocratic relationships. The shared practices that bound elites of different religions into stable, empire-wide networks will take center stage in Iranian political history, revealing the dynamic processes through which Iran was made and remade.

In order to consider East Syrian laws as evidence for political practice, we have to situate their production in the political context of a Church of the East whose fifth-century aspirations to ecclesiastical unity had given way to fragmentation. Modern scholarship continues to depict the Christian communities of the Iranian world as sharing uniform doctrines, an ecclesiastical hierarchy culminating in the patriarchate of Seleucia-Ctesiphon, ethical norms, and even social identities. They are also believed to have represented themselves to the Iranian court and to have accessed political power through their ecclesiastical leaders, primarily the patriarch. The events of the sixth century surrounding the tenure of Mar Aba, however, disclosed the contested nature of Christian norms, the frailty of the ties that bound bishoprics, and the vulnerable position of the patriarch, the putative leader of the empire's Christians. Worldly Christians rather than bishops emerged, moreover, as the most powerful intermediaries with the court and even as the leading organizers of Christian communities. The evidence for the activities of the ambitious bishop and his allies in reform provides greater insight into the internal politics of Christian communities than the sources available for the fifth century, revealing the unruly relations among bishops, East Syrian elites, and imperial authorities that hagiographical and canonical texts had hitherto suppressed in favor of idealized representations of ecclesiastical unity. To interpret East Syrian laws, in other words, a foray into the realm of ecclesiastical politics is necessary. Against the backdrop of fragmented, conflict-ridden Christian communities, the law making of Mar Aba appears as aspirational as the synodal proclamations of a united church.

DISCIPLINING THE BISHOPS

In 540, the court of Husraw I dispatched messengers to the School of Nisibis, the emergent center of East Syrian learning, to summon one of its scholars to Seleucia-Ctesiphon to be appointed as its bishop.[7] Mar Aba was reportedly selected to lead the Church of the East on account of his reputation for learning in both Christian and Greco-Roman traditions. The late Sasanian court convened philosophers, physicians, and religious specialists from the neighboring civilizations of Rome and India with a view to re-collecting the corpora of human knowledge that Zoroastrians believed ultimately derived from Iran.[8] In the eyes of cosmopolitan courtly elites, the scholar from Nisibis possessed an impressive background.[9] He had traveled throughout the Roman Empire, studying in the cities of Edessa,

Alexandria, and Athens—at least according to the representations of his contemporaries—which sixth-century Iranian elites recognized as authoritative centers of learning.[10] What the court could not have known was that he had also once been an accomplished student of the Avesta and its exegesis. He had been born in a Zoroastrian house and educated in "Persian literature," attaining honors for his learning and a position in the office of the *āmārgar*, fiscal administrator, of Beit Aramaye.[11] Mar Aba was, in short, an example of the lower-level elites who gained administrative offices in the expanding empire of Kawad I, Husraw I, and their successors.[12] Whatever knowledge he acquired in the hērbedestān and the intellectual circles of Roman cities, however, was harnessed to the goals of an ascetic scholar. Established in the late fifth century, the School of Nisibis combined the study of Antiochene Christian theology, heuristically useful philosophical texts, and some more practical subjects such as medicine with a rigid regime of self-regulation, renunciation, and prayer that transformed its scholars into men as Christlike as the solitaries, *iḥidaye* or *bnai qyama*, of the early Syriac-writing ascetic tradition.[13] Mar Aba became particularly conversant in the thought of Theodore of Mopsuestia, taking his conception of the productive capacity of law in shaping Christian communities as an instrument of reform.[14] In Nisibis, Mar Aba adapted his worldly learning to the spiritual life, becoming an ascetic scholar in the East Syrian sense of the word *eskolaya*.[15]

But unlike the solitaries who withdrew from the world into either domestic or deserted places, the scholars of Nisibis entered the world, with a pan-Mediterranean intellectual formation, rhetorical techniques, and textual instruments to create strictly Dyophysite and asceticized Christian communities. Mar Aba played an important role in this process, as a figure around whom aspiring ascetic leaders and their supporters rallied. The selection of an ascetic scholar as the patriarch was a departure from the common practice of choosing ecclesiastical leaders with expertise in domains useful to the court, such as medicine or astrology, and ties with imperial elites.[16] Frequently married and moneyed, the bishops of Seleucia-Ctesiphon—and other major cities—tended to lead from within, rather than without, the networks of Iranian society. As an ascetic scholar, Mar Aba stood apart from the relations of kin, commerce, and patronage in which the East Syrian bishoprics were typically embedded. His elevation marked the first time that an ascetic scholar attained the most authoritative ecclesiastical office, the beginning of a gradual and contested shift toward the preferment of ascetic candidates for the episcopate that continued into the early Islamic period. Scholars from Nisibis and related schools in particular began to take control of bishoprics from the mid-sixth century.[17] Mar Aba was, therefore, in the vanguard of a new generation of ascetic bishops who sought to gain leadership in Christian communities at the expense of leaders whom scholars considered too worldly. Ironically, the School of Nisibis owed its foundation to just such a married and moneyed bishop: Barsauma of Nisibis, a paradigmatically worldly leader, against whom the ascetics defined themselves, endowed the school with its sources of revenue in the 470s.[18] Ecclesiastical leaders with competing visions for the church were more interdependent than the sources admit.

The Iranian court had elevated the patriarch to the see of Seleucia-Ctesiphon in order to discipline the bishops of the empire, who had been embroiled in factionalism for nearly two decades. In 523, the catholicos Shila designated his son-in-law Elisha as his successor, in keeping with a tradition of maintaining episcopates within familial networks. A rival group of bishops, however, elected their own candidate for Seleucia-Ctesiphon and proceeded to make appointments to a parallel episcopal hierarchy in cities throughout the empire.[19] Mar Aba described this ecclesiastical factionalism as "the duality of leadership," the bifurcation of the Christian communities in a particular city into competing factions with their own bishops.[20] In the cities of Mesopotamia, Khuzestan, and Fars, bishops and their constituencies sparred for control of ecclesiastical institutions. The scholar from Nisibis was an outsider whose ascetic and intellectual accomplishments Christians of disparate factions could recognize, and thus he seemed well placed to provide unifying leadership on behalf of a court with an interest in ensuring that Christian communities remained manageable and stable. But the court underestimated how disruptive this new brand of ascetic, scholarly leadership could be. The School of Nisibis transformed individuals of diverse backgrounds into scholars who continually refashioned themselves in accordance with the scriptures and who, in episcopal office, brought their scriptural standards to bear on the Christian communities under their authority. Training at the school also equipped scholars with modes of exegesis, theologies, and, most important, notions of Christian law that were novel in East Syrian Christian communities. The approach of the patriarch Mar Aba toward the Christians and Zoroastrians whom he encountered was more characteristic of an uncompromising ascetic than of a pragmatic bishop.

Although invited to Seleucia-Ctesiphon to unify the Christians of Iran, Mar Aba generated new, equally intractable conflicts through his efforts to reform the church in line with scholarly ideals. Among the most contested of his goals was the establishment of a pyramidal structure of authority. The notion of an empire-wide church with homogenous structures, canons, and beliefs and a hierarchy culminating in Seleucia-Ctesiphon, which the scholars took for granted, was not universally shared. If we are accustomed to describe the Christians of late Sasanian Iran as members of a single "Church of the East," the fifth and sixth centuries witnessed ceaseless controversy over the shape that ecclesiastical unity—or disunity—should take.[21] From at least the mid-fourth century, the bishopric of Seleucia-Ctesiphon endeavored to establish its superiority over its counterparts, with only modest success.[22] It was only through royal patronage and the introduction of Roman concepts and canons that a pyramidal ecclesiastical structure took shape. The Synod of Isaac in 410 fixed the position of the bishop of Seleucia-Ctesiphon at the top of an ecclesiastical hierarchy and required subordinate bishops to obtain his confirmation before assuming office and, ambitiously, to obey his every command.[23] The frequent reiteration of the canons outlining and regulating this monarchical structure throughout the late Sasanian period suggests that their implementation was gradual, inconsistent, and ultimately incomplete. Although Mar Aba and his successors stylized themselves patriarchs on par with those of the ancient Mediterranean sees, their authority over the bishops of Iran was highly contingent and even ignored.[24]

Alternative conceptions of ecclesiastical unity generally prevailed over the centralizing model in the organization of Christian communities. The self-conceptions of most bishoprics have not survived the medieval processes of redaction, but those that appear in the hagiographical sources are uniformly condescending or hostile toward the claims of the capital. The colorful account of a highly mythologized third-century bishop, Mar Miles, who literally bruised a bishop of Seleucia-Ctesiphon for his high-handedness gives a sense of how resistant many ecclesiastical leaders were to a pyramidal vision of the church.[25] This narrative of antagonism toward the patriarchate was among the most influential East Syrian hagiographical texts, included in the *History of Mar Awgen* and read in a Sogdian version even in the monasteries of the Turfan Oasis.[26] Barsauma, the aforementioned bishop of Nisibis, put alternative principles into action at the Synod of Beit Lapat in 484, which restricted the authority of the catholicos to his own metropolitanate and liberated the bishops of the empire to govern themselves.[27] These bishops frequently claimed apostolic traditions superior to those of Seleucia-Ctesiphon. Because of a surfeit of apostolicity in the Iranian world, even the most minor of bishoprics could produce narratives of origins no less apostolic than those of Mar Mari, which the patriarchate began to propagate in earnest in the sixth century.[28] One of the bishops of Arbela claimed to have consecrated the first bishop of Seleucia-Ctesiphon and to have been the source of the apostolic authority of his successors, an argument that many other, undocumented bishoprics might have made.[29] Even bishops who recognized their dependency on a patriarchal superior could turn to Antioch, outside the empire, as the source of episcopal power that flowed ultimately from the apostles.[30]

The patriarch thus made recourse to state power to establish a hierarchical ordering of bishops subject to his authority, to accomplish in practice what the roughly contemporaneous *History of Mar Mari* articulates as aspiration. He initially enjoyed the patronage of the king of kings, whom he lauded as a "new Cyrus, who overcame all kings," surpassing even the Achaemenian in his magnanimity.[31] Immediately upon his elevation, Mar Aba undertook a journey to the episcopal sees whose communities had fractured. He first traveled to Peroz Shapur in northern Mesopotamia and then returned southward to Kashkar, Maishan, Khuzestan, and Fars. In each of these provinces, he either secured the loyalty of an existing bishop or ousted the bishop (or bishops) of a city in favor of a candidate supportive of the patriarch.[32] To achieve such a feat, he depended on the imperial authorities' powers of coercion, as the detailed description of the case of a recalcitrant bishop of Beit Lapat, Abraham bar Audmihr, makes plain. When Abraham created a faction against the patriarch, the rad, āmārgar, ōstāndār (fiscal administrator), mowbed, and other provincial officials—a litany of all the known regional imperial officials, designed to underline the comprehensiveness of Mar Aba's support—brought the bishop to obedience.[33] An ecclesiastical hierarchy loyal to the patriarch of Seleucia-Ctesiphon was the creation of imperial authorities, much as the initial conception of the hierarchy in 410 depended on the personal intervention of Yazdgird I. The patriarch prominently invoked the name of Husraw I throughout the canonical letters that he composed during his sojourn in Khuzestan and Fars.[34] More strikingly, he highlighted the support of mowbed for his project of ecclesiastical reform. When we turn to his polemics, we should keep in mind the collaboration of Zoroastrians and Christians in the establishment and maintenance of a supraregional church with an authoritative patriarchal bishop at its head.

The ecclesiastical pyramid nevertheless remained precarious. The Iranian court withdrew its support for the bishop of Seleucia-Ctesiphon almost as soon as he returned to the capital from Khuzestan. To interrogate him on aspects of his reforms, a party of aristocrats at court summoned him to the aforementioned council. According to the author of the *History of Mar Aba*, who was eager to present the king of kings as a patron of Christians, the initial interrogation of the patriarch took place while Husraw I was on campaign against the Turks in the Caucasus.[35] The courtly opponents of Mar Aba included not only the mowbedān mowbed and other leading Zoroastrian officials but also Christian secular elites opposed to the reforms.[36] On account of his unwillingness both to refrain from rebuking Christians who married the wives of male relatives or consumed the meat of Zoroastrians and to stop actively converting members of the Good Religion to Christianity, the court kept the patriarch confined for the remainder of his tenure. Mar Aba was exiled to Azerbaijan for several years after the interrogations and thereafter remained in the custody of the court in Seleucia-Ctesiphon, during which time he briefly returned to Azerbaijan in 550 while the king of kings was on campaign.[37] Imperial support for his vision of ecclesiastical unity was withdrawn as soon as his reforms were identified as a threat to the interests of the Zoroastrian religious authorities and the empire's aristocracies. Allowed to remain the titular head of the Church of the East, he was deprived of access to both imperial and ecclesiastical institutions. He was thus forced to address and to try to overcome the limits of his power. Law making emerged as the primary instrument at his disposal for binding bishops and their constituencies across an empire of pronounced regionalisms into an enduring structure.

While in Azerbaijan, the patriarch had his earlier canons redacted and disseminated and probably also authored a polemical treatise on Christian laws of marriage, the *Regulations of Marriage*.[38] He creatively developed the canon as the main source of authority available to an ambitious patriarch without access to the state. Starting with the Synod of 410, collections of canons regulating ecclesiastical life, which only a gathering of bishops under the leadership of the patriarch could sanction, were systematically distributed among Christian communities. Even so strident an opponent of Seleucia-Ctesiphon as Barsauma of Nisibis came to regret his decision to call a synod without a catholicos, acknowledging at least the supervisory and organizing role of the empire's primary bishop in the formulation of canons.[39] If imperial authority could unite the church momentarily, adherence to a shared set of principles, processes, and practices could encourage bishops to act in concert, or at least enable patriarchs to hold them accountable to canonical terms. Canons could not easily coerce bishops or lesser clergy who did not consider their own sacerdotal power to flow from a patriarchal center with the authority to excommunicate. But bishops or lesser clergy could nevertheless be persuaded to adopt canonical stipulations as their own and to assume the authoritative position as regulators of Christian communities that canonical texts envision. Canons provided a shared language for authoritative action that ultimately derived from the patriarchate and therefore acknowledged and reinforced its superordinate authority.

It is on account of Mar Aba's law making that he has loomed so large in the history of Christianity in the Iranian Empire. He was not only prodigious but also innovative in producing canons (*qanone*) and laws (*namose*) that created new opportunities for patriarchs and bishops to regulate both clergy and laity.[40] While in the provinces, in the company of allied clerics and imperial authorities, Mar Aba issued canons for the organization of the ecclesiastical hierarchy and for the discipline of lay men and women. These letters and canons have been preserved mostly intact. The letters propagated his original canonical work, while the canons constitute a bricolage of Roman canons from Nicaea to Chalcedon, previously issued East Syrian canons, and citations from his letters.[41] Drawing on rhetorical techniques and theological arguments acquired at the School of Nisibis, the patriarch expanded upon conventional synodal canon making to produce the *Regulations of Marriage,* misleadingly known as his lawbook (*Rechtsbuch*). In any examination of the legal writings of the patriarch, his precarious, even marginal position in the empire's ecclesiastical institutions must remain in the foreground. It was through the production and distribution of canonical texts that he sought to augment episcopal power, for himself and his subordinates, with a novel variety of spiritual authority, dependent less on the state and aristocratic networks than on the moral superiority of ecclesiastical leaders over the worldly men and women of their flocks. The patriarch grounded this spiritual power in the demarcation of specifically ecclesiastical and worldly spheres of authority, the espousal of Dyophysite Antiochene theology, and, most important for this chapter, the active rejection of practices deemed Zoroastrian. The Iranian political practices at issue in his works need to be considered in light of his efforts to create a separate, ecclesiastical space, in which only holders of churchly office could lead Christians and in which the authority of the worldly was constrained.

DISCIPLINING THE WORLDLY

What compelled Christians to support one bishop over another during the decades of factionalism? Ethnic and linguistic differences have often been cited, as some churches maintained distinct liturgies in Greek and Syriac.[42] But ethnic and linguistic loyalties are absent from contemporary accounts of "the duality of leadership," and the argument for separate groups of "Nazarenes" and "Christians" has now been definitively undermined.[43] Mar Aba's proposals for reforming communities at Beit Lapat in Khuzestan in 540 provide a different starting point for considering the dynamics of ecclesiastical fragmentation. The patriarch regarded factionalism as the result of inappropriate relationships between lay and clerical leaders. The primary objective of his reforms was to disentangle ecclesiastical officeholders from the network of worldly men who subordinated ecclesiastical institutions to their own sectional interests: "The clergy of the city or country should not make factions, make connections, use words or writings to struggle against their leaders or against one another, nor appeal to the patronage [*prostasia*] of the faithful, whose consciences they trouble with their slanders. It is not permitted to the faithful, for their part, as they have done in the time of trouble, to stir up schisms and disputes."[44] It was the involvement of bishops and lesser clergy in an altogether too worldly web of social obligations, rather than ethnic or linguistic loyalties, that, in Mar Aba's view, prevented Christian communities from cohering around leaders united in their obedience to Seleucia-Ctesiphon. The secular faithful with the power to offer patronage had caused competing factions to emerge, and East Syrian conflicts arose from the misalignment of spiritual and worldly authorities that such relationships entailed.

This was a demarcation of spheres of authority that most East Syrian Christians would not have recognized as readily as ascetic scholars would have. Worldly men occupied particularly powerful positions in the Church of the East. Candidates for the episcopate were, of course, subject to the scrutiny of their constituencies as a condition of their elevation, as in the Roman world. But East Syrian communities institutionalized the role of Christian secular elites in the office of the "head of the believers" (*reš d-mhaymne*), which has gone unmentioned in discussions of ecclesiastical structure.[45] The most famous head of the believers was the great aristocrat Yazdin, who was extolled as the leader of all the Christians in the empire.[46] However rhetorical, this boast signals that the authority of worldly men over ecclesiastical structures was widely recognized. The supremacy of the patriarch over the most powerful Christian aristocrat was not self-evident in the early seventh century, and the position of the former was, as we have seen, no stronger in the sixth. In a letter of Ishoyahb III, the case of a more humble bearer of the title appears, with an indication of its formal as opposed to its rhetorical function. The patriarch wrote to confer with the reš d-mhaymne of the city of Arbela regarding candidates for the episcopal see, showing that his assent was required for the election of a bishop.[47] The office of the head of the believers here invested the traditional popular declamation in a single worldly man from the ranks of the provincial aristocracy of the region, which features in the following chapter. If the head of the believers played a legitimate role in governing the church in the correspondence of a patriarch as strident an advocate of patriarchal power as Mar Aba, more-permissive bishops recognized the authority of the worldly in a wide range of affairs. The reformist Synod of Joseph, for example, complained in 554 of worldly men who assumed positions "in the first place" during ecclesiastical councils and judged the actions of clerics.[48]

The church was far from independent of the ties of kinship that bound together the powerful in the empire. Episcopal office was very much a familial affair. The prosopographical evidence for individual bishops is limited, but we know of several instances of an episcopal office passing from relative to relative, and until the rise of the ascetic episcopate—of which Mar Aba was an early representative—such family monopolies seem to have been the norm. The successor of the martyred fourth-century bishop Simeon, Barbashmin, was his kinsman, and the pattern recurs in other known episcopal genealogies.[49] At the Synod of 410, the bishopric became not only a position of Christian leadership but also an imperial office that could, under certain circumstances, gain its holder alliances with the highest officials or even access to the court. Although Christian aristocrats do not seem to have pursued episcopal careers on a large scale until after the Islamic conquests, they were keen to keep bishoprics within allied families and loath to relinquish control of the appointment of their representatives to either a metropolitan or a patriarch.[50] The marriage of bishops and lower clergy facilitated the integration of both into local social networks and the intergenerational transmission of their offices. Despite the Encratite tendencies of Syriac-writing Christian communities, East Syrian bishops continued the apostolic practice of marrying and creating families.[51] The Synod of Aqaq in 486 and the Synod of Babai in 497 reaffirmed the permissibility of marriage for every ecclesiastical officeholder, even the patriarch, against ascetic critiques.[52] Bishoprics, like relics and shrines, were the possessions more of particular families and factions than of a supraregional church.[53]

A clear distinction between the ecclesiastical and the worldly was thus not easily achieved. The scholar-patriarch did not impose his ascetic conception of ecclesiastical leadership on the bishops, although his creation of clear procedures for electing the bishop of Seleucia-Ctesiphon aimed to ensure the elevation of likeminded leaders.[54] Nor did he exclude worldly Christian officials from ecclesiastical decision-making processes. The council that convened to condemn Abraham of Beit Lapat included a "master of the artisans" (*kirrōgbed*), a "military commander" (*artēštārānsālār*), and the chiefs of guilds for merchants, goldsmiths, and tinsmiths.[55] Instead of seeking the complete asceticization of the episcopate or the marginalization of the worldly, Mar Aba endeavored to construct a space of distinctively ecclesiastical authority that would allow bishops to place ecclesiastical interests ahead of sectional ones. Nevertheless, apart from several unspecific condemnations of worldly men who unjustly intervened in ecclesiastical affairs, the patriarch issued only one canon that directly separates clerics from seculars. In it, Mar Aba prohibits ecclesiastical leaders from associating themselves intimately with the worldly, declaring that they should "not go around among the houses or be foster fathers [*mrabyana*] or guardians for the worldly, to shame the priesthood and bring sins upon the worldly faithful."[56] In addition to introducing a general restriction on informal sociability, which might refer to the pleasures of the banquet, the patriarch proscribed the clerical practice of fosterage, an important Iranian institution, as we saw in the previous chapter, for establishing relations of kinship between those related by neither blood nor affinity. This canon is the earliest indication that East Syrian elites practiced fosterage to tie their ecclesiastical leaders intimately to themselves through the placement of sons in their care. For Mar Aba, the practice generated precisely the personal loyalties and sectional interests that prevented bishops and lesser clergy from acting in concert with their superiors as representatives of an empire-wide universal church. To disentangle ecclesiastical and secular networks, however, he relied as much on polemics against the practices of the worldly as on the regulation of the clergy.

BISHOPS AND IRANIAN LAW

At Beit Lapat in 540, Mar Aba employed a rather different strategy than canon making through synods for augmenting ecclesiastical authority, one that he refined in subsequent years: censuring the worldly for engaging in Iranian political practices that could, because of their origin and cosmological significance, be deemed Zoroastrian. He generally referred to the regulations that he crafted to discipline the worldly as *namose*, a Syrian term that, we will see, in the context of episcopal law making in the sixth century designates customary rather than authoritative, enforceable laws. But before we turn to the content and significance of these laws, the question of their authority needs to be raised. For more than a century, scholars have interpreted the legal writings of bishops as evidence of a distinctive Christian legal system that regulated conflicts and policed behavior in East Syrian communities, which experienced neither the interference of Zoroastrian mowbed nor the influence of Iranian law. Studies of Iranian law and East Syrian canon law alike agree that Christians constituted an autonomous, self-governing community within the empire, in which bishops made laws, presided over courts, and enforced their decisions with ecclesiastical bans.[57] This reading of the legal evidence has contributed in no small measure to the prevailing representation of Iranian society in late antiquity, discussed in the introduction, as one of separate religious communities insulated from one another: Compilations of Zoroastrian, Jewish, and Christian laws provided clear frontiers for believers, and mowbed, rabbis, and bishops were empowered to correct the wayward and to preserve the integrity of their communal boundaries. Only in exceptional cases, such as apostasy, would Zoroastrian judges interfere in the affairs of autonomous communities. The sources surrounding Mar Aba's judicial activities, however, suggest that the relationship between law and society in the Iranian Empire was hardly so straightforward. The patriarch's laws brought him into direct conflict with Zoroastrian judges, and the resulting debate concerning the nature of episcopal judicial authority in the empire provides rare insight into the relationship between Zoroastrian and East Syrian legal cultures.

If his laws have normally been regarded as evidence of Christian legal autonomy, Mar Aba made plain that he considered his community subject to, not independent of, the authority of Zoroastrian judges. His regulations, laws, and canons operated at a level beneath the courts of the mowbed and in no way rivaled their authority. This was in keeping with Zoroastrian expectations, according to the *History of Mar Aba* and Zoroastrian sources. During the aforementioned interrogation at court in 541, a mowbed accused Mar Aba of luring Christians away from Zoroastrian courts and of violating Zoroastrian judgments: "He summoned away from the house of judgment [*beit dina*] many Christians who had judicial disputes [*dine*] with one another [resolved by] a *bōxtnāmag* with the seal of the mowbedān mowbed, and he broke the *bōxtnāmag*. He judges all the judicial disputes we should judge, and we suffer much violence from him."[58] If the principal charge was that the bishop had broken the seal of a mowbed's declaration of innocence (bōxtnāmag), the Zoroastrian judge also expressed anxiety about bishops as possible competitors for judicial disputants. The mowbed were concerned both to maintain their authority over Christians, who could turn to alternative sources of judicial authority for the settlement of lawsuits, and to attract as many disputants as possible. Since justice was a service for which fees were expected, Zoroastrian courts also had an economic interest in extending their remit to Christian elites.[59]

"The law of the kingdom is the law," declares one of the best-known passages of the Babylonian Talmud, which enjoins Jews to adhere to the law of the Iranian Empire.[60] This law was the jurisprudence of Zoroastrian religious professionals. Although a wide variety of judicial authorities flourished in late antique Iran, ranging from informal mediators to rabbis and bishops trained in their own legal traditions, Zoroastrian judges occupied a uniquely authoritative position. From the beginning of the Sasanian dynasty, the kings of kings invested judicial authority in Zoroastrian priest-exegetes, such as the great third-century mowbed Kerdir. He boasted in his inscriptions of the power to sanction "contracts, treaties, and judgments," to hold a judicial office, and to authenticate documents with seals.[61] Both the sigillographic evidence and the early seventh-century *Hazār Dādestān*— our only collection of late antique Iranian legal decisions—demonstrate that subsequent mowbed and other Zoroastrian religious professionals continued to enjoy royally sanctioned judicial authority in addition to their control of religious institutions such as fire temples.[62] The judges, known as *dādwar*, rad, and mowbed or mowbed-dādwar like Kerdir, drew heavily on Avestan literature and cosmological thought to create an increasingly sophisticated body of legal knowledge and specialist vocabulary over the course of the empire's history.[63] By the sixth century at the latest, Zoroastrian judges had come to distinguish between decisions reached *pad čāštag*, on the basis of religious doctrine, and those reached *pad kardag*, on the basis of norms arising from judicial practice and custom.[64]

Despite the religious nature of their office, Sasanian judges restricted neither their authority nor their services to coreligionists. The *Hazār Dādestān* presumes the presence of unbelievers (agdēn) in Zoroastrian courts.[65] According to one judgment, the same set of principles and regulations that governed Zoroastrians applied in cases involving agdēn, with one exception: "Although no substitute successor [*stūr*] is to be appointed for [unbelievers] . . . other laws apply for them just as for the members of the Good Religion."[66] This exception was important, for, as we will see from Mar Aba's discussion of the practice, substitute successorship, or *stūrīh*, was a basic strategy of elite reproduction in Iranian society. Because stūrīh was closely linked with Zoroastrian doctrines of fertility, unbelievers could not establish substitute successors in a Zoroastrian court. But otherwise, Christians, Jews, and others could appeal to the same principles as Zoroastrians to settle their disputes, transfer properties, contract marriages, or make arrangements for inheritance. The high degree of familiarity with Iranian law evident in contemporaneous East Syrian and Talmudic literatures and especially in East Syrian legal writings from after the Islamic conquests implies that unbelievers frequently took advantage of the expertise and authority of Zoroastrian judges.[67] A seventh-century treatise of Simeon, the bishop of Revardashir, who freely drew on Zoroastrian jurisprudence, gives the impression that East Syrian Christians in the region of Fars considered Iranian law their own.[68] Indeed, so complete was the Christian appropriation of Iranian law after the Islamic conquests that the legal compendium of the East Syrian bishop Ishobokht, composed circa 775–79 in Fars, serves as a source for the laws of the Iranian Empire alongside the *Hazār Dādestān*.[69] Christians, Jews, and Zoroastrians occupied overlapping, not separate, juridical communities.

Even as he issued regulations for Christian behavior that provoked the concern of imperial religious authorities, Mar Aba clearly distinguished between the authority of Zoroastrian judges and the authority of bishops. The latter was not commensurate with the former. The author of the *History of Mar Aba* highlighted the difference between the two in the literary representation of the accusation against the patriarch quoted above. A mowbed claims that the bishop broke the seal not merely of a judge but of the empire's supreme judge, the mowbedān mowbed. Because the mowbedān mowbed served as the ultimate source of law and his decisions were considered infallible, the allegation was self-evidently implausible.[70] A bishop would no more break the seal of a local mowbed than that of the mowbedān mowbed, for his office was of an entirely different nature. In response to the rad of Fars's accusation that he had misused "restraints," the patriarch elaborated on the limits of episcopal coercive powers: "I am not commanded by the divine scriptures to restrain or strike anyone or to confiscate anything of his, but rather we pray and beseech God concerning those who err to return to true knowledge."[71] Where a mowbed had the power to imprison, disenfranchise, or inflict corporeal punishment to enforce his decisions, the bishop had the capacity only to rebuke or excommunicate. Mar Aba prescribed purely liturgical punishments for those who transgressed his canons, ranging from donations to the poor to outright excommunication, depending on the severity of the offense.[72]

The contrast with Armenia, where fourth-century Christian kings and powerful aristocratic houses had allowed bishops to displace Zoroastrian religious specialists as a judicial elite, is telling. At the Synod of Shahapivan in 444, the Armenian bishops adopted the coercive powers of their Zoroastrian predecessors. Thereafter, they administered harsh corporeal and financial punishments to those who disobeyed their canons.[73] For contracting consanguineous marriages, nobles were fined up to three hundred drachms and female commoners were imprisoned for ten years in a leprosarium. For other offenses, precise numbers of lashings were specified as punishments. Apostates were to be executed by stoning. Fines, lashes, and execution were punishments that Zoroastrian judges inflicted. In Zoroastrian jurisprudence, precisely enumerated fines and/or lashes could expiate the crimes of an offender, with the exception of the *margarzān* offenses, such as apostasy, that we encountered in chapter 1. In explicitly renouncing any right to inflict corporeal punishment or to confiscate goods, Mar Aba recognized the authority of Zoroastrian judges over East Syrian Christians. Unlike their Armenian counterparts, East Syrian bishops were enjoined to remain subject to the mowbedān mowbed and his subordinates in matters of justice. If Zoroastrian judges worried that bishops were infringing on their authority, Mar Aba—and his associates who produced the *History of Mar Aba*—carefully demarcated a sphere of episcopal judicial authority that precluded episcopal judges from interfering with a mowbed's powers of coercion or authentication. The East Syrian episcopal court was to operate in a distinct domain beneath the uniquely authoritative Zoroastrian courts.

The episcopal judges, who gained prominence in Iran beginning in the sixth century, were, Mar Aba insisted, complementary rather than inimical to their Zoroastrian superiors. Bishops such as Sabrisho, who provided the inhabitants of Lashom with "correct laws and just judgments," might have attracted disputants who would otherwise have sought out the mediation of a Zoroastrian judge, precisely as the mowbed had feared.[74] But as recent work on the Roman Empire has shown, ancient societies had systemic shortages of justice, which episcopal courts served to alleviate.[75] The focus of historians of Roman legal culture has shifted from the jurists of the Justinianic Code to the masses of disputants who sought judicial expertise and authority from local aristocrats, village headmen, military officers, monks, and bishops as well as those with formal legal training.[76] Their demand for dispute settlement far outpaced the capacities of the Roman bureaucracy. The episcopal courts that took shape in the fourth century were just one element of a society with multiple sources of judicial authority, not competitors of state-sanctioned judges.[77] In their capacity as mediators of Christian conflicts, bishops necessarily became familiar with the Roman civil laws and procedures that structured the disputes of their flocks. This model of bishops participating in a broader legal culture rather than creating autonomous, rival courts fits well with the East Syrian evidence. Although the surviving East Syrian sources preserve only laws considered distinctively Christian, the judges who consulted these texts, like their rabbinic counterparts, will have engaged with a wide range of contracts, judgments, principles, and laws relevant to the property and personal status of the disputants before them, including both Iranian law and largely invisible local traditions. It was only after the Islamic conquests that bishops forbade Christians from using the courts of "outsiders," extending to the entire Christian community a canon that from 484 had applied only to clerics and monks.[78]

Instead of providing evidence for a comprehensive, peculiarly Christian system of family law, the writings of Mar Aba on marriage show, as the following section demonstrates, how similarly Christians and Zoroastrians arranged their marriages and inheritances. As bishops more enthusiastically embraced their informal and unofficial role as mediators of disputes, they found themselves implicated in the worldly business of contested marriages and inheritances formulated in terms of Iranian law. Into the existing mixture of legal traditions, the patriarch introduced regulations for marriage that expressly opposed Iranian principles without challenging the authoritative seals of official judges or demanding that Christians refrain from availing themselves of Zoroastrian courts. His regulations, laws, and canons did not preclude the use of Iranian judicial principles, authorities, or institutions in other domains of social life. Indeed, the creation of distinctive Christian laws might have facilitated the incorporation of Iranian law into the episcopal court. For bishops uncomfortable with the cosmological language of Iranian contracts and judicial decisions, the militant rejection of incestuous marriage might have helped to assuage anxieties over the Christian adaptation of Iranian law. Yet aristocratic Christians could not straightforwardly abandon the practices that the patriarch sought to restrict with his laws. Behind the horrors of incest, Mar Aba obscured a complex system of marriage and inheritance law that gave solidity and stability to the aristocratic networks that underpinned Iranian imperial power. Given their lack of binding force, his laws could equally be characterized as polemics, directed against worldly Christians unable or unwilling to conform to the expectations of an emergent ascetic episcopate.

INCEST AND INHERITANCE

In a compilation redacted in 544 during his exile in Azerbaijan, Mar Aba included a canon—probably first issued in 540 in Khuzestan—defining the forbidden forms of marriage. A Christian man could not marry the wife of his father or uncle, his aunt, his sister, his daughter, or his granddaughter, "like the Magians." Nor could a believer marry the wife of his brother, "like the Jews."[79] The union of a Christian man and an unbelieving woman was also proscribed. Although the synod that Barsauma of Nisibis convened in 484 had condemned Christians who "imitated the Magians through impure marriage," Mar Aba was the first canonically to specify which unions were forbidden to Christians.[80] He drew the greatest attention to the incestuous union known as *xwēdōdah*, which Zoroastrian texts advocate as cosmologically beneficial.[81] *Xwēdōdah* refers to the marriage of brother and sister, of father and daughter, or of other equally proximate kin, an exceptional practice in ancient Eurasian societies, which were generally observant of the incest taboo that modern anthropologists have made the basis for their analyses of kinship.[82] But the patriarch equated an entirely customary practice with incest: marrying the wives of one's patrilineal relatives. Christianity, Jack Goody famously argued, introduced prohibitions on the marriage of close kin that were without precedent either in ancient societies or in the Christians' sacred scriptures. Such marriages were above all "strategies of heirship" that secured the transmission of names and properties, so ecclesiastical laws against incest could disrupt traditional flows of wealth across generations.[83] In the case of Iran, the principal strategy of heirship was stūrīh, or substitute successorship, the instituting of a man in the place of a man who had died without sons to produce a male heir on his behalf. Despite his rhetorical emphasis on Zoroastrian incest, the patriarch intended to regulate the inheritance strategies of East Syrian Christians.

Mar Aba developed laws on marriage into a strategy for remodeling Christian communities and redefining the authoritative position of their ecclesiastical leaders vis-à-vis secular Christian elites in his treatise the *Regulations of Marriage*, composed during his exile in Azerbaijan. If the canon states the collective decision of a synod, the regulations (*thume*) and laws (namose) of the treatise are the product of Mar Aba's exegetical scholarship. It is an example of the Antiochene school's historical exegetical method of evaluating the implications of the scriptures in light of the specific historical contexts of contemporary Christians.[84] The treatise is an interpretation of the Book of Leviticus's categories of deviant sexuality, which the patriarch compared to and contrasted with practices in the Iranian world of his time.[85] In the Book of Leviticus, he found a model for creating a close-knit community of believers through the proclamation of common laws, an appealing possibility for a leader who had been deprived of access to the institutional structures of his office.[86] The authors of the *Martyrdom of Simeon* and the *History of Simeon* had already deployed Israelite history as a model for a Christian "people of God," with bishops as its Levites.[87] Building on such foundations in Seleucia-Ctesiphon, Mar Aba composed "distinguishing laws" on marriage that set Christians apart from their neighbors and subordinated them to their priestly leaders, much as the Israelites had cohered around the laws of the Levites.[88] It was their role as lawgivers that separated the priestly Levites from the remainder of the Israelites and authorized the former to command the latter.

In polemicizing against incestuous Zoroastrians, Mar Aba joined a chorus from across Eurasia, ranging from Buddhist monks and Chinese envoys to Roman historians, that condemned Iranian sexual deviance.[89] But his treatise is distinct both for its scriptural sources and for its familiarity with the Zoroastrian doctrine of xwēdōdah. The Book of Leviticus treats incest as one form of unnatural sex among others, including homosexuality and bestiality.[90] The treatise thus describes regulations against homosexual and bestial relations as well as the incest condemned at Beit Lapat, an equating of varieties of sex that Iranian society understood as very different from one another. Mar Aba presented men who married their brother's wife, married their daughter, had sexual relations with another man, or violated an animal as practitioners of equally unnatural forms of deviance. If the canon of Beit Lapat permitted a bishop or a priest to rebuke a Christian for incest, this treatise equipped ecclesiastical leaders with a more colorful palette of rhetorical options for persuading the uncooperative to recognize their Levite-like authority. As a polemic against Zoroastrianism, his Levitical account allowed Mar Aba the convert to draw on his knowledge of the Good Religion to present its tenets as perversions of its own cosmological order. The patriarch rightly recognized that the purpose of xwēdōdah was to maximize human social and political goods.[91] In Zoroastrian thought, close-kin marriage served to recreate the world in the pristine state of Ohrmazd's primordial creation. Although the prevalence of incestuous marriages in late antique Iran is unclear, belief in the cosmological benefits of the practice—in particular its capacity to increase knowledge, as the patriarch suggested—was unambiguous.[92] Mar Aba, however, equated incest with sodomy, its diametrical opposite in Zoroastrian cosmology. If Ohrmazd brought creation into being through xwēdōdah, Ahreman created deceit through homosexual sex, *kūnmarz*.[93] But sex that imitates Ohrmazd's act and sex that imitates Ahreman's are identically unnatural in the Book of Leviticus. According to the *Regulations of Marriage*, Iranians who practiced incest were, moreover, equivalent to Arabs and Hephthalites—the empire's nomadic, Ahremanic enemies—who all practiced homosexuality.[94] The patriarch described outlandish cases of men marrying their daughters, taking boys as wives, and reclining with cattle, all acts of these nomadic civilizational inferiors, perhaps meant to recall polyandry, widespread in Hephthalite-controlled Bactria.[95] These are not, however, the underlying concern of the treatise. Amid examples of deviance that few Christians would have countenanced, the treatise discusses forms of marriage that East Syrian Christians typically accepted: marrying the wife of a deceased paternal uncle and marrying the wife of a deceased brother (levirate marriage), practices of substitute successorship in general, if not stūrīh in particular, that were indispensable for the reproduction of patrilineages in Iranian political culture. Framed as a polemic against close-kin, homosexual, and bestial sex, the treatise targets a fundamental political institution, to whose background we now turn.

The Zoroastrian injunction to practice xwēdōdah was only the starting point for the development of a complex system of marriage and inheritance law. Once elevated to authoritative positions in the early Sasanian period, Zoroastrian religious specialists elaborated on Avestan passages and principles to create legal institutions that maximized fertility and ensured the continuity of patrilineages, fundamental obligations for practitioners of the Good Religion. Close-kin marriage was an extreme manifestation of a more general emphasis on human reproduction as the most cosmologically beneficial of acts. A man was to seek as many opportunities as possible to reproduce himself without doing harm to a social order that acts of adultery or abandonment could undercut. The potentially contradictory requirements to reproduce oneself and one's patrilineage were harmonized through institutions of marriage that aimed to enable elite men to make full use of their capacities, while safeguarding the status of women and guaranteeing the unambiguous transmission of lineages. In the pursuit of maximum fertility, elite males could not only practice polygamy but also contract a union for a predetermined period, a so-called temporary marriage.[96] Whether permanent or temporary, different kinds of contract produced different reproductive strategies. In addition to the familiar *pādixšāy* marriage, in which a wife was entitled to a portion of the inheritance and the children were legitimate, there was the option of *čagar* marriage, which permitted a man to contract a union whose progeny were not considered his own.[97] The wife in a čagar marriage remained a member of her natal lineage and did not enter the husband's clan. She was thus without access to its patrimony. Seemingly counterproductive in a patrilineal society, the čagar marriage in fact resolved its contradictions.

In a society where social status derived from the blood of one's father and one's father's father, sonlessness was the most acute problem that a man—often along with his agnates—could face.[98] As studies of ancient demography have demonstrated, delayed marriage and premature male death combined to make the production of a male heir within a man's lifetime the exception rather than the rule.[99] In Zoroastrian cosmological thought, moreover, sonlessness was the greatest of evils. If the prospect of the return of his patrimony (theoretically—and often in practice—first collectively inherited from the father) to agnates and the loss of his name and fame were not sufficient motivation, the Good Religion denied men who failed to produce a male heir access to Chinwad Bridge, the path to paradise. But Zoroastrian jurists tried to guarantee that such a calamity would never befall an elite male. Every man who possessed a patrimony worth at least sixty staters (two hundred drachms) of silver would be provided with a substitute successor if he were to die sonless. This institution maximized the reproductive capacities of men and women and ensured the continuity of patrilineages. If the deceased were to leave a wife, unmarried daughter, or unmarried sister, she was to serve as his *ayōkēn*, a natural stūr, which entailed contracting a čagar marriage with another man and producing sons who would be considered—legally and spiritually—the heirs of the deceased.[100] As an alternative, a man could appoint a man or a woman as a proxy stūr, who would fulfill the same obligations. In the event that a man failed either to leave an ayōkēn or to make arrangements for a proxy, judges in concert with the king of kings would appoint a substitute successor. Women serving as stūr in čagar marriages were compelled to satisfy the demands of Zoroastrian ideology for fertility, which required them to subject themselves frequently to the hazards of childbirth. Through their labors, men who failed to produce a son on account of either infertility or ill fortune were able to satisfy the Good Religion's demand for the transmission of lineages.

The innovation of stūrīh was an essential feature of the aristocratic politics of the empire. For members of aristocratic houses, whose wealth resided in patrimonies and whose lineages earned them office, stūrīh ensured the validity of their names as political currency across generations. As an unusually flexible form of substitute successorship, the institution was far more important politically and economically than incest.[101] Despite the representations of Mar Aba and the later jurist Ishobokht, the economic benefits of incestuous unions were meager, especially as close-kin marriages tended to be temporary.[102] For those who wished to acquire and retain wealth and social status in the Iranian Empire, securing the intergenerational transfer of patrilineages and patrimonies, which took time to build, was a paramount concern. If discussions of Sasanian society tend to depict an aristocratic social order with stable hierarchies, the realities of male death introduced a high degree of instability into the lives of elite men who could not call upon the services of Zoroastrian judges. Even a man with sons could leave his fatherless heirs subject to the predations of outsiders, including agnates, eager to appropriate their lands. The situation was all the more precarious for men who left no males to succeed them. Women without husbands were equally vulnerable. Those with patrilineages and patrimonies to protect and perpetuate stood to benefit from the services of judges who provided guardians and, when necessary, established substitute successors.

Some Zoroastrian judges refused to institute a stūr for agdēn. As we have seen, the *Hazār Dādestān* singles out stūrīh as a service available exclusively to Zoroastrians, an unsurprising restriction given its cosmological context. That a jurist needed to compose a judgment on this question nevertheless suggests that at least some Christians, Jews, or others appealed to Zoroastrian judges to establish stūr. Some likely complied. But those who considered the Hebrew Bible a source of law did not require stūrīh to arrange for substitute successors. The Book of Deuteronomy 25:5–6 enjoins a man to marry the wife of his brother if the latter dies without an heir, the institution of levirate marriage. A son born from such a union would carry the name of the deceased brother. The practice had fallen into desuetude in the late Roman Palestine of the Yerushalmi, but the rabbis of the Babylonian Talmud customarily continued to require the brothers of men who died sonless to contract levirate marriages in fourth- through sixth-century Iranian Mesopotamia.[103] Although Christians were familiar with the practice from their sacred texts and possibly their Jewish neighbors, there was no corresponding religious obligation for them to produce an heir. The need to transmit land and lineage across generations in order to participate in Iranian aristocratic politics, however, was sufficient motivation to develop cognate practices.

Mar Aba included levirate marriage in his list of incestuous, homosexual, and bestial acts. Historically, he argued, the practice had satisfied the Israelites' desire to provide heirs for sonless men and found justification in Genesis 38:8's injunction to approach the wife of one's brother. Christians, however, "consider establishing the seed of those who have died superfluous, insofar as many have chosen even of their own will to forgo marriage for the sake of the kingdom of heaven." Christians whom the patriarch styled as "spiritual" held the transmission of their seed in slight regard, unlike the "worldly" Israelites, "on account of the weakness of their faith in the resurrection."[104] Given the exceptional nature of the ascetic life even in the highest ranks of the ecclesiastical hierarchy, this passage reminded its readers that not all Christians are equally spiritual. The label *worldly*, moreover, was the same term that Mar Aba had employed in his early canonical works for the secular Christian elites whose powers he sought to constrain. In another section of this treatise, we find an explicit acknowledgment of the value that East Syrian Christians ascribed to their seed and its transmission. After a litany of quotations from the Hebrew Bible and the New Testament proscribing the marriage of a man with the wife of his paternal uncle, the patriarch reported this practice as common among Christians in Iran. Although he deemed such a union forbidden and held that it should be nonexistent, "the deeds performed among us are the opposite."[105] What is more, earlier ecclesiastical leaders did not consider marrying the wife of one's uncle a sin worthy of comment or censure. The patriarch frankly admitted that Christians normally married the wives of their paternal uncles, self-evidently with a view to perpetuating their patrilineages and preserving their patrimonies. Christians were as interested in the transmission of their seed as Israelites and practiced a form of substitute successorship similar to, albeit less flexible than, stūrīh. This is the earliest indication of Christian patrilineal practices that are well documented and described in later East Syrian judicial compilations, which help to reveal the political significance of Mar Aba's polemic against men marrying the wives of agnates.

In the first two Islamic centuries, East Syrian bishops compiled collections of judgments to consolidate their judicial authority. Once Zoroastrian judges lost the support of the state, ambitious bishops sought to occupy their positions and authoritatively to regulate matters of marriage and inheritance.[106] Their compilations reveal the diversity of East Syrian legal principles and institutions at the time of the Iranian Empire's collapse. In contrast with Mar Aba's pretension to have promulgated a single set of laws for all Christians, even at the beginning of the ninth century—after a century and a half of compilation and codification—Ishobokht reported that just judgments "are left to the knowledge and examination of the leaders of the church, and the manner of judgment differs and contrasts in accordance with the difference and divergence in the knowledge and will of each one of them."[107] This range of judgments—some permitting varieties of substitute successorship, others condemning such unions as consanguineous—is characteristic of post-Sasanian legal texts, and there cannot have been greater harmony in the preceding century. The opposite was clearly the case, as bishops worked without written sources and under the shadow of Zoroastrian courts. The situational decision making of individual East Syrian bishops, who drew on different bodies of legal knowledge depending on both their immediate environment and the details of the case at hand, forms the backdrop to Mar Aba's treatise on marriage.

The East Syrian episcopal judges agreed on one important principle: patriliny.[108] In the formulation of their judgments, these bishops aimed to ensure that sons succeeded to their fathers' estates. At the most basic level, this entailed maintaining the Iranian law of inheritance, which privileged sons in the partition of a father's estate, in contrast with the Roman law, according to which sons and daughters inherited equally.[109] Although the Roman law of inheritance was known among East Syrian Christians, Iranian judges writing in the immediate aftermath of the Islamic conquests resolutely insisted on the prevailing Iranian law. Simeon of Revardashir, the port city of Fars, wrote in the 650s that "everywhere sons are the holders of the inheritance of their fathers and not daughters, because a greater portion of the property of their father comes to them in inheritance. Therefore, a complete share is given to a son, while a half share [is given] to a daughter, for her maintenance, nourishment, and clothing."[110] In Mesopotamia, the patriarch Henanisho made an identical judgment three decades later.[111] The principles that Simeon, Henanisho, and later Ishobokht enunciated correspond perfectly with the laws of the *Hazār Dādestān*. In Iranian law, unmarried daughters each received half a share of the inheritance (*bahr ī duxt*), whereas legitimate sons were each entitled to a full share (*bahr ī pus*).[112] As married daughters had already obtained a dowry, a share of the inheritance given in advance (*pēšigān wāspuhragān*), their exclusion from the estate was absolute. While insisting on Iranian law as normative, the bishops also attested to Christians who desired to endow their daughters with greater shares, perhaps an indication of the declining importance of patriliny in an Islamic society.[113] Even in these cases, however, the bishops required the daughters to receive only their half shares, demonstrating that the preservation of patrimonies had been elevated to a foundational principle of East Syrian inheritance law. Ishobokht explained that a daughter could receive only half a share because she did not contribute to the continuation of her family's male lineage.[114] Patrilineages and patrimonies were inextricably intertwined in the thought of East Syrian bishops.

If East Syrians were no less interested in patriliny than their Zoroastrian peers, we would expect them to have labored over the problem of sonlessness equally energetically. The controversial question on this topic that animated East Syrian judicial writings was whether a wife, the nearest agnates, or other relatives should inherit a sonless man. There is thus a symmetry between the *Hazār Dādestān* and the East Syrian lawbooks. There was a strong tendency among Christians to permit the wife to inherit, a practice that contradicts patrilineal principles only apparently. The patriarch Ishoyahb III described a case that lasted from 650 to 658 and reveals the parameters of the debate. The bishop of an unspecified province had condemned a marriage between a man and the wife of his dead maternal uncle, which was intended to provide the deceased man with heirs. As there was no agnatic relationship between the husband and the deceased, we are dealing here not with a levirate marriage but rather with either a čagar marriage contracted for the purpose of stūrīh or an informal arrangement of a substitute successor in imitation of stūrīh. But Ishoyahb III framed the question solely in terms of a wife's inheriting, to present this practice as contradicting both Christian and Iranian law. The inheritance of wives was "foreign to the will of the divine book and to the teaching according to which this kingdom was ruled until now."[115] This is a misrepresentation of Iranian law, as in cases of sonlessness a wife would temporarily inherit her husband before transferring his estate to his substitute successor. Where we find the inheritance of a wife in East Syrian law, an institution of substitute successorship was available to the sonless.

"From where is it known that when a man dies and has a wife and brother and no children, his property is due to his wife, not his brother?"[116] Writing contemporaneously with Ishoyahb III, Simeon of Revardashir judged that the wife was always to inherit the sonless husband. In the only judgment of his treatise in which he invoked Christian language, the bishop argued that the wife inherited because she and her husband had formed "one flesh," contradicting a statement more characteristic of Iranian law that "a Christian wife becomes foreign to the family of her husband" after his death.[117] In different circumstances, each principle could apply. If her husband left male heirs, any future children of the wife would need to be excluded from his patrimony. If the man died sonless, the wife would contract a marriage with a substitute successor through the formal institution of stūrīh or, more probably, through customary practice. According to Ishobokht, who presided over the same episcopal court as Simeon a century and a quarter later, substitute successorship was the norm:

> The Christians who are in our land, because they reside among Magians, who give the inheritance of a childless man in the way that we have described above, also give the inheritance of a childless dead man to his wife, because they do not recall that they ruled thus for the sake of levirate marriage [*yabmuta*], in which the father and brothers of a man are permitted to marry his wife or someone else who is related to him from among the members of his family. When children are born, they are considered to belong to the dead man. The property is his and does not belong to the one who married his wife.[118]

Despite misinterpreting flexible forms of substitute successorship as levirate marriage, Ishobokht recognized the connection between the wife's inheritance and the continuation of the patrilineage through an institution similar to stūrīh. He, like his associate the patriarch Timothy, condemned the practice but freely admitted its prevalence among the Christians of Fars and its acceptance by episcopal judges.[119] There were bishops in the Fars of Simeon and Ishobokht and the Mesopotamia of Ishoyahb who worked to secure the inheritance of the wife in cases of sonlessness in order for a substitute successor to be produced.

East Syrian episcopal judges thus placed themselves in the service of Iranian political institutions, allowing elite households to reproduce themselves through a form of substitute successorship. Although aristocratic houses with common ancestors formed the ruling classes of the empire, these clans were segmented into individual households. The household rather than the clan was the site of the transmission of wealth and status. Men of imperial office could expect advancement for their sons, not their brothers. The currency of aristocratic names, moreover, was of uneven exchange value. The reversal of a man's wealth to his brothers negated his accomplishments and his name, even if their ancestral lineage continued. The rapacity of brothers who sought to profit from the deaths of sonless men or men with puerile heirs was legendary, particularly in the East Syrian hagiographies that emerged from the milieu of lesser or middling noble houses, more vulnerable than their grander counterparts.[120] The alternative to substitute successorship was a stark one in this context. Henanisho both described and recommended a very different solution to the problem of sonlessness: the return of the dead man's land to his surviving agnates.[121] Sitting upon the same episcopal throne that Mar Aba and Ishoyahb III had occupied, this patriarch opposed substitute successorship while supporting the preservation of patrimonies. His straightforward solution was doubtless a customary one, always an option in Iranian society. The Zoroastrian architects of stūrīh may even have been reacting to such a practice that secured the integrity of ancestral properties but not the continuous transmission of patrilineages. For landowning Christians in an early Islamic political system that did not distribute power according to lineage, Henanisho's solution may have been adequate. But for ambitious late Sasanian Christians busily constructing the patrilineages that were the prerequisite for status and office in the Iranian Empire, the topic of the next chapter, some form of substitute successorship was indispensable to address the inevitable eventuality of sonlessness.

Mar Aba therefore proscribed a fundamental Iranian social practice that East Syrian Christians had generally regarded as permissible. In referring merely to the marriage of a woman with her paternal uncle, the patriarch addressed the most common form of substitute successorship, which we know from Ishobokht could involve a wider range of agnates standing in the place of the sonless deceased. Ishobokht's description of this practice as widespread and even accepted among East Syrian bishops demonstrates that the institution, which Simeon advocated in the early seventh century, already prevailed in the sixth. Even if Zoroastrian judges restricted stūrīh to wehdēn, Christians also ensured the successful transmission of their names and lands through the institution of substitute successors, sometimes even under the judicial authority of bishops such as Simeon. East Syrian Christians could not participate in the patrilineal politics of the empire as effectively as Zoroastrians, who had access to the more flexible institution of stūrīh, which guaranteed a male heir regardless of circumstances. But the use of a wider range of paternal male relatives as substitute successors than traditional levirate marriage allowed provided most sonless men with heirs. If the passages of Mar Aba's treatise concerning substitute successorship stood on their own, we would be under the impression that this practice was comparatively unproblematic. But the patriarch juxtaposed a defensible and accepted form of marriage to acts that were inconceivably loathsome either to Christians (sex with one's daughter or mother) or to Christians and Zoroastrians alike (bestial or homosexual sex). Of the marital and sexual practices that he condemned in his treatise, only substitute successorship was common, and indeed necessary for the reproduction of aristocratic Christians.

The case of substitute successorship reveals the method of the patriarch. He regulated with canons and laws a practice that he recognized as widespread and legitimate within Christian communities. A generally accepted form of marriage thus became incest. If the treatise on marriage defines no punitive measures for illicit sex, the canon from Beit Lapat requires the excommunication of those guilty of contracting incestuous marriages, a punishment that entailed the public rebuking of the offender. Canons and laws possessed the same authority, residing in the performative speech acts of individual bishops. The highly rhetorical nature of the *Regulations of Marriage* alerts us to the ways in which canons were applied and served to consolidate the episcopal position in decidedly multipolar Christian communities. Laws on marriage empowered bishops not simply to excommunicate, a drastic measure corrosive to communal cohesion, but also to censure and rebuke, to call the sinful to account. Polemics and laws were of a piece. Acknowledging the ubiquity of substitute successorship, the patriarch did not expect Christians uniformly to obey his proscriptions. He rather deployed laws as instruments to distinguish the worldly from the spiritual and to subordinate the former to the latter in ecclesiastical institutions. It was on account of the indispensability of the practice to aristocratic Christians that the patriarch could identify substitute successorship—now labeled a variety of incest—as the defining mark of their worldliness. The laws on marriage therefore offer an ideal point of departure for the practice with which the *History of Mar Aba* pairs them: the consumption of Magian meat.

MAGIAN MEAT

In the polemical literature emanating from the circle of Mar Aba, incest was paired with the consumption of meat subjected to Zoroastrian rites as the two abhorrent Zoroastrian practices that Christians were obliged to reject. Although a canon concerning the consumption of "meat of murmur" has not survived, the *History of Mar Aba* reports its condemnation as a fundamental feature of the patriarch's reforms.[122] His courtly interrogators, we should recall, offered to close their inquest if Mar Aba would refrain from condemning Christians who contracted marriages according to Iranian laws or consumed Magian meat, as well as stop converting Zoroastrians to Christianity.[123] This is an important indication of the interest of Zoroastrian religious professionals in securing the participation of Christians in their festive meals. If Zoroastrians opened their feasts and banquets to unbelievers, a vocal body of ecclesiastical leaders in the sixth and early seventh centuries polemicized, in canonical and hagiographical texts, against Christians who joined them. And if this controversy was reported to have emerged first in the course of Yazdgird II's conflicts with the Armenian aristocracy in the middle of the fifth century, polemics against the consumption of Zoroastrian meat began to appear only in the sixth, when East Syrian and Armenian authors came stridently to equate the practice with apostasy.[124] Drawing on the Roman martyrologies that were increasingly available in Syriac and Armenian translations, these authors presented commensality with Zoroastrians as an act of idolatry that Christians worthy of the name could not perform. In East Syrian communities, Mar Aba's associates were the first to propagate polemics against Christians who partook of Zoroastrian meals, as part of the program to circumscribe the powers of worldly Christians. In the patriarch's vision of the church, Magian meat and incest served as the linchpins of a distinctively Christian habitus. Neither of these practices was, however, as peculiarly Zoroastrian as Christian authors represented them. To comprehend the significance of these novel Christian polemics, we need to consider the role of meat consumption in Iranian imperial institutions.

Eating was an unavoidably religious activity in Iran. Before consuming food, Zoroastrians were to recite a brief prayer, the *wāz*, which rendered the act of eating a part of the system of rituals that culminated in the Yasna.[125] The consumption of meat in particular was highly ritualized in a religion whose foundational texts, the Gathas of Zoroaster, malign the cruelties of animal slaughter and constitute a bloodless sacrificial liturgy in the Yasna. Animals were only to be slain in a sacrificial rite that entailed the stunning of the victim with a wooden club before its slaughter, the offering of its head to the god Haoma, and the communal distribution of its meat.[126] In a debate with a Christian preserved in the fifth book of the *Dēnkard*, an early ninth-century mowbed explained that the ritual was compassionate in intention, designed to minimize the fear and pain of the animal.[127] One should not slaughter an animal lightly, he added, whenever or wherever a desire for the taste of meat arose. Animal sacrifice was rather an occasion for communal consumption. In the Middle Persian translation of the *Hōm Yašt*, a cow curses the sacrificer who failed to share his flesh: "Thus may you be childless and likewise may dishonor be with you, who do not distribute wealth for my sake to the worthy but . . . withhold me for your wives, sons, and your own belly."[128] Cattle who forfeited their bodies for the welfare of a human community expected collective recognition of their sacrifice. Ancient Zoroastrianism's concern for the well-being of beneficent animals gave rise to rituals of collective feasting, which Iranians developed into political institutions for the creation and reorganization of communities through the consumption of cosmically significant meat.

The late Sasanian translator of the *Hōm Yašt* modified the original Young Avestan text with the qualification that the cow's wealth should be distributed "to the worthy" (*ō arzānīgān*). Who was worthy to partake of an animal's sacrificed meat? Although some scholars forbade the offering of meat to unbelievers, in Iranian society neither sacrificed meats nor the feasts at which they were consumed were restricted to Zoroastrians. Nor was the consumption of sacrificial meat ever taken as evidence of one's status as wehdēn, as Christian martyrs were forced to partake during the Roman persecutions of the third century—at least according to the martyrologies to which East Syrian hagiographers so often turned for their models. The report of the *History of Mar Aba* that a council of Zoroastrian religious authorities insisted on the liberty of Christians to partake of their communal meat accords well with the evidence for Zoroastrian festivals, which were broadly inclusive affairs.[129] The most important occasions for commensality were the pan-imperial festivals of Nowruz and Mihragan, which structured the experience of time and space in the empire and convened its diverse populations in a common celebration of the political and social order of Iran.[130] In the sixth century, however, East Syrian leaders sought to restrict Christian participation in Iranian feasts. The Synod of Ishoyahb I in 585 forbade believers from attending non-Christian feasts, as part of its continuation of Mar Aba's reforms.[131] Hagiographers writing in Mesopotamia, Iberia, and Armenia described the celebration of these festivals in the provinces and dramatized the potential contradictions that Christians participants could experience. The *History of Gregory the Commander*, the *Martyrdom of Eustathius of Mtskheta*, and the *Martyrdom of Yazdbozid* recount stories of Zoroastrians who publicly apostatized at festivals, with a view to condemning Christians who partook of Zoroastrian meat. The *History of Gregory* was composed in Mar Aba's immediate circle as another vehicle for the propagation of his polemics.[132] Even as the authors of these texts railed against the evils of commensality with Zoroastrians, their intimate familiarity with the customs and religious, political, and economic significance of Nowruz in particular suggests that Christians were active participants in these festivities. Their earnestness equally implies a reluctance of Christians to abandon the communal pleasures of the New Year. Despite the protestations of bishops, the feasts of Nowruz and Mihragan were such fundamental occasions for the Christian population of Iran that the Church of the East modeled its own calendar after the schedule of Zoroastrian festivals.[133]

The great feasts had begun at court. The kings of kings were believed to have instituted the festivals and served on these occasions as the hosts of all their subjects.[134] Although the New Year's celebration derived ultimately from ancient Mesopotamian rites, the Iranian mythical-historical tradition understood Nowruz and Mihragan as the institutions of the primordial kings Jamshid and Fereydun intended to mark moments of cosmic restoration. On these days, the kings of kings stood in the place of their mythical predecessors to perform their role as cosmologically beneficent rulers. The principal cosmological action that the kings of kings undertook on Nowruz was giving hierarchical order to the population of the empire, arranging persons great and small in appropriate positions of service. Courtly historiographers and Christian hagiographers emphasized the importance of the day for the reordering of imperial ranks. The royal table was the preeminent site for the according and withdrawal of privileges. The Middle Persian treatise *Sūr ī Saxwan* has preserved a speech delivered in the course of the blessing, the wāz, at the royal banquet, in which a king of kings enumerated in a normative order the titles of the grand officials invited to the royal table, including the *wuzurg framādār* (chief administrative commander), the four head military commanders, and the greatest Zoroastrian ritual and judicial authorities. This document has recently been described as Iran's nearest surviving equivalent to the Roman *Notitia Dignitatum*, the emperors' handbook for comprehending their bureaucracy.[135] Similar announcements and arrangements placed holders of titles and offices beneath the exalted ranks of those entitled to dine at the royal table in a precise order that authoritatively fixed each man's status in relation to his peers. Through the offering of gifts, moreover, a king of kings indebted to his magnanimous self political subordinates, who in the course of the year would repay their debt through imperial service. Royal gifts, such as robes of honor, could also equip men with the means to display and to authenticate the ranks that they received. Through the orchestration of the celebration of Nowruz, Iranian kings of kings demonstrated that wealth and power were products of the cosmologically appropriate ordering of persons, which only they could achieve. So closely linked were these festivals with the functions of Iranian rulership that kings of kings were normally crowned on either Nowruz or Mihragan, and the former marked the beginning of the fiscal year.[136]

Microcosms of the courtly feast were performed, the Christian hagiographers reveal, throughout the empire. Their works provide precious insight into the unfolding of the feasts in the provincial societies that great nobles, middling officeholders, and their collaborators would have experienced. In the *History of Gregory*, we have an account of the celebration of Nowruz in a military context in the Caucasus in 529. Pirangushnasp, a great noble of the house of Mihran, was expected to preside over the festivities for the field army that he commanded. His soldiers appealed to him in eager expectation of the pleasures of the feast, "The eyes of all of us are directed toward you. Rise and perform the *yašt*. We have one day for eating and drinking. Honor us with great honors from the great wealth that Ohrmazd has given you. Make yourself the head and leader of us all."[137] Opening with a recitation of the Avesta, this festival of Nowruz entailed banqueting, the distribution of gifts, and the hierarchical ordering of the soldiers beneath their "head and leader." The royal ceremony was here reduplicated at the level of a field army, with a military commander as the symposiarch who convened, reorganized, and rewarded his forces, which would have included aristocrats and their retinues. Such rehearsals of the royal feast took place in every imperial institution. Officials commemorated Nowruz as a collective subordinate to their chief, the āmārgar in the case of the sixth-century Armenian *Martyrdom of Yazdbozid*.[138] Even the masters of comparatively humble guilds were expected to orchestrate festivities, as the feast of the Iranian sandal and other shoe makers of Mtskheta in the Georgian *Martyrdom of Eustathius of Mtskheta* attests.[139] For the empire's fundamental institutions—the military, the fiscal administration, and artisanal workshops—feasting linked their mundane work to the cosmological purpose of Iran, demonstrated the essential benevolence of imperial hierarchies, and ensured the effective collaboration of men of very different social classes and cultural backgrounds. A flow of gifts and mutual obligations extended from the courtly banquet to the most humble of provincial workshops, entangling persons great and small in a pan-imperial web of reciprocities.

Feasts displayed and demanded popular recognition of a social hierarchy that, as we shall see in the following chapter, was far from static. Congregants at a festival constituted an audience that expected a performance of status from men who claimed to be worthy of wielding authority over others. In its description of soldiers eyeing their commander, the *History of Gregory* gives expression to the status anxieties that a feast could occasion. On the one hand, the organizer of the feast had to reestablish precious bonds of reciprocity with his subordinates, the generally nameless infantry, scribes, artisans, and other laborers who provided the manpower for the operation of imperial institutions. On the other hand, each man had to impress his peers. Whether at court or at an artisanal workshop, men of rank gathered together not only to enjoy but also to evaluate one another. Feasts were the preeminent occasions for aristocratic sociability, as congregants—many of whom will have traveled from a distance—boasted of their exploits and vied for positions and prestige while sharing meat. Alliances could be formed, others abandoned. The emphasis on hierarchy in Christian accounts of provincial feasts suggests that the normative listing and positioning of men according to their rank was characteristic of banquets beneath the court. If a man gained or lost rank, he did so in the sight of his peers. Participation in the banquets of Iranian festivals was a prerequisite not only of maintaining a position in imperial institutions but also of earning the recognition of one's name that was needed to attain an office and to move up in the imperial hierarchy.

To demand that a Christian forgo feasting was to demand that he extricate himself from Iranian political institutions and networks. This is precisely what the authors of the Christian hagiographies and Mar Aba proposed. The *History of Gregory* plainly equates the rejection of festivals with the rejection of social status and power. Declaring Nowruz a "feast of Satan," Pirangushnasp frames his conversion to Christianity as a repudiation of the social and political structures that the feast represented: "I renounce Ohrmazd, wealth, and leadership because he has neither wealth nor power. I am a Christian and I worship our lord Jesus Christ, and I do not serve demons."[140] The author of this hagiography was eager to demonstrate that refusing the wealth and leadership that derived from service to Ohrmazd did not imply disloyalty to the king of kings. As we saw in chapter 1, this aristocrat—now named Gregory—served Husraw I as the commander of a campaign against the Romans even after his abandonment of both the feast and the Good Religion. But the personal relationship with the king of kings that a member of the Mihranid house enjoyed was not available to the middling aristocrats who constituted the audience for antifestive polemics. The secular authorities targeted by Mar Aba's polemics—the inspiration of the author of the *History of Gregory*—included the masters of artisanal workshops and military commanders operating at the provincial level, officials in command of precisely those imperial institutions in which feasting played so important an organizing role. These men needed to navigate imperial aristocratic networks that cohered in space and time at feasts that did not reaffirm so much as reposition aristocrats in relation to their peers. For Christian officeholders, participation in festive banquets was an inevitable and indispensable component of their political practice, and a failure to partake of Magian meat would have insulted their peers, disappointed their inferiors, and caused irreparable damage to their status.

Not all Christians were willing to renounce wealth and leadership as readily as Pirangushnasp, Yazdbozid, or Eustathius. The proliferation of Christian aristocrats suggests, to the contrary, their increased involvement in imperial institutions. Ecclesiastical leaders thus strenuously condemned the eating of Magian meat in canonical and hagiographical polemics throughout the sixth century and into the seventh. In the absence of an offering to idols or a profession of loyalty to Zoroastrian deities at these feasts, the equation of meat consumption with pagan worship that these polemicists made on the basis of Roman martyrologies did not persuade holders of fiscal, military, artisanal, or courtly office to abandon commensality with members of the Good Religion. The efforts of these authors, moreover, demonstrate how routinely Zoroastrians included agdēn in their festive banquets. The great festivals of Nowruz and Mihragan were occasions for classifying men in imperial hierarchies according to status, not religious identity. Despite their polemics, these sixth-century hagiographies reveal the importance of feasting in the aristocratic politics of the empire, in which Christians sought to participate more actively. Like the exilarch, the leader of the Jewish community at court, Christian elites adopted the practices of the Iranian aristocracies, regardless of episcopal criticism.[141] Condemnations of commensality constitute evidence of its prevalence and its centrality to political life. Consumption of Magian meat was thus of a piece with Zoroastrian practices of marriage and inheritance.

THE RECEPTION OF CHRISTIAN LAWS

At the interrogation of Mar Aba, two worldly elite Christians were present, according to the *History of Mar Aba*. If one openly supported the patriarch, the other opposed him and "conspired together with the Magians."[142] Even in portraying these two as only superficially Christian, the hagiographer acknowledged that not only Zoroastrians but also worldly Christians opposed the bishop's reforms and appealed to the court to have him constrained. It was, in the representation of a contemporary associate of Mar Aba's, the combined interests of Christians and Zoroastrians that caused the patriarch's imprisonment and exile. The *History of Mar Aba* thus suggests that his reforms precipitated dissent rather than consensus, conflict rather than coherence, in the ranks of the East Syrian faithful. The worldly appear to have continued to contract marriages and join feasts according to Iranian customs. The ongoing participation of Christians in courtly life and banquets, the enduring importance in East Syrian communities of Zoroastrian festivals such as Nowruz, and the recurrence of polemics against commensality throughout the late Sasanian period imply that the patriarch's ban on Magian meat failed to discipline Christian aristocrats. Likewise, the writings of the post-Sasanian episcopal judges that describe the ubiquity—and even permissibility—of forms of marriage that Mar Aba deemed incestuous demonstrate that the *Regulations of Marriage* did not become normative. But the laws of the patriarch were not therefore without influence. Ecclesiastical leaders increasingly embraced his canons as ways of articulating their distinctively spiritual authority vis-à-vis their worldly counterparts. Even if surviving sources cannot be taken as representative of ecclesiastical views, the prevalence of Mar Aba's laws in hagiographical texts and synodal decisions of the late sixth and early seventh centuries document their impact on the thought and practice of a significant—and highly influential—segment of East Syrian bishops. Ascetic ecclesiastical leaders such as Ishoyahb III invoked the model of the Levites in moments of tension between spiritual and worldly authorities in the Church of the East.[143] They repeated Mar Aba's laws without any pretense concerning the enforceability of their strictures, respecting the suzerain authority of the Iranian court and its judges that the patriarch had outlined. The worldly who accepted the laws did so voluntarily.

The ninth-century legal treatise of Gabriel of Basra has preserved a rare testimony to the self-regulation of a worldly Christian community. This document contains the statutes of an association of artisans in a city, unfortunately unnamed, which were compiled at some point between the middle of the sixth and the end of the seventh century.[144] These statutes reproduce the canons of Mar Aba in the context of an artisanal workshop, identifying the rejection of incest as the distinguishing characteristic of a Christian collectivity: "We abstain from adultery, fornication, sorcery, murder, and the abominable marriage of two women, from the impure union with a mother, daughter, daughter-in-law, mother-in-law, the wife of a brother, and the wife of an uncle [or] with the other [relations] that are despised, abhorred, and rejected in the law of Christianity. We abstain from giving our daughters, sisters, kin, and daughters of our family to pagans, unless they have converted beforehand. We consent to and observe all the holy laws that were established by the leaders of the church, without compulsion."[145] The artisans' espousal of a "law of Christianity" is more characteristic of the first Islamic century than of the Sasanian period, but some artisanal workshops—which unlike fiscal and military institutions could have been entirely Christian in composition— might have recorded the canons of the patriarch in their books during his sojourn in Khuzestan. What is significant for the question of the reception of these canons is the phrase "without compulsion." This artisanal community voluntarily incorporated them into its statutes. Laws, in the understanding of its members, were the distinguishing marks of the pious, the symbolic boundaries of a particular vision of Christian unity that separated them not only from Zoroastrians who practiced close-kin marriage but also from worldly Christians who practiced substitute successorship.

CONCLUSION

Writings that purport to constitute impassible boundaries between Christians and Zoroastrians reveal, on closer inspection, the East Syrian faithful in profoundly mixed states. The canons, regulations, and laws that Mar Aba promulgated in the sixth century served not as the foundations of a distinctive legal system that separated Christians from Zoroastrians but rather as interventions in debates concerning the extent to which Christians could involve themselves in Iranian political institutions. The subordination of East Syrians to the authority of Zoroastrian judges went unquestioned, and the services of Zoroastrian courts were available to agdēn and wehdēn alike, albeit on somewhat different terms. As a consequence, these Christians participated simultaneously in two legal cultures that shared much more than the polemics of the patriarch immediately suggest. The formal, state-sanctioned jurisprudence of the Zoroastrian religious professionals regulated the transmission of patrilineages and patrimonies. The informal jurisprudence of the bishops regulated the spiritual states of the faithful, a remit that came to include mediating conflicts between Christians in which Iranian laws of inheritance, among other topics, played a prominent role. Mar Aba sought not to remove Christians from the judicial authority of the Zoroastrian officials, whose powers he recognized, but to persuade his flock to reject particular practices that he deemed unworthy of Christians. He significantly identified practices that the powerful Christians whose authoritative roles within the church he aimed to circumscribe could not abandon without also abandoning their political positions. With a view to endowing allied bishops and lesser clergy with greater room for maneuver within their respective constituencies, the patriarch composed and disseminated new norms for the marital and dining practices of Christians, according to which their moral and spiritual states could be measured. Their marrying the wives of agnates or partaking of Zoroastrian meats implicated the Christian aristocrats of the Iranian Empire in the defilements of a sinful world that had not yet accepted the redeeming teachings of Christ, from which ecclesiastical leaders—

even those undisciplined by the ascetic life—kept themselves pure. These aristocrats' practices rendered them unmistakably worldly and, in the eyes of reformist clerics, unworthy of leading Christian communities.

It is their worldliness that is of greatest interest for the history of the Iranian Empire. In the polemics of Mar Aba, as in the hagiographical works of northern Mesopotamia discussed in the following chapter, we have a rare glimpse of what has hitherto been a highly elusive phenomenon: the participation of the lower and middling aristocrats of the provinces in the political life of the empire. Here institutions and their corresponding practices, not identities, were the conduits of power. If the importance of Iranian family law for the reproduction of the greatest aristocratic houses has been recognized, the patriarch's writings on marriage suggest that marital and inheritance strategies were of equal consequence for Christian aristocrats. Even without access to the specifically Zoroastrian institution of stūrīh, Christians worked to transmit their patrilineages and patrimonies across generations, through a simplified version of substitute successorship. If accounts of courtly life attest to the importance of the feast for kings of kings and their greatest aristocratic officials, the antifestive polemics of Mar Aba and his circle show the involvement of even the humblest provincial aristocrats in an empire-wide festive economy. The feast, like the court of a Zoroastrian judge, was inclusive of persons irrespective of their religion. These institutions nevertheless required compromises from the Christian faithful. A pious Christian may have bristled at the Avestan recitation that inaugurated the festival, but the ensuing banquet was an occasion for the commensal celebration of an empire held in common. Knowledge of the cosmological underpinnings of Iranian family law may have given some pause over the conceptual links between substitute successorship and incest. Such considerations, however, did not prevent Christians from adapting stūrīh's principles to their own purposes. Despite their shrill tone, the legal writings of Mar Aba demonstrate the importance of the shared practices that allowed Christian and Zoroastrian aristocrats alike to create, maintain, and reproduce powerful houses in the late Sasanian period.

It was, after all, during the tenure of Mar Aba that Christian elites came to participate most visibly in Iranian aristocratic politics. In 551 one of Husraw I's sons, Anushzad, launched a campaign to seize the throne from his father, an example of the intradynastic contestation that characterized the Iranian court throughout its history.[146] What was unprecedented in Anushzad's revolt was the source of his economic and political support: the cities of Khuzestan, with their prominent Christian elites, rather than the great aristocratic houses.[147] The right of rebellion against a Sasanian deemed ineffective in favor of another member of the dynasty was a privilege of Iran's leading houses, such as those of Mihran and Suren.[148] In the sixth century the urban Christians of Khuzestan considered themselves powerful enough to lay claim to this aristocratic privilege and supported the efforts of their own Sasanian candidate for the throne. Anushzad reportedly converted to Christianity, or at least presented himself as a Christian to gain the confidence of the inhabitants of towns and cities such as Beit Lapat/Jundishapur. The Christians of Khuzestan, however, miscalculated their political capital. With the support of the great houses and Mar Aba himself, Husraw I quickly suppressed the rebellion, putting a definitive end to the ambitions of these East Syrians if not to their hopes for a Christian Sasanian.[149] The courtly response to the political aspirations of the Christians of Khuzestan sought to deny them any claim to authority in the empire. They were of ambiguous origins and hence unable to command others, unlike the great aristocrats, whose noble lineages endowed them with power and legitimate political authority.[150] Christians, the opponents of Anushzad contended, could not be nobles. In converting, the rebellious Sasanian departed from "the religion of his ancestors" (*dīn-e niyāgān*) and exhibited his "bad seed" (*bad nižād*).[151] As we have seen, East Syrian elites were already attempting to construct the lineages and houses that were the foundations of political power and authority in the Iranian Empire. If the abrupt attempt to appropriate so exalted an aristocratic privilege as the right of rebellion failed catastrophically in Khuzestan, more gradual processes of accumulating economic and cultural capital were at work in East Syrian communities, especially in urban contexts. In the following chapter, we turn to the East Syrian elites in the towns and cities of northern Mesopotamia, who were more successful than the Christians of Khuzestan at creating aristocratic houses worthy of the recognition of the court.

4

Creating a Christian Aristocracy

Hagiography and Empire in Northern Mesopotamia

CITIES AND SAINTS

At a shrine on a tell just outside the city of Karka d-Beit Slok, modern Kirkuk, Christians from the surrounding region of Beit Garmai in northern Mesopotamia gathered annually in the sixth and early seventh centuries to commemorate martyrs from among their ranks (see figure 3).[1] The congregation of the faithful processed from the worldly city, whose monuments ancient pagan kings had built and whose inhabitants included Zoroastrian aristocrats, to the wholly spiritual tell known as Beit Teta, "the place of the fig tree," named for a tree that had sprung from a site of martyrdom (see figure 4).[2] During the reigns of Shapur II and Yazdgird II, martyrs had fallen victim to the violence of the Sasanian authorities, being executed upon the tell, in its immediate environs, and in the undulating landscape that surrounded the city. In the same way that Mount Bisutun had become a relic of the saints through contact with their bodies (see chapter 2), the blood of the martyrs had rendered the tell an object of veneration by suffusing this more modest hillock at Karka d-Beit Slok and its vicinity. Beit Teta became "a second Sinai," a place where the Christian God had manifested himself to believers through the martyrs who had imitated Christ.[3]

A similar relationship between worldly city and spiritual tell took shape near the contemporary city of Arbela, approximately ninety kilometers (fifty-six miles) north of Karka d-Beit Slok, in the region of Adiabene. There Christians convened at a shrine upon the tell known as Melqi, a site regarded as supernaturally potent from the Neo-Assyrian period onward.[4] Although Melqi has not been located, the tell stood in close proximity to Arbela, like Karka d-Beit Slok an ancient founda-

FIGURE 3. View of the citadel of Kirkuk, ancient Karka d-Beit Slok, in 1911. The Gertrude Bell Archive, Newcastle University, Q_194.

tion and a center of Sasanian administration (see map 3). The congregants there commemorated a martyr, Mar Qardagh, legendarily stoned to death by crowds of Zoroastrians and Jews at the gate of his fortress on the tell at the behest of Shapur II. Melqi, like Beit Teta, became a specifically Christian site in an environment that Christians, Zoroastrians, and others had to share. The construction of shrines of martyrs on the tells of cities that were centers of imperial authority introduced a new technology with which ecclesiastical leaders could redefine relations between Christian and Zoroastrian elites in northern Mesopotamian regions undergoing far-reaching social and political transformations.

Attending the commemorations of the martyrs were not only ecclesiastical leaders but also northern Mesopotamian Christian aristocrats, a subset of the imperial elite who played a key role in late Sasanian politics. The two hagiographical works that recount the histories of these martyrs, the *History of Karka d-Beit Slok and Its Martyrs* and the *History of Mar Qardagh*, foreground the social and political dimensions of their ritualized feasts in hitherto unparalleled ways. These texts explicitly segment the Christian communities that gathered at the sites into aristocrats and commoners, with ecclesiastical leaders belonging to the ranks of the former almost without exception. As Gernot Wiessner and Joel Walker have shown, the author of the *History of Mar Qardagh*, writing around the year 600, was fluent in the cultural discourse of the Iranian court and aristocracies, richly

FIGURE 4. Nave of the so-called Church of Mar Tahmazgerd, at the site of the shrine of the martyrs of Karka d-Beit Slok, a Sasanian foundation reconstructed numerous times before its partial destruction during World War I. The elongated hall with niches is characteristic of late antique Iranian monumental buildings, Sasanian palaces as well as East Syrian churches. The Gertrude Bell Archive, Newcastle University, Q_202.

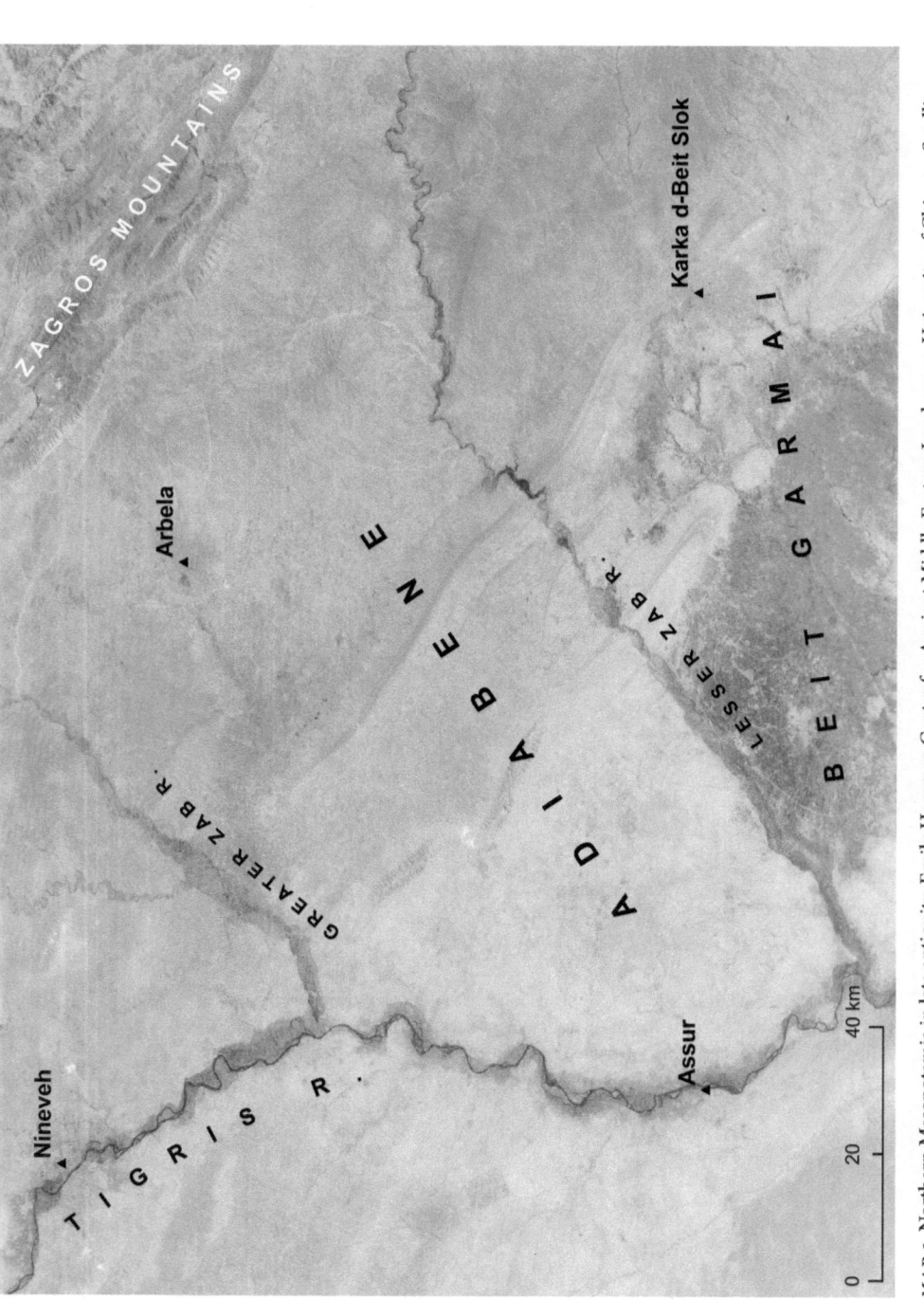

MAP 3. Northern Mesopotamia in late antiquity. Emily Hammer, Center for Ancient Middle Eastern Landscapes, University of Chicago. Satellite imagery from Google Earth.

describing the hunts, games of polo, and feats of martial valor in which Qardagh excelled as a "Christian warrior."[5] The author of the *History of Karka*, this chapter argues, similarly molded aspects of its narrative in distinct ways in accordance with the expectations of Iranian elites. Exploring the dialogic relationship of the hagiographer of Karka d-Beit Slok with his aristocratic audience provides a social and political context for the related *History of Mar Qardagh*. The contemporaneous hagiographers of these works both sought to demonstrate, in Iranian terms, that Christians could be no less noble than their Zoroastrian counterparts, while rooting their claims to aristocracy in cities that were also the loci of episcopal authority. Their works thus offer an opportunity to explore some fundamental questions of Sasanian social history that have remained unanswered. How did provincial elites earn recognition as nobles from their Iranian peers? How did Christian and Zoroastrian elites find bases for collaboration within imperial institutions? What was the relationship between landed aristocratic houses and the cities of the empire? If scholars have long lamented the lack of evidence for provincial societies or relations between provincial elites and the court, these two hagiographical texts permit, through the mediation of their ecclesiastical leaders, the reconstruction of the perspective of the aristocracies of Karka d-Beit Slok and Arbela on the late Sasanian political landscape.

The histories of these martyrs were recited during the course of annual feasts at sacred places within view of their respective cities. If the Christian inhabitants of Karka d-Beit Slok and Arbela fully participated in the mixed rituals, institutions, and practices of Iranian society, including the feasts of Mihragan and Nowruz, against which Mar Aba railed (see chapter 3), on one day each year they came to constitute a distinct group demarcated from their Zoroastrian, Jewish, Manichaean, and polytheist counterparts. As they departed collectively from the walls of their cities for their shrines on the tells, they physically instantiated the clearly defined communities that their bishops and priests could otherwise demarcate only symbolically. During the feasts of the martyrs, Christians were more Christian than on other occasions. Commemorations of martyrs and the physical structures of the shrines at which they took place were, therefore, important instruments for the construction of ecclesiastical authority. In particular, the bishop's leading the community to the shrine and selecting a script to be recited before this congregation provided an occasion for the communication of a narrative that could underpin not only episcopal authority but also a novel vision of community appropriate for its contemporary social and political context, as chapter 2 shows. The *History of Karka* constitutes the earliest evidence for the urban development of the package of institutions—relics of martyrs, shrine structures, hagiographical texts, and ritualized commemoration—that made saints such potent presences in Iranian society in the late Sasanian period. At the Synod of Joseph in 554, East Syrian leaders were enjoined to build churches, monasteries, and martyr's shrines in cities, a departure from earlier canonical regulations that had prohibited such structures from appearing in urban centers.⁶ The date at which a shrine was constructed on Beit Teta remains unknown, but the commemoration of the martyrs at the site during a three-day feast was instituted in the late fifth century. Maron, the bishop of Karka d-Beit Slok, established this feast together with the catholicos Baboi—whose death in 484 provides the terminus ante quem—and the bishops of Beit Garmai and Adiabene.⁷ Specific dates are absent from the *History of Mar Qardagh*, but the text and the shrine seem to have been joined in the late sixth or early seventh century.⁸ If there were likely countless saints' shrines in rural and urban contexts in Iran, the literary expertise that the well-established bishoprics of Arbela and Karka d-Beit Slok enjoyed gave their martyrs more influence than cults elsewhere in northern Mesopotamia.

The hagiographers of these two works were at least as innovative as the author of the *Martyrdom of Pethion, Adurohrmazd, and Anahid* (see chapter 2). Composed in the late Sasanian period, most likely during the reign of Husraw II (590–628), the *History of Karka* is an amalgam of the Christian literary genres of hagiography and historiography.⁹ Its author drew on martyrologies, diptychs, and other records in the archive of the bishopric, as well as the *Chronicle* of Eusebius, which a contemporary translated from Greek into Syriac at Karka d-Beit Slok, and other written sources.¹⁰ At the same time, he responded to Iranian mythical histories, which likely circulated primarily orally in northern Mesopotamian milieux. The resulting work begins with the ancient history of the city under Assyrian, Achaemenian, and Seleucid rulers before proceeding to recount the interwoven histories of the martyrs and bishops of the city. This is the only East Syrian hagiographical text to incorporate secular and ecclesiastical historiography. The *History of Mar Qardagh* adheres more closely to hagiographical conventions but similarly draws on Iranian mythical histories in the portrayal of its saint. This work also includes references to the ancient Assyrian past that depend on Hellenistic historiography. Its author was, moreover, familiar with intellectual trends in the Roman world, in particular the cosmological thought of John Philoponus.¹¹ The authors of these two texts thus bore witness to the cultural cross-pollination taking place in the literary and intellectual circles of late Sasanian northern Mesopotamia. They stood at the eastern terminus of what Paul Peeters has called "bilingual Syria," a trans-Mesopotamian set of Greek- and Syriac-writing textual communities, and marked the beginning of an Iranian literary culture in which oral transmissions were at least as important as texts for the dissemination of stories and ideas.¹² They were, in a word, products of transimperial Christian intellectual networks and Iranian imperial structures. Their works therefore offer an institutionally specific, highly informative perspective on the shifting position of provincial Christian elites in the Iranian Empire.

CHRISTIANS IN AN EXPANDING EMPIRE

The reforms of Mar Aba make plain how active Christians had become in Iranian politics by the middle of the sixth century (see chapter 3). In the aftermath of Hun invasions that threatened the ideological foundations and territorial integrity of the empire throughout the fifth century, the Sasanian court reorganized and intensified its structures of rule, incorporating the provinces more thoroughly into the networks of the fiscal and military administration. As a result, the sixth-century kings of kings not only kept hostile Hephthalite Huns and Turks in check but also conducted repeated military campaigns against the Romans that secured symbolically important tributary concessions.[13] Under Husraw I, the empire expanded into the western Caucasus and southern Arabia, the first large-scale augmentations of the imperial landmass since Shapur II's retaking of Nisibis in 363 (see chapter 1).[14] This extension required the cooperation of men in the provinces, who organized the extraction of resources and served in the cavalry-based armies that the Sasanians summoned with unprecedented frequency for lengthy campaigns throughout the fifth, sixth, and early seventh centuries. The regions most strategic for the military, with which the fiscal administration was usually paired, were largely non-Zoroastrian in population. If the Iranian military commanders stood at the head of the imperial administration in the Caucasian, Arabian, and northern Mesopotamian frontier regions, Christians were prominent—and sometimes even predominant—among the provincial aristocracies and their subordinate populations.

In Armenia, the great house of the Mamikoneans, which had rebelled against the Iranian court in 451 and 484, became a steadfast representative of the empire in the sixth century, working in league with Zoroastrian commanders to consolidate control over the contested Caucasian and eastern Anatolian frontiers.[15] It was in this age of Armenian aristocratic collaboration with Iran that hagiohistoriographers produced the legendary accounts of Armenian rebellions against purportedly persecutory Zoroastrians that have shaped perceptions of the Sasanian period in the region.[16] In Arabia, Iranian elites at al-Ḥīra, closer than Armenia to Seleucia-Ctesiphon, formed interaristocratic ties, through fosterage and shared spaces of sociability, between their houses and those of resident Arab tribes, which worked to extend imperial authority deep into the Arabian Peninsula, even as far as the Hijaz.[17] Although Christianity was not necessarily predominant at al-Ḥīra, the number of Arab elite Christians there was sufficient for the Church of the East to develop this frontier city into a second sacred center, the site of the interment of the bishops of Seleucia-Ctesiphon.[18] Christians were among the representatives of Iran and al-Ḥīra at Najran, a strategic crossroads between southern Arabia and the Hijaz.[19] The success of the religion among the Arabs culminated in the late sixth century with the conversion of the Lakhmid king al-Nuʿman III (ca. 583–602).[20] In northern Mesopotamia, the cities, towns, and villages of the provinces of Beit Garmai (Middle Persian Garmegān), Adiabene (Middle Persian Nōd-Ardaxšīragān), and Beit Arbaye (Middle Persian Arbayestān) played fundamental roles as staging grounds for the campaigns against the Roman Empire that typified sixth-century Iranian political culture. With Kawad I's invasion of Roman Anatolia in 502, more than a century of comparative peace between the two empires came to a close. Sixth-century Sasanians repeatedly marshaled their field armies for campaigns against Rome, with which the court rallied the aristocracies around the idea of Iran.[21] Northern Mesopotamia was therefore once again at the center of the empire's political history, and its provincial aristocracies gained unprecedented prominence at court. During the reign of Husraw II, a Christian aristocrat from Karka d-Beit Slok, Yazdin, became the chief fiscal administrator for Mesopotamia and/or the empire, occupying the office of *wāstaryōšansālār*, "master of the cultivators."[22] More impressively, his son Shamta reportedly participated in deposing the king of kings, taking advantage of the right of legitimate rebellion that the great Iranian aristocrats of the kingdom regarded as their exclusive prerogative.[23] Even if exceptional, the presence of a Christian aristocratic house from Beit Garmai at the heights of courtly influence and power suggests the importance that non-Iranian provincial elites had obtained. The members of the houses of Yazdin, the Mamikoneans, and the Lakhmids are nevertheless only the best known of the myriad, mostly nameless Christians who came to serve Ērānšahr as administrative officials and soldiers in the late Sasanian era and whose identities appear on seals.

The corpus of Sasanian seals and bullae, clay moldings used to validate access to goods or documents, has grown markedly over the past several decades and provides a more varied and representative perspective on the men whom the court enlisted in its networks than literary texts. Personal seals reveal how individuals represented themselves to their peers, because unlike official seals, which give only the title of an office and its associated province(s), personal seals have space for the bearer's name, official title, and religious sentiments, as well as various symbols that underpinned the owner's claim to authority. Although a precise chronological typology for Sasanian sigillography remains a desideratum, comparisons of the seals and bullae excavated from the sixth- and early seventh-century strata at Takht-e Suleyman and elsewhere allow the majority of such surviving materials to be dated to the late Sasanian period.[24] Their owners ranging from the highest officials, such as the *wuzurg framādār* (chief administrative commander) and the *spāhbed* (military generals), to humble scribes, seals document the participation of individuals at the middling levels of imperial administration, which the literary sources, for the most part, ignore. A remarkable number of personal seals display Christian imagery, often drawing upon a Mediterranean repertoire of styles and symbols.[25] Those who produced these seals creatively combined Christian and Iranian elements, slightly modifying traditional Middle Persian formulae to accommodate monotheism and juxtaposing imperial symbols—such as the ram, a representative of the royal xwarrah—to Christian crosses. Such experimentation took place in contexts of political consequence, as Christians collaborated with Zoroastrians in imperial institutions. If the majority of seals of officials show little symbolic variation, even in overwhelmingly Christian regions such as Armenia and Georgia, a handful of participants in the administration placed crosses alongside their state-sanctioned titles. A *šahrab*, chief administrator of a province, of the town of Husraw-šād-Ohrmazd in the vicinity of Seleucia-Ctesiphon, for example, had a cross placed on a seal with his official title, beneath the more conventional symbol of a bull.[26] Imprinted on administrative bullae were similar seals with Christian themes: Daniel in the lions' den together with a cross on an example discovered at the site of Ak-Tepe, near Iran's easternmost frontier; a simple cross on the bulla of the *ōstāndār* in Iberia; and the reduction of the plural *yazdān*, "gods," to *yazd*, "god," in the stock phrase *yazdān ī abzūd az ī weh*, "gods who increased from that which is good," on the bullae of the *āmārgar* of Khuzestan and northern Mesopotamia.[27] Christian seals on bullae are particularly significant as evidence not only of Christian participation in administrative structures but also of the deliberate display of their distinctive religious affiliation in the space of imperial institutions. Presenting the cross as one's symbol did not hinder one's ability to serve as an *ōstāndār* or *āmārgar*, high offices typically though not exclusively held by Zoroastrian aristocrats, or even to serve as a *šahrab*.

Rika Gyselen has, however, highlighted a peculiarity of the Husraw-šād-Ohrmazd *šahrab*'s seal that is suggestive of the ambiguities that could surround Christians in such exalted positions.[28] Where the seals of other known *šahrab*—including one of the same administrative center—represent them wearing a *kolāh*, the traditional headgear of Iranian nobles, the Christian official elected to place a bull on his seal instead of his own bust. In similar fashion, a *naxwār* (regional military commander) represented himself with a ram in place of the bust with kolāh that his counterparts displayed, although his religious affiliation went unspecified. The reluctance of the Christian *šahrab* to portray his face implies, as Gyselen suggests, that he was not a member of one of the recognized great noble houses, whose representatives were entitled to wear a kolāh. On the one hand, his seal points to the newfound prominence of Christians in offices that members of the great nobility had hitherto nearly monopolized. On the other hand, it foregrounds the problem of recognition that Christians taking on novel political positions in a burgeoning administrative structure will have encountered. Whence did Christians obtain the authority to command and organize men and material on behalf of the empire? What made the provincial aristocrats whom literary and sigillographic sources show participating in and even presiding over imperial institutions worthy to hold such power? The bearers of seals offered their own answers to these questions, describing themselves as pious, faithful, and hence trustworthy, associating themselves with animals that were widely recognized emblems of strength and imperial loyalty, and emphasizing possible convergences between Zoroastrian and Christian professions of belief.[29] A Christian could display a cross while declaring his "trust in the gods," *abestān ō yazdān*, a traditional Zoroastrian formulation.[30] The dilemmas discernible in such seals and bullae were particularly urgent in late Sasanian northern Mesopotamia, where a culturally diverse, highly stratified elite cooperated to put the resources of the region in the service of an Iran that was mobilizing its aristocracies for campaigns against Rome.

NORTHERN MESOPOTAMIAN ARISTOCRACIES

Even among the multifarious provinces of the Iranian Empire, northern Mesopotamia stood out for its peculiarities. When the early Sasanians incorporated this region, it had long-standing traditions of political autonomy, an Aramaic-speaking local elite, and a strategic position at the Roman frontier. Under the Parthians, the province had been a kingdom, Adiabene, with an urban center of political authority at Arbela, an arrangement that the Sasanians appear to have kept in place at least into the fourth century.[31] The disappearance of Parthian kingship, however, did not eradicate memories of northern Mesopotamian political unity: the late Sasanian hagiographers whom we will consider recounted its distinctive political history, a tradition that the medieval compiler of the *Chronicle of Arbela* continued. The social composition of the province in the third, fourth, and fifth centuries is poorly documented. What is clear is that, alongside the Parthian dynasts, a class of landowning, Aramaic-speaking nobles known as *bnai ḥere*, "sons of free men," dominated its hinterlands.[32] If these individuals, such as the *māre*, "lords," in the inscriptions of Assur, appear only sporadically in the Parthian period, bnai ḥere of Arbela and Karka d-Beit Slok feature in East Syrian accounts of the fourth-century "Great Persecution."[33] These sources represent the nobles of northern Mesopotamia as mostly Christian, with Manichaean and polytheist deviants among their ranks, already in the fourth century. But attempts to measure religious loyalties in the province on the basis of exclusively Christian sources are imprudent. Were we to possess Manichaean, Zoroastrian, or Mesopotamian polytheist sources for the northern Mesopotamian elite, our knowledge of its cultures would be much richer. There is no reason to believe that Christians eclipsed other groups in the region, as Manichaeans and polytheists appear among the bnai ḥere even in sixth-century accounts. Christianity was nevertheless the predominant religion of the indigenous northern Mesopotamian aristocracies discernible in late Sasanian sources. As bnai ḥere, however, these Christian nobles were different from their coreligionists in the towns of Khuzestan, who neither recalled histories of provincial political autonomy nor recorded claims to nobility in their contemporaneous hagiographies. In the plains between the Tigris and the mountains of the upper Zagros, the Sasanians encountered an unusually confident local aristocracy that spoke Aramaic, traced its roots to the Parthian period, and practiced religions other than Zoroastrianism.

Into this already stratified region, the kings of kings introduced a new elite: "Iranian," in the meaning of the term described in the introduction, great aristocratic families, especially from the province of Fars.[34] Throughout the centuries of Sasanian rule, we find Iranian nobles, officials, and religious professionals in the principal towns of northern Mesopotamia and in rural settlements there that sometimes surpassed urban centers in political importance. Their aristocratic houses appeared abruptly in the region with its incorporation into the Iranian Empire. If the early Sasanians transferred laboring populations from Roman cities to Iran (see chapter 2), they also deported nobles to frontier regions such as northern Mesopotamia. After the Romans ceded the frontier city of Nisibis to the Sasanians in 363, great nobles were reportedly transferred from Istakhr, Isfahan, and elsewhere in Fars to repopulate the abodes that the Romans had abandoned, and were, according to a late Sasanian East Syrian text, granted extensive lands between Nisibis and the Tigris.[35] We will henceforth refer to the descendants of such houses as "Persians," designating persons who believed that their lineages had an origin in Fars. Similar installments and endowments of Iranian aristocratic clans appear to have taken place at Arbela, Karka d-Beit Slok, and other key settlements during the Sasanian period, perhaps through more gradual processes.[36] Iranian nobles occupied the highest levels of the empire's administration, as marzbān, naxwār, and spāhbed, and Zoroastrian religious professionals supervised the administration of royal justice, as mowbed, rad, and dādwar, between the fourth and seventh centuries.[37] Despite their monopolization of the highest ranks of political authority, the Iranian great nobles did not constitute an exclusive elite ruling a non-Iranian and non-Zoroastrian population. A small group of noble families were unable single-handedly to dominate a region as geographically, socially, and culturally complex as northern Mesopotamia. Rather than a self-sufficient ruling minority, these Iranian nobles should be considered brokers between the royal court and the local nobility of the province.[38] The successful extraction of resources required the cooperation of local intermediaries, such as the local nobles, whose possession of land and labor placed them well to either facilitate or obstruct the extension of Sasanian structures of rule. The Sasanians depended on nobles of the most trustworthy origins, such as men of their native Istakhr, to cultivate the necessary ties to bind men of the northern Mesopotamian plains to the imperial center at Seleucia-Ctesiphon. The Iranian nobles of the province laid the foundations for negotiation with established local hierarchies rather than their direct domination.

Iranian and indigenous aristocrats stood between cities such as Nisibis, Nineveh, Arbela, and Karka d-Beit Slok and their rural estates in the fertile, rain-fed plains that extend from the Zagros Mountains to the Tigris River.[39] East Syrian hagiographical works constitute the only literary evidence for the aristocratic exploitation of land and labor in the region, whose archaeology, at least in the Sasanian period, remains understudied. The basic unit of exploitation was the village (Syrian *qrita*) of dependent laborers, whom landowning aristocrats could command at will.[40] Syriac texts often characterize these villagers as *'abde*, "slaves," a term that collapses the distinctions between Middle Persian *bandag*, "subordinate, servant," and *anšahrīg*, "slave."[41] *'Abde* could be slaves, the possession of at least a few of whom was a sign of aristocratic status. But they were more often dependent villagers who cultivated the lands of their superiors. The centers for the administration of these lands were rural estates that were typically named after an aristocratic house, such as Husrawān, the estate of the house of Aqeblaha, a bishop of Karka d-Beit Slok in the latter half of the fourth century.[42] Although the bulk of these estates likely took shape independent of the court, those that appear in the literary sources were established at Sasanian initiative. Aqeblaha's ancestors, for example, exploited one of their estates with laborers whom Shapur II was reported to have deported from Maishan in southern Mesopotamia.[43] According to a late Sasanian hagiographical work from Nisibis, the same king of kings apportioned the rural districts surrounding the city among Iranian noble houses.[44] The author of the text specified the territories, which rivers clearly demarcated, suggesting that the rural landscapes of northern Mesopotamia were perceived as a mosaic of aristocratic landholdings. The fragmentary Sasanian decorative stucco (see introduction)—characteristic of well-known rural estates such as the site of Chal Tarkhan, south of modern Tehran—found at Qara Tepe outside Kirkuk shows that at least some aristocrats in the region erected palatial abodes on their lands.[45] Imperial administration, however, brought these noblemen into the cities that housed military, fiscal, and religious institutions and their officials. Even if the aforementioned military commanders possessed landed estates, contemporaneous sources associate them with cities. At least in northern Mesopotamia, fire temples and Zoroastrian religious authorities were to be found in Arbela, Karka d-Beit Slok, and other urban centers. The Christian ecclesiastical hierarchy was organized in the same cities.

The social boundaries, relations, and locations of northern Mesopotamian elites were fluid rather than fixed. The leading military commanders who descended from the houses of Fars were uniformly Zoroastrian, but other Persian houses at Nisibis, Karka d-Beit Slok, and, most likely, Arbela, were Christian. These houses shared a conception of their nobility even as they differed in religion. This chapter shows, moreover, that Christian elites who imagined themselves indigenous to the region sought to identify genealogically with the Persians. The authors of the *History of Karka* and the *History of Mar Qardagh* constructed places for Christians within Iranian categories of nobility. Before turning to their narrative interventions in late Sasanian society, let us consider a counterexample from the same region to highlight the significance of their literary work. The *History of Sultan Mahduk*, composed in the late seventh century, recounts the history of a royal dynasty at Hirbet Glal, in the vicinity of Karka d-Beit Slok. This royal house, whose progeny were martyred under Shapur II, comprised the descendants of Arioch, an opponent of the kings of Sodom and Gomorrah in Genesis 14.[46] East Syrian exegetes located Arioch's kingdom at Nippur in southern Mesopotamia, which the *Synodicon Orientale* notes was known for its noblemen.[47] Writing after the Islamic conquests had undermined the preeminence of Iranian elites in the region, the Hirbet Glal hagiographer provided his city's nobles with a genealogy that is distinctly biblical and Mesopotamian, perhaps directly to rival the claims of their counterparts at Karka d-Beit Slok. There were, the *History of Sultan Mahduk* shows, literary resources available to communicate the distinctive political history of northern Mesopotamia and the nobility of its inhabitants in ways that rendered Iran and its great nobles irrelevant. The hagiographers of interest in this chapter selected modes of representing the pasts of their cities and of men in terms that create convergences between Iranian and provincial histories. In the acts of recalling and recording the ancient kingdoms of their region, the following sections show, the East Syrian authors of Karka d-Beit Slok and Arbela located their communities in an Iranian social and political imaginary that could include elites Christian and Zoroastrian, Mesopotamian and Persian.

HISTORIES FOR CHRISTIAN NOBLE HOUSES

Among the dozens of hagiographies that East Syrian authors produced between the fourth and the seventh century, the *History of Karka* and the *History of Mar Qardagh* are exceptional in one important respect: both of their hagiographers commenced with the ancient origins of the Christians whose martyrdoms are the primary focus of their works. The northern Mesopotamian martyrs whose histories they related were, moreover, largely representatives of the noble families that dominated the hinterlands of Karka d-Beit Slok and Arbela. While narrating the deaths of men and, in less detail, women on account of their faith, the hagiographers simultaneously expounded the ancient, noble, and powerful origins of the martyrs' families, which likely retained private traditions and rights of commemoration alongside the public cults.[48] The fixation of these histories on the nobility is characteristic of late Sasanian hagiography more generally, which concentrates on the conversion, contests, and eventual martyrdom of members of the great nobility. Histories of aristocratic converts participated in broader East Syrian debates—in which the laws of Mar Aba intervened (see chapter 3)—on the potential perils of the increasing involvement of Christians in imperial institutions in the late Sasanian period. It was primarily through the production of hagiographical narratives that late Sasanian Christian clerics attempted to negotiate the confrontation of Iranian aristocratic and Christian religious cultures, much as their contemporaries in Merovingian Gaul composed the *Adelsheilige* to shape the practices of the emergent Frankish aristocracy.[49] Unlike the authors of histories of late Sasanian converts, the ecclesiastical leaders of Karka d-Beit Slok and Arbela crafted hagiographies that create convergences between aristocratic and Christian cultures while foregrounding potential conflicts. Rather than concentrate on great noble converts' abandonment of Iranian aristocratic culture together with Zoroastrianism, their histories celebrate the commitment to Christianity of the northern Mesopotamian martyrs in terms that attribute their steadfastness in the faith to their nobility. Where hagiographies traditionally relate the origins of a saint, these hagiohistoriographers developed complex historical introductions that root the heroism in the face of persecution of the martyrs in the ancient, mythical origins of their noble lineages.[50] Amid the debates of both Sasanian elites and Christian leaders concerning the relationship between Christianity and nobility, the bishoprics of Karka d-Beit Slok and Arbela produced narratives that insist on the authenticity, power, and even sanctity of Christian noble lineages.

"This is Karka the great." Thus commences the archaeology of the *History of Karka*, an account of the ancient history of the city that preceded its Christianization at the hands of apostles, bishops, and martyrs. The deeds of Assyrian, Achaemenian, and Seleucid monarchs are recounted in juxtaposition to those of the city's bishops and martyrs: they all equally magnified the great city, whose name we will henceforth abbreviate as Karka. What unites these seemingly disparate accounts is the continuous history of the city's nobles (bnai here), who served the Assyrian, Achaemenian, and Seleucid kings, presided as the city's most distinguished bishops, and perished as martyrs to defend the Christian faith. Noblemen made Karka great. While the historical introduction of the work has received the most attention as a source for Karka's ancient history, its primary concern is the narration of the origins of the city's noble families, not the comprehensive political history of the settlement.[51] Three ancient kings had shaped Karka: Esarhaddon/Sargon, Darius III, and Seleucus Nikator. These were historical kings reimagined through the legends of Hellenistic historiography, the Hebrew Bible, Iranian mythical histories, and northern Mesopotamian oral traditions. Despite the name of the city, which means "Karka of the house of Seleucus," the Assyrian king Esarhaddon, the son of Sennacherib, was said to have founded it as an administrative outpost against the incursions of a Median king.[52] The *History of Karka* identifies Esarhaddon with both the Sardana of the Hellenistic tradition and the Sargon of the Bible, a confusion that exemplifies its intermingling of historical traditions. It presents the Assyrian as a pious king, who submitted to the preaching of Jonah and declared a fast at Nineveh.[53] But his piety did not secure the support of divine providence against the Medes, who came against "Nimrod," here synonymous with Assyria. Karka was restored by Darius, "who fought with Alexander son of Philip and was conquered by him."[54] If Darius was credited with ornamenting the city, an alternative, perhaps competing account of its foundation places Karka among the illustrious civic foundations of Seleucus Nikator, an attribution evident in its name: "He built five walled cities [*karkin*]; Antioch the city of Syria, the Seleucia of Syria, Seleucia of Pisidia, Sliq the great city of Beit Aramaye, and the city Karka d-Beit Slok."[55] In the précis of ancient Near Eastern history at the opening of the *History of Karka*, the city occupies a central place in the imperial struggles among Assyrian, Achaemenian, and Seleucid kings. As we will see, the self-representation of the settlement was highly aspirational.

The most enduring legacy of these ancient kings was their contribution to the population of the city. Each installed aristocratic families within its walls.[56] When Esarhaddon/Sargon built Karka, he transferred "a great family from the land of the Assyrians from among the notables of the kingdom, one known by the name of Burzin," and another unnamed "great lineage" (*tuhma raba*).[57] The remainder of Karka's aristocrats originated in Istakhr, an authoritative place of origin for Sasanian nobles. Darius "brought five families from the land of Istakhr . . . whose names are written in the archives of the kingdom of Persia."[58] Seleucus, for his part, installed additional men from the famous city of Fars: "He brought five notable families from Istakhr . . . and gave them arable property [*'arata*] and vineyards in the land."[59] The authority of Karka's twelve noble houses was mapped onto the layout of the city, which Seleucus had reportedly divided into twelve districts, each named after one of the aristocratic families that Esarhaddon/Sargon, Darius, or Seleucus himself had installed. With solid symbolic foundations for their authority in the city and landed estates in its hinterland, the aristocracies of Karka were well positioned to outlive their dynastic patrons. One need not accept the historicity of this account to admit its plausibility to a sixth-century audience. Long after the Assyrian, Achaemenian, and Seleucid dynasties had disappeared, their aristocracies continued to wield power in northern Mesopotamia in the *History of Karka*'s vision of the mythical-historical landscape of the region. Through these legendary stories, its hagiographer drew a distinction between nobles with Mesopotamian and those with Persian—in the sense of deriving from Fars—lineages, which reflected the self-conceptions of the late Sasanian houses in the city.

This distinction recurs in the *History of Mar Qardagh*, hitherto studied in isolation from the *History of Karka*. The archaeology of the latter provides a wider, northern Mesopotamian context for the legendary history of the family of the martyr Qardagh. The *History of Mar Qardagh*'s interest in ancient history is not nearly as extensive as that of the *History of Karka*, but both hagiographies concern themselves with ancient lineages, kings, and landscapes and seek to conflate provincial, northern Mesopotamian and transregional, Iranian histories. Where the *History of Karka* traces the varied pasts of an entire local nobility, the *History of Mar Qardagh* addresses the origins of a single man, Mar Qardagh, supposedly a victim of Shapur II in the fourth century: "Mar Qardagh was from a great family from the stock of the kingdom of the Assyrians. His father was descended from the renowned lineage of the house of Nimrod, and his mother from the renowned lineage of the house of Sennacherib. And he was born of pagan parents lost in the error of Magianism, for his father, whose name was Gušnōy, was a prominent man in the kingdom and distinguished among the Magi."[60] Much as the nobles of Karka originated from both Assyria and Fars, the "great family" of Qardagh could claim both northern Mesopotamian descent, through Sennacherib, and Iranian descent, through Nimrod, a characteristically Iranian—in the sense of genealogically related to the Avestan ēr—mythical figure in the region, discussed in greater detail below. The identification of Qardagh's residence with the ruined fortress outside Arbela anchored his origins in an ancient landscape—in this case, a suburban one. Here too, association with ancient kings supports an account of noble lineage. Direct descent from the kings, however, made Qardagh's family rather grander than their counterparts at Karka, merely "free," not "great," men.

The *History of Karka* makes plain that the ancient noble houses continued to dominate the settlement and its hinterland in the late Sasanian period. Seleucus Nikator's division of its urban space accounted for the distribution of power in sixth-century Karka among twelve noble lineages that traced their origins either to the Assyrian kingdom or to the province of Fars. Members of these noble families recur throughout the text, as martyrs and bishops. The narrative presumes their Christian loyalty and celebrates their martyrdoms but provides only occasional insight into the history of these families' Christianization. If there were undoubtedly Christians within their ranks before the outbreak of Shapur II's persecution, some had adopted Christianity more recently. The late fourth- or early fifth-century bishop Shapur Braz, from the noble "house of Ardashir son of Shapur Braz," converted one of the families that Seleucus had transferred from Istakhr. Its members' commitment to Christianity was, however, less than uniform. Some of their ranks continued to practice Manichaeism into the sixth century, a remarkable example of aristocratic religious diversity at the provincial level.[61] At Karka, we nevertheless find a largely Christian provincial nobility that traced its origins to Assyrian and Persian aristocracies. The *History of Mar Qardagh*, by contrast, does not expressly link the martyr's lineage with sixth-century noble houses in Arbela. There were, however, Christian nobles in the region who will likely have claimed lineages similar to those of their counterparts ninety kilometers (fifty-six miles) to the south, at Karka. The way in which the contemporaneous *History of Karka* associates particular noble families with the Assyrian and Persian lineages that appear in the *History of Mar Qardagh* suggests a similar situation in Adiabene. Sennacherib and Nimrod were not simply figures of legend but also figures of lineage. Although the *History of Mar Qardagh* tells a story of aristocratic conversion along the lines of contemporaneous hagiographical works, the projection of Qardagh's apostasy into a distant past would have permitted sixth-century auditors of the history to identify with a noble lineage that the martyr had successfully rendered Christian. Indeed, some Christian elites of Adiabene claimed descent from fourth-century martyrs: Abraham of Nethpar, a seventh-century monk from Adiabene, descended from "a lineage [tuhma] of martyrs whom Shapur the king killed."[62] The cultural hybridity of Qardagh, moreover, might have enabled multiple noble families to identify with the saint. If families with diverse histories of origin—similar to those of Karka—from both Assyria and Fars constituted Adiabene's local nobility, Qardagh's inclusive genealogy with both Assyrian and Persian components, will have enabled the region's noble Christian houses unanimously to recognize him as one of their own.

These histories were written not merely about noble families but on their behalf. Nobles emerge from their pages as the heroes of Christian communities, as their primary sources of sanctity, leadership, and patronage. Prior to the composition of these hagiographies, the nobles of northern Mesopotamia had a reputation for perfidy, not loyalty, to the Christian faith. Fourth- and fifth-century accounts of the "Great Persecution" soberly reminded Christians of the potential contradictions between aristocratic and religious loyalties. When Shapur II enjoined the bnai here of Karka to stone their bishop to preserve their positions, they willingly complied, a story frequently repeated in early northern Mesopotamian hagiographical works.[63] Against such tales of aristocratic betrayal, the *History of Karka* and the *History of Mar Qardagh* elaborate on the manful resistance of Christian nobles to Zoroastrian persecutors. In the course of its account of the purported persecution of Yazdgird II (r. 438–56), whose aristocratic context chapter 1 discusses, the *History of Karka* records the names and families of the nobles who perished. Isaac son of Hormizgard was the first to fall after boldly defending the faith, and his fellow martyrs were chiefly fellow nobles, such as Ardashir son of Arzanaya, the entire "house of Stephanos," and other bnai here.[64] As if directly to correct accounts of fourth-century noble apostasy at Arbela, the *History of Mar Qardagh* provides a painstakingly detailed description of the valiance of the martyr.[65] Like contemporary Armenian historiographers of the battle of Avarayr, the sixth-century hagiographers of northern Mesopotamia attributed to nobles an ability to endure the most painful of torments. The connection between martyrdom and landscape that transformed Beit Teta and Melqi into sacred sites also appeared on aristocratic estates. The members of the "house of Stephanos," among other nobles, were executed on the slopes of a place called Kenar, in the "habitation of Nikator," that is, on the property of one of the houses descended from Seleucus Nikator.[66] These nobles were likely martyred on their own lands, like Mar Qardagh. As the most manful martyrs, noblemen stood at the center of the symbolic constructions of Christian community in northern Mesopotamia, an imaginative space that ascetics and clerical martyrs had previously occupied.

Noble families also provided the foundations for Christian institutions. With the arrival of the "holy apostles" Addai and Mari in Karka, the *History of Karka* shifts its focus from ancient kings and nobles to the history of bishops. But even if the first bishop of Karka was a refugee from the Roman East, the histories of the episcopate and the nobility were rarely distinguishable.[67] The few bishops of Karka whose biographies were recorded were uniformly of noble origin. Aqeblaha, who ruled in the latter half of the fourth century, belonged to the noble house of Husraw, and his father occupied an exalted position at court in Seleucia-Ctesiphon.[68] His successor, Shapur Braz, was a member of "the family [*šarbta*] known as the house of Ardashir son of Shapur Braz."[69] The names of both of these families correspond with those of the Sasanian dynasty and high aristocracy, implying that these clans of Husraw and Ardashir son of Shapur Braz either originated in Fars or constructed genealogies linking themselves with the noble houses of the Iranian Plateau. Regardless, these bishops were nobles. The institutions of Christian community emerged largely through the intersecting interests of the nobility and the episcopate. With the wealth of the house of Husraw, Aqeblaha rebuilt Karka's principal church, adorned its liturgy with gold, silver, and silk, and donated his patrimonial "treasure" to the church.[70] Shapur Braz not only brought his familial resources to the episcopal throne but also persuaded another noble house to place its wealth in the service of the church: "He turned the descendants from the family [*šarbta*] that Seleucus brought from the land of Istakhr into pure vessels in the name of the creator. He built on their patrimony a house for the *aksenaye* (outsiders), where the sick, the oppressed, the poor, and the needy were received and rested. He donated the house and designated it a property [*qenyana*] for the wages of the physicians who were in it and for the present provision of the goods that were fitting for those who came to be healed."[71] In Karka, the institutions that facilitated the liturgical celebrations and charitable activities through which Christianity was realized rested on the patronage and leadership of the city's noble houses. The *History of Mar Qardagh* similarly emphasizes the magnanimous endowments of the saint's aristocratic wealth. Qardagh had the fire temples that his house had constructed converted into churches and monasteries.[72] It was nobles, whether acting as martyrs, bishops, or pious lay men, who erected the institutions of the Christian community in northern Mesopotamia. In foregrounding the nobility of the best men among the ranks of the Christians at Karka and Arbela, the hagiographers of the *History of Karka* and the *History of Mar Qardagh* emphasized these nobles' possession of a commodity that brought access to status and office in expanding imperial institutions.

NOBLE LINEAGE: A CURRENCY OF POWER

Noble lineage was a prerequisite for power and privilege in Iranian political culture. From the foundation of the empire in 226 until its dissolution, great noble houses largely of Parthian descent dominated the highest ranks of the court, and their corresponding offices. Rather than seek to expand their authority at the expense of these noble dynasties, the Sasanians co-opted men whose patrimonies and patronage networks rivaled their own, enlisting the resources of the great houses in their service. The Mihranids, Karenids, Surenids, and other great houses organized and commanded armies, supervised taxation, and managed Zoroastrian institutions on behalf of the king of kings.[73] On account of the interdependence of royal and aristocratic dynasties, historians have generally considered the Sasanians unsuccessful at constructing stable transregional fiscal and military administrations.[74] The ability of noblemen to call upon their own resources and authoritative names has been viewed as inimical to the consolidation of royal power. But recently published seals and bullae indicate that by the sixth century, the court was employing āmārgar to levy taxes and was effectively supervising the activities of its officeholders in disparate regions of the empire.[75] The sixth-century court, moreover, created a quadripartite set of military administrations.[76] The extent to which these structures resulted from specific reforms undertaken during the reign of Husraw I or from a more gradual series of developments that unfolded over the course of the fifth and early sixth centuries remains debatable. What is clear is that these structures enabled the court to expand the remit of the fiscal and military administrations—and, indeed, to expand the empire itself—throughout the late Sasanian period.[77] The high officials who presided over these structures of imperial rule were invariably men of great noble lineage. Although historians have argued that the empire could expand only by constraining the great noble houses and creating a new service aristocracy (*Dienstadel*), the personal sealings of the spāhbed at the apex of the administration show that royal and aristocratic powers expanded in concert rather than in competition.[78] The known spāhbed were of Parthian and Persian lineages, and some were specifically from the house of Mihran. If James Howard-Johnston has argued that religious and linguistic differences prevented provincial elites from collaborating with the great nobles, especially in northern Mesopotamia, the genealogical identities that elites of different strata and religions claimed could provide the basis for enduring, reproducible relations.[79]

With the language of lineage as their primary means of distinguishing among men, spāhbed and other leading military-cum-fiscal officials, such as the marzbān and naxwār known from late Sasanian northern Mesopotamia, endeavored to create similarly collaborative relationships with the members of the less exalted strata of the nobility in the provinces. In the Iranian taxonomy of humanity, princely, *wispuhr,* and great noble, *wuzurg,* men stood above a class of lesser nobles, the *āzād*.[80] These "free men" corresponded with the bnai here whom we have encountered in Aramaic texts and encompassed a wide variety of provincial nobilities, including the *dahigān,* or local landowners.[81] Although they are conventionally believed to have been a product of Husraw I's reforms, the appearance of dahigān in the *Martyrdom of Pethion* suggests that such lesser nobles did not come into being but merely became more prominent as a result of late Sasanian administrative developments.[82] The diverse aristocracies of the provinces emerge with striking consistency in late Sasanian sources, ranging from the great nobles of Armenia known fromEłishe, Łazar, and other writers to the more modest dahigān of Middle Persian, Arabic, and New Persian sources and the bnai ḥere of northern Mesopotamia.[83] The aristocratic community—of Sasanian and Parthian dynasts in the early Sasanian period—expanded markedly in the fifth and sixth centuries to include more and more men in the ranks of nobility. The reasons for this tendency are straightforward. The military threat of Iran's new nomadic enemies from the north and northeast required the mobilization of as many *aswār*—cavalrymen typically drawn from the ranks of the āzād—as possible and the costly provisioning of armies almost continuously on campaign. If historians have seen the rise of the dahigān as a sign of the weakness of the great noble houses and thus of increased centralization and efficiency, the ongoing leadership of the great nobles points to a different role for their lesser peers in the reorganization of the empire's limited resources. Just as the kings of kings relied on the authority of the great nobles to command men and material, the great nobles in turn depended upon middling and lesser nobles whose names were authoritative at the local level to assist in the extraction of surplus and in the raising of cavalry. The basis for such collaboration was the conception of shared, if differentiated, nobility, which distinguished both wuzurg and āzād from the mass of nameless commoners.

Nobles articulated their relations with one another through genealogy. The more ancient and accomplished one's ancestors, the more authoritative—and thus more worthy of power—one's name was. If the Sasanians were entitled to rule as the descendants of the primordial kings and the Kayanians, the great nobles drew their power from heroic ancestors whose origins were no less ancient, such as Rustam, Karen, and Nawdhar.[84] The Kayanians were the mythical kings of the Avesta who had served as the patrons of Zoroaster, not a historically identifiable dynasty.[85] The ancestors of the great nobles were similarly epic rather than historical figures. In the *Book of Kings* (*Xwadāy-nāmag*) that the late Sasanian court produced, mythical and historical accounts are interwoven and inextricable.[86] Courtly literary specialists thus identified the historical Achaemenians, known through Greek sources, as the mythical Kayanians.[87] Such mythical-historical writing reflects not deficient historiographical capacities but rather a set of priorities that distinguished the Iranian tradition from its Greco-Roman equivalent. Mythical histories provided the basis for declarations of genealogical prestige. Specific houses claimed descent from legendary figures whose mythical-historical functions they believed themselves to fulfill in the present. The Mihranids and Surenids, for example, claimed Rustam as their ancestor, and the Karenids their eponym, Karen.[88] But textual references to noble lineages are only the dimmest reflections of a lively culture of genealogical conversation, construction, and comparison. Both before and after the compilation of written royal and aristocratic histories in the late Sasanian period, the past was primarily a matter for tellers of tales. Noblemen were expected to give an account of their patrilineage in the company of their peers, to boast of their ancestors' heroics, especially at banquets. But specialists known as *gōsān*, who recited mythical histories on festive occasions, continually provided the aristocracies with new materials with which to reshape the past.[89] Connections between mythical ancestors could be drawn and redrawn according to the circumstances, with implications for how their contemporary successors interacted. The *Book of Kings* reimagines relations between mythical-historical royal and aristocratic dynasties in ways that established paradigms for cooperation in the late Sasanian period. Men whose forefathers had collaborated were necessarily bound to one another. The myths that gave structure to relations of power in the Iranian world were, moreover, highly malleable.

Northern Mesopotamian materials reveal how provincial aristocrats participated in the culture of genealogical politics. If the accounts that dahigān elsewhere in the empire gave of themselves are lost, the histories of noble genealogies that hagiographers compiled and constructed for bnai ḥere are preserved in Christian institutions, such as contemporaneous Armenian histories.[90] There was a fundamental genealogical disparity between Armenian and East Syrian Christian nobles. The former could claim descent from Parthian houses and lineages among the greatest in the empire. The status of the northern Mesopotamian aristocracy was more ambiguous. Even if they were "free men," great aristocrats called into question their ability to hold power. The sixth-century *History of the Armenians* of Łazar P'arpec'i, an author very much in touch with the attitudes of the great nobles, portrays the inhabitants of Mesopotamia in the most unflattering terms. To persuade a group of Iranian aristocrats of his worth, the great Armenian nobleman Vahan Mamikonean contrasts the manly and faithful Armenians with the deceitful "Syrians": "You compared the Armenians to the most cowardly and weakest in battle—first to the Syrians, then to deserters, slackers, and cripples."[91] If Iranians and Armenians were known for valiance, Syrians were known for cowardice. It is thus unsurprising that northern Mesopotamian hagiographers avoided the appellation *Syrian*, an adjective notable for its rarity in their works at a time when their Syriac-writing counterparts across the frontier in Roman Mesopotamia were constructing and disseminating a peculiarly "Syrian" collective past.[92] A strong connection between lineage and land gave rise to ethnic arguments by Armenians, Parthians, and Persians who rooted their aristocratic communities in the landscapes of their mythical-historical ancestors. Northern Mesopotamians did not venture to make ethnic claims of this kind, which would have distanced them from the great nobles in their midst. In concert with Christian literary specialists, however, they constructed accounts of ancient lineage that guaranteed their ability manfully and faithfully to serve Ērānšahr.

A POTENT PAST

The hagiographers of Karka and Arbela created new histories of noble lineage that trace northern Mesopotamian houses from authoritative ancient figures. Their accounts were artifacts of the late Sasanian period that reshaped oral tales circulating in the region concerning ancient kings on the basis of a historiographical tradition common to Christians on both sides of Mesopotamia's political frontiers. To account for the appearance of Sennacherib (r. 705–681 BCE) and Esarhaddon (r. 681–669 BCE) in these texts, scholars have argued that orally transmitted, folkloric memories of the Assyrians continued to be associated with particular sites, such as Assur, Nineveh, Arbela, and the shrine of Mar Qardagh at Melqi, more than a millennium after the collapse of the Neo-Assyrian dynasty.[93] The Neo-Assyrian kings loomed large in a landscape that had once formed the heart of their empire, long after its collapse.[94] Even in the absence of a local historiographical tradition, these kings and their accomplishments were widely known and associated with the region's tells and ruins. Nevertheless, East Syrian hagiographers introduced new sources for ancient Mesopotamian history into a culture of tale telling already alert to the deeds of ancient kings. In addition to the Hebrew Bible's account of Nimrod, the *History of Karka* and the *History of Mar Qardagh* depend on a text that had become available to Syriac-writing communities just before they were composed: the *Chronicle* of Eusebius, originally written in Greek but surviving only in Armenian.[95] According to the eleventh-century historiographer Elias of Nisibis, a certain Simeon Barqaya made a translation of Eusebius's *Chronicle* at Karka during the reign of Husraw II, that is, roughly contemporaneously with the writing of the *History of Karka*.[96] Unlike other Christian works of history in late antiquity, the *Chronicle* treats the ancient political history of the Near East in detail on the basis of Hellenistic histories in an effort to demonstrate the accuracy of the Hebrew Bible's historical narratives. The work of Eusebius interested northern Mesopotamian writers as a repository of the kind of ancient historical knowledge that was so important in Iranian political culture. East Syrian and Armenian writers embraced it as a source for the past of their regions and their aristocratic patrons.

The *Chronicle* of Eusebius enabled hagiographers to refashion the history of northern Mesopotamia in one potent way. The authors of the *History of Karka* and the *History of Mar Qardagh* focused on only one of the various narratives of ancient Mesopotamian kings in this work: the account of Nimrod's relationship to the Assyrians. In keeping with his aim of demonstrating the historicity of biblical figures, Eusebius had presented Nimrod as the founder of the Assyrian royal capital, Nineveh, which Asshur and later Ninus, the son of Belos, restored.[97] The *History of Karka* develops this account into an identification of Nimrod with Ninus, the son of Belos, whom Hellenistic historiographers had considered the founder of the Assyrian dynasty.[98] The *History of Mar Qardagh*, in turn, presents its namesake saint as the descendant of Nimrod and Sennacherib, now both equally Assyrian, in a further evolution of the account of Eusebius. Just like the Assyrian kings whose tales were widely told, Nimrod was a figure of legend in the region, in particular for Christians, Jews, and others with access to the Hebrew Bible, who knew him as the first Mesopotamian king and "a mighty hunter before the Lord" (Genesis 10:9). But his connection with historic Assyria was only circumstantial. Originally based in the south, Nimrod "went to Assyria, where he built Nineveh, Rehoboth Ir, Calah, and Resen" (Genesis 10 11–12). In late antiquity, this passage gave rise to conflicting interpretations identifying Nimrod with particular cities.[99] The fourth-century poet-theologian Ephrem considered Edessa, Nisibis, Ctesiphon, Hatra, and Reshaina as foundations of Nimrod, while the northern Mesopotamian *Cave of Treasures* includes cities in southern Mesopotamia and Azerbaijan in the remit of the legendary king.[100] The Eusebian genealogy permitted the hagiographers of the *History of Karka* and the *History of Mar Qardagh* respectively to include Karka and Arbela in this evolving list. If the *History of Karka* is the only witness to the claims of the former, the East Syrian exegetical tradition regarded Ninus as the founder of Arbela.[101] The *Chronicle of Khuzestan*, a work from the latter half of the seventh century, completely replaces Nimrod with Ninus as the founder of the cities enumerated in Genesis 10, a historiographical legitimation of a biblical narrative that Eusebius could have constructed.[102] These literary developments suggest the influence of the Karka hagiographer—and the translator of Eusebius's *Chronicle*—not only on his counterparts at Arbela but on East Syrian scholars more generally. The *History of Karka* and *History of Mar Qardagh* hagiographers went beyond the account in the Book of Genesis to make Nimrod the primordial source of kingship in northern Mesopotamia, from whose patrilineage legitimate political power flowed. On the basis of the *Chronicle* of Eusebius and the Hebrew Bible, and likely in dialogue with local oral accounts, these hagiographies recast Nimrod as an Assyrian, joining two ancient historical traditions that had previously been distinct.

The reinvention of Nimrod served to make the Assyrian ancestors of the northern Mesopotamian aristocracies a branch of the Iranian genealogical tradition. Nimrod was, after all, widely known as an Iranian in late antiquity, reflected in Syriac, Greek, Caucasian, and Iranian sources.[103] Early Islamic historiographers who drew on the *Book of Kings* identified Nimrod with the mythical rulers Fereydun, Zahhak, and Tahmuras.[104] Although such parallels between biblical and Iranian traditions are normally regarded as Islamicizing topoi, akin to the attempts of Eusebius to ground the Hebrew Bible in Greco-Roman historiography, the ubiquity of Nimrod the Persian in pre-Islamic sources suggests that this identification did not begin with the early Islamic historiographers.[105] In northern Mesopotamia, the connection between Nimrod and Persians was particularly strong. In a ninth-century collection of biographies of sixth- and seventh-century monks, Ishodenah of Basra included accounts of Qardagh, said to be from a "family of Persians of the house of Nimrod," and of Joseph of Hazza, a "Persian" from the village of Nimrod.[106] Settlements named after the mythical king in the region conform to a pattern common in the Iranian world, whereby aristocrats gave their names, frequently combined with the suffix –*abad*, "settled," to their residences and associated villages.[107] This identification of Joseph's village and the known settlement of Nimrodabad reinforce the evidence of the hagiographies for Nimrod's importance as an ancestor for men claiming Persian descent. As the preeminent mythical king and hero of a Mesopotamia that had been transformed into the heart of the Iranian Empire, Nimrod was assimilated into the Iranian historical tradition by the late Sasanian period at the latest, presumably in an effort to appropriate a figure who could rival those in the Iranian account of the primordial past. He became, alongside Darius III, a representative of the mythical Iranian historical tradition in northern Mesopotamia. Arbela and Karka, as foundations of Nimrod, became monuments to the melding of Iranian and Christian traditions, much as the shrine of the prophet Daniel at Susa also became a shrine of the Kayanian king Kay Husraw.[108]

The adjective *Persian* in these contexts refers, as we have seen, to those who traced their lineage to houses from the province of Fars. But northern Mesopotamian Persians who were Zoroastrian were likely also to have regarded themselves as ēr. Because ērīh is an ethnic conception whose parameters are sacred history, genealogy, and ethics, Iranianness and nobility are frequently intertwined in Zoroastrian sources (see chapter 1). In normal cases, only ēr could attain the highest ranks of nobility in the empire. Being Iranian was nevertheless not a precondition for laying claim to noble lineage, and elite anēr and agdēn could argue for their genealogical prestige to circumvent the question of their religious deficiencies.[109] In northern Mesopotamia, the hagiographers of the *History of Karka* and the *History of Mar Qardagh* avoided directly labeling the aristocratic houses ethnically, focusing instead on their specific genealogies, which combined Iranian and Assyrian elements. If Nimrod could be identified with one of the kings of Iranian mythical history, making him the father of the Assyrian lineage provided a link between the provincial and imperial traditions. The aristocracies of Karka and Arbela included, we should recall, men descended from the noble houses of Fars and from those of the Assyrians. In these hagiographers' invention of the past, both lineages were equally Iranian, that is, derived from the mythical-historical primordial and Iranian kings and their aristocratic associates, whom the royal and aristocratic dynasties of the Sasanian era succeeded. Although the Iranian Christian nobles were decidedly anēr, they were genealogically related to ēr.[110] Their lineages were worthy of recognition from their grander aristocratic peers. While the great Parthian houses were boasting of ancient lineages, which the court inscribed in the *Book of Kings*, the descents of bnai ḥere from ancient kings and aristocrats who represented a derivative branch of the Iranian royal genealogy were being recorded in writing and recited at the feasts of the martyrs at Karka and Melqi.

The implications of such potent lineages were, moreover, written on the body of Mar Qardagh. "Handsome in his appearance, large in build, and powerful in his body," the descendant of Nimrod and Sennacherib epitomized the ontologically superior status that men of ancient lineage were believed to have achieved.[111] Smbat Bagratuni, a leading military commander in the early seventh century, is described in almost identical terms.[112] In the course of the *History of Mar Qardagh,* the saint performs his manly valiance in contests of archery and polo and in a victorious military campaign against the Romans.[113] As Joel Walker has demonstrated on the basis of a masterly comparison of the text with Armenian and Iranian materials, the hagiographer made his subject conform precisely with the expectations of contemporary epic literature, "a cultural language of power."[114] In his hagiography, Mar Qardagh executes the same heroic deeds as mythical Kayanians, historical Sasanians, and their respective aristocratic collaborators, whose accomplishments in martial athletics were recorded in rock reliefs, inscriptions, silver bowls, and literature. These narrations of bow shots, hunts, and conquests point to the corporeal, performative dimensions of nobility. If a narrative of origins was the basis for claiming noble status, aristocrats were expected continually to demonstrate their physical superiority and their capacities expertly to fulfil the function of their class, namely military service. The noble body was as much a product of training as of the seed of its ancestors. These narratives were not engaged in imaginative self-representation. In the early seventh century, an aristocratic youth from Hazza in Adiabene was instructed in "the archery of the king of Persia" before being selected to serve Husraw II.[115] The bnai ḥere of northern Mesopotamia could have had their sons educated in martial arts to form men worthy of service in the retinues of the marzbān and naxwār of the region. Mar Qardagh provided a model for the combination of Christianity and aristocratic manly valiance that captured, validated, and communicated the aspirations of a late Sasanian class of Christian elites.

The immediate audience for these narratives was the Christian communities whose members congregated "in all their ranks" to commemorate the martyrs. Nobles who descended from Persian, Assyrian, or hybrid lineages gathered alongside one another in the company of subordinate populations to hear their ecclesiastical leaders recount reworked versions of their own histories. But if redeployed during the course of a cultic feast, these narratives could be introduced into the quotidian interactions of nobles great and middling, Christian and Zoroastrian. Tales of one's ancestors, as discussed above, were communicated orally, as men gave accounts of their pasts to position themselves vis-à-vis their peers. The primary context for such aristocratic sociability was the banquet, whether on festive or commonplace occasions, at which the recounting of epic tales was a basic form of entertainment. As we saw in the previous chapter, royal and aristocratic feasts were the institutional spaces in which elite hierarchies were continually reestablished. The feasts of the martyrs served as complementary spaces for the ritualized performance of status within Christian communities. But unlike the festivals of Nowruz or Mihragan, the Christian feasts included the recitation of texts—in the northern Mesopotamian cases, accounts of nobility delivered before communities that were segmented at the very moment of their congregation. The author of the *History of Mar Qardagh* explicitly evoked the culture of aristocratic banqueting, describing the histories of martyrs as "banquets for the holy church."[116] If individual aristocrats could have recounted such stories at the banquets of the worldly, the written nature of the hagiographical banquets suggests that these tales possessed the distinct authority of text. It was not only the status of the nobles that was displayed at the martyrs' feasts but also the texts themselves, as the authoritative witnesses validating the nobles' ancient and Christian histories. In the late Sasanian period, written accounts of noble origins increasingly authorized and gave shape to the oral tales that men told of themselves or heard recited on their behalf.

PROVING NOBILITY: WRITING AND RECOGNITION

Written accounts came to eclipse oral tales as vehicles for the communication of authoritative history in the sixth and early seventh centuries, as the Iranian court began to compile an official history of the dynasty and its allied aristocratic houses from their origins in the primordial past to the present, the so-called *Book of Kings*. It would be more accurate, as Timothy Greenwood has recently argued on the basis of Armenian versions, to speak of books in the plural, since the court continually revised its accounts of both mythical and historical periods according to the particular circumstances in which the dynasty found itself.[117] Although a precise date for the first composition of a *Book of Kings* at court remains elusive, references to royal histories in sixth-century sources, such as the Roman historian Agathias, suggest that the court was already disseminating such texts during the reign of Kawad I and possibly earlier.[118] The surviving narratives of mythical-historical dynasties encountering hostile enemies from the steppes mirror the political circumstances of fifth, sixth, and early seventh-century Sasanians facing the Huns and the Turks.[119] At the same time as written mythical histories were being produced, their Avestan sources were being transcribed in writing, an innovation that required the invention of a new script and the translation of the corpus into Middle Persian.[120] The Avesta continued to be recited orally, but an official text could be used to test and regulate its interpretation and to make available its accounts to literary specialists, such as the historiographers at court who composed—and recomposed—the *Book of Kings*. As noted above, the royal histories featured the great aristocratic houses as the associates of the kings of kings and traced their lineages from the primordial past. In this respect, the *Book of Kings,* Armenian histories, and northern Mesopotamian hagiographies all shared a common purpose, despite their disparate authors, audiences, genres, and overall content. Whether the compositions of Christians or Zoroastrians, written accounts of mythical history in the late Sasanian period served to document the antiquity of aristocratic lineages in textual form.

This novel enthusiasm for textual evidence of nobility emerged against the backdrop of lingering anxieties concerning the stability of the social order in the aftermath of the Mazdakite revolt.[121] During the first part of his reign (488–96), Kawad embarked on an experiment in the Iranian economy of reproduction, embracing the view that women should be held in common, sexually available to men in general rather than just to specific husbands. Wife sharing was an outgrowth of the same Zoroastrian juridical thinking that had generated the institutions of stūrīh and temporary marriage.[122] The royal promotion of the institution has been represented often as an attempt to weaken the ability of the aristocracy to preserve its lineages, even as the desperate bid of an embattled king of kings to liberate himself from a constraining aristocracy.[123] The patrilineal principles that governed elite reproduction, however, held that the father, not the mother, was the determinant of personhood, leaving the identity of the latter at least theoretically irrelevant to the perpetuation of the lineage. Kawad's interest in sharing the sexual potential of women was not necessarily antiaristocratic. It was nevertheless the starting point for the revolutionary thought of the Zoroastrian exegete Mazdak, who, in the first decades of the sixth century, developed an alternative vision of the social order based on the communal sharing of property and women.[124] He took the idea of communal property from a deviant exegete of the third century, Zaradusht of Fasa, whose views were apparently prevalent in late Sasanian northern Mesopotamia, indeed at Karka.[125] Unlike Kawad, Mazdak expressly intended to dismantle the hierarchies of nobles and subordinates through which imperial institutions were organized, and his followers appear to have rebelled against the court. The scope of the revolt is unclear, but as chapter 1 notes, Mazdak was sufficiently influential for Husraw I to repress his followers violently and for Zoroastrian religious professionals to produce extensive polemics against this advocate of the undoing of Iran.

Regardless of the practical consequences of the Mazdakite revolt, its envisioning of an alternative order for Ērānšahr in cosmological terms indicates that skepticism concerning the legitimacy of aristocratic authority was not unknown even in Zoroastrian scholarly circles. More consequential for Iranian society than the violence of either the rebels or Husraw I's suppression were the efforts of the court to establish aristocratic authority on a more stable footing. The *Letter of Tansar* describes, through an apology for the paradigmatic figure of the first king of kings, late Sasanian attempts to repair aristocratic hierarchies that had undergone "degradation" (*tahjīn*). Ardashir I "established a visible and general distinction between men of noble birth [*ahl-e darajāt*] and common people," ordaining particular clothes, houses, and place settings for particular grades of nobility, forbidding intermarriage between nobles and nonnobles, and recording noble ranks in the royal archives.[126] Late Sasanian rulers developed an ideology of the poor and of reciprocity between the powerful and the poor.[127] Husraw I represented his administrative reforms as palliative measures intended to unburden the poor of their oppressions. He claimed to have established the ideal, reciprocal relationship between the powerful and the poor and to have instituted judges and mowbed—the "advocates of the poor" (*driyōšān jādag-gōw*)—to monitor their relations.[128] With their focus on upholding aristocratic authority in their communities, the northern Mesopotamian hagiographers of the *History of Karka* and the *History of Mar Qadargh* were implicitly participants in the same imperial project of reinforcing the boundaries between nobles and commoners.

The author of the *History of Karka*, indeed, explicitly invoked the discourse of the court. The late fourth-century bishop of Karka Isaac, the hagiographer reminded the audience of the text, had eradicated the teachings of Zaradusht, on which Mazdak depended, from the city.[129] Isaac's successors therefore stood in the tradition of militant opposition to the deviant Zoroastrian school of thought that had so upset the stability of the empire. The ecclesiastical leaders of Karka also acknowledged the importance of the "books and archives" that the *Letter of Tansar* reports had been newly established to record nobles and their ranks.[130] The names of the aforementioned five families that Darius III had legendarily deported from Istakhr to Karka were inscribed in the royal "archives" (*beit 'arke*).[131] The *History of Karka* not only confirms the testimony of the *Letter of Tansar* but also demonstrates that provincial elites were attentive to the records of nobility that the court maintained. They were also aware of the distinction between nobles from the genealogically prestigious city of Istakhr, whose mythical-historical origins the court had documented, and nobles whose origins the court had not recorded or validated. The references to a royal archive of lineages raise the question of how an aristocratic house—of, for example, lesser bnai here—proved its nobility in a political culture that was beginning to use official records to authenticate the origin accounts underpinning claims to elite status. The great bulk of the nobles at Karka and, presumably, Arbela could not have found their names in the court's archives of nobles. They will have had to prove their nobility on the basis of evidence that their peers could evaluate and recognize as authoritative. If the oral tales of the gōsān were no longer sufficient vehicles for claims of an ancient, manful lineage, written texts akin to the documents preserved in the "books and archives of the court" were needed. It is in the context of this dilemma that the authors of the *History of Karka* and the *History of Mar Qardagh* adapted their ancient-history sections—otherwise anomalous in East Syrian literature—to the imperatives of the late Sasanian court. Christian elites no longer had to rely on oral tales to demonstrate their nobility but could now provide textual evidence of their aristocratic ancestry.

The problem of recognition nevertheless remains. Could Zoroastrians have found texts that were composed in provincial languages and describe martyrs persecuted at the hands of mowbed compelling as sources of aristocratic history? A passage from the tenth-century *History of the Albanians* shows how a work of Christian hagiographical literature could serve as historical evidence of an ancient lineage. The compiler of this history, like the transmitters of the *Book of Kings*, drew on written accounts from late Sasanian Caucasian Albania.[132] A key staging ground for campaigns against the Huns and the Turks of the southern Russian steppes, the province was as militarily strategic and culturally diverse as northern Mesopotamia.[133] Here too, Iranian great nobles from the imperial core came to collaborate with Christian provincial aristocracies in the fifth, sixth, and early seventh centuries.[134] The Armenian-writing aristocrats of Albania also had to prove their claims of nobility. The account preserved in the *History of the Albanians* retrojects the debate on their status into the fourth century, when Shapur III (r. 383–88) reportedly initiated an investigation to determine which men should be entrusted with the ranks and honors of imperial authority. At a banquet where he convened men from all the great lineages, Shapur expressed doubts concerning the Armenian nobles, who lacked ērīh:

> I am well acquainted with the true Pahlavis among the Persians and Parthians and the order of precedence of these nobles, but I have been unable to discover anything concerning the noble family of Armen and their order of precedence either from my royal ancestors or from books. You nakharars of Armenia are faced with a choice of two things: either you show me an ancient book giving the degree and rank of each house, whereupon you shall again receive from us your outstanding positions of honor, or, if you cannot bring this to the eyes of our Iranian [*arya*] assembly, we shall bestow your highly placed cushion, honors, house, earth, and water and all your possessions upon Iranian noblemen.[135]

The scenario so imagined was set at the paradigmatic site in time and space at which a man was measured: the courtly banquet. The Armenians were compared in genealogical terms with their great noble counterparts with origins in Fars or Parthia and were to be accorded honors, offices, and even lands on the basis of their ability to prove their ancestral relationship with the Iranians.

To satisfy the demand of the king of kings for textual evidence, the Armenian nobles supplied the *History of the Armenians* of Agatangełos, which was promptly translated at court into Middle Persian. When Shapur discovered the name of Ardashir, the first Sasanian, in the text, he restored the Armenians to their positions in the imperial hierarchy of noblemen. Purportedly a description of a late fourth-century encounter between the court and provincial nobles, this narrative reveals what the Armenian nobles of Albania believed that texts could accomplish in the late Sasanian period. The history of Agatangełos is a product of the fifth century, and this account must have postdated its composition. From the perspective of late Sasanian Albania, a work of hagiographical history could be deployed in the context of a royal banquet to support claims of noble status: neither the Christian character of the work nor its language of composition would be an obstacle to its reception by the court. Nevertheless, Agatangełos's *History of the Armenians* was a curious choice. This earliest Armenian ecclesiastical history is an account of Armenian hostility toward the Sasanians, specifically King Khosrov's resistance to Ardashir I.[136] But if it does not overlook occasions of antagonism between Armenian and Sasanian dynasties, its narratives record the Parthian lineages of the Caucasian Armenian noble houses. What the *History of the Armenians* provided these nobles with was evidence that their houses were linked genealogically and historically with those of Persians and Parthians, despite their self-evident cultural differences. It was the literary demonstration of genealogical prestige and shared history that earned the non-Zoroastrian and non-Iranian nobles of Caucasian Albania recognition as worthy of privilege and brought them palpable perquisites of power, namely positions in the martial hierarchy and endowments of land.

To extend the network of aristocratic relationships through which the resources of the empire were channeled, the late Sasanians, like the imagined Shapur III in the above episode, sought out men whose genealogical and historical interconnectedness with their own mythical-historical ancestors could be proved. And as the court worked to put its mythical histories into writing, texts became a privileged form of evidence. Beyond the *History of the Armenians*, there are strong signs that the court took an interest in alternative historiographical traditions, such as the Hebrew Bible and the *History of Alexander*.[137] This was a multilingual, intellectually open court that prided itself on its cosmopolitanism, hosting Roman philosophers, Indian sages, and Jewish and Christian religious professionals from within the empire. The presentation and translation of an Armenian history—and, by extension, the products of other provincial literary cultures—is entirely in keeping with its known tendencies. The introduction of writing into Iranian political culture thus opened possibilities for those with access to novel sources of historiography, especially Christian literary specialists who could tap into pan–Mediterranean literary networks. East Syrian and Armenian hagiohistoriographers seized the opportunity with zeal, composing histories of provincial Christian noble houses that fused Christian, Hellenistic, and Iranian sources and modes of representation to document their lineages and heroic deeds. As courtly histories validated the pasts of the greatest houses, hagiographies came to support the claims of equally ancient and intertwined genealogies of their lessers. Such texts did not have to be read or translated to reinforce the positions of their protagonists. Even if the *History of Karka* and the *History of Mar Qardagh* were submitted to the banquets of neither the kings of kings nor the great nobles in the same manner as the history of Agatangelos purportedly was, the inscription of their accounts on parchment placed in the archives of their authors' respective bishoprics lent the authority of writing to the oral boasts of northern Mesopotamian bnai here.

Despite the hagiographers' concerted construction of accounts connecting imperial and provincial pasts in the domain of aristocratic genealogy, their works remain martyrologies, with narrative concerns and functions at variance with those of the compilers and consumers of royal historiography. The primary objective of such a narrative was to commemorate the violent deaths of men and women who perished for their faith, who were the victims of the very kings with whose histories the nobles identified. There is a dissonance in these works between demonstrating how Christians could be included in imperial networks and remembering their violent exclusion at the hands of Zoroastrian generals, religious professionals, and kings of kings, the leading representatives of Iran. The hagiographers gave written expression to commonalities between Christian and Zoroastrian nobles in the literary form of martyrology, which is intended primarily to articulate religious difference. Paradoxes of this kind, however, are characteristic of the literary production of ecclesiastical leaders whose authority depended as much on their self-positioning within social, economic, and political structures as on their ascetic rejection of worldly power, as the previous chapter shows. We should not underestimate the ability of ancient persons to disentangle these narratives and to draw upon different aspects of a text according to the circumstances. The interest of the hagiographers in documenting genealogies suggests that the *History of Karka* and the *History of Mar Qardagh* were designed to provide textual proof of nobility in settings beyond the martyrological celebration. And the *History of the Albanians* shows that in the view of late Sasanian provincial nobles, their grander counterparts could receive a Christian hagiohistoriographical text as evidence of the former's descent from authoritative lineages. To understand the role of ecclesiastical leaders as the mediators of such claims, we need to locate these writings and their ritual performances in the urban contexts that their authors emphasized.

ARISTOCRATIC CITIES

Northern Mesopotamian aristocrats were, according to the hagiographers of the *History of Karka* and the *History of Mar Qardagh*, representatives not only of their houses but also of their cities. The *History of Karka* enlists the ruins of Karka and its environs as a means of proving the antiquity of the noble lineages of its houses, describing its walls, palaces, streets, and markets—not implausibly—as constructions of the ancient kings who had established their foundations. If the work was recited during the feast of the martyrs on the tell of Beit Teta, a specifically Christian sacred site, its opening lines turned the attention of the audience toward the monuments of the city, clearly visible from the neighboring tell as an amalgam of walls and buildings. Among the structures that stood within the lines of sight of the late Sasanian auditors were Assyrian, Achaemenian, and Seleucid constructions. Esarhaddon/Sargon established two buildings within the city, including the "house of the kingdom of Sargon" (*beit d-malkuta d-sargon*), and a "small wall" (*šura za'ura*) and a "fortress" (*ḥesna*).[138] The temple of idols for the worship of an eagle and a lion that the Neo-Assyrian king was believed to have constructed continued to attract devotees in the late Sasanian period.[139] Darius III reportedly expanded the fortifications and built houses and a fire temple (*beit nura*). The Hellenistic ruler Seleucus Nikator, however, was supposed to have had the greatest impact on the cityscape. He erected a robust wall with sixty-five towers and two gates, one of which retained an inscription attesting to its antiquity.[140] With the addition of a royal palace, squares, and streets, Karka gained attributes of a Hellenistic city. The self-evidently ancient monuments surrounding the audience of the *History of Karka* provided incontrovertible proof of the singularly ancient origins of the noble houses whose histories the hagiographer interwove with ruins. In this respect, the author participated in an empire-wide process of rooting claims of mythical-historical ancestors in monuments perceived to have been their constructions.[141] At the same time, the *History of Karka* identified aristocrats with a city in an entirely novel way.

In addition to having their nobility affirmed, the aristocrats who attended these feasts took on a role as members of the larger community of the *karkaye*, "inhabitants of Karka."[142] If they emphasized the distinction of nobles from others throughout their texts, the hagiographers of northern Mesopotamia simultaneously affiliated aristocrats horizontally with their fellow urban inhabitants. In the formulation "the city of Arbela of the Assyrians," the *History of Mar Qardagh* similarly identifies the aristocracy with the city.[143] Such a connection was unusual in Iranian society and political culture in late antiquity. The aristocratic houses of Iran whose networks the middling nobles of northern Mesopotamia aspired to join were based in rural estates and imagined their lineages as inextricable from their lands.[144] The aristocrats of late Sasanian northern Mesopotamia also maintained rural lands and estates, as we have seen, whose importance the *History of Karka* and the *History of Mar Qardagh* both emphasize. But the continued centrality of the rural estate to the economic strategies and cultural practices of landed elites did not preclude them from adopting new urban roles. The nature and functions of the Sasanian city remain poorly documented and accordingly little studied. Cities nevertheless seem to have gained importance as administrative centers, at least in some regions, especially in the course of the reforms of Husraw I.[145] Great noble houses were known to have resided in Seleucia-Ctesiphon, Nisibis, Karka, and other cities while maintaining ancestral estates in the hinterlands of these cities or elsewhere in the empire.[146] The sigillographic evidence of the late Sasanian period shows that fiscal, judicial, and religious officials were generally based in cities with regional circumscriptions.[147] Major urban centers expanded thanks to the imperial intensification characteristic of the sixth century and at the expense of more modest towns and villages, as the surveys of Robert McC. Adams have demonstrated.[148] Cities in the late Sasanian period were becoming arenas as important for the aristocratic pursuit of power and status as the rural estates with which noble houses were traditionally associated.

The contemporaneous mobilization of the ancient histories and landscapes of Arbela and Karka contributed to this reshaping of the role of the city in Iranian political culture. For the author of the *History of Karka* in particular, the city was the primary locus of political authority. The account of ancient kings endowing Karka with urban infrastructure and ruling families authenticated the power of late Sasanian noble houses only insofar as they accepted their place in a reimagined city. Thanks to the Assyrians, Karka took on the capacity to grant political authority. The king who built the city intended its inhabitants to rule over its hinterlands: "Sargon ordered that the city be built in his name for leadership . . . [and] that the entire land be subject to him as if to a master."[149] The land in question was Beit Garmai, a subkingdom of the Assyrians whose limits were defined under Esarhaddon/Sargon: "From the Zab River to the Tigris River, from the Tigris River as far as the mountain called Awrok, [from] the mountain as far as the river Aterqon, which is also called Turmara, as far as the land of Lareb and the mountain of Sharan and as far as the lesser Zab."[150] Authority over the region extending from the Zab to the upland fringes of the Diyala and from the Tigris to the Zagros was invested in Karka and its inhabitants. The "subjugation" that Esarhaddon/Sargon established evokes the language widely used in northern Mesopotamian Syriac literature to characterize relations between aristocrats and laboring populations. The Assyrian was therefore supposed to have made the inhabitants of Karka the lords and masters of Beit Garmai. In a reversal of traditional Iranian social and political roles, to be an aristocrat was to reside in the city. In the same way, the *History of Mar Qardagh* precisely defines the territory over which its namesake noble wielded authority: "[Shapur II] made him *bidaxš* and marzbān [over the land] from the Tormara River up unto the city of Nisibis."[151] Arbela, the hagiographer asserted, was to control the entirety of Adiabene.

Such claims, however, were grandiloquent. Karka, after all, had had to vie with the otherwise unknown, apparently humble settlements of Hirbet Glal and Shahrgard to become the center of imperial authority and the seat of the suzerain bishop.[152] If we have thus far reproduced the text's description of Karka as a "city," *mdinta*, neither the ancient tell nor its Hellenistic features were sufficient to merit such a designation or the domination over other provincial centers that the author arrogated to its inhabitants.[153] The so-called city could perhaps distinguish itself only with difficulty from the settlements—also called cities in contemporaneous sources—that the *History of Karka* rendered subordinate to it.[154] There were, as we have noted, the Iranian aristocrats and officials residing within its confines, and an artisanal quarter for the production of commodities along the lines of those in the more familiar centers in Khuzestan.[155] But until excavations or surveys of the Sasanian period in the region appear, reconstructing the hierarchical relations among these settlements will remain simply a desideratum.[156] In the interim, a recent survey of the western bank of the Tigris, including Nineveh and its hinterland, provides a plausible counterpoint to the *History of Karka*'s aspirational account. Nineveh enjoyed the prestige of a bishopric in a strategic location at a ford of the Tigris, and the excavation of ornately decorated Sasanian helmets points to its importance in the military administration.[157] The late Sasanian foundation of Shahrabad, approximately forty kilometers (twenty-five miles) to the north, nevertheless surpassed this ancient city in size and administrative importance.[158] Moreover, a series of middling settlements only marginally smaller than Nineveh or Shahrabad appear to have served administrative functions, rivaling the more prominent centers. A survey of the eastern Jazira has unveiled a landscape of roughly equivalent settlements that stands in contrast to the representation of their sees as cities sovereign over their regions in the Christian sources that emerged from the metropolitan bishoprics of Nineveh, Arbela, Nisibis, and Karka.[159]

The *History of Karka* author was therefore creating a political imaginary rather than describing the position of Karka in relation to its neighbors. The *History of Mar Qardagh* similarly vaunts Arbela at the expense of the nearby settlement of Hazza, known to have been at least as consequential politically in the late Sasanian period.[160] In both cases, settlements with ancient ruins and metropolitan bishoprics asserted their superiority over sites that possessed administrative importance but lacked cultural distinction. The hagiographies of northern Mesopotamia thus suggest that administrative reforms of the sixth century precipitated competition among cities—or, perhaps more accurately, among villages and towns—for more powerful positions in the fiscal networks that the court was consolidating. The seal of an āmārgar in charge of both Beit Garmai / Garmegān and Adiabene/Nōd-Ardaxšīragān for example, highlights the fluid, shifting character of administrative structures and civic hierarchies.[161] What made a city worthy of the recognition of the Iranian authorities? The *Cities of Iran*, a text that preserves late Sasanian political geography in courtly views of the empire's urban centers, evaluates cities in terms of the selfsame mythical-historical categories with which the court measured men. Kayanian and Sasanian kings of kings, the heroes of Iranian epics, and the Achaemenian Darius were the most industrious founders of cities, from Herat and Samarqand to Nisibis and Ctesiphon.[162] This courtly compilation also acknowledges Alexander the Great as the important builder of the Iranian cities of Merv and Isfahan.[163] Neither Karka nor Arbela features in the text, a reminder of their modest significance in late Sasanian political culture.[164] The northern Mesopotamian cities that do appear in the *Cities of Iran* are accorded distinctly Iranian origins: A mythical hero, Gurāzak ī Gēpakān, built Nisibis. Neither Nimrod nor

Seleucus but rather Narseh the Parthian was the founder of the Roman city of Edessa. An otherwise unknown Sasanian dynast, Peroz the son of Shapur, established Nineveh.[165] The fusing of Assyrian and Iranian pasts that the hagiographers accomplished thus had significance for civic and aristocratic histories. Karka and Arbela could be represented as Iranian—or Hellenistic—foundations whose histories were as grand as those of Nineveh and Nisibis. In this respect, the activities of hagiographers with access to the literary resources of the major bishoprics might have allowed Karka and Arbela to distinguish themselves from competing settlements in their respective regions.

These cities gained ascendancy at least in ecclesiastical, if not imperial, politics in the late Sasanian period. The feast of the martyrs at Karka was also a celebration of its bishop's domination of the ecclesiastical leaders of Beit Garmai's other centers. According to the *History of Karka*, the preeminence of this bishop was a comparatively recent achievement. When the bishop of Shahrgard purportedly refused to present himself as the leader of the Christians of the region before Iranian authorities, out of fear of violence, during the reign of Yazdgird II, a boy from Karka exhorted him to remain steadfast in the faith. The boy was appointed the metropolitan bishop of Beit Garmai for his courage, and the office was henceforth invested in the representatives of his city. This legendary tale was designed, in the context of the feast, to humiliate the ecclesiastical authorities of Shahrgard, for they were compelled to attend the commemoration of the martyrs together with the other bishops rendered subordinate to Karka in the fifth or sixth century. The catholicos of the Church of the East and the bishops of Adiabene and Beit Garmai had signed a contract, preserved in the episcopal archive, that required the subordinate bishops, under the threat of excommunication, to attend the feast.[166] The coercion needed to convince the ecclesiastical leaders of the rival settlements of Hirbet Glal and Shahrgard suggests their disrespect of their neighbor's ambitions, not without justification. These bishoprics regarded themselves as cities whose apostolic origins were no less distinguished than those of their metropolitanate.[167] The presence of so many great noble houses and high officials at Karka seems to indicate that the leading role of the city in the imperial administration precipitated its rise in the ecclesiastical hierarchy. An understanding of the precise relationships among the settlements of Beit Garmai will, however, require an archaeological basis. The position of the bishop of Arbela vis-à-vis his peers in Adiabene was more secure, but his city's administrative role was more ambiguous, as Hazza remained the aristocratic center. In the domains of civic and aristocratic history, the *History of Mar Qardagh* responded to the literary model that its metropolitan counterpart produced, with a view to achieving a similarly predominant position over the settlements of Adiabene.

The reimagining of cities as the loci of power wielded over their hinterlands could reinforce the authority of aristocrats and bishops alike. Through the interweaving of aristocratic, civic, and ecclesiastical histories, the hagiographers identified the Christian aristocracies with urban bishoprics.[168] As we have seen, the bishops whose genealogies the *History of Karka* outlines were nobles. If they abandoned the wealth of their houses, they retained their genealogical distinctions, social networks, and, in a word, aristocratic authority. Asceticism was, moreover, the exception rather than the rule. The *History of Mar Qardagh* includes no bishops in its narrative, but the known leaders of late Sasanian Arbela were members of the region's noble houses, such as Ishoyahb—the best documented leader of the Church of the East—who was the bishop of Nineveh and the metropolitan of Arbela before becoming the patriarch. He is a paradigmatic example of an ascetic bishop who could mobilize aristocratic resources in the service of the church.[169] But if the authority of the bnai ḥere extended across villages, rural estates, and cities, the bishops focused on what the hagiographers established as the symbolic centers of elite, imperial power in northern Mesopotamia. From the first, legendary second-century bishop, Theocritus, the bishops of Karka adorned the city with churches decorated with silk and gold, as well as the hospital, or *xenodocheion*, that the bishop Shapur Braz constructed in the early fifth century. In their roles as builders of monuments in the city, these bishops continued the work of making Karka into "Karka the great" that Esarhaddon/Sargon, Darius, and Seleucus Nikator had begun. The archaeology of the city with which the *History of Karka* commences is of a piece with its subsequent accounts of bishops and martyrs. If the valiance of martyrs continued the traditions of ancient aristocracies, the urban patronage of the bishops continued the traditions of ancient kings. The bishops under whose authority the cults at Karka and Arbela were orchestrated stood at the center of symbolic constructions of community that exalted the powers of the region's aristocracies. The texts and rituals that placed bishops at the head of communities simultaneously religious and civic long outlived the noble houses on whose behalf they were originally produced.[170]

CONCLUSION

The views from the tells of Beit Teta and Melqi fundamentally alter our understanding of the late Sasanian political landscape. The intensification of imperial rule characteristic of the period gave rise to the remarkable literary creativity of East Syrian authors in northern Mesopotamian cities, who made use of Greek historiography, Iranian mythical histories, and their own hagiographical tradition to produce texts that are simultaneous histories of ancient kings, saints, cities, and aristocrats. Histories of Sennacherib, Seth Richardson has argued, were a free-floating resource with which provincial imperial elites could define the terms of their loyalty to their kings while articulating their autonomy.[171] The hagiographical turn to ancient history—and to Sennacherib in particular—was one such act of political self-definition by the ecclesiastical leaders of northern Mesopotamia. In their melding of three literary traditions, the texts recited at the feasts of the martyrs fuse Christian and Iranian modes of self-representation that historians have often considered incompatible for an audience of East Syrian aristocrats who routinely cooperated with Zoroastrian elites in the project of empire. The nobles of Karka and Arbela will have departed from these annual feasts acutely aware of the distinctive Christian pasts of these cities, which include martyrs whom tyrannical kings of kings had slain and saintly bishops and aristocrats who had endowed their churches, shrines, and monasteries. These nobles will have left with an awareness of the fundamental untruths of Zoroastrianism and, if they had been at Melqi, a set of arguments to make against the false religion. They will have heard stories of the peculiarly distinguished Mesopotamian, Iranian, and Hellenistic kings and kingdoms that had adorned their cities long before the Sasanians, stories of a kind that Iranian texts such as the *Cities of Iran* and the *Wonders of Sistan* have preserved. But in the very act of recalling their difference they asserted their commonalities with the Zoroastrian nobles of the region and across the empire. Whether of Mesopotamian or Persian lineage, they shared an ancestor in Nimrod. They were as capable of the manful arts of cavalry warfare as their Iranian and Armenian counterparts. They ruled over the hinterlands of the cities whose monuments constituted icons of their authority in league with the Zoroastrian noble houses, which were absent from the feasts of the martyrs. Bnai ḥere of northern Mesopotamia became simultaneously wholly Christian and wholly noble at these tells, as their ecclesiastical leaders publicly acknowledged the compatibility of the distinct practices and self-conceptions that accompanied the two social roles. The documentation of their lineages on the basis of archival research, such as the study of the *Chronicle* of Eusebius, placed their aristocratic identities on solid, textual ground. The cults of the saints at Karka and Arbela served as an institutional vehicle for the integration of Christian elites into Iranian political culture. As we shift our perspective from the tells of northern Mesopotamia to the palaces of Seleucia-Ctesiphon in the following chapter, the interdependence of the actions of comparatively humble hagiographers and kings of kings to create a synergy between Christian and Iranian institutions will become plain.

5

The Christian Symbolics of Power in a Zoroastrian Empire

CHRISTIAN KINGS OF KINGS?

In the eyes of Christians in both the Iranian and the Roman Empire, Zoroastrian kings of kings became Christian in the late Sasanian period. The arrival of Husraw II Aparwez at the court of the Roman emperor Maurice in Constantinople in 590 as a refugee from the rebellion of Wahram Chobin inspired reports of the conversion of the Sasanian that were not easily put to rest.[1] To cement an alliance between their two dynasties, Maurice adopted Husraw II as his son through a rite of *adoptio per arma* that normally presumed the Christian identity of its participants.[2] At the time, Pope Gregory the Great accurately assessed the situation: "I lament that the emperor [*imperatorem*] of the Persians was not converted" despite the best efforts of the leading Roman bishops.[3] But seventh-century historiographers from Iranian Armenia to post-Roman Frankia preserved accounts of the king of kings' conversion to Christianity, showing how widely narratives of the Christianized Sasanian dynasty circulated during his reign.[4] He was, moreover, not the first Sasanian to convert, according to Christian writers. In the *History of Pseudo-Sebeos*, a compilation of a late seventh-century Armenian historiographer, Husraw I Anushirvan recognizes the truth of the Christian faith, accepts baptism, and partakes of Holy Communion immediately before his death.[5] In a parallel strain of Roman historiography, the seventh-century Egyptian chronicler John of Nikiu preserved an account of the baptism of Husraw I that is modeled on Christian narratives of the conversion of Constantine the Great, suggesting that some Romans believed a Sasanian could occupy the position of legitimate Christian ruler, once the exclusive preserve of the emperors.[6] Building on accounts of the Magi of the New

Testament, who brought the good news of Christ to the East, Christian authors in the Iranian world claimed—with notable indifference to chronology—that these wise men had converted the founder of the Sasanian dynasty, Ardashir I.[7] In the imaginations of Christians from across the Mediterranean and the Middle East, the Sasanians came to constitute a dynasty of believers.

Such accounts were historically baseless. The late Sasanians were unwavering advocates of the religion that provided the ideological and infrastructural foundations of their empire. In the media that the Iranian court produced to articulate its rule—coins, silver plates, mythical histories—the Sasanian commitment to Zoroastrianism, which Ardashir had established, remained consistent until the fall of the dynasty. The silver coinage constitutes the best contemporaneous evidence for courtly ideological developments, as drachms produced at regional mints with centrally controlled, royally designed dies communicated a uniform message to the kings of kings' subjects who handled silver. Shifts in their symbolism or rhetoric attest to innovations in imperial ideology of consequence for aristocrats of all strata and of all regions. The modifications that the court of Husraw II made to the silver coinage only emphasize the empire's dependence on Zoroastrian deities, in particular Wahram, the deliverer of victory, placed on coins after the 591 defeat of Wahram Chobin, and the court's possession of xwarrah, the supernatural force that accompanied legitimate rulers.[8] There are signs of Christianity's heightened significance for the court in a small collection of silver drachms with crosses engraved on their fringes.[9] But these were merely additions to the prevailing Zoroastrian imagery, perhaps the modifications of provincial mints with or without courtly permission. The examples are few and their chronological frame is narrow, suggesting that either these issues were unpopular or the court forbade their production. Along with the coinage, the literary texts that the court produced, principally histories and advice literature, and the stone sculptures of Husraw II at Taq-e Bustan (see chapter 2) make the supremacy of the Zoroastrian ideology of empire unambiguous.[10] The primary modalities of self-representation that the late Sasanians deployed, in the tradition of their predecessors, drew exclusively on the Zoroastrian framework of cosmological kingship. This is entirely in keeping with what both Iranian and Roman sources—apart from the abovementioned accounts—report of the kings of kings. The regime of Husraw II was no less Zoroastrian than those of his predecessors.

Narratives of the Christianization of the Sasanians nevertheless gained traction among Christians who experienced the favors of the king of kings. Husraw II associated himself with Christian powers—both worldly and supernatural—and their institutions to an unprecedented degree. He depended, in the first instance, on Roman Christian forces to take the throne. Crowned suddenly as an alternative to his father, Ohrmazd IV, in 590, he fled the army of the usurper Wahram Chobin, which would have overwhelmed him at Seleucia-Ctesiphon.[11] Romans lent the king of kings forces, which allowed him to defeat the rebel and to restore the Sasanian dynasty. An intimate relationship between Christian Rome and Husraw II ensued, leading the king of kings, in the first decades of the seventh century, to consider himself capable of conquering the Roman Empire and incorporating its lands into Iran. The provinces of the Christian Roman Near East were indeed, for anywhere from a decade to a quarter of a century, components of the Iranian Empire, until the deposition and execution of the king of kings in 628 in the face of the successful campaigns of the emperor Heraclius (r. 610–41) against Iran.[12] But Husraw II's interactions with Christianity went well beyond his relations with the Roman emperors and their subjects. He married two Christian wives, one a Roman, Maria, and another a Mesopotamian, Shirin.[13] He constructed several prominent churches and contributed to the erection of many more.[14] Along the royal road on the way to the monuments commemorating his victories, including Taq-e Bustan at Bisutun, he had a monastery built at Qasr-e Shirin.[15] And as we will examine in detail, he allied himself with a Christian saint and a living holy man, took the True Cross into the Iranian court's possession, and performed according to the expectations of a Christian ruler in the conquered Roman territories. On account of these acts, Christians of different sectarian affiliations in both the Roman and the Iranian Empire came to regard him as a Christian king of kings. At the same time, his court insisted on the inseparability of the Zoroastrian religion and Iranian kingship.

This chapter first traces Husraw II's innovative use of Christian symbols to represent his rule, then turns to the acts through which the king of kings and his court communicated the supremacy of an imperial Zoroastrianism undiminished by the admixture of Christian saints and crosses and the empire's ideological apparatus. The same king of kings who cultivated a personal relationship with Christ and his saints also wished to be known for policing with the sword the boundary between the Good Religion and an inferior religion, Christianity. The apparent paradox of a ruler simultaneously elevating and suppressing Christianity is the main topic of this chapter. Both actions, it argues, worked to stabilize relations between the elites of the different religions in ways that allowed Husraw II to realize his expansionist ambitions. To return to a theme of chapter 1, a hierarchical conception of humans and their religions provided the basis for cross-cultural symbolic experimentation and its counterpart, cross-cultural collaboration in an imperial political project.

THE THRONE OF OHRMAZD IV

During the reign of Ohrmazd IV (579–90), the court began to innovate models for the relationship between Zoroastrianism and Christianity. In a narrative preserved in al-Ṭabarī's *History of Prophets and Kings* (*Ta'rīkh al-rusul wa al-mulūk*) and the *Chronicle of Seert*, both of which draw upon the traditions of the *Book of Kings*

(*Xwadāy-nāmag*; see chapter 4), the king of kings articulates a vision of political community in which Christians provide indispensable supports for Sasanian rule. When certain Zoroastrian priests petitioned Ohrmazd IV to do some unspecified harm to Christians, he reportedly appealed to them to recognize the contributions of these unbelievers to the realization of Zoroastrian empire:

> Just as our royal throne cannot stand on its two front legs without the two back ones, our kingdom cannot stand or endure firmly if we cause the Christians and adherents of other faiths, who differ in belief from ourselves, to become hostile to us. So refrain from harming the Christians and become assiduous in good works, so that the Christians and the adherents of other faiths may see this, praise you for it, and feel themselves drawn toward your religion.[16]

The metaphor of the throne rendered Christianity one foundation of the empire, one of the four legs, without which the kingdom could not stand, of the royal throne.[17] In the Christian recension of al-Ṭabarī's tale, the *Chronicle of Seert* interprets the metaphor as stipulating the counterbalancing of religions that were, from the king of kings' perspective, of comparable status: "A throne has four legs and cannot stand on two inner legs without the two outside. Thus the Zoroastrian religion [*dīn al-majūs*] will not stand without an opponent [*maqāwim*]."[18] The term *opponent* corresponds with the Middle Persian *hamēmār*, whose semantic range encompasses positive and negative stances, from associate to antagonist.[19] The author of the East Syrian account of Ohrmazd's throne developed the metaphor to represent the upward mobility of his religion at court, from a subordinate position in relation to the Good Religion to one of parity as its—sometimes cooperative, sometimes competitive—counterpart.

There is, however, no question of an equivalence between Christianity and Zoroastrianism in the version of al-Ṭabarī, who, unlike al-Dīnawarī and some other early Islamic historiographers, disregarded Christian reworkings of the *Book of Kings*. Not only do the two front legs stand in a superior position, but the body of the king of kings on top of the throne was believed to join religion and kingship, to embody this twinship that was at the heart of the idea of Iran. Christians, in this political metaphor, could contribute to the operation of the empire without jeopardizing its Zoroastrian framework. The passage in al-Ṭabarī enjoins Zoroastrians to attend to the essential tasks that the Good Religion imposes on them, their good work, or *xwēškārīh*, rather than harm human resources crucial for the maintenance and extension of Sasanian structures of rule. If the report of Zoroastrians seeking to harm Christians betrays the anxieties of some religious specialists concerning increasingly powerful Christians and ecclesiastical institutions, the courtly authors of the throne metaphor articulated a new model of collaboration on the basis of the Zoroastrian conceptions of human difference and hierarchy discussed in chapter 1. Political life in anticipation of the cosmic restoration of the world would of necessity entail the coexistence and cooperation of humans who attained different measures of goodness. Even those unpracticed in the arts of the Good Religion were not entirely devoid of the capacity to do good work, and any viable political system would have to harness their efforts. What Ohrmazd IV's court formulated for the first time was a metaphor for such a state of mixture that recognized the vital importance of the activities of inferior humans, which also underpinned the authority of the throne, while pointing to the ultimate cosmic function of Zoroastrian kingship. The good work of the kings of kings and their subjects would, in time, bring all humans to the Good Religion. In the interim, all subjects, Christians included, should attend to their xwēškārīh.

The throne metaphor accurately represents the political situation of the late Sasanian period. In chapter 4 we saw how Christian elites became increasingly crucial components of the imperial administration. The reign of Husraw II was the apex of Christian aristocratic fortunes under the Sasanians, and Christian elites were ubiquitous in military and fiscal contexts during the age of the Islamic conquests.[20] Christian Armenian noble houses occupied some of the most strategic—and prestigious—military commands in the empire. During the rebellion of Wahram Chobin, a leading Armenian nakharar, Mushel Mamikonean, rejected the blandishments of the usurper, remaining loyal to the king of kings. His service earned him a place in the *Book of Kings* for abandoning his native land to campaign diligently on behalf of Husraw II, the first and only Christian aristocrat whom courtly historiographers commemorated.[21] Another Armenian, Smbat Bagratuni, rose to occupy the frontier commandery of Gorgan, perhaps the most contested and militarily important region of the empire. For his successes in the East, Husraw II appointed him the chief of the military administration in the Caucasus and established his noble house, the Bagratunids, as a cornerstone of Sasanian rule in the region.[22] Its fiscal administration reportedly came under the authority of the noble Yazdin whose northern Mesopotamian background we examined in the previous chapter. Even if Christian sources exaggerate the scope of his authority and activities, there can be no doubt that this East Syrian Christian was instrumental in organizing imperial revenues at a time when grandiose military campaigns put the fisc under enormous strain. Yazdin was important enough to be executed for political reasons in the late 620s. And after 609, in addition to the Christian aristocrats of the Iranian world, the Christian elites of the conquered Roman territories needed to be co-opted, to extend the empire's fiscal and military structures into lands that the Sasanians had never previously attempted to govern. The throne metaphor was as much a project to be realized as a reflection of late Sasanian circumstances.

The Christians whose authority to organize soldiers, scribes, and fellow aristocrats on their behalf the late Sasanians in general and Husraw II in particular depended on placed their confidence not only in the court but also in an assemblage of objects that channeled supernatural powers. In the course of the sixth century, Christ, the saints, and their relics came to participate more directly in political life in the Mediterranean world. Christian Roman emperors had long consulted holy men, patronized saints and their shrines, and regarded Christian supernatural forces as agents of empire. These unseen actors made themselves palpable through relics—either the bodies of saints or materials with which they had come into contact—and images. These objects were believed not merely to represent Christ or his saints but to make them physically present in the world. Relics and images came, not without controversy, to translate supernatural forces into mundane affairs.[23] The Mandylion of Edessa, a cloth on which Christ purportedly imprinted his face, provides a paradigmatic case of how a relic could act politically. During the campaign of Husraw I, this image of Christ prevented the Iranians from taking the city of Edessa, at least in late sixth-century reports.[24] In the following decades, Roman elites experimented with ways of enlisting the powers of relics and images, especially to motivate soldiers, a trend that culminated with the procession of an icon of the mother of God around Constantinople in 626 while the Iranians and Avars were besieging the city.[25] As we have seen repeatedly, the Christian communities of Iran tended rapidly to adopt the cultural innovations of their Mediterranean counterparts, and relics came to loom large in the political life of the Iranian Empire at the provincial level before reaching the imperial stage. Chapters 2 and 4 show how the presence of the saints, in their shrines and their bodies, contributed to the reshaping of Christian communities that facilitated their integration into the empire. But Christian sources of supernatural power could contribute more directly to Iranian imperialism.

Relics of the True Cross came to play a role in Iranian armies almost as soon as the Roman emperor Maurice dispatched an example to Sabrisho—then the bishop of Lashom in the region of Beit Garmai, before his 596 elevation to the patriarchate—as a sign of Roman-Iranian collaboration.[26] The gift marked a departure from Roman imperial efforts to monopolize the cult of the cross in Jerusalem and Constantinople, and thereafter the locus of Christian imperial power was increasingly detached from the Roman Empire.[27] At the beginning of the seventh century, an Armenian was reported to have uncovered a fragment of the True Cross on the body of a soldier on a battlefield in Gorgan.[28] Christians serving in Iranian armies, in this episode, drew strength from Christ by means of a relic of his cross, much as Roman soldiers did. This fragment, moreover, was granted to Smbat Bagratuni and his house. The aristocrat who secured some of Husraw II's most consequential victories did so with a relic of Christ's cross in his possession, an instrument of unparalleled potential for a military commander rallying Armenian Christian nakharars in defense of Iran. The idea that Christ would intervene through his cross on behalf of the Iranian Empire also appeared in contemporaneous northern Mesopotamian. Mar Qardagh, the legendary saint who features in chapter 4, is reported in the *History of Mar Qardagh* to have defended the city of Arbela and the surrounding region from an invasion of—Christian—Romans and Arabs by means of the cross. When he resumed the role of military commander, which he had abandoned together with the Good Religion, the noble saint sprinkled *ḥnana*—dust that had come into contact with saintly relics—on his horse and soldiers and "hung on his neck a cross of gold in which was fastened the Holy Wood of the Crucifixion of our Savior."[29] Thus equipped, Mar Qardagh decisively defeated the Romans and Arabs and expelled them from Iranian territory. To reinforce the origins of the power whereby the victory was obtained, the hagiographer had a holy man display "the glorious sign of the cross" before Mar Qardagh while saying, "Behold, my son, the great sign of your victory. Be strong and powerful because the Lord has handed over your enemies into your hands."[30] The sign by which Constantine—and his successors—had conquered now secured the victory of Iran over Rome, in the eyes of the Christian provincial elites of the Iranian Empire.

But if the historical Smbat Bagratuni was a loyal servant to the Sasanians in every respect, the legendary Mar Qardagh took his military victory on Iran's behalf as an opportunity to demolish the fire temples of his region. The Christian cross was, in his late Sasanian hagiographer's view, a symbol of his religion's triumph over the falsehoods of Zoroastrianism. Even if the True Cross could bring about an Iranian triumph over the Romans, Christians could continue to see their faith as defined in opposition to the Good Religion, which East Syrian Christians—unlike Zoroastrians including the Sasanians—sought to disassociate from an ideally secular royal power. Even if Zoroastrians recognized the fundamental place of Christianity in the empire, the vocal militancy of ecclesiastical leaders who employed saint's cults and their associated media as vehicles for anti-Zoroastrian polemics will have led even those Zoroastrians most favorably inclined toward Christians to question whether Christianity's symbols could help to rally elites in the service of the Iranian Empire. The vision of a Christianity allied with albeit subordinate to imperial Zoroastrianism, which the throne metaphor outlines, overestimates the ease with which Christian institutions could be made to complement the court's primary religious foundations. But with saints and relics beyond the state's control organizing human collectivities with or without Sasanian participation, the ideological work that the courtly authors of the throne metaphor undertook was indispensable.

The court could not render Christianity a foundation of the empire without also harnessing the supernatural powers to which its institutions offered access, and those forces were identified more often with Roman than with Iranian rulers. The symbols of Christianity—holy men, saints, and relics—were storehouses of supernatural potency that served a variety of political actors simultaneously: the architects of orthodox Christian communities, irrespective of their worldly sovereigns; Roman emperors; and, farther afield, the Christian monarchs of Ethiopia and the Caucasus.³¹ Rather than allow East Syrian leaders to retain a monopoly on the powers of Christ and his saints, Husraw II sought to channel their forces into the service of the Iranian Empire, to place the Sasanian throne on a more solid footing. Unlike his contemporaries who employed similar assemblages of sacred bodies and objects, this Zoroastrian ruler was vulnerable to opposition, from both Zoroastrians and Christians, to the use of the same institutions that the most militant advocates of Christian orthodoxy, such as the author of the *History of Mar Qardagh,* employed to articulate Christian supremacy over Zoroastrianism. Courtly literary specialists would have to overcome, through arguments akin to those embodied in the throne metaphor, the apparent contradictions in the manipulation of holy men, saints, and crosses by a Zoroastrian king of kings. It is this ambivalence of Christian symbols in Iranian political culture during the reign of Husraw II that the following sections explore.

HUSRAW II AND THE SAINTS

The earliest account of a king of kings working in concert with Christ and his saints concerns Kawad I's conquest of the Roman city of Amida in 502. The *Chronicle of Pseudo-Zachariah of Mytilene,* which a West Syrian monk composed in the vicinity of Amida in 569, recounts how the Sasanian had a vision of Christ during the siege of the city.³² The Christian God encouraged Kawad, who had begun to doubt the ability of his army to triumph over the Romans, to remain steadfast.³³ Christ promised to deliver Amida into his hands within three days, and after this happened, the Iranian army sacked the city and plundered its wealth. But as a sign of the connection between Christ and the king of kings, Kawad spared the city's Great Church of the Forty Martyrs and the Amidenes who had taken refuge within its walls. He was even believed to have honored an icon of Christ.³⁴ This narrative developed in northern Mesopotamian Syriac literary circles, which crisscrossed the imperial frontiers, and survives in an East Syrian version in the *Chronicle of Seert* that further emphasizes the personal relationship between the ruler and Christ.³⁵ Its importance resides less in its possible historicity than in its revelation of a thoroughgoing reconception of the relationship between Sasanians and Christianity in the Fertile Crescent in the course of the sixth century. Sasanians, once regarded as persecutors of Christians, could now be considered, in Roman and Iranian sources alike, believers in the power of Christ and his saints, if not in Christianity as a whole. Even if Kawad did not confess the Christian faith, a step which subsequent Christian historiographers claimed that some of his successors took, he was regarded as capable of finding support in Christ for a victory over the most Christian of empires. Christ had hitherto been the exclusive protector of the Romans. In the near contemporaneous *Chronicle of Pseudo-Joshua the Stylite,* for example, supernatural Christian powers are frequently invoked to defend the

Romans against the campaigns of Kawad, especially at Edessa, where the Mandylion of Christ rendered the city invincible.[36] By 569, however, the Christian God had become more promiscuous in the eyes of Christians on both sides of the frontier, ultimately leading to his yielding even of Edessa to an Iranian king of kings in 609.

The saint most closely associated with the Sasanians was Sergius. A military saint whose cult proliferated widely across political and cultural frontiers in the fifth through seventh centuries, Sergius became a key participant in interimperial politics with Justinian I's reconstruction of the city of Rusafa in a liminal zone where Romans and Ghassanid Arabs coruled, near the borderlands of Iran.[37] A shrine city whose churches overwhelmed its civic structures thus took shape in the steppe, attracting Roman, Arab, and Iranian devotees of a saint believed to bring military strength. Among the patrons of the saint and his shrine was Husraw II.[38] He made recourse to the saint on two occasions, through grand gestures directed not only toward Sergius but also toward the Sasanian court and army and the Roman allies who brought the king of kings to power. The first invocation of the saint took place during the joint Roman and Iranian campaign against the rebel Wahram Chobin in 591. Before confronting the forces of the usurper, Husraw II "supplicated Sergius ... [and] solemnly promised to offer as first fruits of victory the famous symbol of the Lord's Passion (this is designated a cross), to fashion it from beaten gold and to cover it with pearls and radiant Indian stones."[39] After his triumph over Wahram, the king of kings returned to the shrine of Sergius the gem-encrusted cross that his father, Husraw I, had appropriated from Sergiopolis (Rusafa) in 542. Husraw II made his second petition to Sergius in 593/94, after his marriage with the Christian queen Shirin, when he appealed to the saint to grant him a son. As recompense for the ensuing birth of a son to Shirin, the king of kings again dispatched gifts to the shrine. In place of the cross that Shirin wore, which he had promised to send, Husraw II delivered five thousand silver drachms. He wanted to retain the cross in the possession of the royal household, he stated in a letter to the saint, an indication of his interest in the cross as a Sasanian symbol.[40]

Two letters of dedication accompanied these royal gifts. The king of kings addressed the first to the ministers of the shrine, the second to the saint. The Roman historians Theophylact Simocatta and Evagrius Scholasticus recorded versions of these letters which modern commentators agree are precise transcriptions of the original messages, providing precious insight into the self-presentation of the Sasanian.[41] In these letters, Husraw II emphasizes the personal nature of his relationship with the saint. Having heard of "the fortune of the most holy and renowned St. Sergius," he had requested the latter's support against a particular enemy, the rebellious military commander Zadesprates, the delivery of whose head he regarded as a sign of the saint's favor.[42] An even more intimate experience of Sergius attended the conception of the king of kings' son:

And from the time when I had the said petition [that Sergius help Shirin to conceive] in my mind ... ten more days did not elapse and you, holy one, not because I am worthy but because of your goodness, you appeared to me in a dream at night and thrice declared to me that Shirin had conceived in her womb. And in the dream itself, I thrice answered you in return and said, "Thank you, thank you." And because of your holiness and charity, and because of your most holy name, and because you are the grantor of petition, from that day Shirin did not know what is customary for women.[43]

These professions of faith in the power of a Christian saint could not have been more public, associated as they were with trains of extravagant gifts on par with those of the grandest diplomatic exchanges between Rome and Iran. The king of kings did not discreetly supplicate Sergius—either to please Iranian or Roman Christians in his army or out of personal piety—but rather vaunted the peculiarly intimate relationship between Sasanian and saint, suggesting that the former had displaced the Roman emperor as the preeminent ally of the Near East's most influential Christian cult figure. He was the privileged recipient of Sergius's invisible assistance in battle and prophetic dreams sent by the saint. Husraw II adopted Sergius as a supernatural partner in rulership.[44]

The king of kings simultaneously brought a living holy man into the royal entourage as an intermediary between himself and Christian supernatural powers: the patriarch Sabrisho I.[45] This particular bishop came to the episcopal throne of Seleucia-Ctesiphon as the protégé of Husraw II and Shirin. In the course of the sixth century, the prayers that the patriarchs had promised to utter on behalf of their rulers since the Synod of 410 became more potent in the eyes of the Sasanians. When he returned to the throne of Iran, Husraw II was openly hostile toward the patriarch Ishoyahb I (r. 581–85), for having failed to join him in flight and for having supplicated the Christian God on behalf of the wrong ruler, the usurper Wahram.[46] While his predecessors had frequently called upon bishops to render a variety of administrative, diplomatic, and even economic services, Husraw II was equally interested in their capacities of intercession with Christian forces. An ascetic graduate of the School of Nisibis (see chapter 3), Sabrisho is believed to have been elevated to the patriarchate only after having helped Husraw II to secure a military victory.[47] While on campaign against the rebel Wistahm in 594, the king of kings had a vision of a monk, the *Chronicle of Seert* reports, who encouraged him to join battle, leading to a Sasanian triumph. The monk revealed himself as Sabrisho in a dream, and the king of kings brought him from the humble bishopric of Lashom to the imperial capital.[48] In another version of the narrative, the *Chronicle of Khuzestan* places Sabrisho's intercession on behalf of the Sasanian during his confrontation with Wahram rather than Wistahm.[49]

Regardless of their differences, these narratives reveal a common understanding among Christians of the late Sasanian period of the king of kings' interest in

Sabrisho's supernatural powers. Given his recognition of Sergius's assistance in battle and appearance in a dream, the claim of Christian authors that Husraw II attributed a victory to the ascetic bishop Sabrisho should not be disregarded. The holy man played, after all, a leading role in the next major campaign. When the king of kings gathered his forces for an invasion of the Roman Empire in 604, he included Sabrisho, mounted on an ass, in the train of men who marched northward to Nisibis.[50] The patriarch on campaign with Husraw II attracted the attention of Christian communities for the implicit or explicit approval of imperial warfare that his presence signaled. For East Syrian authors, this episode elicited tensions over the possibility of a saint sanctifying violence. According to the *Chronicle of Seert*, Husraw II embarked upon the campaign only because he believed that the prayers of Sabrisho would ensure an Iranian victory. After declaring that the king of kings would triumph, the patriarch tempered his prophecy with injunctions to treat the Roman Christians moderately and justly.[51] For Husraw II, the presence of a living holy man in his retinue was a sign that Christian powers could be placed in the service of his empire, designed to persuade both conquerors and conquered of the feasibility of incorporating the Christian Roman Empire into Iran.

THE CONQUEST OF CHRISTIAN ROME

In 615, with the formidable army of the Iranian commander Shahin encamped outside Constantinople, the Roman Senate dispatched three envoys to the court of Husraw II. They offered nothing less than the full submission of the Roman emperor, Heraclius, to the king of kings, in terms that James Howard-Johnston has described as "grovelling": "We beg too of your clemency to consider Heraclius, our most pious emperor, as a true son, one who is eager to perform the service of your serenity in all things.... And hereafter we shall be in enjoyment of tranquillity, through your gifts, which will be remembered forever, receiving an opportunity to offer prayers to God for your long-lasting prosperity."[52] A Roman emperor, who occupied the role of Christ's representative on earth, now recognized, in the name of the same God, his subordination to an Iranian ruler. For the first time in their nearly four centuries of interaction—sometimes conflictual, sometimes peaceable—the Roman state recognized Iran's claim to universal dominion and accepted a subject position. The reasons for this humiliating about-face were plain. From 603, Iranian forces had campaigned against the Romans with the startlingly novel ambition of conquering their empire.[53] Iranian forces had previously targeted individual Roman cities, only to withdraw upon the rendering of tribute. The early seventh-century Iranian campaigns, by contrast, incorporated entire provinces into Iran.[54] After crossing the Euphrates in 610, the Iranians entered Syria, Anatolia, and Palestine, seizing Antioch and Caesarea in 611 and Damascus in 613.[55] With the Iranian conquest of Egypt in 619, the Romans forfeited more than 30 percent of their fiscal revenues, together with the great bulk of their agriculturally productive lands.[55] But they yielded more than merely material resources to Iran. After the Iranian conquest of Jerusalem in 614, the True Cross—the most potent sign of Roman sovereignty—was in the hands of a ruler whom the Christian Romans regarded as a pagan. The God in whose name the emperor ruled had turned against the Romans for their sins, as a monk of the Palestinian monastery of Choziba had foretold: "Lord God of mercies and lord of pity ... take up your staff and strike this people, because they walk in ignorance."[57] Even the most dedicated advocates of Christian *Romanitas* began to lose faith in the empire. As the imperial court considered the Iranian army assembled across the Bosporus at Chalcedon in 615, the loss not only of the revenues, resources, and infrastructures necessary for organizing resistance but also of all of the signs of forthcoming divine assistance was self-evident. The Romans thus turned to the ruler God whom seemed to favor.

Husraw II spurned their offer of submission. The envoys were imprisoned, their proposal ignored. This response marked a shift in the Iranian understanding of Rome's place within its world order, which was no less dramatic an ideological innovation than the Senate's acceptance of subordination. Until the beginning of the seventh century, the Iranian court had considered the Roman Empire a tributary state. If the early Sasanians had demonstrated Rome's subject status through military victories over emperors, fifth- and sixth-century kings of kings had used Roman tributary payments secured either diplomatically or militarily as key symbols of Iranian universal sovereignty.[58] A mythical-historical account of Rome's relationship with Iran began to circulate from at least the fifth century according to which Roman rulers descended from the Kayanian king Fereydun's son Salm.[59] Roman and Iranian monarchs were, from the Sasanian perspective, genealogically related, a paradigm that could be deployed selectively in the service of either cooperation or conflict, depending on the circumstances. It is not accidental that Husraw II was the king of kings with both the most intimate and the most antagonistic relationships with Roman emperors. The amiable relationship between him and Maurice abruptly gave way to conflict in 602 when a military officer, Phocas, usurped the Roman throne and eliminated the reigning emperor and his house.[60] In response to the destruction of this lineage—whose members Husraw II, with his limited knowledge of Roman history, regarded as the legitimate rulers of Rome, genealogically intertwined with the Sasanians—the king of kings initiated the campaigns that culminated in the arrival of his forces at Chalcedon.[61] Given the opportunity in 615 to accept Rome as a tributary power on Iranian terms with the Roman emperor as a client, the Iranian court fatefully decided to incorporate the Roman Empire directly in an enlarged Iran, which would momentarily reachieve its extent under the Achaemenians, extending from the Nile to the Oxus.[62]

The conquerors accordingly aimed to subordinate rather than to devastate Roman infrastructures. Roman literary accounts describe the destruction of churches, monasteries, and cities, including, most shockingly, the torching of the holy city of Jerusalem: "The Lord's tomb was burned and the far-famed temples of God, and, in short, all the precious things were destroyed."[63] The conquests were, of course, violent, entailing assaults on defensive architecture and resistant populations and punitive measures of appalling scope.[64] Excavations around Jerusalem have uncovered mass burials, in which women and children outnumber adult males, that can be firmly dated to the decade of the city's capture; the account of Strategius, a Greek-writing Palestinian monk, graphically describes the massacre of Christian captives at one such site, Mamilla.[65] But the archaeology of the Levant more generally has revealed more continuity than discontinuity during the era of Iranian rule. Throughout this period, although the cities of Anatolia that were contested began to devolve into fortified towns, the fully conquered urban structures of Syria and Palestine remained intact.[66] The rapidity with which a Roman city could rebound is clearest at Jerusalem. The famed burning of the city that captured the Roman imagination appears to have occurred only at a section of the northern wall.[67] If the new rulers put churches or other buildings to the torch, as the literary sources claim, they immediately repaired any damage that the holy places sustained, leaving no trace of a destructive conquest.[68] Beyond the holy city, in Transjordan, inscriptions from sites in the Hawran and elsewhere show that church construction, rather than destruction, continued apace.[69] Narratives of the conquerors as slayers of Christians and torchers of churches were responses to Iranian actions that were a greater danger to Christian Roman ideology—namely, the appropriation of the symbolic foundations of Christianity in its holiest places.

If the loss of the empire's most productive lands drained the Roman fisc, the fall of Jerusalem called the very idea of a Christian Roman Empire into question. To rally the Romans in defense of what remained of their empire, the emperor Heraclius and his associates mobilized objects and texts in novel ways to reaffirm their Christian mission and to demonstrate the ongoing intervention of God and the saints on their behalf. The war against Iran was cast as a war on behalf of the Christian faith, to a much greater extent than earlier Roman-Iranian confrontations had been.[70] Heraclius had arrived in Constantinople to seize power from Phocas in 610 on "ships that had on their masts reliquaries [of the saints] and icons of the Mother of God," announcing the intensified participation of supernatural agents in imperial politics that was characteristic of his reign.[71] When the Iranians joined forces with the Avars to besiege Constantinople in 626, the icon of the Mother of God of Blachernai, which was paraded around the city, was believed to have repulsed the invaders.[72] With the True Cross in Iran, alternative objects such as icons were deployed to channel divine power in the service of Rome. The procession of the icon of Blachernai constituted a performance of the narrative simultaneously disseminated in sermons, poems, and hagiographies according to which the Iranians were the enemies of the Christian God, whose identification with the Roman Empire was inviolate. The Heraclian reaction thus entailed the demonization of an empire that sixth-century Romans had often regarded as a partner and even a civilization worthy of admiration.[73]

Roman poets, historians, and hagiographers transformed Iran into God's enemy in the aftermath of 614. Contemporary witnesses, as noted above, considered Roman defeat a consequence of Christian sin, a collective failure to fulfill the obligations that God demanded of them. The Romans, in this view, merited the conquests as punishment, and the Iranians were mere pedagogical instruments of divine will. As Phil Booth has recently shown, Jerusalem's fall caused some prominent ascetics to work to purify Christian communities to appease a malcontent deity, while others placed responsibility on the Iranians and their paganism, which necessarily rendered them barbarians. In his poems recounting the conquest, Sophronius of Jerusalem, a leading ascetic thinker of the age and a future patriarch of Jerusalem, depicted the Iranians as murderous, demonically inspired barbarians seeking the destruction of Christianity.[74] This was the representation around which Heraclius rallied what remained of his empire. In an echo of this kind of rhetoric, the eighth- and ninth-century chronicler Theophanes Confessor reported that, on receiving envoys in 615, Husraw II had demanded that Heraclius renounce Christ and worship the sun.[75] It was not merely the survival of the empire but also its religion that was at stake. To propagate this message in elite circles, the court poet George of Pisidia produced poems for the emperor that present him as God's representative waging war against a wicked reincarnation of Exodus's Pharaoh.[76] The destruction in 628 of Zoroastrianism's most sacred site, the fire of Adur Gushnasp at Takht-e Suleyman, was celebrated as a pious act. Because of the Iranians' enmity toward Christianity, Heraclius could promise his troops eternal life in exchange for death in battle, eliding the distinct categories of soldier and martyr: "When God wills it, one man will rout a thousand. So let us sacrifice ourselves to God for the salvation of our brothers. May we win the crown of martyrdom so that we may be praised in the future and receive our recompense from God."[77] The emperor's appeals to Christ and the saints were intended not only to unite what remained of the Romans but also to counter perceptions that the Christian God had abandoned Rome in favor of Iran. The object that embodied the bond between empire and religion was, after all, now at the court of the king of kings.

THE TRUE CROSS IN IRAN

The True Cross was the sign by which Constantine the Great had conquered, and since its purported discovery by his mother, Helena, and its installation in Jerusalem, its wood had embodied the soteriological purpose of the Roman Empire in the divine economy.[78] If the breaking of the bond between the cross and Roman victory led some to question God's identification with the Roman emperor, Heraclius's advocates emphasized the taking of the cross as the clearest indication of the Iranian intention to destroy the Christian religion, not merely its Roman, sacred-historical repository. The cross loomed large in the aforementioned authors' reactions to 614. Writing in the 630s, after the cross had been returned to Jerusalem, Strategius composed the most detailed account of Iranian treatment of the relic, known as the *Capture of Jerusalem,* which has survived in an Arabic and a more reliable Georgian translation. Strategius aimed to commemorate the events of the previous decades in terms that would place the renewed pact between Christianity and Roman imperialism, represented in Heraclius's restoration of the cross in 630, on a solid historical footing.[79] In his representation, the Iranians had captured the cross to prove the falsehood of Christianity and to drain the object of its supernatural, empire-sustaining power. The Christians who had been exiled from Jerusalem to Mesopotamia were required, Strategius reported, to trample upon the cross as they departed the city.[80] The Iranians had presided over its ritual humiliation, whereas the emperor Heraclius had introduced, by the time of the text's composition, the feast of the exaltation of the cross.

But even as he depicted the conquerors as wicked enemies of the faith who had sullied the cross, Strategius intimated that the Iranian court had made rather creative use of the object's potency. The relic, he reported, was installed at court when Zachariah, the exiled patriarch of Jerusalem, was brought there for questioning. The *Capture of Jerusalem* thus reveals that Husraw II placed the earthly manifestation of Christ's religiopolitical power in intimate proximity to himself for an audience of Roman Christians, a narrative in keeping with what other East Syrian sources have reported concerning the ruler's manipulation of the cross. Strategius acknowledged that Iranians honored the cross in ways that the East Syrian *Chronicle of Khuzestan,* to be discussed momentarily, has documented. To explain the court's recognition of its power, Strategius described the seemingly miraculous exploits of Zachariah during a disputation with a mowbed, after which "no one dared to approach the Lord's cross and the wood of our Savior, for fear seized all of them on account of this sign."[81] Because of Zachariah's demonstration of its capacity to triumph over Zoroastrianism, the king of kings entrusted the holy cross to Shirin, who reverently safeguarded it in a royal palace. There is a hint here of what Roman authors generally either ignored or suppressed: the translation to Iran not only of the symbols of Christian Roman power but also of the supernatural support of the Christian God and his saints, which relics, holy men, and holy places now in Iranian hands were believed to mediate. Strategius had to demonstrate that the power of the cross resided with the holy man Zachariah, not with the "evil king." He expressly stated for his uncertain readers that Husraw II was "not a Christian king" but the "king of Persia."[82] The bishops, monks, and poets who worked to communicate God's unfailing support of Heraclius in the face of the loss of hitherto reliable signs of divine favor were also addressing a greater challenge to the continued existence of the Christian Roman Empire. In his efforts to reinforce the position of the Christian churches and to mobilize Christian powers both heavenly and earthly, Husraw II built on a long tradition of Sasanian patronage of Christianity to incorporate previously Roman Christian institutions into Iran. There was truth, from the Iranian perspective, in the Roman anxiety that the Christian God had abandoned Rome and chosen a Zoroastrian king of kings as the executor of his will.

Acquiring the True Cross, the sign of divine favor, was a clear objective of the conquering forces. According to accounts of Jerusalem's capture, the elites of the city buried the relic in a vegetable garden in an attempt to prevent the Iranians from plundering it.[83] But the conquerors were not content to despoil the Jerusalemites of only the gold, silver, and other high-value goods discovered in their churches. An object of singularly immaterial value was their chief interest. Shahrwaraz, the commander of the conquerors in the Levant, had Jerusalem's bishop and notables tortured until they revealed its location. Brought from the garden to the victorious general, Christianity's most sacred relic entered Zoroastrian hands. For an early seventh-century East Syrian historiographer whose work came to be included in the *Chronicle of Khuzestan*, the revelation of the cross to Shahrwaraz was the clearest sign of divine favor for the Sasanians, more significant even than their unprecedented victories: "Because divine power had crushed the Romans before the Persians because they had shed the innocent blood of Maurice and his sons, God left no place unknown that the Romans did not reveal to them."[84] So supportive was the Christian God of Husraw II, the historiographer contended, that he allowed his cross to be revealed to the Iranians, to be translated from Rome to Iran.

In Seleucia-Ctesiphon, the capture of the cross was also taken a sign of the Christian God's support for Iran. While Roman narratives portray its humiliation and violent seizure, the East Syrian historiographical tradition represents the translation as the deliberate, cautious installation of the relic at the symbolic center of the Iranian Empire. The *Chronicle of Khuzestan* recounts the respectful delivery of the cross from Jerusalem to the Iranian court: "[The conquerors] prepared a number of chests and sent [the True Cross] together with countless vessels and precious objects to Husraw. When [the convoy] reached Yazdin, he organized a great feast. With the permission of the king, he took a piece of [the cross] and then sent it to the king. [The king] placed it in a position of honor with the sacred vessels in the new treasury that he had built at Ctesiphon."[85] It was the task of the administrator of the fisc, Yazdin, to receive plunder from the conquered territories, including the cross. But the relic was not regarded as conventional plunder. If the Christian aristocrat organized a feast for its arrival on his own authority, the king of kings honored the cross before a courtly audience, according to the chronicler. The *Chronicle of Khuzestan* has preserved an East Syrian perspective on the translation of the cross to Seleucia-Ctesiphon which considers this act the legitimate transfer of the symbol of Christian political power to Husraw II.[86] Some East Syrians, such as the author of the *History of Mar Qardagh*, might have seen in their newfound access to relics of the True Cross a sign of divine favor for the joining of Christianity and empire in Iran. East Syrian ecclesiastical and secular elites were both now able to participate in the distribution of fragments of the cross, a process that gathered pace in the Roman world in the latter half of the sixth century.[87]

The most important aspect of the above passage, however, is its mention of the installation of the cross in a "new treasury" at Ctesiphon. Victorious Sasanians typically celebrated their triumphs over Rome with elaborate architectural projects. The early Sasanians constructed complexes around rock reliefs in Fars. Husraw I erected the storied palace known as Ayvan-e Kisra to the south of Ctesiphon, which likely included mosaics and stuccos depicting his victories. Husraw II commissioned an extraordinarily ambitious interlinked set of palaces and monumental rock reliefs along the royal road in Walashfarr, not least the masterful representation of the triumphant ruler at Taq-e Bustan (see chapter 2). But the architectural projects of this king of kings in the royal cities remain undocumented, both textually and archaeologically.[88] The reference to the construction of a new treasury raises the still unanswerable question of how the ruler transformed the capital to reflect the enlarged horizons of the Iranian Empire.[89] The unfinished excavations of Ctesiphon and its environs have revealed considerable development in the areas immediately surrounding the palace of Husraw I, where this treasury would have been constructed. Archaeologists without knowledge of the *Chronicle of Khuzestan*'s account have long suggested that the complex at Tell Dhahab was a treasury, but any such precise connections will remain speculative until excavations resume.[90] What is certain is that the treasury was in the expansive complex of palaces, paradises, and hunting grounds that constituted the locus of royal authority. This was the space where kings of kings performed for their various constituencies of aristocrats and religious specialists. One instrument for the performances that a king of kings who ruled from the Oxus to the Nile would wish to undertake was the object most sacred to the Christians who now formed a major component of the imperial elite. Once transferred to Seleucia-Ctesiphon, the True Cross became an indispensable part of the court's ideological tool kit, an incontrovertible sign that the Christian God and his saints were advocates of Ērānšahr. In an empire whose western provinces were overwhelmingly Christian, the cross as a symbol that all Christians could recognize as endowing legitimacy and supernaturally sanctioned authority was a resource full of potentiality for a king of kings anxious to consolidate his power over recently conquered territories and East Syrian and Armenian elites.

IRANIANS AND ROMANS: A SASANIAN EMPEROR

For anywhere from ten to upward of twenty years, the provinces of the Roman Near East were territories of Iran. This is commonly known as an era of occupation, but the inhabitants of the conquered regions could not have known that Iranian rule would be temporary. The facts on the ground pointed in a rather different direction. If historians have focused on the damage done to Roman political institutions in advance of the Islamic conquests, the ways in which the Iranians consolidated their rule have received less attention. There are two fundamental methods that the new rulers used to integrate conquered territories and populations into the empire: the installment of an Iranian governing elite and the cultivation of an indigenous elite loyal to Iran. Alongside the great generals, marzbān were stationed in cities that had previously served as the centers for the Roman administration, such as Caesarea Maritima, Edessa, and Alexandria.[91] The corpus of Middle Persian papyri documents the presence throughout Egypt circa 619–29 of cavalry forces, together with their commanders and ancillary officials, who policed traffic on the Nile and supervised the extraction of the region's resources.[92] A certain Shahralanyozan, the so-called steward of the court (*kār-frcmān ī dar*), directed the coordination of the already existing network of Roman officials and a team of Iranian scribes and officials to collect taxes in gold in Egypt.[93] Although Iranians displaced the highest levels of the Roman administration in the conquered territories, they depended on the collaboration of myriad intermediaries between themselves and provincial populations. They thus turned to already authoritative Roman elites who had remained in their cities during the course of the conquests and were willing to place themselves in the service of the king of kings. If the Egyptian papyri reveal the results of such collaboration, the pro-Roman historiographical literature tends to obscure the forging of alliances between conquerors and conquered. The one exception is the West Syrian historiographical tradition, which, as we will see, could regard Husraw II favorably. At Edessa, the well-known house of the Rusafoye, major patrons of the West Syrians, remained in power. Husraw II was reported to have dined in the palace of Johannes Rusafoyo while on his way to Constantinople in 580, and after the conquest, Johannes's son Sergius was brought to court to become "one of the companions of his table" before returning to power as an agent of Iran in Edessa.[94] There were doubtless many such Roman elites invited to the banquets of the king of kings, military commanders, and other Iranian aristocrats, who have gone undocumented.

The Iranian regime in the West sought to gain legitimacy in the eyes of the conquered populations on the basis of its patronage of Christians and their institutions.[95] In contrast with Roman narratives of the anti-Christian violence of the Iranians, they presented themselves, at least through particular actions, as no less supportive of the Christian faith than their Roman predecessors, much as Husraw I represented himself as a patron of the Roman people.[96] Historians have downplayed the possibility of Roman Christians' adapting to Iranian political structures or recognizing the king of kings as the rightful successor of the Christian Roman emperor.[97] But the systematic appropriation of the accoutrements of Christian supernatural power—the selfsame saints and relics that Heraclius so ostentatiously deployed—permitted the new rulers to attempt to overcome the obvious religious distinctiveness of the invading empire, with a view to cultivating constituencies of Christian Romans. The elites of Iran, Christian or otherwise, were no longer the only audience for Husraw II's communicative acts. The overwhelmingly Christian elites of previously Roman territories needed to be integrated into the imperial network, and courtly symbolic innovations addressed the aristocratic houses of Edessa, the urbane citizens of Alexandria, and the diligent officials of Upper Egypt, among countless others. The relationship with Christianity that Husraw II had constructed enabled him to be so audacious as to seek to rule the Roman Empire. With the legitimacy of the Christian Roman head imperial office vitiated in the aftermath of the conquest, the king of kings, who was a friend of the saints and a kinsman of the house of Maurice, was well placed to stand in the line of the successors of Constantine. Developing the strategies that their ruler had deployed during the first decades of his reign, the Iranian governing elites worked to communicate their support for Christianity and, vice versa, the unfailing sanction of the Christian God for Iran's expansion into Roman lands, as the Christian historiographical traditions discussed below make plain. To include the Roman Near East in Ērānšahr in the sixth century, the king of kings and his representatives in the provinces acted in the manner of Roman rulers, consolidating their authority through the construction of churches, the oppression of Jews and other unbelievers, and the negotiation of conflicts over Christian orthodoxy.

Though known for causing the destruction of Jerusalem, Husraw II cast himself as the restorer of the holy city. Roman Christian texts describe the efforts of an abbot, Modestos, whom Iranian authorities brought to power as the vicar of the exiled patriarch Zachariah in 616, to rebuild the city's ecclesiastical monuments in the wake of 614.[98] Although the archaeological reports discussed above show Roman accounts of the razing of Jerusalem to be exaggerated, the violent seizing and plundering of the city left considerable damage. There was grassroots fundraising among the conquered to make repairs. John the Almsgiver, the Chalcedonian patriarch of Alexandria, dedicated vast amounts of Egyptian wealth to the project. The extent of Modestos's mobilization of the network of bishops crisscrossing the Iranian Empire is clear from the letter he sent appealing for financial assistance from Komitas, the Armenian catholicos—whom the patriarch of Jerusalem regarded as a Miaphysite heretic.[99] Within several years of the conquest, the bulk of the churches in Jerusalem were once again in use, even if the Church of the

Anastasis remained in disrepair.¹⁰⁰ What the emphasis on the patriarchal vicar's activities has ignored is Sasanian support for the renovation of the holy city. The reported restorations of Modestos would have taken place under the auspices of the Iranian authorities. Husraw II, moreover, ordered and funded Jerusalem's reconstruction, according to Pseudo-Sebeos and the *Chronicle of Khuzestan*.¹⁰¹ The latter reports that Yazdin dispatched large sums of silver to Jerusalem at the order of the king of kings and presided over the renewal of its sanctuaries and the construction of new monasteries and churches. Emerging from Iranian contexts, these two histories are more aware of courtly acts and representations than are Roman accounts, and they have preserved an important aspect of Husraw II's policies in the conquered territories. The king of kings positioned himself as the rebuilder of a Jerusalem whose monuments embodied Roman Christian imperial power, implicitly to continue the tradition of Christian rulers patronizing the holy city. Modestos might well have cooperated with the Iranian authorities, but given his subsequent renown, Roman authors could not include this aspect of his tenure.¹⁰² Like Constantine and Justinian, Husraw II aimed to leave his mark on the city, whose imperial symbolism he had harnessed to Ērānšahr.

For Roman emperors, the construction of ecclesiastical buildings at Jerusalem entailed the suppression of Jews, through the erasure of the Jewish past or more direct forms of violence.¹⁰³ In tandem with the increasing dependence of the emperors on Christ and the saints for legitimacy, Jews were ever more forcefully excluded from the political community of Roman Christians. In the seventh century, Roman anti-Judaism culminated in forced conversions and expulsions during the reigns of Phocas and Heraclius.¹⁰⁴ The latter forbade Jews from residing within three miles of Jerusalem when he restored the cross to the city in 630. As Gilbert Dagron has observed, "the logic of the victory of the cross" precipitated this reissuing of a decree that the emperors Hadrian and Constantine had once promulgated.¹⁰⁵ But when Husraw II had restored Jerusalem, he had expelled the Jews from its confines, according to Pseudo-Sebeos.¹⁰⁶ In applying a traditionally Roman edict of expulsion to communicate the divinely sanctioned nature of a victory, the king of kings had preempted Heraclius. The Roman returned to a Jerusalem that, Dagron has suggested, had been emptied of Jews more than a decade before.¹⁰⁷ This marked a sea change in Iranian policies toward Jewish communities in the conquered territories. Jewish elites in the cities of the Levant tended readily to accept Iranian rule as a welcome respite from Roman persecution.¹⁰⁸ Roman authors developed episodes of Jews collaborating with the new regime into polemical accounts of their inveterate hostility toward Christians and the Roman Empire, but Jewish sources represent the conquests as a new beginning. When Shahrwaraz took Jerusalem, the era of Christian domination came to an end. Contemporaneous piyyutim, Jewish liturgical poems, celebrate the Iranian victory as a liberation from Edom, the biblical archetype of a persecutory state, and as a portent of the

Messiah's imminent arrival.[109] But within three years such hopes were dashed. The Temple, which had reopened in 614, was closed and the recently empowered leader of the Jewish community slain.[110] The Sasanians, according to one contemporaneous piyyut, came to suppress Jews just as their Roman predecessors had.

If Roman authors overlooked Iranian measures against the Jews in Jerusalem, the accounts of the piyyutim find confirmation in the works of Christian chroniclers of the Iranian world. The *Chronicle of Khuzestan* recounts how the Jews, in league with the resident Iranian commander, plundered the shrines and reliquaries of Jerusalem in the aftermath of the conquest, until Yazdin—ever the leading patron of the Christians in the eyes of this work's historiographer—reported their deeds to the king of kings. Husraw II then commanded that the Jews of the city be dispossessed and crucified.[111] But the *History of Pseudo-Sebeos* describes their expulsion rather than execution. Its Armenian historian, moreover, connected the sudden reversal of Jewish fortunes with the restoration of Jerusalem's Christians to a position of dominance: "Then a command arrived from the king to have mercy on those who had fallen prisoner, to rebuild the city, and to reestablish [its inhabitants] there in each one's rank. He ordered the Jews to be expelled from the city. And they promptly carried out the king's command with great alacrity. They appointed a certain archpriest over the city by the name of Modestos."[112] Together with the rebuilding of Jerusalem's ecclesiastical structures and the elevation of its Christian elite, the Iranian court undertook an operation unprecedented in its history: the forcible expulsion of an entire community on the basis of its religious identity. This was a departure from the court's long-standing collaboration with Jewish religious leaders, from the established exilarch of Babylonia to the rabbis of conquered Roman cities. Husraw II's command recalls the measures of Hadrian and Constantine. Expelling the Jews of Jerusalem rendered the king of kings a more Christian ruler than the emperors who had immediately preceded him. In proclaiming his edict of 630, issued on behalf of the Christian leaders who came to power under the Sasanian, Heraclius was imitating Husraw II as much as Constantine.

The Iranian regime's actions in Jerusalem reveal some of the self-conscious ways in which the conquerors cultivated the loyalty of Roman Christians. The conquered populations, however, hardly formed uniform or unified Christian communities, as the Christian Roman emperors had come to realize. The sectarian landscape of the Roman Near East was decidedly more complex than the familiar mix of East Syrian, Caucasian, and West Syrian communities in Iran. Controversies over the definition of Christ's nature at the Council of Chalcedon in 451 had divided Christians throughout the eastern half of the empire, leading to the formation of institutionalized communities—West Syrian or Syrian Orthodox and Coptic churches—that had their own bishops and monasteries but were united in their rejection of Chalcedon and the Roman emperors who sought to enforce its

Dyophysite language as the touchstone of orthodoxy.[113] The Iranian court had had knowledge of the West Syrian church as an entity distinct from the Church of the East since Simeon of Beit Arsham, a propagandist of Miaphysite orthodoxy, had brought the former's beliefs to the attention of Kawad I in the early sixth century.[114] The West Syrian movement gained ground in Iranian Mesopotamia throughout the Sasanian era, but its religious leaders did not attain political prominence until the Roman conquests, at which point they rivaled the Church of the East.[115] Once vast numbers of Chalcedonian, West Syrian, and Coptic Christians entered the Iranian Empire, the king of kings came face to face with the same dilemma that the Roman emperors had encountered of how to unify Christian communities prone to centrifugal controversies.

With firsthand experience of Roman society and political culture, a Christian spouse as an intermediary, and intimate relationships with ecclesiastical leaders, Husraw II was better placed than his predecessors to comprehend and to transcend the differences of his Christian subjects. Kawad had reportedly solicited statements of divergent Christian doctrines in the first quarter of the sixth century, and the question of Christ's nature became ever more urgent at the synods that the Church of the East held at the behest of the court in Seleucia-Ctesiphon.[116] But Iranians directly intervened in Christian controversies only in the course of the conquests. The conquerors were particularly concerned with the relationship between the East Syrian Church and the West Syrian Church, which were in the process of dividing some of the most strategic populations of the empire, including the inhabitants of northern Mesopotamian and the Arabian frontier. The West Syrians' prevalence in Syria and alliance with the Egyptian Church made their variety of orthodoxy particularly interesting to the king of kings. His wife Shirin was known to have favored their leaders, in addition to the East Syrian hierarchy traditionally associated with the Sasanian dynasty.[117] If Iranian elites gained knowledge of the nuances of intra-Christian conflicts on an informal basis, through conversations and negotiations with ecclesiastical leaders in the cities they conquered, the court quickly adapted instruments for regulating doctrinal controversies characteristic of Justinian and other effective emperors as the conquests gathered pace. Ultimately, at least one formal discussion and disputation was convened in the presence of Husraw II, in the 610s, to which leading representatives of both Syrian Churches and an Armenian contingent aligned with the West Syrians presented their distinctive versions of orthodoxy. It was not only in Constantinople that a ruler sought to undo the divisions that Chalcedon had generated.

The conquerors carefully distinguished between Chalcedonians and non-Chalcedonians as they established structures of rule in formerly Roman cities. Ecclesiastical leaders who adhered to the creed of the emperor were frequently displaced in favor of bishops whom Roman authorities considered heretical.[118] In Edessa, the Iranians initially placed an East Syrian on the episcopal throne, the same strategy that the court had deployed to discipline the Christian communities of Armenia in the fifth century. But once the potential of garnering the loyalty of the Syrian Orthodox Church became evident, a West Syrian was elevated as the bishop of the city, where Christological controversies had incited violent contestations of ecclesiastical power throughout the preceding century.[119] The transfer of ecclesiastical leadership from Chalcedonian to West Syrian bishops took place throughout Syria, even in the great see of Antioch. West Syrian leaders had already laid the foundations for a rapprochement with Iran. In response to the Romans' systematic repression of the opponents of Chalcedon, they began to imagine a world without a Roman Empire decades before the conquest, effectively disassociating Christianity from Romanitas.[120] The hagiographer, historian, and bishop John of Ephesus, for example, had come to regard the Sasanian dynasty as a possible ally of the West Syrian Church in the mid-sixth century.[121] The communities of this church, moreover, spanned the Fertile Crescent, their networks easily crisscrossing the boundaries of the Roman and Iranian Empires. The conquerors thus viewed the leaders of these communities, which were not closely identified with the Roman Empire, as worthy of their confidence. Chalcedonians were not, however, uniformly displaced. In strongholds of Roman orthodoxy, such as Jerusalem, they remained in power. In Alexandria, John the Almsgiver continued to represent the Constantinopolitan Church, even as the Egyptian Orthodox gained greater room for maneuver. Iranian patronage of West Syrians nevertheless marked the beginning of a period of ecclesiastical institution building for the non-Chalcedonians, of a kind not seen since Theodora, the wife of Justinian, extended her support to them. It was in the first decade after the conquest that the Syrian Orthodox and Egyptian Churches first articulated a common, Miaphysite doctrine, which became the basis for institutional cooperation. In 616 Athanasius of Antioch sailed to Egypt to unite the two churches, which the Roman state had kept separate: "The truth has appeared from the land of Egypt, and righteousness has arisen from the East. Egypt and Syria have become one in doctrine."[122] The Iranian regime inaugurated an era of triumph for Miaphysite orthodoxy.

Apart from simply suppressing Chalcedonians in the way that Maurice and Phocas had suppressed West Syrians, the Iranian regime addressed the debates over doctrine that caused Christian communities to fracture. At the outset of the conquests, the court recognized that its privileging of the patriarch of the Church of the East could hinder its efforts to cultivate the loyalty of Christians in Roman territory. Husraw II therefore refused to appoint a successor to the patriarch Gregory after the latter's death in 609. For the first time since 410, the Iranian court did not identify with one particular church, giving it greater flexibility in its negotiations with Christian communities.[123] The Church of the East remained without a suzerain bishop for the next eighteen years, during which the aristocrat Yazdin was among its most powerful representatives, together with some leading clerics such as the abbot Babai the Great.[124] Also in this period, the most influential Christian leaders in the Iranian Empire came to stand at opposite ends of the doctrinal spectrum, as the East and West Syrians were diametrically opposed on the question of Christ's nature. An inadvertent consequence of the expansion of the empire was the accelerated fracturing of Christian communities that had, from the court's perspective, seemed solid. Antagonistic relations between the East and West Syrians only intensified in the 610s, leading the court to intervene more directly in Christian controversies just a few years after suspending the East Syrian patriarchate. Neither East nor West Syrians were content to leave the position of the supreme bishop vacant, and rival sectarians attempted to persuade Husraw II to appoint someone from their ranks as patriarch. When the court physician Gabriel of Sinjar, whom the West Syrians considered their Constantine, recommended that a Miaphysite be appointed to the see, the East Syrian bishops dispatched a mission of scholars to Seleucia-Ctesiphon to keep the position in Dyophysite hands.[125] The result was a formal disputation, a synod on a modest scale, organized under the auspices of the court in 612.[126]

According to the *History of George the Priest*, which the contemporary Babai the Great composed, the king of kings invited representatives of the sects to present their competing doctrines in writing, in translation from Syriac to Middle Persian.[127] He then supervised the ensuing Christological debates, requiring the disputants to articulate their understandings of the nature of Christ and his relationship with the Mother of God, as well as the historical development of their respective doctrines. Babai, an eyewitness to these events, reported that Husraw II sought out potential middle ground between Miaphysite and Dyophysite doctrines, demanding, for example, that the East Syrians avoid invoking the highly controversial theologian Nestorius (386–451).[128] The king of kings acted in a manner that recalls the efforts of a theologically engaged emperor such as Justinian to design a Christological compromise. He even allowed his wife Shirin to favor the West Syrians while he himself attempted to achieve a transcendent equilibrium, much as Theodora had patronized the anti-Chalcedonians on behalf of her avowedly Chalcedonian husband. Unlike his Roman counterparts, however, Husraw II recognized that the intransigence of the most militant members of these communities was insurmountable. Neither doctrine was endorsed, nor was a third Christology innovated. The seat of the patriarch at Seleucia-Ctesiphon remained vacant until the end of the king of kings' reign. Instead of crafting a compromise, such as the Monothelete doctrine of Heraclius, he seems to have enjoined theological moderation upon the Christians at court. A few years after the debate of 612, the learned, ascetic, militantly Miaphysite Maruta found East and West Syrians at court partaking of the same Communion, the preeminent expression of Christian unity.[129] The studied ambiguity of a court that invited definitions of orthodoxy without approving a single normative formula of Christian belief allowed the empire's various Christian sects to claim royal sanction for their peculiar doctrine. Nonetheless, the king of kings positioned himself as the arbiter of Christian orthodoxy, taking from the Roman emperors the authority to validate theological truth.

In the aftermath of the conquests, Husraw II appropriated the sacred-historical sacred role of the Christian emperors, fulfilling the obligations that accompanied the possession of the True Cross: to restore Jerusalem, to subordinate the Jews, and to regulate Christian doctrine. The effects of this package of measures on the populations of the conquered territories are difficult to discern, as the bulk of the surviving literary evidence was composed from a pro-Roman perspective, in the service of Heraclius's project of reconquest. Nevertheless, the West Syrian historiographical tradition views the Iranian conquest of the Near East as precipitating the victory of orthodoxy. The Iranians were the instruments with which God banished the memory of Chalcedon from the region, according to the twelfth-century compiler Michael the Syrian.[130] And the rapid dissemination of the account of Husraw II's conversion, which emanated from Roman Chalcedonian milieux in Syria, in both Chalcedonian and anti-Chalcedonian communities in the early seventh century suggests that many Christians, even literary elites, could consider the Sasanian a Christian ruler. Through the exercise of the functions of a Christian emperor, he gained support as a legitimate ruler over Christians even among those who did not regard him as a convert, part of a long Christian tradition of accepting the overlordship of unbelievers in anticipation of the completion of the religion's universalizing mission. At the level of quotidian practice, a Coptic papyrus well illustrates the ease with which Christian and Iranian ideologies of rulership could be married. Fourteen villagers promised an Iranian official that they would provide him with the merchandise they owed "by God and the good fortune of the king of kings." Their statement, Andrea Gariboldi has observed, "curiously seems to mix Christian elements with the mythical Persian concept of the king's *xwarrah*."[131] The Iranians appropriated not only the infrastructures of the conquered empire but also its religious ideology.

HUSRAW'S CROSSES IN THE *BOOK OF KINGS*

Thus far this chapter has primarily been concerned with the evolving role of the Iranian court vis-à-vis its Christian subjects. How did Zoroastrians, especially the great nobles and religious specialists who formed the most powerful actors in the governing elite, perceive the manipulation of Christian symbols? Did they accept the metaphor of a throne that legs of different religions upheld as a viable vision of a Zoroastrian empire? As chapter 1 emphasizes, the wehdēn were hardly unanimous in their attitudes toward the adherents and institutions of other religions. Reconstructing the full range of responses to the mixing of Zoroastrian and Christian symbols is impossible, given the parlous state of our evidence for the late

Sasanian aristocratic and priestly classes. What remains are the narratives of political history that early Islamic historiographers preserved, reflecting the ways in which the royal court, or an aristocratic faction, purposefully reshaped the past. In the various recensions of the *Book of Kings*, courtly literary specialists trained in the Avesta and its interpretation endeavored to recount events in a manner that demonstrates the kings of kings' successful exercise of cosmological kingship in their historical circumstances but in the writers' terms. Among their counterparts were the aristocratic authors of a literature of rebellion—such as the *Book of Wahram Chobin*, which recounts the 590–91 rebellion of its namesake—which survives only in fragments.[132] The *Book of Wahram Chobin* was composed in opposition to the *Book of Kings*—that is, in order to demonstrate that Ohrmazd IV, Husraw II, and indeed the entire Sasanian dynasty had failed to practice kingship properly and had thereby forfeited their claim to the throne. Both of these historiographical traditions address Husraw II's relationship with Christianity, indicating that his ideological innovations in this domain were a central feature of his reign for Christian and Zoroastrian elites.

As part of its assault on Sasanian kingship, the *Book of Wahram Chobin* makes use of an account of the conversion to Christianity of Ardashir I that had begun to circulate in the sixth century. Its East Syrian author, Alexander Schilling has shown, modeled Ardashir's conversion on Zoroastrian accounts of the turn of the Kayanian king Wishtasp to the teaching of Zoroaster, with the aim of demonstrating that the Christian faith could provide a source of legitimizing xwarrah for the dynasty.[133] The appearance of this story, which originated in Christian circles, in a narrative that emerged from an aristocratic milieu attests to its remarkably wide diffusion. Aristocratic communities that supported the rebellion of Wahram Chobin against the dynasty, however, found in the account an example of the Sasanian abrogation of the obligations of legitimate kingship.[134] According to al-Dīnawarī, who based his work on the *Book of Wahram Chobin*, aristocratic rebels evoked Ardashir's conversion to raise the specter of the Sasanians and their court abandoning Zoroastrianism for Christianity. In Iranian political culture, the aristocratic houses possessed the authority legitimately to displace a ruler who failed to fulfill his obligations, which included the maintenance of the Good Religion.[135] If earlier rebellions had sought to replace one Sasanian with another, Wahram Chobin and his allies were the first to try to eliminate the dynasty and to place the Mihranid house on the throne.[136] For such a purpose, the story of the founder of the Sasanian dynasty converting to Christianity was highly convenient. The court's very public use of Christian symbols in the decades of the *Book of Wahram Chobin*'s composition, moreover, would have lent credibility to the claims of anti-Sasanian aristocrats that Husraw II was a closet Christian.

Courtly historiographers responded to criticisms of the Sasanian embrace of Christian symbols. Because of the catastrophic nature of Husraw II's defeat at the hands of Heraclius, narratives of the Roman conquests were either suppressed or only selectively included in surviving versions of the royal histories.[137] There are no traces of the campaigns in Firdawsī, and only skeletal accounts in al-Ṭabarī and al-Dīnawarī. We thus lack a courtly perspective on the translation of the True Cross or the behavior of the king of kings and his agents in the conquered territories. In accounts of Roman-Iranian relations in the decades preceding the conquests, however, Husraw II's controversial engagement with Christian materials is a leading theme. The alliance with Maurice put him in possession of potentially authoritative Roman regalia, gifts that the emperor had sent to mark the definitive defeat of Wahram Chobin. Among the precious goods that the Romans dispatched were a bejeweled cross and brocade robes decorated with crosses, according to the *Šāhnāme*.[138] In an account that well captures the ideological conundrum of his reign, the king of kings reportedly sought the guidance of Zoroastrian advisers as to what should be done with such overtly Christian objects. The wearing of "garments of patriarchs," Husraw II stated frankly, was not a custom of Iranian nobles but rather "a custom of Christians" (*āyīn-ī tarsā*). If the king of kings refused to don them, the emperor would take this as a rejection of a diplomatic gift and would suspect him of disloyalty. But if Husraw II were to wear the crosses, the nobles at court would take this as evidence of his conversion to Christianity. Displaying the cross would help to forge an alliance with the emperor—or any Christian whose cooperation was needed—at the risk of the Iranian nobles raising precisely the objections that the *Book of Wahram Chobin* makes to Sasanian rule. The guidance of a Zoroastrian counselor provided a resolution. Religion does not reside in garments, he insisted: "You remain in the religion of the prophet Zoroaster even if you are allied with Caesar." The symbols of Christianity could be displayed without compromising the dynasty's adherence to the Good Religion. The king of kings, according to Firdawsī, donned the vestments for audiences of Iranians and Romans alike. Yet doubts about the innovation lingered. Some realized that he wore the garments to satisfy his Christian audiences. Others wondered aloud "whether the ruler of the world has become a Christian in secret."

An account of the fate of a fragment of the True Cross further reveals anxieties concerning the court's use of Christian symbols. In the course of the diplomatic correspondence between the emperor and the king of kings that followed their alliance, Maurice requested one gift in exchange for the convoys of gold, embroidery, and jewels that the Romans had sent, "the wood of Christ [*dār-ī masīhā*] that is in your treasury."[139] The origins and nature of this wood went unspecified. The redactors of the *Book of Kings* appear to have confused the requested object with the True Cross—seized after Maurice's death—in the new treasury of Husraw II or to have deliberately rendered this wood a representative of the complete relic whose recapture the historiographers had to ignore. The episode, in either case, provided an occasion to articulate the court's justifications for possessing a cross in its treasury that were directed to the great aristocrats, the primary audience for royal narratives. In his imagined response to Maurice, Husraw II insists on his loyalty to the "pure [*pākīzeh*] religion" and "the religion of Hushang," one of the primordial ancestors of the Sasanians.[140] He was nevertheless unwilling to release the relic. In his view, it was merely a piece of wood, not worthy of its position in the royal treasury in the first place, still less of serving as a diplomatic gift.[141] The king of kings thus refused the emperor's request. What this narrative proclaiming "the wood of Christ" worthless obscures is the reason for its preservation in the royal treasury. But the inherent contradictions of the account did not concern the courtly historiographers, who were interested in explaining how a king of kings could keep a Christian cross. The purpose of their narration was to silence detractors of the royal policy of holding the True Cross—whether a mere fragment or the relic in its entirety—in honor at court. In a manner characteristic of Iranian historiography, courtly literati could include criticism of the king of kings in their texts even as they insisted on the legitimacy of his actions within a Zoroastrian framework.

An account in the *Šāhnāme* of Husraw II's encounter with a Roman envoy most clearly communicates the terms on which a Sasanian could employ Christian symbols. At a banquet to which he had invited the Romans at court, the king of kings wore the gold-embroidered, cross-emblazoned garments that Maurice had given him. While Husraw II intoned the wāz prayer before the meal, an envoy known as Neiathous threw his bread in annoyance, proclaiming that "[mixing] the wāz and the cross is to insult Christ through Caesar."[142] The wearing of the cross was, in an accurate representation of Roman Christian ideology, incompatible with the saying of Zoroastrian prayers. To this objection to the royal mixing of religious practices, Husraw II replied unequivocally, "No one should conceal the religion of the gods. From Gayomard to Jamshid to Kay Kawad, no one has recalled Christ."[143] Abstention from the saying of the wāz would have constituted an unthinkable act of apostasy for a king of kings. Husraw II encharged his wife Maria with persuading Neiathous to recognize that the king of kings would never abandon the Good Religion and to refrain from impetuously propagating Christianity. Accepting these terms of participation in courtly affairs, Neiathous responded, "Continue in the religion of your ancestors; a wise man does not turn from religion [*kīš*]."[144] Here we find encapsulated two principles that, the next section shows, were generally normative in late Sasanian political culture and provided the necessary foundations for Husraw II's experimentation with Christian institutions: imperial Zoroastrianism was to be unquestioned and inviolate, and conversion from Zoroastrianism to Christianity was accordingly impermissible. The imagined figure of a Roman envoy assailing a Zoroastrian practice provided an opportunity for courtly historiographers to articulate the conditions under which an unambiguously Zoroastrian king of kings could wear crosses on his person. Christianity had a legitimate place at court only as long as the superior position of Zoroastrianism was secure.

CONVERSION, BOUNDARIES, AND IMPERIAL VIOLENCE

In East Syrian literature, in contrast with courtly historiography, the late Sasanian period was an age of Zoroastrian decline. With kings of kings so actively supportive of Christianity, more and more Zoroastrians were supposed to have abandoned the Good Religion to become Christians. The *History of Rabban Mar Saba*, composed during the reign of Husraw II, recounts how the namesake saint converted village after village, town after town, to Christianity from Zoroastrianism, with only sporadic interventions from Iranian authorities.[145] But even the highest levels of the Sasanian elite were reported to have drawn closer to the Christian faith, on the example of the kings of kings Husraw I and Ardashir I, whom late Sasanian Christian authors claimed to have been covert converts. A work of hagiography written in the most powerful East Syrian circles in the first quarter of the seventh century, the *History of Sabrisho*, expressly equates the court's support for Christian institutions with an increased rate of conversion under Husraw II:

> A merciful command was given by the king that whoever wishes to become Christian from any religion [*deḥlta*], or wishes to build a monastery [*daira*] wherever he wish, was allowed to do so according to his will, without anyone interfering. For this reason, many of the members of the house [of the king] abandoned their previous error and became Christians. The notables of his kingdom built many churches and monasteries, and even the king built a monastery and named it in the name of the faithful queen Shirin.... In every royal house and every noble house the name of Christ triumphed on account of [Sabrisho], and all took refuge in his prayers.[146]

This account is a misrepresentation of the policies of Husraw II that nevertheless captures some of the ambitions to which his reign gave rise among ecclesiastical leaders.

According to triumphalist hagiographers, the empire stood on the brink of total conversion. A number of modern studies have accepted this claim to varying degrees. One recent study speaks of "dwindling numbers of Zoroastrians" in the late Sasanian era.[147] Geo Widengren and Gernot Wiessner went so far as to argue counterfactually that the Iranian Empire would have become Christian had the early Islamic conquests not brought its ruling house to a premature end.[148] There were, however, few documented converts from Zoroastrianism to Christianity in the late sixth and early seventh centuries. As chapter 2 discusses, in Middle Persian sources, converts joined the Good Religion as commonly as they departed it, and acts of apostasy were not always definitive. Only the Christian hagiographical literature records cases of unambiguous conversion, and if we accept its accounts as historical, the number of Zoroastrian apostates was paltry. In the fifth century, East Syrian hagiographers, such as the author of the *Martyrdom of Pethion, Adurohrmazd, and Anahid,* turned toward narrating the martyrdom of converts, developing works of increasingly complex style and theology. These texts shared the aim of defining the truth of Christianity in relation to the falsehood of Zoroastrianism, with each author attuned to the intellectual and political concerns of his particular environment. Despite what their polemical purposes might suggest, the late Sasanian hagiographical works tended to be composed in the immediate aftermath of the martyrdoms in question and in ecclesiastical circles whose members were familiar with the circumstances. Their authors thus retained historicity even as they reframed events to suit their narrative goals, allowing for the reconstruction of cases of conversion. If we disregard reports of generalized, large-scale conversion that lack substantive details such as names, dates, and places, there were scarcely a dozen converts in the sixth and early seventh centuries whose cases hagiographers documented.[149] This was hardly the swelling tide of elite conversions that the author of the *History of Sabrisho* described. There were doubtless other individuals who joined the Christian churches, perhaps a great many. The ways in which hagiographers made the social and cultural dilemmas of converts—how to extricate oneself from a disapproving family, what to do with one's Zoroastrian spouse, whether to continue observing Zoroastrian regulations of purity—central themes of their works suggest that these predicaments were not uncommon.[150] But there may have been as many Christians who apostatized in favor of the Good Religion, like the famous philosopher Paul the Persian during the reign of Husraw I.[151] The martyrological narratives should not, therefore, be regarded as paradigms of the experiences of untold thousands of Zoroastrian apostates. They may nevertheless be paradigmatic of a particular kind of convert: those who were prosecuted and executed by Iranian authorities for their conversion to Christianity.

The same court that so actively embraced the institutions of the Christians also orchestrated the killing of prominent members of their ranks for apostasy from Zoroastrianism.[152] The new Cyrus, Husraw I, and the partner of Sergius, Husraw II, are thus known, in both ancient Christian and modern historiographies, as persecutors of the very Christians they patronized. Even though some of the most famous converts of the era, such as Mar Aba and the legendary Rabban Mar Saba, escaped execution, the bulk of the documented converts found themselves subject to violence at the hands of Zoroastrian authorities. Some of these were historical figures, such as Gregory the Commander, Yazdpaneh, George the Priest (d. 615), Ishosabran (d. 620/21), and Anastasios the Persian (d. 628).[153] Others were legendary, such as Mar Qardagh, Sultan Mahduk, and Mar Saba. As we saw in chapter 1, historians have taken narratives of prosecuted apostates as evidence for the systematic enforcement of the law of apostasy, according to which those who abandoned the Good Religion merited death. But the question of whether such a law was applied can be addressed only on the basis of the hagiographical works that document particular, historical—as opposed to legendary—cases of execution for apostasy. Given the importance of martyrs and their commemoration to Christians, the late Sasanian hagiographical works can be regarded as reliable sources for the frequency of execution for apostasy. Had more Christians been slain for converting, accounts of their martyrdom would have been composed. Therefore, very few apostates were executed. If the principle that apostates from Zoroastrianism should be slain was applied only exceptionally, the precise circumstances of its invocation bear examining.

Aristocratic anxieties about the effects of conversion on their patrilineages and patrimonies were an important impetus behind violence against converts. The bulk of known martyrs in the late Sasanian era were members of aristocratic houses, whose patrilineal relatives initiated the proceedings against them. There were two ways that conversion could endanger the integrity of a house. Abandoning the Good Religion rendered aristocratic men and women ineligible for marriage—whether endogamous or with allied houses—that would ensure the reproduction of a Zoroastrian clan and its properties. As aristocratic houses understood their political authority to derive from their mythical-historical roles, moreover, the rejection of religion was an affront to the power of the entire clan and a threat to its reputation in the highly competitive politics of the period. Houses ranging from provincial clans in northern Mesopotamian to the great family of the Mihranids demanded that the court intervene to punish converts in their ranks in the sixth and early seventh centuries. However rare such episodes of execution were, their political resonance extended well beyond the Christian communities that commemorated the martyrs, to the great houses that, as the *Book of Kings* suggests, were concerned that the court's embrace of Christian symbols might undercut the foundations of their own authority. Such anxieties appear to have been unwarranted, in light of the limited number of identifiable aristocratic converts. The high-profile presence at court of Christian symbols and leaders—including some apostates from Zoroastrianism—who boasted of their expansionist ambitions nevertheless gave Iranian elites cause for concern about the state of their patrimonies in the early seventh century.

Conversions attracted the attention of the court only if they challenged the foundations of imperial order, such as the aristocratic houses or the ideology of Ērānšahr, publicly—that is, in the presence of decision-making elites. The story of Rabban Mar Saba freely converting villages in the Zagros Mountains is plausible, as there were countless settlements in the empire that only rarely encountered imperial elites. Acts of apostasy that took place in an aristocratic household were necessarily public, because the houses were effectively the arms, indeed the very constituents, of the state. Among the other spaces where conversions could be made public were the institutions of the military, the religious administration, and the court. It is in these locations that the two best-known cases of execution for apostasy during the reign of Husraw II occurred, namely those of Anastasios the Persian and George the Priest. Originally a Zoroastrian from the region of Rayy, Anastasios was enlisted in the conquering armies, and the sight of the True Cross attracted him to Christianity and, ultimately, inspired him to convert.[154] He withdrew from his fellow conquerors unmolested but returned to the site of the Iranian administration in Caesarea Maritima to humiliate Zoroastrianism publicly. He found a group of Zoroastrian priests and interrupted their performance of the Yasna to ridicule their religion and to enjoin them to convert to Christianity. The marzbān in the city accordingly intervened, discovered Anastasios's apostasy, and dispatched him to Seleucia-Ctesiphon for prosecution and punishment.[155] Anastasios was executed at the command of the king of kings in 628.

The apostasy of George the Priest, born a Zoroastrian noble, similarly only became consequential politically when the facts of his conversion became known to elites. Invited to represent the East Syrians at the disputation of 612, discussed above, George became a victim of the machinations of Gabriel of Sinjar, the secular leader of the West Syrians.[156] Gabriel exposed George as a convert before the entire court in an effort to discredit his East Syrian rivals. The ensuing investigation produced a document that proved incontrovertibly that the monk had been a Zoroastrian, and the court took action in a case whose details had become widely known in elite circles of Seleucia-Ctesiphon.[157] The execution of George in 615 communicated clearly to elites across the empire that the court would preserve the Good Religion inviolate and police its boundaries with violence if necessary.

The site of George's martyrdom underlines the communicative dimension of the act. Unusual among martyrs under Iranian rule, his death took place as publicly as his apostasy had been revealed, at a symbolic center of the royal cities. The killing was orchestrated at the hay market of Weh-Ardashir, known as Koxhe in Syriac, one of the constituent cities of Seleucia-Ctesiphon.[158] Weh-Ardashir was, legendarily since the arrival of the apostle Mari, the seat of the bishop of the royal cities and thus the patriarchate. It was unambiguously the center of Christianity in the empire. In selecting a market, a crossroads of the city, as the site for George's execution, the court aimed to reach as wide an audience of Christians as possible. The advocates of conversion from Zoroastrian, such as the author of the *History of Sabrisho*, were to understand that however much the king of kings supported the churches, Christians would not be permitted to expand their ranks at the expense of the Good Religion. Husraw II's unprecedented embrace of Christian symbols was not to be mistaken for an increase in the flexibility of the boundaries of the imperial religion. At the same time, the case of George would have been known throughout Seleucia-Ctesiphon, since Weh-Ardashir housed the heart of its commerce. The significance of this execution becomes clear only in its temporal and spatial relation to the arrival of the True Cross in the city. The installation of the cross in the new royal treasury just across the Tigris from Weh-Ardashir occurred within months of George's death in January 615. The convert was, moreover, crucified at the market, an unusual and possibly unprecedented form of capital punishment in Iran. References to the use of crucifixion by Iranian officials prior to the era of Roman conquest are, according to Christelle Jullien, ambiguous.[159] The decision to execute the convert on a cross appears to have been intended to put the death in dialogue with the True Cross in the treasury. Husraw II simultaneously disciplined and honored the Christians of Iran by means of the cross.

While refraining from pursuing converts, the court systematically punished, sometimes spectacularly, their acts. There was a concerted effort by the regime to prevent the attrition of the Zoroastrian ranks and, more productively, to communicate the peculiar, unquestionably superior status of the Good Religion through the violent policing of its boundaries at the very moment when Christian institutions were giving expression to imperial rule. The kings of kings of the fourth and fifth centuries occasionally had apostates executed, on an apparently ad hoc basis. Their late Sasanian counterparts, however, developed the normative judicial procedures for disciplining apostates that we examined in chapter 1. The courtly political advice literature that enjoins kings of kings to preserve the position of Zoroastrianism and to ensure that apostates are brought to justice is difficult to date precisely but reflects the conditions of the reign of Husraw II quite as much as those of Husraw I. The inquests into the conversions of Anastasios, George, and Ishosabran followed the procedures in the *Letter of Tansar* (see chapter 1), suggesting that the court aimed to enact the principles that its Zoroastrian religious authorities had articulated in matters of religious boundaries.[160] The Armenian *History of Pseudo-Sebeos* indeed reports that Husraw II issued an empire-wide decree against conversion: "Let none of the impious dare to convert to Christianity, and none of the Christians to impiety, but let each one remain firm in his own ancestral tradition."[161] We encountered a distorted echo of such a proclamation in the *History of Sabrisho*, according to which the king of kings had issued an edict permitting anyone to convert to Christianity.[162] What is significant is not that the hagiographer misrepresented the decree but rather that Christian authors both Armenian and East Syrian could regard the pronouncement of a legal principle forbidding conversion as an act of benevolence.[163] The reported decree recognized the legitimate position of Christianity in the empire, with institutions and boundaries that were to be respected as much as those of the Good Religion. At the same time, the king of kings insisted on the inviolability of Zoroastrianism, and the actions of his court in the early seventh century exhibited his commitment to the supremacy of this religion. The execution of George in Weh-Ardashir's market was a logical consequence of the decree that the Armenian chronicler recorded.

CONCLUSION

After the death of Husraw II in 628, even an observer with firsthand knowledge of the Iranian court, Babai the Great, hoped for an end to Zoroastrian kingship.[164] The Roman emperor Heraclius took a more optimistic view of the place in the Christian *oikoumene* of Iran, which the Roman court had depicted as inveterately evil, in the immediate aftermath of his victory over it. Having become acquainted with Iranian elites, practices, and institutions, the emperor, Cyril Mango has argued, embarked upon the project of Christianizing Iran's ruling dynasty and Iran as a whole.[165] In 629 he arranged a meeting with the commander Shahrwaraz, the famous conqueror of Rome, who had apparently developed affinities with Christianity in the course of his career. His son bore a Christian name, Niketas.[166] Heraclius agreed to provide Shahrwaraz with a Roman army to seize power from Ardashir III (r. 528–29), the grandson of Husraw II, to replace the Sasanian house with a royal dynasty that would be Christian rather than Zoroastrian. Had this occurred, Iran would have become another satellite state subordinate to the most Christian emperor, its king of kings on par with the Ethiopian negus or the Christian kings of the Caucasus.[167] Shahrwaraz did indeed triumph over the Sasanian, momentarily establishing a new house, which was closely allied with Rome, on the Iranian throne. Before gaining the throne in 630, he had returned the True Cross to the Romans.[168] But the aristocracies of Iran refused to accept him, deposed him, and restored to the throne a Sasanian house that, at this stage, had only daughters to offer. Boran (r. 630–31), the daughter of Husraw II, proclaimed herself "the restorer of the lineage of the gods."[169] The attempts of ecclesiastical leaders, however tentative, to Christianize the fundamental institutions of the empire lasted only as long as the aristocratic houses required to organize their martial forces. A reassertion of the supremacy of Zoroastrianism that had pertained under Husraw II followed. Until the death of Yazdgird III in 651, and even beyond, the rulers of Iran sought to realize Ērār-šahr in self-conscious imitation of Husraw II.[170] Despite the embarrassment of his defeat in 628, that king of kings left a legacy as the embodiment of the ideals of Iranian, Zoroastrian kingship. The alliance of Heraclius with Shahrwaraz thus reveals striking contradictions in the perceptions of Christians and Zoroastrians of the relationship between religion and empire in Iran in the early seventh century. Among Christians across the Near East and the Mediterranean, the association of Husraw II with Christ and his saints had given rise to reports of his clandestine conversion, to the extent that even the Roman emperor could imagine a Christian Iranian state. For Zoroastrians, the possibility of a Christian king of kings was as unimaginable as at any point in the history of the dynasty, and Husraw II's use of Christian symbols in no way undermined his position as an ideal Iranian ruler.

The apparent paradoxes of Husraw II's reign were the result of Christian misinterpretations of Iranian symbolic actions. Christian religious specialists, as we have seen throughout the preceding chapters, regarded the adoption of the practices of another religion as a self-evident sign of apostasy. They brought the same understanding of identity to bear on the adherents of other religions. A king of kings who petitioned a saint, invited a holy man into his entourage, honored the True Cross, expelled Jews from Jerusalem, and organized an inquiry into Christian orthodoxy appeared obviously to be a Christian. But Zoroastrians did not share this exclusive understanding of religious identity. The question for wehdēn was not whether one participated in the institutions of another religion but whether such participation contradicted or complemented Zoroastrian institutions. As long as one worked to realize the cosmological project of the Good Religion, one could adapt the practices and institutions of another religion in one's practical, everyday social and political life. Christianity's proselytizing tendencies did pose a challenge to this cosmological project, at least theoretically. The Iranian court accordingly took decisive action to contain this aspect of the religion while remaining supportive of its leaders and their institutions.

Conclusion

If this book began with a king of kings according honors to a holy man, an account of monks venerating the body of an Iranian ruler provides its conclusion. The last king of kings, Yazdgird III, perished in 651 in the vicinity of Merv after a decade and a half of organizing resistance to the Arab Muslims whose conquest of the Iranian Empire was now complete.[1] Like his early fifth-century namesake, he was slain at the hands of revolting Iranian nobles of Khurasan rather than by conquerors. When taken captive, according to Firdawsī, Yazdgird III was searching for a barsom, the bundle of pomegranate twigs used in the Yasna, for a final performance of the ritual that had sustained Ērānšahr. The marzbān of Merv, Mahoe, responded to the piety of the ruler with what in Zoroastrian terms was a profoundly impious act: the throwing of the royal corpse into a river, polluting its sacred waters.[2] With the aristocracy having abrogated empire and religion simultaneously, only Christians remained, in this account, to treat the body of the sovereign appropriately. On the discovery of the floating corpse, monks from a nearby monastery recognized the ruler and took him to shore. They pronounced a curse upon Mahoe and a paean to the last Sasanian, lamenting the loss of a "warlike" ruler and the "lineage of Ardashir."[3] They gave the king of kings a resting place in a towering tomb, in a garden adorned with silk and musk. Even in the face of the overwhelming Muslim conquests and the rebellion of the leading aristocrats, these Christian monks insisted on their loyalty to the king of kings and accorded him the honors worthy of a ruler, in Christian if not Zoroastrian terms. In the great epic of the Iranian Empire, Firdawsī had Christian ascetics bring Ērānšahr to a ceremonious conclusion. Whether monks actually took possession of the body of the last king of kings and constructed a monument in his memory is less important than the fact of the historical memory that Christians were the unwavering allies of Iran, even potentially more committed to the Sasanian dynasty than were the Iranian aristocrats who had abandoned Yazdgird III. Iranian elites, whether the courtly literati who compiled the *Book of Kings* or the aristocratic storytellers on whom Firdawsī often drew, commemorated the Christian contribution to their empire.[4] Such a narrative derives its plausibility from the developments that the previous chapters have charted. As a memory, the account of the Christian custodians of the last Sasanian captures, in a succinct episode, the relationship between the Church of the East and the Iranian Empire, which had gradually taken shape over the course of the preceding two centuries.

By the time the Arab Muslims began their conquests, the Iranian court had harnessed the elites and institutions of East Syrian communities in its service, in positions subordinate to the elites and institutions of the Good Religion. In the fourth and fifth centuries, the kings of kings struggled to come to terms with the new religious professionals in their midst, as bishops sought to lead nascent communities on the model of their peers in the Roman Empire. What began as an invitation from Shapur II to bishops to serve alongside the Zoroastrian priestly elite in the Iranian fiscal administration marked the beginning of nearly a century of sometimes violent negotiation over the role that the ecclesiastical elite played in an expanding imperial network. With the mutual recognition of their distinct political and religious spheres of authority in 410, kings of kings and bishops came to collaborate more closely throughout the fifth century, precipitating further conflict concerning the boundaries between Christians and Zoroastrians. The court selectively employed violence to set limits on Christian ambitions, preventing East Syrians from assaulting fire temples and from converting adherents of the Good Religion to their own. These limits remained in place throughout the late Sasanian era, requiring periodic reinforcement when Christians attempted to transgress them. Norms communicated through violence—and its communal remembrance—allowed Christians to be included in imperial institutions without weakening the superior position of Zoroastrianism. Underpinning such differential inclusion was Zoroastrian cosmological thinking, which categorizes human populations hierarchically in accordance with the quality of their religion, genealogy, and place of origin. Although beneath the incommensurably superior Zoroastrian Iranians from exalted regions such as Fars and Parthia, Christians could surpass polytheists of various kinds in their religion, middling and laboring populations in their lineages, and the inhabitants of regions beyond Iran—and less esteemed ones within its confines—in their homelands. Despite their inferiority to great noble wehdēn, Christians could nevertheless attain elite status, recognition, and office in a Zoroastrian empire. The integration of Christian elites and institutions into the imperial network culminated during the reign of Husraw II, when the Iranian court sought to incorporate the Christian Roman Empire into an enlarged Ērānšahr. The Good

Religion, with its hierarchical rather than binary vision of culturally disparate populations, paradoxically facilitated the inclusion of East Syrian Christians and their shrines and bishoprics.

The political ascendancy of East Syrian elites, however, depended on their actions within the room for maneuver that Iranian political culture afforded them. The institutions of the Church of the East, once thought to insulate Christians from the empire, served as vehicles of integration. The evolving literary tool kits of ecclesiastical writers gave the organizers of saints' cults instruments with which to locate Christian elites in Iranian social and political taxonomies without compromising the particular religious identities that these selfsame authors were constructing. Even the polemical aspects of Christian texts contributed as much to the assimilation of East Syrian Christians as to their distinction. In the Iranian highlands, the hagiographer of the most thoroughgoing deconstruction of Zoroastrianism, the *Martyrdom of Peṭnion, Adurohrmazd, and Anahid*, appropriated the Iranian concept of "land"—a region imagined as a set of signature features in the landscape interpreted through mythical accounts of its history—as the focus of social and political loyalties that Christians and Zoroastrians could share. The deracinated diaspora of Christian "captives" thus acquired, through the literary efforts of this hagiographer, a narrative of its belonging to a land that was a constituent component of Iran. Similarly, hagiographers of northern Mesopotamia crafted accounts of the aristocratic status of East Syrian elites and located them in an Iranian taxonomy of nobility, as manful bnai ḥere / āzād of ancient lineage naturally predisposed to cooperate with their superiors, the Zoroastrian great nobles. The literary development of shared social and political imaginaries thus attended the integration of East Syrian elites and institutions into the imperial network. The cults of the martyrs became, in these instances, institutional mechanisms that rendered aspects of Iranian elite culture legitimate in Christian terms and melded Iranian and Christian cultures to create new communal imaginaries better suited to the political culture of the late Sasanian period. When their activities are discernible in the writings of Mar Aba, bishops appear, in their role as judges, to have been involved in the brokerage of Iranian and Christian laws, in express deference to the superior authority of Zoroastrian judges. Even when distinct Christian laws began to circulate in Iran in the sixth century, episcopal judges continued to appropriate Iranian legal practices necessary for the success of aristocrats in Iranian political culture, such as substitute successorship. Rather than separate Christians from the Zoroastrian elite, the institutions of the cults of the martyrs and the episcopal courts alike facilitated their assimilation and political integration.

East Syrian elites participated fully in Iranian political culture. They conceived of their past, present, and future within the framework of the mythical history of the *Book of Kings*, as the loyal servants of the kings of kings. They understood themselves in patrilineal terms, as the products of their fathers and forefathers, organized their resources in patrimonies, and developed and refined their genealogies in light of their present circumstances. The seed of their patrilineal ancestors had endowed them with the capacities that were the prerequisites for the wielding of imperial authority on behalf of the court. They joined in the aristocratic banquets and empire-wide feasts that were the principal sites of elite sociability and the making of claims to status. They believed that religious rituals, whether Zoroastrian or Christian, sustained the prosperity of an Iran that the benevolent deities, or deity, favored. They even laid claim to the aristocratic privilege of deposing a cosmologically deficient king of kings, in league with Zoroastrian aristocrats in the case of Husraw II. Interpreting the cosmological politics of their empire in Christian terms, they regarded their holy men and saints as the guardians of Iran, whose prayers ensured imperial victory as efficaciously as those submitted on behalf of the Christian Roman Empire. When Iran integrated much of the Roman *oikoumene* in the early seventh century, they looked to the king of kings to fulfill the functions of a Christian ruler. East Syrian Christians never became Iranian in name as long as the religious significance of ērīh predominated. But in their political practices, self-conceptions, and principles, East Syrian elites were as Iranian as aristocrats wehdēn and ēr or indeed the Christian aristocrats of the Caucasus. Between the death of the bishop Simeon in 351 and that of Yazdgird III in 651, the openness of the Iranian court and its Zoroastrian elite combined with the adaptability of ecclesiastical institutions to render East Syrian communities reliable ancillaries of the empire.

East Syrians were, therefore, as much the heirs of Iran as were their Zoroastrian peers. More than a century after the Islamic conquests, a Christian scholar on a journey to Constantinople left a Middle Persian inscription in which he described his native land as Ērānšahr.[5] The use of this archaic term as a marker of political belonging by an eighth-century East Syrian suggests that the appropriation of Iranian elite culture continued apace after the collapse of the empire. The incorporation of Iranian territories into the caliphate removed Zoroastrianism from its position of political superiority, even though the mowbed, fire temples, and hērbedestān continued to thrive into the ninth century, thanks to the support of their aristocratic adherents, institutional resources, and the Muslim ruling elite.[6] Nevertheless, East Syrian ecclesiastical leaders who enjoyed particularly intimate ties with *amīr*s were well placed to claim forms of authority on which Zoroastrians had had a monopoly. The perquisites of the Zoroastrian elite, including their political power and symbolic capital, were available for the taking, and East Syrian bishops were precocious adapters to the new political culture. They composed lawbooks in Middle Persian that harmonize Christian and Iranian laws and claimed to serve as the paramount judicial authorities over East Syrian communities, a role that the mowbedān mowbed had once occupied.[7] The combination of Christian and Iranian symbolism in the local coinage of Fars and Khuzestan during the first Islamic century attests not only to East Syrian control of the minting process in at least some cities but also to experimentation with new modes of representing political authority. Crosses of Roman and East Syrian styles accompany traditional Iranian symbols and formulae on copper coins that East Syrian authorities minted for local consumption.[8] Unambiguously to emphasize the appropriation of the office of the mowbed, one copper coin depicts a bishop wearing a kolāh, the headgear exclusive to the members of the Zoroastrian aristocracy, emblazoned with a cross.[9] As the symbols of the Iranian elite became free-floating resources, more and more East Syrians took the names of the great aristocratic houses, such as Surēn, and claimed noble status.[10] Even the baseborn inhabitants of Mesopotamia presented themselves as being of Iranian aristocratic descent, and a verb for such bluster, "to fashion oneself a dahigān," *tadahaqana*, appears in early Arabic.[11] Alongside these aristocratic houses, which largely converted to Islam in the eighth and ninth centuries, East Syrian communities were bearers of the Iranian imperial legacy in early Islamic society.[12] Ninth-century Christians could thus still regard Ērānšahr as their homeland.

The legacy of the politics of mixture extended well beyond the frontiers of the Iranian world. Before the end of the seventh century, the Church of the East far surpassed its Western counterparts in geographical reach, including not only its ancient communities of South India but also its comparatively recent communities in Tang China. The Asian micro-Christendoms that looked to the patriarch of Seleucia-Ctesiphon—and later Baghdad—bore a distinctly Iranian imprint, both superficially and structurally. The Christians of Kerala prominently displayed Middle Persian inscriptions in their sanctuaries, expressing an identification with the empire from the Sasanian period to the end of the first millennium CE.[13] East Syrian Christianity in China was similarly known as Bosi jiao, the "scriptural religion from Persia," even if ecclesiastical leaders there came to identify with the Christian Roman Empire in the middle of the eighth century after the hope for a Sasanian revival had definitively evaporated.[14] Whether in the ports of Kerala or the Chinese capital of Chang'an, the Church of the East was recognizably an institution of Iran. East Syrian communities in China and India therefore established relations with non-Christian political authorities and other religious communities on Iranian models, distinctly unlike the Roman and post-Roman churches, which aspired to religious and political uniformity in their territories, leaving increasingly narrow spaces for religious others. By contrast, the East Syrian stele erected in Chang'an in 781 acknowledges the sovereignty of the Tang emperors, to whom ecclesiastical leaders attributed the success of their church in Chinese territory.[15] For East Syrians accustomed to recognizing the sacred-historical legitimacy of Iranian kings of kings, the interdependence of their so-called luminous religion (Jingjiao) and the Tang court was entirely unproblematic. In South India, East Syrian copper plates from Quilon, on the coast of Kerala, demonstrate the ubiquity of cooperation among Christians, Zoroastrians, and Jews—as well as Muslims—of a kind that the previous chapters have shown characterized Christian-Zoroastrian interaction in the Sasanian period. As the local ruler granted an East Syrian bishop, Sabrisho, and his community far-reaching commercial privileges, representatives of Jewish, Zoroastrian, and Muslim communities pledged to assist the church in its administration of trade in what emerged as a key Indian Ocean emporium.[16] A bishop working on behalf of a Hindu ruler and in league with Zoroastrian, Jewish, and Muslim peers to place the East Syrian community on a solid material footing well captures the distinctive dynamic of the Christianity to which the Iranian Empire gave rise.

NOTES

INTRODUCTION

1. He had previously served as the bishop of the northern Mesopotamian town of Lashom: *Chronicle of Seert*, vol. 2, pt. 2, 474–81; *History of Sabrisho*, 289–301.

2. *Chronicle of Seert*, vol. 2, pt. 2, 482–85; *History of Sabrisho*, 306; P. Wood 2013, 194–96. The term *Iran* always appears as a shorthand for the Iranian Empire, or Ērānšahr, a Middle Persian concept whose significance is discussed later in the introduction.

3. *Chronicle of Seert*, vol. 2, pt. 2, 487–91.

4. Ibid., 489. For the experience of the court, see A. de Jong 2004a; Canepa 2009, 138–44; Azarnouche 2013a.

5. *Chronicle of Seert*, vol. 2, pt. 2, 488.

6. Ibid., 489.

7. Becker 2009, 326. See Garsoïan 1984 on the parallel situation in Armenia.

8. Lukonin 1969, 27–50; Huff 2008.

9. Howard-Johnston 1995b, 180–97; Haldon 2010.

10. Pourshariati 2008, 37–59; Mosig-Walburg 2010a.

11. For a critique of the application of modern liberal concepts and ideals to Iranian political culture, see Becker 2014.

12. Gnoli 1980; 1989.

13. Daryaee 2005.

14. Canepa 2009, 59–68, 100–110; Overlaet 2013.

15. Macuch 1994; 2004, 188–95.

16. For a critical overview, see Mahé 2002.

17. See chapter 5.

18. Gruzinski 1999, 33–57; Stewart 1999. The terms *syncretism* and *hybridity* will be avoided for their positive connotations in contemporary liberal political discourse. The

term *mixture* has the advantage of comparative neutrality in the present and, most important, of evocation of the cosmological language of Iranian discourse. It is thus best suited to capture the "tense, contradictory and unstable field of conflictual engagement, in which every signifier is a site of encounter, maneuver, advance, retreat and negotiation," that is the subject of the best studies of syncretism (Lincoln 2001, 457).

19. Wiessner 1967a.

20. Labourt 1904: 98; Sachau 1916, 969–73; Fiey 1968; Fiey 1969a; Fiey 1971; Fiey 1973a; Fiey 1973b; Gyselen 2003, 163.

21. For the state of the Sasanian period in twentieth-century archaeological scholarship, see Hauser 2001a; Hauser 2001b; Whitcomb 2007.

22. Hauser 2007a, 95–96.

23. Simpson 2005; Gaibov and Koshelenko 2006, 143–53; Hauser 2007a, 96–104; Hauser 2008; Amen Ali 2008; Toral-Niehoff 2014, 180–83; al-Kaʿbi 2014. For archaeological evidence of Christian communities in Central Asia beyond the limits of Iran, see Semenov 1996, 57–68; Naymark 2001, 81–90.

24. Cassis 2002, 67–68, 76–78.

25. Ibid., 68; Hauser 2008, 40–42.

26. Steve 2003, 87–130; Carter 2008; Payne 2011b.

27. Bayly 1983, 141–42.

28. Harrak 2002.

29. Hunter 1995. For historical reconstructions of the earliest Christian communities, see Chaumont 1988; Koshelenko, Bader, and Gaibov 1995.

30. See chapter 2.

31. Hopkins 1998; Bagnall 2003, 278–85.

32. Labourt 1904, 87–99; E. K. Fowden 1999, 52–54.

33. *Synodicon Orientale*, 17/254; McDonough 2008b, 130. The contemporary Ethiopian negus was similarly represented in Constantinian terms as "victorious": Bowersock 2010.

34. The contested nature of ecclesiastical structures is a leading theme of chapter 3.

35. The Christianization of the Roman imperial apparatus gave bishops a potentially destabilizing role in its operation: Drake 2000, 393–440.

36. Brock 1982, 15.

37. On the inappropriateness of the label Nestorian as a description of East Syrian doctrine and on the role of Nestorius in its articulation, see Brock 1985; Brock 1996; Pinggéra 2004; Seleznyov 2005, 35–58. Lange 2012, 490–516, provides a helpful overview of the development of East Syrian Dyophysite theology in the context of the sixth- and seventh-century Christological controversies.

38. Sachau 1907, 79; Selb 1981, 164–65.

39. Morony 1974; 1984, 364–72.

40. Brock 1982, 12; Frye 1988; Daryaee 2005, 127.

41. Russell 1987; Garsoïan 1996; Garsoïan 1997.

42. Hewsen 1997.

43. S. H. Rapp 2001; Martin-Hisard 2008; S. H. Rapp 2009.

44. Gafni 2003, 140–61; Elman 2007; Herman 2013. See also chapter 3 on the hazards of Zoroastrian feasts.

45. Herman 2005; Kiperwasser and Shapira 2008; Secunda 2014, 115–43.

46. Berger and Luckmann 1966, 65–109; Douglas 1986; Swidler 2001, 160–80.

47. Gignoux 1979; Shayegan 2003. For an overview of Middle Persian epigraphic and documentary texts, see Huyse 2009, 90–105.

48. Graus 1965, 60–61.

49. Wiessner 1967b, 9–10.

50. Peeters 1950; Brock 1994; Taylor 2002; Dickens 2009.

51. Asmussen 1984; Orsatti 2003; Panaino 2007; Sims-Williams 2009, 267–70; Dickens 2013.

52. Sims-Williams 2009, 271–37.

53. On the reorientation of research in Syriac hagiography, see Debié 2012, 28–39.

54. Patlagean 1968.

55. Concise accounts of martyrs and martyrologies likely already circulated in the fourth century: Brock 1978. For the influence of third- and fourth-century Syriac accounts from Edessa on early East Syrian literary production, see Rist 2009.

56. Baumstark 1922, 55–57; Peeters 1925; Wiessner 1967b, 10–20.

57. See chapter 1.

58. Hagiographers tended to obscure their identities out of humility: Krueger 2004, 3–9.

59. P. Brown 1971; P. Brown 1995, 59–65; P. Brown 1998; Cameron 1999 Castelli 2004, 25–28; Moss 2012, 8–18.

60. Graus 1965, 68–69; P. Brown 1983.

61. Sizgorich 2009.

62. Krueger 2004, 94–109.

63. Kreiner 2014, 16.

64. Fouracre 1990, 6–8. Bowersock 1995, 27–28, demonstrates the reliability of the historical details, if not the narratives, of some early accounts of Roman martyrs.

65. Selb 1981, 63–66.

66. Wickham 2005, 384–85.

67. Cantera 2004, 207–20; Elman 2010, 22–25; Secunda 2012.

68. Yarshater 1983; Shahbazi 1990; Daryaee 1995; Macuch 2009, 172–81.

69. Rubin 2005; Rubin 2008a; Rubin 2008b; Pourshariati 2010a; Pourshariati 2010b. Shayegan 2012, 109–55, shows how the discourses of royal inscriptions and Firdawsī's version of the *Xwadāy-nāmag* overlap in significant ways.

70. Rubin 1995; Rubin 2004 Rubin 2007; Pourshariati 2008, 13–17; Howard-Johnston 2010b, 341–53.

71. Greenwood 2002, 330. See also Kreyenbroek 2013.

1. THE MYTH OF ZOROASTRIAN INTOLERANCE

1. Grenet 1990; Gignoux 1991 17–32; Huyse 1998.

2. Kerdir, *Inscription at the Ka'aba-ye Zardosht*, 46/69–70 (modified translation). On the identity of these groups, see Elois 2002, 5–11. The Nazarenes and Christians are unlikely to have been distinct religious groups. The latter term is merely a polemical epithet for the former: C. Jullien and F. Jullien 2002b.

3. Asmussen 1962, 2–3; Chaumont 1988, 111–20; Schwaigert 1989, 42–44; Rist 1996, 26–29; Gignoux 2001b, 99–100; Stausberg 2002, 243; Bruns 2008, 85–91; Daryaee 2009, 77.

4. See Kalmin 2006, 127–29, for the lack of evidence for Jewish persecution in the third century.

5. A. de Jong 2004b, 51. For amiable early Sasanian relations with Christians, see Wiesehöfer 2007b, 167–68. Mani, unlike his Christian and Jewish counterparts, explicitly framed his religion in Iranian terms and worked to supplant Zoroastrianism in elite circles and even at the court: Hutter 1993. Manichaean communities were likely more robust in Iranian society throughout the Sasanian period than has been assumed, as the *History of Karka d-Beit Slok and Its Martyrs*, discussed in chapter 4, suggests. See also Lieu 1992, 106–11; Colditz 1992.

6. Mackenzie 1971, 51; Gignoux 1972, 26.

7. Boyce 1970, 331–36.

8. Wiesehöfer 1993, 380; Williams 1996, 38–41; Baum and Winkler 2000, 10; Rubin 2000, 650–51; Stausberg 2002, 239–41; A. de Jong 2004a, 347–48; Daryaee 2010a, 95–96; Wiesehöfer 2010, 132–33; McDonough 2011a, 303–5; Herman 2012, 39–49.

9. Some recent characterizations of Zoroastrians as intolerant and/or of kings of kings as variably tolerant and intolerant: Morony 1984, 332–33, 342; Wiesehöfer 1993, 377; Walker 2006, 109–12; Jany 2007, 360; McDonough 2011a, 291; Herman 2012, 42–49.

10. Garnsey 1984; P. Brown 1995, 29–54; Ando 2012. For a critique of tolerance that undermines its ethical as well as analytical value, see W. Brown 2008.

11. Nirenberg 1996, 227–30.

12. For the centrality of cosmogony in Zoroastrian political thought, see now the case studies of Lincoln 2012. Shaked 1994, 5–26, has a survey that restores religious and intellectual dynamism to Zoroastrian cosmogony in the Sasanian period. See chapter 2 for a critical consideration of the so-called Zurwanite cosmogony that is often supposed to have rivaled this account.

13. Shaked 1971, 70–72.

14. Kellens 2009, 41–43. The alternative, four-age schema appears to have been an innovation of the early Islamic period: Vevaina 2011, 245.

15. *Bundahišn*, 20–31.

16. Ibid., 46–53; *Wizīdagīhā ī Zādspram*, 34–39. If Ahreman worked through material creations, Zoroastrian scholars denied materiality to evil: Shaked 1967.

17. *Bundahišn*, 272–83.

18. MacKenzie 2002; Vevaina 2011, 254–55.

19. *Bundahišn*, 292–99; *Dādestān ī Dēnīg*, 40–42; *Wizīdagīhā ī Zādspram*, 56–61; Gnoli 1989, 144–48.

20. *Dēnkard V*, 32–34.

21. *Dēnkard VII*, 10–12.

22. Perikhanian 1983b, 9.

23. Shaked 2008, 106, 109; 2010a, 332.

24. The argument of Daryaee 2010a, 103–6, that Christians could become ēr, based on a Middle Persian inscription at Constantinople, downplayed its ninth-century date. Once Zoroastrianism lost its imperial foundations, its institutions, including its political vocabulary, were open to appropriation.

25. *Dēnkard VI*, 14–15, defines religion as "that which one always does" (*dēn hān ī hamē kunēd*).

26. Ibid., 100/101.

27. *Dēnkard VII*, 4–6.
28. For Mašyā and Mašyānē's fall into sin, see Shaked 1987, 244–47; Choksy 2002, 52–55.
29. Shaked 1994, 39; Stausberg 2009, 232–33.
30. A. de Jong 2005, 203.
31. Bartholomae 1904, 44–45; Lankarany 1985, 62, 170–71. The term continued simultaneously to designate the psychopomp of individual souls: Gignoux 2001b, 12–16.
32. Boyce 1970, 326–28.
33. MacEvitt 2008, 21–25.
34. Ibid., 21, distinguishes tolerance as a practice from ideologically grounded means of including religious others.
35. *Dēnkard III*, 24/46, 29/51.
36. Forrest 2011, 44–82.
37. Choksy 1989; A. de Jong 1999; Choksy 2002, 58–64.
38. A. de Jong 1997, 432–44; Meytarchiyan 2001, 54–64.
39. Meytarchiyan 2001, 65–101; Huff 2004.
40. Huff 1989; Hauser 2007a, 105; Hauser 2008, 43–44.
41. *Martyrdom of the Ten Martyrs*, 187–88.
42. Simpson and Molleson 2014, 78.
43. Herman 2010, 37–52; Payne 2011a, 94. On the Christianization of burial practices more generally, see A. Schmidt 1994, 46–62.
44. Brody 1990, 58; Kalmin 2006, 138; Herman 2010, 52. See Shaked 1994, 41–42, for a critique of such views.
45. Forrest 2011, 54.
46. Ibid., 55.
47. Elman 2005, 16–17.
48. *Widēwdād*, 179/149; Elman 2005, 18.
49. Elman 2005, 18; *Widēwdād*, 180/149.
50. For an overview, see Boyce 1975a, with Gnoli 1980, 221–22, and Schilling 2008a, 99–109. Although images and statues were present in Zoroastrian shrines of the Achaemenian and Parthian periods, these do not appear to have played a central role in their cults: A. de Jong 1997, 350–52.
51. *Mēnōg ī Xrad*, 34–35/23–24.
52. Russell 1987, 123–24; A. de Jong 2006, 235–37.
53. *Hazār Dādestān (MHD)*, 594; Boyce 1975a, 107.
54. *History of Karka*, 516.
55. The deities of Babylon, Borsippa, and elsewhere continued to be associated with the sites of their temples, even if these were no longer functioning: Müller-Kessler and Kessler 1999, 68–84.
56. *History of Karka*, 510.
57. Stavisky 1993–94; van Bladel 2011, 49–57.
58. Crone 2012a, 30–32, 36–37.
59. *Martyrdom of Peroz*, 256–57.
60. Molé 1960–61.
61. See, e.g., *Dādestān ī Dēnīg*, 42–43.
62. *Sīrat Ānūšīrwān*, 188–89/15–17.

63. Ibid., 191–92/18–19. See also *Dēnkard III*, 218–19/11; Grignaschi 1966, 32.
64. Al-Ṭabarī, *Ta'rīkh al-rusul wa al-mulūk*, vol. 2, 894/149, vol. 2, 897/155; Ibn Miskawayh, *Tajārib al-umam*, 182–83; Crone 1991, 23.
65. *Letter of Tansar*, 22/47.
66. Shaked 2010a, 332–33, 339.
67. *Mēnōg ī Xrad*, 64/56.
68. Ibid., 29/21.
69. *Pursišnīhā*, 68.
70. Ibid., 58.
71. *Widēwdād*, 100/97. See also Elman 2005, 18.
72. Kalmin 2006, 121–48.
73. See Brock 2008a, 78–81, for a list of surviving accounts.
74. *Martyrdom of Aqebshma*, 361–62.
75. Wiessner 1967b, 169–75; Gignoux 1983, 256.
76. Schwaigert 1988; Wiesehöfer 1993, 379; Walker 2012, 1000–1002. A recent survey regards the violence under Shapur II as "the bloodiest persecution of Christians in all of antiquity": Hage 2007, 273. Similar views appear in recent popular syntheses: Baumer 2006, 68–71; Wilmshurst 2011, 14–17.
77. *Oxford English Dictionary*, s.v. "persecution."
78. Labourt 1904, 43; Christensen 1944, 267–68; Fiey 1970a, 87–88; Boyce 1979, 119; Brock 1982, 7–10; Widengren 1984, 25; Schwaigert 1989, 120–14; Baum and Winkler 2000, 10–11; Stausberg 2002, 237; McDonough 2005, 246–51; Daryaee 2009, 77–78; Walker 2012, 1000. Asmussen 1962, 9–10, provides a dissenting view that has gone unappreciated, and Wiesehöfer 1993, 373–77, stresses internal political factors.
79. Eusebius of Caesarea, *Life of Constantine*, 466–71; Barnes 1985, 130–33; Frendo 2001; E. K. Fowden 2006, 389–90.
80. *History of Simeon*, 782–83/70.
81. *Martyrdom of Baboi*, 631–34. See also the nearly contemporaneous case of the scholar Narsai, who fled to Antioch after being accused of sedition: Barhadbeshabba Arbaya, *Ecclesiastical History*, 612–14.
82. Mosig-Walburg 2007, 174–76.
83. Wiessner 1967b, 178–98.
84. Ibid., 166–67.
85. Mosig-Walburg 2007, 178–82; Smith 2011, 265–73.
86. *History of Simeon*, 790–91/76.
87. *Martyrdom of Simeon*, 726–38/14–24; Smith 2011, 244–53. The Maccabees were also adopted as a literary model in fifth- and sixth-century Armenia: Thomson 1982, 137.
88. Christensen 1944, 234–36; Mosig-Walburg 2002. The political position of Shapur II was highly vulnerable: Pourshariati 2008, 56–57.
89. Schindel 2004, 219–39.
90. Metzler 1977, 219–33, 239–59; Pourshariati 2008, 38–43.
91. Whitcomb 1984; Gyselen and Gasche 1994, 26; Daryaee 1999b; Daryaee 2003b.
92. Schwaigert 1989, 22–33, 109.
93. *Martyrdom of Pusai*, 210.
94. Macuch 1987b, 177; Rubin 1995, 255–56.

95. *History of Simeon*, 793/78.
96. Smith 2011, 273–76.
97. Ishoyahb III of Adiabene, *Correspondence*, 268–69; Payne 2009, 400–401.
98. Schwaigert 1989, 135–36, 147.
99. *History of Simeon*, 779–82/68. For the date, see Stern 2004.
100. Seleucia-Ctesiphon: *Martyrdom of Shahdost*, 278–79; *Martyrdom of Barbashmin*, 296–97; *Martyrdom of Azad*, 253–54. Kashkar: *Martyrdom of the Forty Martyrs*, 327–39. Arbela: *Martyrdom of Barhadbeshabba*, 314; *Martyrdom of 111 Men and Women*, 291; *Martyrdom of Zebina and Companions*, 52; *Martyrdom of Badai the Priest*, 163; *Martyrdom of John the Bishop and Jacob the Priest*, 128; *Martyrdom of Bishop Abraham*, 130; *Martyrdom of Jacob the Priest and Azad the Deacon*, 137–38. Karka d-Beit Slok: *History of Karka*, 512–15; *Martyrdom of Narsai and Joseph*, 284. Khuzestan: *Great Slaughter of Khuzestan*, 246–47. The northern Mesopotamian hagiographical traditions—discussed further in chapter 4—are distinct from the Simeon cycle and lack their historically verifiable content: Wiessner 1967b, 276–88.
101. See Peeters 1925, 297–98, and Fiey 1964b, 203–8, for favorable opinions of the reliability of the northern Mesopotamian martyrologies. These collections would repay reconsideration.
102. Secular elites were comparatively rare among fourth-century martyrs and tended to be close associates of martyred bishops and priests: *History of Simeon*, 878–90/142–54; *Martyrdom of Hnanya the Worldly*, 131; *Martyrdom of Pusai*, 225–29. The last text is dependent on the Simeon cycle: Wiessner 1967b, 96–98. For the development of narratives of the two eunuchs both known as Guhishtazad, see Peeters 1910.
103. Griffith 1995, 229–34.
104. McDonough 2005, 284.
105. Garsoïan 1973–74; Sako 1986, 71–89; McDonough 2005, 273–84; McDonough 2008a.
106. For the development of anti-Zoroastrian polemics, see chapter 2.
107. Brock 1982, 5; Schrier 1992, 77–78; van Rompay 1995; Rist 1996, 32–33. Roman sources represent acts of violence against Christians in Iran as part of general persecutions for their own political purposes: Holum 1977, 155–56.
108. The Romans only gradually introduced religious rhetoric into the Iranian wars: Holum 1977, 162–67; Millar 2006, 68–76; Weisweiler 2009.
109. Grenet 2002; Howard-Johnston 2010a, 41–46; Payne 2014.
110. *Martyrdom of Jacob the Notary*; Labourt 1904, 113–17.
111. *History of Karka*, 521–27; McDonough 2006.
112. For the Armenian perception of the Central Asian frontier as a "distant foreign land," see Ełiše, *Vardan and the Armenian War*, 9/63.
113. *History of Karka*, 518–19.
114. Garsoïan 2009a.
115. Christensen 1944, 272–73; Devos 1966, 219–20; van Rompay 1995, 365–67; F. Jullien 2011a; P. Wood 2013, 39–44.
116. *Martyrdom of Mar Abda*, 251, 252.
117. Theodoret of Cyrrhus, *Ecclesiastical History*, 450–91; van Rompay 1995, 367.
118. Devos 1966, 218–19; van Rompay 1995, 367–68; P. Wood 2013, 44–46.
119. *Martyrdom of Narsai*, 172–73.

120. Ibid., 174.
121. Macuch 2004, 189–93.
122. Sizgorich 2009, 108–43; Lopez 2013, 102–26.
123. Kristensen 2009.
124. Ascetics acting independently of the state could nevertheless invoke its laws: Emmel 2008, 178–81.
125. Theodoret of Cyrrhus, *Ecclesiastical History,* 490–91; Gaddis 2005, 198.
126. The sole subsequent Sasanian narrative of the destruction of a fire temple, in the late sixth- or early seventh-century *History of Mar Qardagh* (67–68/53), projects the event into a distant, legendary past. Nathaniel of Shahrazur was the only historical East Syrian to destroy a fire temple in the early seventh century, a deed that earned him execution, like the abovementioned martyrs: *Chronicle of Seert,* vol. 2, pt. 2, 520. P. Wood 2012, 68, and P. Wood 2013, 48–50, importantly emphasize the opposition between the actions of the martyrs and the political interests of the catholicate. Herman 2014, 88–89, suggests that the author of the *Martyrdom of Narsai* sought to minimize the influence of Narsai's actions.
127. Peeters 1910. Ascetics were supposedly executed for proselytism in fourth-century Fars: *Martyrdom of Bar Shebya,* 281.
128. *Martyrdom of Shapur,* 125–27; *Martyrdom of the Ten Martyrs*; Herman 2013, 122; van Rompay 1995, 369–70; Devos 1965, 312–14.
129. For a Roman perspective, see John of Ephesus's account of those whom Simeon of Beit Arsham reportedly converted during the reign of Kawad I: *Lives of the Eastern Saints,* 140–41.
130. See Bruns 2008, 90, for a critical discussion.
131. *Martyrdom of Peroz,* 257–58; *Martyrdom of Jacob the Sliced,* 541–42.
132. For the pedagogical and ritual aspects of conversion, see Schwartz 2013, 17–25.
133. *Martyrdom of Narsai,* 171–72.
134. *Mēnōg ī Xrad,* 48/36.
135. *History of Yazdpaneh,* 414–15. Rabban Mar Saba, discussed later, also escaped prosecution and execution.
136. *Hērbedestān,* 62/63; *Hazār Dādestān (MHD),* 303/319.
137. East Syrian authors focused almost exclusively on cases of apostasy from the latter half of the fifth century onward: C. Jullien 2010, 282–84.
138. *History of Yazdpaneh,* 397–98; *Martyrdom of Anastasios the Persian,* 56–59; Babai the Great, *History of George the Priest,* 520–22. See the discussion of the latter two in chapter 5. The idea of voluntary martyrdom was well established in late Sasanian hagiography: *History of Saba Pirgushnasp,* 227–29.
139. *History of Rabban Mar Saba,* 636–39.
140. Ibid., 644–46.
141. *History of Gregory the Commander,* 350–51. Rayy was a stronghold of the Mihranids: Christensen 1944, 105.
142. Becker 2009, 305–8.
143. *History of Gregory the Commander,* 362.
144. Ibid., 367.
145. *Martyrdom of Shirin,* 113–14/17–18; Devos 1994, 6–15.
146. *Martyrdom of Shirin,* 119–21/22–23.

147. Babai the Great, *Martyrdom of Christina*, 206–7; Binder 2012, 18.
148. Ishoyahb III of Adiabene, *History of Ishosabran*, 510–11
149. Ibid., 516.
150. See, e.g., *History of Yazdpaneh*, 414–15.
151. Brock 1982, 5.
152. *Sīrat Ānūširwān*, 191–92/18–19.
153. Wikander 1966; Sundermann 1976, 173.
154. *Letter of Tansar*, 16/41.
155. Ibid., 16–17/42; Jany 2007, 360.
156. *Martyrdom of Pethion, Adurohrmazd, and Anahid*, 563.
157. *History of Gregory the Commander*, 353–54.
158. *Martyrdom of Shirin*, 118/21.
159. Ishoyahb III of Adiabene, *History of Ishosabran*, 511–12.
160. For the date, see F. Jullien 2004, 172.
161. See, e.g., Kolesnikov 1970, 45, on the antiaristocratic violence during the reign of Ohrmazd IV (r. 579–90).
162. Christensen 1944, 313; MacMullen 1986.

2. BELONGING TO A LAND

1. Luschey 1996a.
2. Al-Muqaddasī, *Aḥsan al-taqāsīm fī maʿrifat al-aqālīm*, 353.
3. Markwart 1931, 70–71. For the continued veneration of the mountain into the Sasanian period, see Boyce 1991a, 91–99; for open-air liturgies, see Boyce 1975a, 94–95.
4. Azarpay 1982; Movassat 2005, 19–62, 136–43; Gall 1990.
5. For the identification of the temple at Kangavar with Anahid, see Lukonin 1977; Russell 1986. For its late Sasanian date, see Azarnoush 2009.
6. Gropp 1995, 159–61; Boyce 1967; Boyce 1975b, 464; Russell 1987, 164. On the development of the fire temple, see Choksy 2007, 251–62; Schippmann 1971, 499–514. Minov 2013, 255–57, suggests that the representation of paradise as a mountain encountered in the Syriac exegetical tradition was produced under the influence of Zoroastrian models.
7. *Supplementary Texts to the Šāyast-nē-Šāyast*, 79. See also *Hōm Yašt*, 82–85.
8. *Martyrdom of Pethion, Adurohrmazd, and Anahid*, 628.
9. For the route of the road, see Levine 1974, 100–101; Kleiss 1977. On its Achaemenian origins, see Graf 1994.
10. Frankfurter 2003, 364–67; Caseau 2001a; Caseau 2001b.
11. Gyselen 1989, 61.
12. Fiey 1995, 333–34; Devos 1965, 315.
13. For the place of fire temples in the landscape and their connections with aristocratic houses, see the case study of Huff 1995.
14. Sims-Williams 1985, 31–68.
15. On account of the author's creativity, the text has been dismissed as "epic" rather than historical: Devos 1966, 221; Fiey 1970a, 92.
16. For the importance of Karka d-Beit Slok as a literary center, see chapter 4.
17. Cantera 2004, 11.

18. *Martyrdom of Pethion*, 584, 599; Ciancaglini 2008, 209, 148. Gippert 1993, 345–350, argues that such Iranian administrative terminology entered Georgian directly from Middle Persian, without Armenian intermediaries, suggesting that even in a comparatively distant province, encounters with imperial authority were conducted in Middle Persian.

19. For Syriac–Middle Persian bilingualism, see Ciancaglini 2008, 19–20; Gignoux 2011.

20. P. Brown 1995, 69.

21. Sachau 1916, 961–65; Chaumont 1988, 54–160. An archaeological survey in the region has revealed the concentration of settlement in urban centers that could have included captives like the counterparts of those in Khuzestan: Abdi 1999, 41.

22. Pigulevskaya 1963b, 125; Metzler 1977, 213–33; Morony 2004a; Canepa 2009, 27–28, 55.

23. *Chronicle of Seert*, vol. 1, pt. 1, 220–21; Chaumont 1988, 71–83.

24. Morony 2004a, 167–69.

25. Mosig-Walburg 2010b, 130–44.

26. Sachau 1916, 964; Peeters 1924; Schwaigert 1989, 19–23. The conquest of Antioch appears to have taken place in 253, not 260 as has usually been stated: Barnes 2009.

27. Guidi 1889, 407–14; Sachau 1916, 969–71; Wiessner 1967a.

28. Gyselen 2003, 163.

29. Schwaigert 1989, 45–102; Tubach 1997. See also chapter 3.

30. *Martyrdom of Miles*, 266–67.

31. Like the *History of Simeon,* on which its author depended, the text insists on Christian loyalty to the king of kings while recounting violence at his hands: Wiessner 1967b, 97.

32. *Martyrdom of Pusai*, 209. See also Mosig-Walburg 2010b, 150–53; C. Jullien 2011, 287–88. For the foundation and its economic functions, see Gyselen and Gasche 1994.

33. Lieu 1986, 484.

34. Smith 2011, 292–320.

35. *Martyrdom of the Captives*, 316–18.

36. Macuch 2010c, 199.

37. Gnoli 1989, 151.

38. Bogolyubov 1971; Blois 1990.

39. *Martyrdom of Pethion*, 560.

40. Widengren 1967a, 64–95; Bedrosian 1984.

41. For Christian nobles and notables in Beit Lapat, see *Martyrdom of Peroz*, 255, 257; *Martyrdom of Badma*, 347.

42. *Martyrdom of the Captives*, 324. See Fiey 1970c, 372–73, on the region and its Christian communities.

43. *Martyrdom of Pethion*, 562.

44. Gignoux 2001a; Gignoux 1998; Bruns 2009c. For a post-Sasanian East Syrian defense of ascetic specialization in medicine, see *History of Mar Yonan,* 473–75. The East Syrian monks of Turfan possessed a pharmacological treatise, composed in New Persian in Syriac script: Sims-Williams 2011, 361–67.

45. For the functions of these officials, see Gyselen 1989, 34–35; Macuch 1981, 15.

46. *Martyrdom of Pethion*, 617.

47. Williams 1996, 39; Gignoux 2001b, 100; Walker 2012, 1004. McDonough 2011a, 303, encapsulates the literature in speaking of "the inexorable spread of Christianity."

48. Kreyenbroek 1985, 101–2, offers a discussion of the term *kilīsyāg*.
49. For an overview of the legal benefits that conversion brought, see Cantera 2010.
50. *Hērbedestān*, 62/63 (modified translation). See also Macuch 2005a, 94; Shaked 2008, 107.
51. *Hērbedestān*, 80/81 (modified translation). See also Secunda 2005; 2014, 47–50.
52. Such statements provide context for the efforts of the sixth-century court to restrict access to the hērbedestān: Rezania 2012, 486–87.
53. On Abarag as a fifth-century scholar, see Macuch 1993, 13; Elman 2010, 23–24. Xrad ī ahlawān involved the study of ritual power (*nērang*): *Nērangestān, Fragard* 2, 280–81.
54. *Hērbedestān*, 62/63 (modified translation). The reading of *tarsāgīh* is not without ambiguity but finds support in the subsequent reference to *kilīsyā*.
55. Ishodenah of Basra, *Book of Chastity*, 23/21. As there is no mention of schools in the *History of Bar Shabba*, about Merv's legendary first bishop, of the fourth century, the Bar Shabba in question seems to have been the bishop who appeared at the Synod of 424: Brock 1995; Brock 2011; *Synodicon Orientale*, 43/285.
56. *Husraw and the Youth*, 51/54. See Azarnouche 2013b for the techniques of memorization and recitation in hērbedestān. The question of the frequency of literacy in Iranian society remains unexplored. But Weber 2010 presents materials for a study of the teaching of *dibīrīh*. Christian Arab elites in sixth-century al-Ḥīra were known to have acquired literacy in Middle Persian in Zoroastrian schools: Toral-Niehoff 2010, 332.
57. Elman 2006, 27.
58. Potter 1993; Bowersock 1995, 41–57; Buc 1997, 73–80.
59. Widengren 1956, 122–36.
60. Christensen 1944, 15–17; Blois 2003; Colditz 2005.
61. Menasce 1956, 424–26.
62. Macuch 1993, 346; Perikhanian 1983a, 634.
63. *Zand ī Wahman Yasn*, 138.
64. Pigulevskaya 1963b, 150; Macuch 1981, 79–84.
65. *Wonders and Magnificence of Sistan*, 261–63.
66. Chaumont 1974, 82–84.
67. Huff 1999, 27–28, considers the ancestral tombs of an unidentified "Dynastie lokaler Kleinfürsten" in the region in the late Parthian and the Sasanian period.
68. Kawami 1987, 160–62; Gall 1996. A Parthian inscription identifies the ruler: Gropp and Nadjmabadi 1970, 200–201.
69. *Martyrdom of Pethion*, 574–76.
70. See chapter 4.
71. *Martyrdom of Pethion*, 594.
72. Caseau 2001b, 43.
73. Markus 1994; Sotinel 2005, 420–21.
74. *Martyrdom of Pethion*, 598.
75. Ibid., 623–24.
76. Ibid., 627.
77. Ibid., 599–600.
78. Ibid., 602.

79. See C. Jullien and F. Jullien 2010 and F. Jullien 2013, 344–49, on the idea of ḥnana and its associated practices.

80. Macuch 2003; Moazami 2005.

81. Insects harmful to agriculture are a common theme in Christian hagiography: P. Brown 1995, 61. Egyptian saints similarly demonstrated their prowess over animals traditionally regarded as demonic, such as crocodiles: Frankfurter 2003, 372–74.

82. *Martyrdom of Pethion*, 601.

83. Ibid., 626–27.

84. *Martyrdom of Miles*, 275. See Brock 2008c, 185–86, for the disarmingly early date of the text and Sundermann 2002 for its influence.

85. *Martyrdom of the Captives*, 323–24.

86. For examples of cults of water and rainmaking in the Iranian highlands, especially at the recently excavated site of Čāle Ğār, see Overlaet 2011.

87. Walker 2004; Walker 2006, 166–72; Tubach 1998, 414–15; Bruns 2014.

88. Becker 2006b, 33.

89. After Nöldeke (1893) translated the relevant cosmological expositions, discussed later in this chapter, studies of Zurwanism continually interpreted them in this way.

90. *Martyrdom of Pethion*, 565.

91. Ibid., 589.

92. See Gignoux 1976, 106–8, and Gignoux 2005 on such compound names.

93. *Martyrdom of Pethion*, 588; Boyce 1967, 36.

94. *Martyrdom of Pethion*, 577. See also Nöldeke 1893, 35–36.

95. *Martyrdom of Pethion*, 592. See also Nöldeke 1893, 36.

96. Nyberg 1931, 87; 1937, 427.

97. Rezania 2010, 281–315.

98. Shaked 1992, 226–27.

99. Nyberg 1937, 424–34; Widengren 1965.

100. Christensen 1944, 435; Zaehner 1955; Boyce 1957b, 306–8; Morony 1984, 288–91; Hutter 1993, 10–12; Boyce 1996, 15–17; Blois 2000, 5–7; Stausberg 2002, 247. See Molé 1959, Frye 1959, and Menasce 1962 for early criticisms of this literature, which went largely unheeded.

101. Rezania 2010, 12–24, and A. de Jong 1997, 330–38, provide critical surveys.

102. Shaked 1992, 228.

103. See the response of Boyce 1996 to Shaked 1994.

104. A. de Jong 1997, 68; Boyarin 2007.

105. Eznik of Kołb, *Treatise on God*, 156–59; Mar Aba, *Regulations of Marriage*, 264–66/265–67. Chapter 3 considers the latter in greater detail.

106. Mariès 1924, 41–47; Nyberg 1929, 238–41; Asmussen 1962, 12.

107. Photios, *Bibliotheca*, 187. See also A. de Jong 1997, 337.

108. Becker 2006a.

109. Van Rompay 1984.

110. Shaked 1992, 235; Shaked 2008, 111; Rezania 2008.

111. The problem of time suffused Zoroastrian cosmological speculation in the Sasanian period: Rezania 2010, 105–48.

112. Sundermann 1979, 112; Hutter 1993, 10–11; Colditz 2005, 20.

113. Becker 2006b, 32–33. See Debié 2010a, 338–41, for the theme elsewhere in East Syrian hagiography.

114. Assmann 2008, 53–75, 83–86.

115. Skjærvø 2007.

116. Nau 1927, 184–90, argues on the basis of the *Martyrdom of Pethion*'s references to the Avesta that there was no written version in the fifth century. For its redaction in the sixth, see Cantera 2004, 135–62; Huyse 2008, 145–46.

117. *Martyrdom of Pethion*, 572.

118. Bailey 1943, 39–40.

119. *Martyrdom of Pethion*, 577.

120. Ibid., 580.

121. The frog too was a xrafstar allied with Ahreman: *Bundahišn*, 184–85.

122. *Martyrdom of Pethion*, 578–79; Nöldeke 1893, 36–37.

123. Menasce 1937–39, 591.

124. *Bundahišn*, 70–81.

125. Shaked 2004, 339. See also Menasce 1962, 184, on Kerdir's anxieties about the possibility of worshiping demons.

126. *Nērangestān, Fragard* 2, 230–31.

127. *Dēnkard III*, 297/283.

128. *Ardā Wirāz Nāmag*, 78. See also Shaked 1999.

129. For the role of such spiritual journeys in Zoroastrian thought and literature, see Gignoux 2001b, 65–68.

130. Forrest 2011, 55–60. See Lincoln 2009, 53–54, for the intellectual anxieties of the scholars who worked to reconcile evil forces lacking in existence with such irruptions in the material world.

131. MacMullen 1986.

132. Gobrecht 1967, 397–403; Perikhanian 1979; Macuch 1993, 133–36.

133. Macuch 1987a; Cantera 2004, 120–22.

134. *Ardā Wirāz Nāmag*, 79.

135. *Dēnkard V*, 70–71.

136. *Dēnkard VII*, 62–63.

137. C. Jullien 2004 provides a useful overview of the modalities of torture in East Syrian martyrs' accounts without considering their dependence on Roman hagiographical models.

138. Shaw 1996.

139. For the penitential and punitive functions of beating with the *srōščaranām*, "belt of obedience," see *Nērangestān, Fragard* 2, 52–53, 54–57, 234–35; *Widēwdād*, 112–26/107–13. For punishment in Iranian law more generally, see Jany 2007.

140. *Martyrdom of Dado*, 220–21; *Martyrdom of Gubralaha*, 254; Gignoux 2000.

141. *Chronicle of Seert*, vol. 1, pt. 2, 164–66.

142. *Martyrdom of Pethion*, 613.

143. Ibid., 614–15.

144. Ibid., 616.

145. *Dēnkard III*, 399/372–73; Bailey 1934, 282–83.

146. Boyce 1991b, 284; MacKenzie 1971, 58.

147. *Ātaxš Niyāyišn*, 106–9. For the role of this hymn in the Yasna, see Kotwal and Boyd 1991, 119.

148. *Martyrdom of Pethion*, 617–18.

149. Ibid., 613.

150. Fiey 1970c, 374, mistakenly locates the river farther north, in the vicinity of modern Sanandaj, too far from the royal road that the text describes.

151. *Ardā Wirāz Nāmag*, 85.

152. Buc 1997, 92, argues that the discrediting of social and political rituals was a basic function of hagiographical polemics, a project that could involve the subordination of the transcended ritual: "Les auteurs et les metteurs en scène tenteront de satelliser le ritual de l'autre, de lui imposer une place subordonnée dans leur propre rituel, ou de faire comprendre qu'il n'est intelligible que dans un cadre qu'ils définissent grâce à leur maîtrise de l'interprétation." Land-sustaining rights here become "satellites" of a Christian imaginary.

153. On the possibility of cross-pollination in the realm of ideas, see Asmussen 1968, 170–77; Asmussen 1975; Sundermann 2008.

154. See Huff 1995, 73, for an illustration.

155. *Martyrdom of Pethion*, 571, 574.

3. CHRISTIAN LAW MAKING AND IRANIAN POLITICAL PRACTICE

1. Labourt 1904, 178–80; Peeters 1951, 137; Williams 1996, 50–51; Rist 1996, 38–39; Panaino 2004, 817; Bruns 2008, 107. Mar Aba is, moreover, commonly included in the ranks of the East Syrian martyrs, even though he perished of natural causes in the custody of the court: Brock 1982, 5–6; 2008a, 83.

2. The charges of conversion and proselytism were juxtaposed to other accusations: *History of Mar Aba*, 228–29, 237–38.

3. Ibid., 233–34.

4. Ibid., 235–36.

5. Ibid., 228–29.

6. By contrast, Hutter 2003, 171–72, views the regulation of these practices as evidence for a "Zoroastrianized Christianity," without considering their social and political dimensions. Elsewhere these practices appear primarily as markers of identity: Walker 2012, 1004–5; P. Wood 2013, 94.

7. *History of Mar Aba*, 224–25.

8. Gutas 1998, 40–45; Hartmann 2007; van Bladel 2009, 27–57.

9. Peeters 1951, 125–33; Pigulevskaya 1979, 207.

10. *History of Mar Aba*, 217–18; Pigulevskaya 1948. Kosmas Indicopleustes famously identified the scholar as his teacher: Kominko 2013, 16–17.

11. *History of Mar Aba*, 210–11, 215–16.

12. Peeters 1951, 121. See chapter 4 for administrative developments.

13. Reinink 1995; Becker 2006b, 77–97. For a survey of the development of East Syrian asceticism, see Griffith 1995. Husraw I endowed a *xenodocheion* in Nisibis, a possible site of medical study in connection with the School of Nisibis: Reinink 2003, 165–67.

14. Weitz 2013, 38–46. On the reception and diffusion of Theodore's works, see Becker 2006a; 2006b, 117–18.

15. Becker 2006b, 36–37; *History of Mar Aba*, 211–14.

16. Morony 1984, 340–41. For ascetic training as an increasingly common prerequisite for spiritual leadership, see C. Rapp 2005, 100–152.

17. Fiey 1965, 55–62; Bettiolo 2007; Camplani 2007.

18. Barhadbeshabba Arbaya, *Ecclesiastical History*, 605–8; Gero 1981a, 60–67.

19. *Chronicle of Seert*, vol. 2, pt. 1, 148–49; Labourt 1904, 160–62.

20. *Synodicon Orientale*, 70.

21. On the East Syrian theologies that underpinned ideas of ecclesiastical unity, see Vries 1955, 39–67, 122–35, 144–49, 151–53; Tamcke 1988, 31–37.

22. Blum 1980.

23. *Synodicon Orientale*, 20, 23, 26–27.

24. Fiey 1967a; Abramowski 2011, 18–31.

25. *Martyrdom of Miles*, 266–68.

26. Schwaigert 1989, 45–102; Schwaigert 1990; Sundermann 2002.

27. Gero 1981a, 74–76.

28. Sachau 1916, 969–75; Tubach 1997; C. Jullien and F. Jullien 1999; C. Jullien and F. Jullien 2003, 102–6; C. Jullien 2006; P. Wood 2010, 110–17.

29. *Chronicle of Arbela*, 43/65. The work is here cited as a medieval compendium of ecclesiastical traditions, not as a modern forgery. See the discussion in C. Jullien and F. Jullien 2001.

30. *History of Karka d-Beit Slok and Its Martyrs*, 512–13.

31. *Synodicon Orientale*, 69–70/320. This was possibly an evocation of a legend that Cyrus had foreseen the birth of Christ: Schilling 2008a, 184–86. Rabbis contemporary with Mar Aba, on the other hand, took a negative view of the Achaemenian: Mokhtarian 2010.

32. *Synodicon Orientale*, 70–73/321–24. The catholicos was unable to secure the obedience of Nisibis, however, on account of the city's opposition: *Synodicon Orientale*, 93/349; Delly 1957.

33. *Synodicon Orientale*, 77/329.

34. *Synodicon Orientale*, 81/334, 86/340, 94/350, 540/551; Peeters 1951, 138.

35. *History of Mar Aba*, 227.

36. Ibid., 228–34.

37. Peeters 1951, 145–59. Azerbaijan was a major center of imperial administration: Ghodrat-Dizaji 2010, 88.

38. His activities in exile included the production of texts and consultation with ecclesiastical leaders visiting from sees throughout the empire: *History of Mar Aba*, 247–48; Peeters 1951, 147. Athanasius of Alexandria had a similarly prodigious literary output during his third exile in the Egyptian desert: Brakke 1995, 129–40.

39. *Synodicon Orientale*, 527/533–34; Gero 1981a, 51–52.

40. Mar Aba tended to respect a distinction between canons (*qanone*) and laws (*namose*), using the former term only for decisions made at synods, but he also eroded the distinction by referring to all principles and decisions to which Christians should adhere as "laws." For the use of *canon* to refer to a synodal decision, especially from the fifth century onward, and the abiding confusion of *kanon* and *nomos*, see Ohme 1998, 380–83, 539–42.

41. On the introduction of Western—including some Chalcedonian—canons, see Pigulevskaya 1979, 206; Selb 1981, 104–5.

42. Garsoïan 1998, 1104.

43. Gero 1981b, 25; C. Jullien and F. Jullien 2002b.

44. *Synodicon Orientale*, 82.

45. *Chronicle of Seert*, vol. 2, pt. 1, 99, 148–49, 157. See also Selb 1981, 148, and Morony 1984, 341–42, neither of which discusses the riš d-mhaimane.

46. *Chronicle of Khuzestan*, 21; Ishoyahb III of Adiabene, *History of Ishosabran*, 577. Gignoux 1999, 85, argues that the term designates Yazdin's role as a tax collector for all Christians, but there is no evidence that Sasanian taxation was levied according to religious affiliation: Goodblatt 1979.

47. Ishoyahb III of Adiabene, *Correspondence*, 98–100.

48. *Synodicon Orientale*, 82/334–35.

49. *Martyrdom of Barbashmin*, 297. The catholicos Aqaq was related to his predecessor, Babowai: *Chronicle of Seert*, vol. 2, pt. 1, 112.

50. Even in the Roman world, where ecclesiastical offices were not normally familial institutions, the appointment of bishops for life exacerbated interelite tensions: Van Dam 2003, 59–63.

51. It has long been argued, most recently in Erhart 2001, 118–19, that the marriage of bishops was a concession to Zoroastrian norms. But the practice was instead rooted in East Syrian tradition: Gero 1981a, 45–47; Gero 1983; Bruns 2005. Some East Syrian leaders argued that episcopal wives could assist in the practice of pastoral care: *Chronicle of Seert*, vol. 2, pt. 1, 137.

52. *Synodicon Orientale*, 56–59/303–6, 63/312.

53. Payne 2011a, 97–102.

54. *Synodicon Orientale*, 543–44/554. See Selb 1981, 122–24, on Mar Aba's arrangement and on the different solutions developed by the synods of Joseph and Ishoyahb I later in the sixth century.

55. *Synodicon Orientale*, 79–80/331–32. For the Syrian *qarugbed*/Middle Persian *kirrōgbed* as "master of the artisans," see Pigulevskaya 1963b, 161; Ciancaglini 2008, 251.

56. *Synodicon Orientale*, 82.

57. Sachau 1907; Perikhanian 1983b, 265; Müller 1975; Morony 1974; Erhart 2001. Early articulations of this view depend on the so-called Syro-Roman law book, now known to have entered East Syrian communities only in the eighth century: Selb and Kaufhold 2002. For the possible influence of Roman law on East Syrians, see Monnickendam 2012.

58. *History of Mar Aba*, 234. For the term *bōxtnāmag*, see Shaked 1975, 216–17.

59. Perikhanian 1979, 192. The costs of justice prevented most Romans from procuring the services of their courts: Kelly 2004, 138–45.

60. Herman 2012, 202–4. Even in formulating specifically Jewish laws, the rabbis imagined that Shapur I had sanctioned their legal authority: Mokhtarian 2012, 165–66.

61. Kerdir, *Inscription at the Ka'aba-ye Zardosht*, 46–47/68–69.

62. Shaked 1990. For the *Hazār Dādestān* as a historical source, see Macuch 2009, 185–90; Corcoran 2011. On later continuities of the titles and powers enjoyed by Kerdir, see Gignoux 1986.

63. Macuch 2005b; Jany 2006.

64. Macuch 1981, 5, 150–51.

65. Perikhanian 1983b, 9–10.
66. *Hazār Dādestān (MHD)*, 409/415. See also Macuch 2010c, 202–3.
67. Macuch 1999; Macuch 2002; Elman 2003; Macuch 2008; Macuch 2010a; Simonsohn 2011, 44–52; Secunda 2014, 90–100.
68. Payne 2015.
69. Pigulevskaya 1958a; Menasce 1985; Macuch 1999. For the bishop in his early Abbasid context, see Weitz 2013, 73–79.
70. *Hazār Dādestān (MHDA)*, 51/190.
71. *History of Mar Aba*, 232.
72. *Synodicon Orientale*, 83/335, 84/336, 549–50/561.
73. *Armenian Book of Canons*, 444–46; Mardirossian 2004, 234–45.
74. *History of Sabrisho*, 300–301; Simonsohn 2009, 196–98. For the development of the East Syrian judge, see Kaufhold 1984.
75. Lamoreaux 1995, 150–56.
76. Gagos and van Minnen 1994; Harries 2003; Humfress 2014.
77. Simonsohn 2009, 194–96; Humfress 2011.
78. *Synodicon Orientale*, 220/485, 623/624; Simonsohn 2009, 200–203.
79. *Synodicon Orientale*, 82–85/335–37, 549–50/561.
80. Ibid., 623–24; *Chronicle of Seert*, vol. 2, pt. 1, 100.
81. Macuch 1991; 2010b.
82. See Hübner 2007 for the rarity of actual incest—as opposed to marriages of fictive kin—in ancient Mediterranean societies.
83. Goody 1983, 204–5. Goody oversimplified a complex process, in which worldly Christians often accepted and even advocated restrictions on the range of permissible marriages, as M. de Jong 1989 shows.
84. The Israelites of the Pentateuch are prominent in the writings of Thomas of Edessa, a close associate of Mar Aba at the School of Nisibis: Hainthaler 2006, 83.
85. The treatise explicitly identifies the Canaanites with the "Persians": Mar Aba, *Regulations of Marriage*, 262/263. Because of Mar Aba's exegetical method, there is little continuity between his work and the *Didascalia*, which uses the Pentateuch to counter the Christian observance of Mosaic law: van Unnik 1983; Visotzky 1990; Fonrobert 2001. For the use of the Pentateuch as a source of Christian law in the early medieval West, see Kottje 1965.
86. Mar Aba, *Regulations of Marriage*, 258/259.
87. *Martyrdom of Simeon*, 738/26; *History of Simeon*, 818/94.
88. Such Levitical modeling was also used to augment ecclesiastical power in post-Sasanian Armenian and East Syrian communities: Mardirossian 2004, 255–68; Payne 2009, 401–2.
89. Silk 2008.
90. The Pentateuch was also a common source for sexual slander in late antiquity: Knust 2006, 58–59.
91. Mar Aba, *Regulations of Marriage*, 264–66/265–67.
92. Macuch 1991, 151; Panaino 2008, 74–76.
93. *Pahlavi Rivāyat Accompanying the Dādestān ī Dēnīg*, 51/11; Skjærvø 2004; König 2010, 284–353.

94. Mar Aba, *Regulations of Marriage*, 280-82/281-83. A text that emerged from the milieu of late Sasanian ascetic bishops considers Arabs "a barbarian people" (*gensa barbaraya*): *History of Sabrisho*, 321. Zoroastrians frequently represented Arabs, Huns, and Turks as Ahremanic, inferior humans: Lincoln 2010; Cereti 2010. For more on nomads and Arabs in Syriac texts, see Segal 1984; Bruns 2003, 61–62; Pietruschka 2009.

95. Mar Aba, *Regulations of Marriage*, 280-82/281-83; Crone 2012, 400–405b. The Iranian historiographical tradition represents polyandry as sodomy: al-Ṭabarī, *Ta'rīkh al-rusul wa al-mulūk*, 873/110.

96. Macuch 1985; 2006a.

97. Macuch 2006b.

98. On Iranian patriliny, see Perikhanian 1968a; 1983a.

99. Hopkins 1983, 31–119; Scheidel 1999; Hübner and Ratzan 2009. These general demographic constraints—rather than a late Sasanian demographic crisis, as Elman 2003 argues—formed the background for the development of stūrīh.

100. Macuch 1981, 7–10; Carlsen 1984; Macuch 1993, 74–76, 345–46; Hjerrild 2003, 15–18; Hjerrild 2006; Hjerrild 2007.

101. Macuch 1995.

102. *Synodicon Orientale*, 82/335; Ishobokht, *Book of Judgments*, 36–37.

103. Weisberg 2000; Satlow 2001, 188.

104. Mar Aba, *Regulations of Marriage*, 278/279.

105. Ibid., 274/275.

106. Payne 2015.

107. Ishobokht, *Book of Judgments*, 8.

108. On post-Sasanian East Syrian judges, see Rücker 1908, 7–21; Selb 1981, 176–77; Tamcke 2008; Payne 2009; Ioan 2009, 32–34, 83–86.

109. For partible inheritance practices that militated against the development of patrimonies in Roman society, see Saller 1994, 155–80; Hopkins 1983, 74–78; Arjava 1996, 70–75.

110. Simeon of Revardashir, *Ecclesiastical Judgments*, 245.

111. Henanisho, *Judgments*, 18.

112. Klingenschmitt 1967; Perikhanian 1968b; Macuch 1981, 85–86.

113. Henanisho, *Judgments*, 48–50/49–51; Simeon of Revardashir, *Ecclesiastical Judgments*, 247/246. The possibility of granting daughters inheritances equivalent to those of sons did exist in Iranian law: *Hazār Dādestān (MHD)*, 311–12/327–28.

114. Ishobokht, *Book of Judgments*, 94.

115. Ishoyahb III of Adiabene, *Correspondence*, 153–54.

116. Simeon of Revardashir, *Ecclesiastical Judgments*, 235.

117. Ibid., 235, 247.

118. Ishobokht, *Book of Judgments*, 100.

119. Timothy, *Correspondence*, 50, 68–69, 79, 105.

120. *History of Rabban Mar Saba*, 644; Ishoyahb III of Adiabene, *History of Ishosabran*, 516.

121. Henanisho, *Judgments*, 34–38.

122. *History of Mar Aba*, 229. See also Hutter 2003, 170.

123. *History of Mar Aba*, 238.

124. Ełišē, *Vardan and the Armenian War*, 20/73–74; *History of Rabban Mar Saba*, 644.

125. Boyce and Kotwal 1971.

126. Gignoux 1994, 20–30; A. de Jong 1997, 357–62; A. de Jong 2002; Daryaee 2012.
127. *Dēnkard V*, 94–97.
128. *Hōm Yašt*, 110.
129. Shaked 1991.
130. Inostrancev 1909; A. de Jong 1997, 371–86. For the role of the court in establishing a calendar of feasts, see Boyce 1970; 2005.
131. *Synodicon Orientale*, 158/417–48.
132. See Becker 2009, 324–25, for its participation in the discourse of fear, *deḥlta*, as a way of conceiving true religion in contrast to rivals, prominent in the writings of Mar Aba's circle.
133. Taqizadeh 1940, 633–37.
134. *Sūr ī Saxwan*, 27–49.
135. Daryaee 2007.
136. Morony 1976, 53; Canepa 2009, 11–15.
137. *History of Gregory the Commander*, 354–55.
138. *Martyrdom of Yazdbozid*, 125.
139. *Martyrdom of Eustathius of Mtskheta*, 876–77. See Martin-Hisard 1998 for its context.
140. *History of Gregory*, 355.
141. Shaked 2010b; Herman 2012, 239–57.
142. *History of Mar Aba*, 234. Mar Aba's advocate, Abrodaq was widely celebrated in reformist circles for his patronage of ecclesiastical institutions: *History of Yazdpaneh*, 410–11; Payne 2011a, 104–5.
143. Ishoyahb III of Adiabene, *Correspondence*, 225–28; Payne 2009, 407–8. For the Israelites more generally as the model of righteous community in Syriac literature, see Morony 2005, 6.
144. Brock 2008b.
145. Gabriel of Basra, *Collection of Laws*, 177/176.
146. *History of Mar Aba*, 263–64; Firdawsī, *Šāhnāme*, vol. 7, 148–57; al-Dīnawarī, *Kitāb al-akhbār al-ṭiwāl*, 69–70; Peeters 1951, 157–59; Pigulevskaya 1979, 206; Bonner 2012, 50–55; P. Wood 2013, 113–14.
147. Pigulevskaya 1963b, 221–28.
148. Rubin 2004.
149. Bonner 2012, 55. See chapter 5 for legendary accounts of the Christianization of the Sasanian dynasty.
150. Firdawsī, *Šāhnāme*, vol. 7, 155.
151. Ibid., 152–53.

4. CREATING A CHRISTIAN ARISTOCRACY

1. For a contemporaneous description of the commemoration, see *Martyrdom of Shirin*, 123–24. The shrine was in a monastery constructed in the late fifth century: *History of Karka d-Beit Slok and Its Martyrs*, 530–31. A tenth-century reconstruction of the shrine complex survived until its destruction during the First World War: Bell 1913, 100–103; Bachmann 1913, 18; Monneret de Villard 1940, 27.
2. *History of Karka*, 514.

3. Ibid., 532.
4. Walker 2006, 249–59; 2006–7.
5. Wiessner 1971; Walker 2006, 121–63, quote on 149. See also Bruns 2009a.
6. *Synodicon Orientale*, 106–7.
7. *History of Karka*, 531; Fiey 1964b, 216–18.
8. Walker 2006, 277–78.
9. Fiey 1964b, 219–22. On account of its mixing of myths, martyrology, and history, Peeters 1925 regards the *History of Karka* as the work of "un faussaire ou un compilateur peu scrupuleux" (270). A recent attempt to categorize the work as historiography rather than hagiography downplays the themes, conventions, and structures derived from the latter genre that pervade the text: Debié 2010c, 60–61. Van Uytfanghe 1993 and Lifshitz 1994 enjoin historians not to allow modern literary classifications to pigeonhole highly creative hagiographers. On account of its chronological distance from the late Sasanian texts, the medieval *Chronicle of Arbela* is not considered here, although it exhibits features similar to those of the *History of Karka*: C. Jullien and F. Jullien 2001, with Walker 2006, 287–90.
10. For the episcopal archive at Karka d-Beit Slok, see *History of Karka*, 531. Episcopal diptychs were fundamental sources of ecclesiastical history: Wiessner 1967b, 240–56; Menze 2008, 26–86. According to Gabriel of Basra, *Collection of Laws*, 233/232, the diptychs of both the living and the dead are to be recited at feasts but only those of the living on Sundays.
11. Walker 2004; 2006, 164–205.
12. Peeters 1950, 49–70.
13. Greatrex and Lieu 2002, 62–181; Gyselen 2003.
14. Kister 1968; Braund 1994, 268–314; Morony 2001–2; Rubin 2007.
15. Thomson 2000, 673; Garsoïan 2009b, 72–76.
16. Thomson 2004, 376–78; Garsoïan 2009a, 81–83.
17. Toral-Niehoff 2010; 2014, 68–74. For more on the political history of the Lakhmids, the Arab tribe whose capital was al-Ḥira, see Fisher 2011, 91–95, 184–86.
18. Hunter 2008; Toral-Niehoff 2014, 183–94; P. Wood 2014.
19. *Book of the Himyarites*, 14/cix–cx.
20. Rothstein 1899, 20–27, 139–43; Pigulevskaya 1964, 274–83; Toral-Niehoff 2014, 199–208.
21. Payne 2013.
22. *Chronicle of Seert*, vol. 2, pt. 2, 458; Christensen 1944, 451; Fiey 1968, 23–38; Pigulevskaya 1979, 211–12; Flusin 1992, 246–54. The sources disagree on the extent of his authority.
23. Thomas of Marga, *Book of Governors*, vol. 1, 63–64 / vol. 2, 112–16.
24. Gyselen 2007, 9–15.
25. Lerner 1977, 8–30; Shaked 1977, 18–24; Gignoux 1980; Gyselen 2006, 30–39; Hauser 2008, 46–49.
26. Gyselen 2006, 40.
27. Ibid., 39–40; Gyselen 2007, 78–79.
28. Gyselen 2007, 40–41; 2009, 169–70.
29. On animals such as the ram, a manifestation of xwarrah, as political symbols, see Simpson 2013.

30. Gyselen 2006, 29–30, 54–55. For the possibility of reading *yazdān* as a singular, see Shaked 1977, 21.

31. Lukonin 1969, 37. Ardashir, the brother of Shapur II, ruled Adiabene as a subkingdom, the way that Armenia and a handful of other regions were ruled: *Martyrdom of the Forty Martyrs*, 333. The royal house of Adiabene plays an important role in the Babylonian Talmud with no connection to the contemporaneous history of the region: Kalmin 2010.

32. See Chaumont 1982, 173, and Reade 1998, 71–72, on the decline of Greek in the region.

33. Beyer 1998, 11–25. See also chapter 1 on the Great Persecution.

34. Morony 1976, 41.

35. *History of Saba Pirgushnasp*, 224; al-Ṭabarī, *Ta'rīkh al-rusul wa'l-mulūk*, vol. 1, 62–63; al-Dīnawarī, *Kitāb al-akhbār al-ṭiwāl*, 50–51.

36. See later in the chapter and Babai the Great, *Martyrdom of Christina*, 207, for the genealogies of nobles at Karka d-Beit Slok who emphasized their origins in Fars.

37. For the military administration, see Kolesnikov 1981; Gignoux 1984b; Gyselen 2004.

38. See Morony 1984, 181–213, for an unsurpassed survey of the evidence of "Persians" in northern Mesopotamia that nevertheless treats Iranian elites as a virtually autonomous "ruling minority."

39. Kennedy 2006, 11–14; 201, 54–58.

40. Pigulevskaya 1958b; Banaji 2009, 78–86.

41. Colditz 2000, 123–34; Macuch 2002.

42. *History of Karka*, 516; Thomas of Marga, *Book of Governors*, vol. 1, 79 / vol. 2, 177; Pigulevskaya 1963b, 139.

43. *History of Karka*, 516.

44. *History of Saba Pirgushnasp*, 224.

45. Kröger 1982, 187–88.

46. *History of Sultan Mahduk*, 3.

47. Ishodad of Merv, *Commentary on the Old Testament*, 157; *Synodicon Orientale*, 247/518.

48. Such private cults were common among late Roman elites, who were often at the vanguard of Christianization and thus in a sometimes uneasy relationship with their bishops: Bowes 2008. For East Syrian elites as the organizers of cults, see Payne 2011a, 102–8.

49. Bosl 1965; Prinz 1967; Noble 2007.

50. Pratsch 2005, 56.

51. The text has nevertheless generally been regarded as historically reliable: Pigulevskaya 1963b, 39–45; Fiey 1964b, 191–94; Chaumont 1982, 160–61; Chaumont 1988, 97–99.

52. See Harrak 2001 on accounts of Sennacherib in Syriac.

53. For the commemoration of this fast at Karka, see Krüger 1933, 32–38.

54. *History of Karka*, 510.

55. Ibid.

56. Pigulevskaya 1963b, 44–45.

57. *History of Karka*, 509.

58. Ibid., 510.

59. Ibid., 511. *Seleucus* is commonly encountered as a personal name in Iranian inscriptions: Bivar 1990; Frye 1966, 85–87.

60. *History of Mar Qardagh*, 13/20.

61. *History of Karka*, 517. This reference suggests that Manichaeism endured beyond the fourth century, which is when scholars typically argue the religion disappeared from Iran: Hutter 2000. The anti-Manichaean polemics of the *History of Mar Mari* also point to its continued importance in sixth-century Mesopotamia: C. Jullien and F. Jullien 2003, 73–102.

62. Ishodenah of Basra, *Book of Chastity*, 26–27/24.

63. *Martyrdom of Shapur of Beit Niqator*, 55; *Martyrdom of Jacob*; *Martyrdom of Aqebshma*, 380; *History of Karka*, 515.

64. *History of Karka*, 521–27.

65. *History of Mar Qardagh*, 100–102/67–68.

66. *History of Karka*, 526–27.

67. C. Jullien and F. Jullien 2002a, 164, dates the arrival of Theocritus, Karka's first bishop, to the 180s, identifying him with a known bishop of Caesarea in Cappadocia.

68. *History of Karka*, 515–16. The text gives the position of Aqeblaha's father as *redya d-bazdai*, a corrupted and indecipherable rendition of a Middle Persian title. See Gignoux, Jullien, and Jullien 2009, 85, for the name of the house.

69. *History of Karka*, 513.

70. Ibid., 515–16.

71. Ibid., 518. See also Pigulevskaya 1963b, 184–85; Bruns 2009c, 51–56. For the diffusion of *xenodocheia*, see Horden 2005; see also ch. 3, n. 13.

72. *History of Mar Qardagh*, 62–68/51–53.

73. Börm 2007, 115–32; Gyselen 2008; Pourshariati 2008, 83–160; Gyselen 2009, 173–78.

74. See, most recently, Rubin 2000; Pourshariati 2008.

75. Gyselen 2007, 11–13, 51–52.

76. Gyselen 2002.

77. The skepticism of Rubin 1995 and Rubin 2000, 657, concerning the efficacy of these reforms downplays the combined numismatic, sigillographic, and literary evidence for fiscal intensification: Kolesnikov 1998a, 234–47; Banaji 2006, 274–76.

78. For Rubin 2004, 252, the late Sasanian administrative reforms faltered on account of a failure to create a service aristocracy, while Wiesehöfer 2007a, 71, and Wiesehöfer 2010, 122–23, argue that they depended on a newly created *Dienstadel*. Börm 2010 helpfully suggests that such a new elite could have coexisted with a well-established, economically autonomous nobility on the basis of a comparison with the later Roman Empire.

79. Howard-Johnston 1995b, 220.

80. Zakeri 1995, 22–31; Colditz 2000, 66–75.

81. Wiessner 1967b, 173–78; Blois 1985.

82. Tafazzoli 2000 and Wiesehöfer 2010, 122, argue for the emergence of the dahigān in the sixth century.

83. For the aristocracies of the Caucasus, see Toumanoff 1963, 108–44.

84. Nöldeke 1920, 8.

85. Christensen 1931; Yarshater 1983; Daryaee 1995. See also chapter 1. Kayanian mythical history was first propagated in the context of Iran's fifth-century wars with the Huns: Payne 2014.

86. Yarshater 1983.

87. Yarshater 1971; Huyse 2002; Canepa 2010. It is not accidental that Alexander the Great's rival Darius III was the only member of the dynasty to find his way into the tradition, given Iranian interest in historical accounts of Alexander: Gignoux 2007. Daryaee 2006a, 496–500, nevertheless seeks to locate the source of Achaemenian history in the Hebrew Bible, of which Jewish—or Christian—scholars were the possible intermediaries.

88. Shahbazi 1993; Foursharia: 2008, 116–18.

89. Boyce 1957a.

90. For the work of Łazar P'arpec'i as a Mamikonean history and other so-called princely biographies in Armenian, see Thomson 1996, 502–4; Greenwood 2002, 355–58.

91. Łazar P'arpec'i, *History of the Armenians*, 167/228.

92. Crone and Cook 1977, 62–65; P. Wood 2010, 178–83.

93. Younansardaroud and Novák 2002; Walker 2006–7. The *History of Mar Behnam*, which has often been invoked in discussions of Assyrian continuity, is a thirteenth-century work: Wiessner 1978; Younansardaroud 2002. See also Salveson 1998 on ancient Mesopotamian elements in Syriac literature. Despite the scholarly emphasis on the oral transmission of this ancient past, authors writing in Greek and Aramaic in Roman Syro-Mesopotamia in the first two centuries CE made extensive use of the Assyrian past to define their communities in relation to Greek culture and Roman imperialism: Andrade 2014.

94. See the identification of the site of Assur in the medieval *History of Mar Behnam*, 407.

95. Becker 2008 emphasizes the importance of the Hebrew Bible as a source for the literary reinvention of the Assyrian past. See Drost-Abgarjan 2006 for the Armenian version of the *Chronicle* of Eusebius as a translation from Greek and Debié 2006 for its influence on Syriac literature. Even if the Armenian version was translated directly from the Greek, East Syrians might have facilitated its transmission. Although this is often neglected, northern Mesopotamia was an important zone of Armenian—East Syrian interaction: Garsoïan 1999, 45–47.

96. Elias of Nisibis, *Chronology*, 99. See also Witakowski 1987, 78; Fiey 1968, 23, 90.

97. Eusebius of Caesarea, *Chronicle*, 25–28.

98. *History of Karka*, 507–8.

99. Ri 2000, 336–37.

100. Ephrem, *Commentary on Genesis*, 65/52; *Cave of Treasures*, 216–17. On the Iranian context of the West Syrian *Cave of Treasures*, see Minov 2012.

101. Theodore bar Koni, *Book of Scholia*, 112/126; Ishodad of Merv, *Commentary on the Old Testament*, 133–34.

102. *Chronicle of Khuzestan*, 35

103. John Malalas, *Chronographia*, 18/47; Walker 2006–7, 502; S. H. Rapp 2009, 653–54.

104. Al-Ṭabarī, *Ta'rīkh al-rusul wa al-mulūk*, vol. 1, 205; al-Dīnawarī, *Kitāb al-akhbār al-ṭiwāl*, 6; al-Tha'ālibī *Ghurar akhbār mulūk al-Furs wa sīyarihim*, 10; Ibn Miskawayh, *Tajārib al-umam*, 55.

105. For early Islamic attempts to synchronize the biblical and Iranian traditions, see Savant 2013, 138–58.

106. Ishodenah of Basra, *Book of Chastity*, 6/7, 64/54.

107. Bulliet 2009, 17–20. The practice was common in northern Mesopotamia: *History of Karka*, 516; Thomas of Marga, *Book of Governors*, vol. 1, 79 / vol. 2, 177; *Chronicle of Seert*, vol. 2, pt. 2, 474.

108. *History of Pseudo-Sebeos*, 35/30; Schilling 2008a, 182.

109. Payne 2012.

110. By contrast, Wiessner 1971, 151–52, argues that the *History of Mar Qardagh* allows that aristocratic converts remained ēr.

111. *History of Mar Qardagh*, 13/20.

112. *History of Pseudo-Sebeos*, 92/39. See also Greenwood 2002, 347–50.

113. *History of Mar Qardagh*, 13–15/21–22, 58–67/49–53.

114. Walker 2006, 121–63, quote on 122. See also Zakeri 1995, 1–12, on Iranian aristocratic conceptions of manly valiance.

115. *History of the Monastery of Sabrisho*, 196.

116. *History of Mar Qardagh*, 11/19.

117. Greenwood 2002.

118. Shahbazi 1990.

119. Cereti 2010.

120. Cantera 2004, 162–63, 201–20; Cereti 2008; Huyse 2008; A. de Jong 2009.

121. Cantera 2004, 160–62; Rezania 2012.

122. Crone 1991, 24–25.

123. Rubin 2000, 657; Pourshariati 2008, 82–83. Neither of these works takes into consideration the foundational disentangling of traditions concerning Kawad and Mazdak in Crone 1991, nor does Gil 2012, which reproduces the fantasies of the medieval Muslim heresiographical imagination.

124. Crone 1991, 26–30; 1994.

125. *History of Karka*, 517.

126. *Letter of Tansar*, 19/44; Macuch 2010c, 204–5.

127. Sundermann 1976. The "poor" (Middle Persian *škōh, driyōš*) were the agriculturally productive population in imperial ideology: Colditz 2000, 204–5. See Marlow 1997, 66–90, for the development of late Sasanian ideologies of social order and reciprocity.

128. *Sīrat Ānušīrwān*, 189–90/17–18, 194–95/20–21, 200–202/25–28. The title "advocate of the poor" was a Zoroastrian honorific that Armenian bishops maintained: Shaked 1975, 213–16; Garsoïan 1981; Gyselen 1989, 31–33.

129. *History of Karka*, 517.

130. *Letter of Tansar*, 20/44.

131. *History of Karka*, 510.

132. Greenwood 2000, 84–104; Howard-Johnston 2010b, 105–8.

133. Bunyatov 1965, 38–59.

134. For the provincial houses of the region, see Toumanoff 1963, 257–59, 476–81.

135. Movses Daskhurantsʻi, *History of the Albanians*, 106–7/61–62.

136. Agatangełos, *History of the Armenians*, 34–53. See also Thomson 1996, 498–501.

137. Daryaee 2006a, 498–500; Weber 2009; van Bladel 2009, 58–62.

138. *History of Karka*, 509.

139. Ibid., 510. Such continuities in religious practice are well known, if still poorly understood: Morony 1984, 384–430; Müller-Kessler and Kessler 1999.

140. *History of Karka*, 510–11.

141. Canepa 2010.

142. *History of Karka*, 526.

143. *History of Mar Qardagh*, 15/22.

144. Garsoïan 1984–85, 75–79; Kennedy 2006, 14. For two excavated examples of an aristocratic rural estate, see Azarnoush 1994; Berghe 1990.

145. Metzler 1977, 198–206. The city was reportedly the site of the reformed fiscal administration: *Sīrat Ānušīrwān*, 194/20.

146. See Kervran 1985, 98–99, for elite residences at Susa.

147. Gyselen 1989, 28–40.

148. Adams 1965, 72–75; Adams 1981, 179–85. See also Morony 1994; Howard-Johnston 1995b, 198–205; Whitcomb 2007; Haldon 2010. See Alizadeh and Ur 2007 for the intensification of settlement in Azerbaijan.

149. *History of Karka*, 508–9.

150. Ibid., 508.

151. *History of Mar Qardagh*, 15/22 (modified translation).

152. East Syrian hagiography also reports these "cities" as the centers of ancient kingdoms: *History of Mar Mari*, 22–23; *History of Sultan Mahduk*, 3; C. Jullien and F. Jullien 2003, 13–14. For the location of Hirbet Glal, see Hoffmann 1880, 261–62; Fiey 1968, 130–38.

153. For the interdependence of symbolic and material elements in defining ancient cities, see Wickham 2009; Haldon 1999a.

154. *Martyrdom of Narsai and Joseph*; *History of Mar Mari*, 22.

155. *History of Karka*, 511; Pigulevskaya 1963b, 159–69.

156. Nováček, Amin, and Melčák 2013 provides an overview of scholarship on Arbela.

157. Simpson 1996, 95–98.

158. Hauser 1994, 502–7.

159. A similar assertion of authority, rooted in aristocratic genealogies, over a precisely defined territory is made in a roughly contemporaneous hagiographical work from Nisibis: *History of Saba Pirgushnasp*, 222–24.

160. Morony 1984, 132–33.

161. See Gyselen 1989, 78–79, on the tendency of the two regions to overlap.

162. *Cities of Iran*, 8–23.

163. Ibid., 11, 21.

164. The compilation was, however, not comprehensive: Gyselen 1988.

165. *Cities of Iran*, 13, 16.

166. *History of Karka*, 531.

167. *History of Mar Mari*, 22–25; F. Jullien 2006.

168. Their vision of the interdependence of aristocratic houses and episcopal sees approaches the Armenian model of rooting episcopal authority in the houses of nakharars rather than cities: Garsoïan 1984–85, 79–81; Hewsen 1997, 102–8.

169. Payne 2009, 404–7.

170. The Karka martyrs were commemorated on the tell outside Kirkuk into the twentieth century: Galletti 2002. The shrine at Melqi endured at least until the thirteenth century: Walker 2006, 279.

171. Richardson 2014.

5. THE CHRISTIAN SYMBOLICS OF POWER IN A ZOROASTRIAN EMPIRE

1. Michael Whitby 1988, 296–67; Schilling 2008a, 251–61.
2. Schilling 2008a, 247–51.
3. Gregory the Great, *Correspondence*, 242/243.
4. *Chronicle of Fredegar*, 7–9.
5. *History of Pseudo-Sebeos*, 69/9. See also John of Ephesus, *Ecclesiastical History*, 316.
6. John of Nikiu, *Chronicle*, 154; Schilling 2008a, 185–89.
7. Schilling 2008a, 91–96. On accounts of the New Testament Magi more generally, see Witakowski 2008; F. Jullien 2014.
8. Daryaee 1997; Tyler-Smith 2004, 43–45.
9. Kolesnikov 2002. Iberian princes subject to the Sasanians also experimented with Christian crosses on drachms: S. H. Rapp 2001, 103.
10. At the same time, the sculptures appropriate Roman imagery to produce a "cosmopolitan visual culture of royalty": Canepa 2009, 221.
11. Christensen 1907, 55–73; Michael Whitby 1988, 297–304; Frendo 2008, 224–26.
12. Howard-Johnston 2010b, 436–45; Wiesehöfer 2013.
13. Hutter 1998, 373–77. Shirin enjoyed a long afterlife in Iranian literature: Baum 2003, 76–100.
14. *Chronicle of Seert*, vol. 2, pt. 2, 466–67; Agapius of Manbij, *Universal History*, 447; Flusin 1992, 99–102; Garsoïan 2012, 27.
15. His monumental complex was never finished: Luschey 1996b; Howard-Johnston 2004, 94–96.
16. Al-Ṭabarī, *Ta'rīkh al-rusul wa al-mulūk*, vol. 2, 991/298. East Syrian authors generally regarded Ohrmazd IV as a patron: Pigulevskaya 1946, 237–38; Kolesnikov 1970, 45; Schilling 2008a, 209–13.
17. On the development of throne imagery, see Gall 1971.
18. *Chronicle of Seert*, vol. 2, pt. 1, 196.
19. Shaked 1994, 112. Schilling 2008a, 214–16, argues that the account originated in the anti-Sasanian propaganda of the usurper Wahram Chobin.
20. *Martyrdom of Anastasios the Persian*, 84–85; *Chronicle of Seert*, vol. 2, pt. 2, 524–25.
21. Firdawsī, *Šāhnāme*, vol. 8, 73–74, 122–23. See also al-Ṭabarī, *Ta'rīkh al-rusul wa al-mulūk*, vol. 2, 1000/313; al-Dīnawarī, *Kitāb al-akhbār al-ṭiwāl*, 90; *History of Pseudo-Sebeos*, 77–79/20–22. For the Armenian tradition's celebration of his service, see Greenwood 2002, 353.
22. *History of Pseudo-Sebeos*, 96/43–44; Garsoïan 2012, 25–27.
23. Dal Santo 2011; Haldon 1990, 281–96.
24. H. J. W. Drijvers 1998, 18–19.
25. Cameron 1978; 1979, 18–24.
26. *History of Sabrisho*, 301–3; Tamcke 1988, 30.
27. Klein 2004b.
28. *History of Pseudo-Sebeos*, 98–99/46–47. The description of the silver box that held the relic corresponds with known early examples of reliquaries of the True Cross: Klein 2004a, 100–103.

29. *History of Mar Qardagh*, 61–62/50. See also Walker 2006, 150–51.
30. *History of Mar Qardagh*, 66/52.
31. Haas 2008.
32. See Greatrex 2009 for historiographical traditions of the siege. The predominantly West Syrian region's relations with Constantinople were uneasy: Harvey 1987, 57–75.
33. Pseudo-Zachariah, *Chronicle of Pseudo-Zachariah of Mytilene*, 25/237.
34. Ibid., 28/240–41.
35. *Chronicle of Seert*, vol. 2, pt. 1, 132–33.
36. Pseudo-Joshua the Stylite, *Chronicle*, 58/71.
37. E. K. Fowden 1999, 67–92.
38. Ibid., 133–41.
39. Theophylact Simocatta, *History*, 188–89/132–33.
40. Ibid., 213–15/151–52.
41. Peeters 1947; Higgins 1955; Olajos 1988, 146–47; Michael Whitby 1988, 235–36.
42. Theophylact Simocatta, *History*, 213/150; Evagrius Scholasticus, *Ecclesiastical History*, 235/311.
43. Theophylact Simocatta, *History*, 214–15/152. Evagrius recorded an almost identical account: *Ecclesiastical History*, 236–38/312–14.
44. For possible echoes of Sergius in courtly historiography, see Scarcia 2000; 2003.
45. According to the *History of Sabrisho*, 302, the patriarch had also been invited to court during the reign of Ohrmazd IV.
46. *Chronicle of Khuzestan*, 17.
47. Tamcke 1988, 29–31; Flusin 1992, 104–6; Hutter 1998, 376–77.
48. *Chronicle of Seert*, vol. 2, pt. 2, 481–83.
49. *Chronicle of Khuzestan*, 16.
50. *Chronicle of Seert*, vol. 2, pt. 2, 499–501.
51. Ibid., 500.
52. Howard-Johnston 2008a, 82; *Chronicon Paschale*, 709/161–62. See also Kaegi 2003, 83–86.
53. Flusin 1992, 70–93; Greatrex and Lieu 2002, 182–97.
54. Foss 2003.
55. Kaegi 2003, 76–78; Olster 1993, 82–97.
56. Hendy 1985, 172; Altheim-Stiehl 1991.
57. Antony of Choziba, *Life of George of Choziba*, 128/62.
58. Payne 2013.
59. Daryaee 2006b; Shayegan 2011, 21–29.
60. Olster 1993, 49–65.
61. *Chronicle of Khuzestan*, 25; *Chronicle of 1234*, 220–21/121–22; Theophanes Confessor, *Chronicle*, 291/418–19; Rubin 2005, 82. The Iranian court also sought to recover the territory lost to Maurice in 591: Shahid 2004, 226; Sarris 2011, 236.
62. Shahid 2004, 226–27, 238–43. The Sasanians, however, did not self-consciously imitate the Achaemenians, as Shahid argued, as we saw in chapter 4.
63. *Chronicon Paschale*, 704/156. See also Strategius, *Capture of Jerusalem*, 19–27
64. Foss 1975, 742–46; Sāwīrus b. al-Muqaffaʻ, *History of the Patriarchs*, 484–85; Agapius of Manbij, *Universal History*, 451.

65. Avni 2010, 36–40; Strategius, *Capture of Jerusalem*, 18. Bowersock 1997, 9, distinguishes Strategius from the Antiochus with whom he has often been associated.
66. Foss 1975; Foss 1997, 261–63; Pottier 2004; Holum 1992, 74; Stoyanov 2011, 12–23; Sarris 2011, 247–48.
67. Magness 2011.
68. Avni 2010; Dauphin 1998, 352–60.
69. Piccirillo 2011.
70. Haldon 1999b, 18–21.
71. Theophanes Confessor, *Chronicle*, 298/427.
72. Cameron 1979, 5–6; Cameron 1978; Howard-Johnston 1995a.
73. Stoyanov 2011, 61–75; McDonough 2011b.
74. Booth 2013, 94–100.
75. Theophanes Confessor, *Chronicle*, 298/427.
76. Howard-Johnston 2010b, 20–25; Mary Whitby 1994.
77. Theophanes Confessor, *Chronicle*, 310–11/442–43. See also Kaegi 2012, 18; Stoyanov 2011, 61.
78. J. W. Drijvers 1992, 81–117.
79. Speck 1997; Frendo 2008, 226–28.
80. Strategius, *Capture of Jerusalem*, 37.
81. Ibid., 44.
82. Ibid., 38.
83. *Chronicle of Khuzestan*, 25. See also al-Ṭabarī, *Ta'rīkh al-rusul wa al-mulūk*, vol. 2, 1002/318.
84. *Chronicle of Khuzestan*, 25. This work stands out in the East Syrian tradition for its systematic inclusion of political history alongside ecclesiastical history: Pigulevskaya 2000, 322–24; Robinson 2004; F. Jullien 2009, 160–61.
85. *Chronicle of Khuzestan*, 25. The *Martyrdom of Anastasios the Persian*, 47/46, also describes the public delivery of the cross to the king of kings, which inspired its namesake cavalryman to convert.
86. Flusin 1992, 170–71.
87. Klein 2004b, 33–39.
88. One Roman account of the conquest describes the transfer of marble from Roman cities to adorn Seleucia-Ctesphon: Agapius of Manbij, *Universal History*, 451.
89. Al-Thaʿālibī, *Ghurar akhbār mulūk al-Furs wa sīyarihim*, 701–2, records an account according to which Husraw II constructed two treasuries for Roman objects, including the True Cross.
90. Fiey 1967b, 417; Fiey 1967c, 10; J. H. Schmidt 1934, 2. Christian objects have been found at the site: Kröger 1982, 40–42.
91. Foss 2003, 156, 159–61; Sāwīrus b. al-Muqaffaʿ, *History of the Patriarchs*, 485.
92. Weber 2007; 2013. See Weber 2010 for fragments of scribal training exercises in Middle Persian from Egypt.
93. Foss 2002; Banaji 2006, 274; Sänger 2011.
94. *Chronicle of 1234*, 221–24/122–24. See Segal 1970, 126–27, on the family and Debié 1999–2000 on the distinctive Edessene historiographical tradition that has preserved their history.

95. Howard-Johnston 2004, 103.
96. Börm 2006 shows how Husraw I self-consciously occupied the position of the Roman emperor in the hippodrome of Apamea during the invasion of Syria in 540.
97. E.g., Kaegi 2003, 97.
98. Flusin 1992, 173–77; Frend 2008, 231–32.
99. *History of Pseudo-Sebeos,* 116–18/70–72.
100. Mango 1992.
101. *History of Pseudo-Sebeos,* 116/70; *Chronicle of Khuzestan,* 27.
102. Dagron and Déroche 1991, 26, argues that Modestos was the architect of a rapprochement between Iranian and Roman Christian elites.
103. Jacobs 2004, 139–99.
104. Dagron and Déroche 1991 18–32; Olster 1994, 84–92; Cameron 1994.
105. Dagron and Déroche 1991, 29; Stoyanov 2011, 68–69. See Dauphin 1998, 330–32, on the Roman decrees, and Drijvers 1992, 143–44, on anti-Jewish elements in the cult of the cross.
106. Jacobs 2004; Sivan 2008, 194–200.
107. Dagron and Déroche 1991, 29.
108. Déroche 1999, 143–45; Wheeler 1991.
109. Sivan 2000; 2004.
110. Sivan 2004, 88–92.
111. *Chronicle of Khuzestan,* 26–27.
112. *History of Pseudo-Sebeos,* 116/70.
113. Menze 2008, 145–93.
114. John of Ephesus, *Lives of the Eastern Saints,* 153–57; Hainthaler 2002. Husraw I reportedly took an interest in Christian doctrinal controversies as well: John of Ephesus, *Ecclesiastical History,* 316–18.
115. Fiey 1970a, 113–43; F. Jullien 2011b, 53–57.
116. *Chronicle of Seert,* vol. 2, pt. 2, 126.
117. Hutter 1998, 378–83.
118. Frend 1972, 336–38; Flusin 1992, 112–14.
119. Michael the Syrian, *Chronicle,* vol. 4, 390–91 / vol. 2, 380–81.
120. P. Wood 2010, 209–56.
121. Ibid., 229.
122. Sāwīrus b. al-Muqaffaʿ, *History of the Patriarchs,* 482.
123. Frend 1972, 338; Flusin 1992, 106–12; Hutter 1998, 379–81; Greatrex 2003, 81–82; Greatrex 2006, 49–50; Binder 2013, 80–89.
124. *Chronicle of Seert,* vol. 2, pt. 2, 530–32.
125. Babai the Great, *History of George the Priest,* 505–13; *Chronicle of Khuzestan,* 23. For Gabriel as a Constantine, see Denha, *History of Maruta,* 76; Reinink 1999, 177–91.
126. Flusin 1992, 114–18; Lange 2012, 510–13.
127. Babai the Great, *History of George the Priest,* 513–14. For Babai as a hagiographer, see Walker 2010.
128. Babai the Great, *History of George the Priest,* 516.
129. Denha, *History of Maruta,* 76.
130. Michael the Syrian, *Chronicle,* vol. 4, 391 / vol. 2, 381.

131. Gariboldi 2009, 339.
132. Christensen 1907, 5–9.
133. Schilling 2008b, 99–101.
134. Rubin 2004, 267; Schilling 2008b, 96–97.
135. Rubin 2004, 263–73.
136. Ibid., 254–63; Pourshariati 2008, 122–30; Christensen 1907, 9–18.
137. Rubin 2005, 82–86; Howard-Johnston 2010b, 82–85, 367–68.
138. The account that follows, including all of the quotes, is in Firdawsī, *Šāhnāme*, vol. 8, 158.
139. Ibid., 251.
140. Ibid., 255.
141. Ibid., 256–57.
142. Ibid., 159.
143. Ibid., 160.
144. Ibid., 162.
145. *History of Rabban Mar Saba*, 667–69. Such accounts were increasingly common in the course of the seventh century: see, e.g., *History of Mar Yonan*, 481–82.
146. *History of Sabrisho*, 306–7.
147. Daryaee 2013, 93, an apparent reversal of the view expressed in Daryaee 2003a, 198.
148. Widengren 1965, 283; Wiessner 1971. Even a historian sensitive to the appeal of Zoroastrianism has claimed that "spiritually dissatisfied upper-class Zoroastrians defected to Nestorian Christianity": Choksy 1997, 70.
149. Brock 2008a, 83–84.
150. Walker 2006, 206–45.
151. Bruns 2009b.
152. Flusin 1992, 118–27, deconstructs the image of Husraw II as a persecutory king of kings. See also Binder 2013, 72–77.
153. F. Jullien 2004, 172; Flusin 1992, 126.
154. *Martyrdom of Anastasios the Persian*, 46–53.
155. Ibid., 56–67, 70–71.
156. Babai the Great, *History of George the Priest*, 520–22; *Chronicle of Khuzestan*, 23; *Chronicle of Seert*, vol. 2, pt. 2, 537–38; Flusin 1992, 124–26.
157. Babai the Great, *History of George the Priest*, 522–26.
158. Ibid., 536–37; *Chronicle of Khuzestan*, 23; *Chronicle of Seert*, vol. 2, pt. 2, 539. For the identification and site of the city, see Hauser 2008.
159. C. Jullien 2004, 260. The imagery of the cross in the *Martyrdom of Christina*—composed, like the *History of George the Priest*, by Babai the Great—suggests that she was crucified: Binder 2012, 19–23. See also the crucifixion of Nathaniel of Shahrazur in the 610s: *Chronicle of Khuzestan*, 21.
160. *Martyrdom of Anastasios the Persian*, 76–87; Babai the Great, *History of George the Priest*, 520–37; Ishoyahb III, *History of Ishosabran*, 518–20, 530–50.
161. *History of Pseudo-Sebeos*, 85/29. See also Fiey 1970a, 98; Flusin 1992, 100.
162. *History of Sabrisho*, 307. Al-Ṭabarī described a decree allowing conversion with the important provision that Zoroastrians were forbidden from converting to Christianity: *Ta'rīkh al-rusul wa al-mulūk*, vol. 2, 1000 / 314.

163. There is even an East Syrian account of the king of kings having a convert to Zoroastrianism killed: *Chronicle of Seert*, vol. 2, pt. 2, 467–68.
164. Babai the Great, *Martyrdom of Christina*, 204; Binder 2012, 14–15.
165. Mango 1985. At the same time, the emperor sought diplomatically and doctrinally to unify the imperial and East Syrian Churches: Seleznyov 2012; Lange 2012, 553–87.
166. Mango 1985, 110.
167. See G. Fowden 1993, 100–137, for Roman pretensions to a Christian "commonwealth."
168. Mango 1985, 112–14; J. W. Drijvers 2002, 177–78.
169. Daryaee 1999a, 79–80; Panaino 2006.
170. Daryaee 2006–7, 26.

CONCLUSION

1. Kolesnikov 1982, 131–43; Pourshariati 2008, 260–71; Daryaee 2010b, 51–52. His descendants took refuge at the court of the Tang dynasty: Compareti 2003; Daryaee 2006–7, 25–26.
2. Firdawsī, *Šāhnāme*, vol. 8, 468.
3. Ibid., 469.
4. Al-Thaʿālibī, *Ghurar akhbār mulūk al-Furs*, 747–48, includes a highly condensed version of this account, which is absent from other narratives, notably the East Syrian histories: see al-Ṭabarī, *Taʾrīkh al-rusul wa al-mulūk*, vol. 2, 1067 / 409–11; Ḥamza al-Iṣfahānī, *Taʾrīkh sinnī mulūk al-arḍ*, 55; *Chronicle of Khuzestan*, 30–31; *Chronicle of Seert*, vol. 2, pt. 2, 531.
5. Bogolyubov 1971; Blois 1990
6. Kreyenbroek 1987; Choksy 1997, 93–106.
7. Simonsohn 2011, 103–14; Payne 2015.
8. Kolesnikov 1998b; Gyselen 2000, 66–68, 120, 168–75.
9. Ibid., 177.
10. Henanisho, *Judgments*, 6–22.
11. Robinson 2000, 107.
12. There were some significant conversions from Zoroastrianism at the time of the conquests, but the ninth century was the tipping point: Choksy 1997, 80–93; Bulliet 2009, 30–32; Savant 2013, 62–59. The Iranian aristocracy played a fundamental role in the development of Islamic imperial structures, elite culture, and even doctrine: Morony 2004b; Khan 2007; Kennedy 2009; Pourshariati 2009.
13. Gropp 1970; Cereti, Olivieri, and Vazhuthanapally 2002, 293–301.
14. Lieu 2012, 27. The self-proclaimed identification of eighth-century Chinese East Syrians with Da Qin, the name of the Roman Empire in Chinese historiography, was likely an attempt to present the religion as favorably as possible to Confucian bureaucrats, for whom Da Qin was a land with "utopian living conditions and the highest standards of morality": Lieu 2013, 132; see also Barrett 2002, 557–59. This identification also obscured the links of the church with the patriarch in the caliphate, with which the Tang dynasty was on uneasy terms: Hunter 2009, 82.
15. Saeki 1916, 167–74.
16. Cereti 2009; Malekandathil 2010, 39–47.

BIBLIOGRAPHY

PRIMARY SOURCES

Mar Aba, *Regulations of Marriage*, in *Syrische Rechtsbücher*, vol. 3, ed. and trans. Eduard Sachau (Berlin: Georg Reimer, 1914), 258–85.

Agapius of Manbij, *Universal History*, ed. and trans. by Alexandre Vasiliev as *Kitāb al-'Unwān: Histoire Universelle*, vol. 2 (Paris: Firmin Didot, 1912).

Agatangełos, *History of the Armenians*, ed. and trans. R. W. Thomson, *Agathangelos: History of the Armenians* (Albany: State University of New York Press, 1976).

Antony of Choziba, *Life of George of Choziba*, ed. by C. House as "Vita sancti Georgii Chozibitae auctore Antonio Chozibita," *Analecta Bollandiana* 7 (1888): 95–144, 336–59; trans. by Tim Vivian and Apostolos N. Athanassakis in *The Life of Saint George of Choziba and the Miracles of the Most Holy Mother of God at Choziba* (San Francisco: International Scholars Publications, 1994).

Ardā Wirāz Nāmag, ed. and trans. by Fereydun Vahman as *Ardā Wirāz Nāmag: The Iranian "Divina Commedia"* (London: Curzon, 1986).

Armenian Book of Canons, ed. by Vazgen A. Hakobyan as *Kanonagirk' Hayoc'* (Yerevan: Patmutyan Institut, 1964).

Ātaxš Niyāyišn, ed. and trans. by Zahra Taraf as *Der Awesta Text Niyāyiš mit Pahlavi und Sanskritübersetzung* (Munich: R. Kitzinger, 1981).

Babai the Great, *History of George the Priest*, in *Histoire de Mar-Jabalaha, de trois autres patriarches, d'un prêtre et de deux laïques, Nestoriens*, ed. Paul Bedjan (Paris: Otto Harrassowitz, 1895), 416–571.

———, *Martyrdom of Christina*, in *Acta martyrum et sanctorum IV*, ed. Paul Bedjan (Paris: Otto Harrassowitz, 1894), 201–7.

Barhadbeshabba Arbaya, *Ecclesiastical History*, ed. and trans. by François Nau as *La seconde partie de l'Histoire de Barḥadbšabba 'Arbaïa* (Paris: Firmin-Didot, 1913).

Book of the Himyarites, ed. and trans. by Axel Moberg as *Book of the Himyarites: Fragments of a Hitherto Unknown Syriac Work* (Lund: Gleerup, 1924).
Bundahišn, ed. and trans. by Behramgore Tehmuras Anklesaria as *Zand-Ākāsīh: Iranian or Greater Bundahišn* (Bombay: Rahnumae Mazdayasnan Sabha, 1956).
Cave of Treasures, ed. by Su-Min Ri as *La caverne des trésors: Les deux recensions syriaques* (Leuven: Peeters, 1987).
Chronicle of Arbela, ed. and trans. by Peter Kawerau as *Die Chronik von Arbela* (Leuven: Peeters, 1985).
Chronicle of Fredegar, partially ed. and trans. by J. W. Wallace-Hadrill as *The Fourth Book of the Chronicle of Fredegar* (London: Nelson, 1960).
Chronicle of Khuzestan, ed. and trans. by Ignatius Guidi as *Chronicon anonymum* (Leuven: Peeters, 1903).
Chronicle of Seert, ed. and trans. by Addaï Scher as *Histoire nestorienne (Chronique de Séert)*, 2 vols. (Paris: Firmin-Didot, 1908–19).
Chronicle of 1234, ed. by J. B. Chabot as *Chronicon ad annum Christi 1234 pertinens* (Paris: Typographeus reipublicae, 1920); trans. by Andrew Palmer in *The Seventh Century in the West-Syrian Chronicles* (Liverpool: Liverpool University Press, 1993), 111–221.
Chronicon Paschale, ed. Ludwig Dindorff (Bonn: E. Weber, 1832); trans. by Michael Whitby and Mary Whitby as *Chronicon Paschale, 284–628 AD* (Liverpool: Liverpool University Press, 1989).
Cities of Iran, in Joseph Markwart, *A Catalogue of the Provincial Capitals of Ērānšahr (Pahlavi Text, Version and Commentary)* (Rome: Pontificio istituto biblico, 1931).
Dādestān ī Dēnīg, ed. and trans. by Mahmoud Jaafari Dehaghi as *Dādestān ī Dēnīg: Part I, Transcription, Translation and Commentary* (Paris: Association pour avancement des études iraniennes, 1998).
Denha, *History of Maruta*, ed. and trans. by François Nau as *Histoire de Marouta: Patrologia Orientalis*, vol. 3 (Paris: Firmin-Didot, 1900).
Dēnkard III, in *The Complete Text of the Pahlavi Dinkard*, ed. Dhanjishnah Meherjibhai Madan (Bombay: Ganpatrao Ramajirao Sindhe, 1911), 1–407; trans. by Jean de Menasce as *Le troisiéme livre du Dēnkart* (Paris: Librairie C. Klincksieck, 1973).
Dēnkard V, ed. and trans. by Jaleh Amouzgar and Ahmad Tafazzoli as *Le cinquième livre du Dēnkard: Transcription, traduction et commentaire* (Paris: Association pour avancement des études iraniennes, 2000).
Dēnkard VI, ed. and trans. by Shaul Shaked as *The Wisdom of the Sasanian Sages* (Boulder, CO: Westview, 1979).
Dēnkard VII, ed. and trans. by Marijan Molé as *La legende de Zoroastre selon les textes pehlevis* (Paris: Libraire C. Klincksieck, 1967).
al-Dīnawarī, *Kitāb al-akhbār al-ṭiwāl*, ed. 'Abd al-Mun'im 'Āmir (Cairo: Al-Idārah al-'Āmmah lil-Thaqāfah, 1960).
Elias of Nisibis, *Chronology*, ed. by J. B. Chabot as *Eliae metropolitae Nisibeni: Opus chronologicum II* (Paris: Otto Harrassowitz, 1909).
Ełiše, *Vardan and the Armenian War*, ed. by E. Ter-Minasean as *Vasn Vardanants' ew Hayoc' Paterazmin* (Yerevan: Izdatelstvo Akademii Nauk Armyanskoi SSR, 1957); trans. by Robert W. Thomson as *History of Vardan and the Armenian War* (Cambridge, MA: Harvard University Press, 1982).

Ephrem, *Commentary on Genesis*, ed. and trans. by R. M. Tonneau as *Sancti Ephremi Syri in Genesimet in Exodum Commentarii* (Leuven: L. Durbecq, 1955).
Eusebius of Caesarea, *Chronicle*, trans. by Josef Karst as *Eusebius Werke: Die Chronik aus dem armenischen übersetz mit textkritischem Commentar* (Leipzig: J. C. Hinrichs'sche Buchhandlung, 1911).
———, *Life of Constantine*, ed. by F. Winkelmann and trans. by Marie-Joseph Rondeau as *Vie de Constantin* (Paris: Cerf, 2013).
Evagrius Scholasticus, *Ecclesiastical History*, ed. by J. Bidez and L. Parmentier as *The Ecclesiastical History of Evagrius* (London: Methuen, 1898); trans. by Michael Whitby as *The Ecclesiastical History of Evagrius Scholasticus* (Liverpool: Liverpool University Press, 2000).
Eznik of Kołb, *Treatise on God*, ed. and trans. by Susanne Zeilfelder as *Eznik von Kołb: Ełc ałandoc'* (Graz: Leykam, 2004).
Firdawsī, *Šāhnāme*, 8 vols., ed. Jelal Khaleghi-Motlagh (New York: Bibliotheca Persica, 1987–2008).
Gabriel of Basra, *Collection of Laws*, ed. by Hubert Kaufhold as *Die Rechtssammlung des Gabriel von Basra und ihr Verhältnis zu den anderen juristichen Sammelwerken der Nestorianer* (Berlin: Münchener Universitätsschriften, 1976).
Great Slaughter of Khuzestan, in *Acta martyrum et sanctorum II*, ed. Paul Bedjan (Paris: Otto Harrassowitz, 1891), 241–48.
Gregory the Great, *Correspondence*, ed. and trans. by Dag Norberg, Pierre Minard, and Marc Reydellet as *Registre des lettres* (Paris: Cerf, 2008), vol. 2.
Ḥamza al-Iṣfahānī, *Ta'rīkh sinnī mulūk al-arḍ*, ed. Yūsuf Ya'qūb Maskūnī (Beirut: Dār Maktaba, 1961).
Hazār Dādestān (MHD), ed. and trans. by Maria Macuch as *Rechtskasuistik und Gerichtspraxis zu Beginn des siebenten Jahrhunderts in Iran: Die Rechtssammlung des Farroḥmard i Wahrāmān* (Wiesbaden: Harrassowitz Verlag, 1993).
Hazār Dādestān (MHDA), ed. and trans. by Maria Macuch as *Das Sasanidische Rechtsbuch "Mātakdān i Hazār Dātistān,"* pt. 2 (Wiesbaden: Harrassowitz Verlag, 1981).
Henanisho, *Judgments*, in *Syrische Rechtsbücher*, vol. 2, ed. and trans. Eduard Sachau (Berlin: Georg Reimer, 1908), 1–51.
Hērbedestān, vol. 1 of *The Hērbedestān and the Nērangestān*, ed. and trans. Firoze M. Kotwal and Philip G. Kreyenbroek (Paris: Association pour l'avancement des études iraniennes, 1992).
History of Gregory the Commander, in *Histoire de Mar-Jabalaha, de trois autres patriarches, d'un prêtre et de deux laïques, Nestoriens*, ed. Paul Bedjan (Paris: Otto Harrassowitz, 1895), 347–94.
History of Karka d-Beit Slok and its Martyrs, in *Acta martyrum et sanctorum II*, ed. Paul Bedjan (Paris: Otto Harrassowitz, 1891), 507–35.
History of Mar Aba, in *Histoire de Mar-Jabalaha, de trois autres patriarches, d'un prêtre et de deux laïques, Nestoriens*, ed. Paul Bedjan (Paris: Otto Harrassowitz, 1895), 206–87.
History of Mar Behnam, in *Acta martyrum et sanctorum II*, ed. Paul Bedjan (Paris: Otto Harrassowitz, 1891), 397–441.
History of Mar Mari, ed. by Christelle Jullien and Florence Jullien as *Les actes de Mār Māri* (Leuven: Peeters, 2003); trans. by Amir Harrak as *The Acts of Mār Māri the Apostle* (Atlanta: Society of Biblical Literature, 2005).

History of Mar Qardagh, ed. by J. B. Abbeloos as "Acta Mar Kardaghi," *Analecta Bollandiana* 9 (1890): 5–106; trans. by Joel T. Walker in *The Legend of Mar Qardagh: Narrative and Christian Heroism in Late Antique Iraq* (Berkeley: University of California Press, 2006), 19–69.

History of Mar Yonan, in *Acta martyrum et sanctorum I*, ed. Paul Bedjan (Paris: Otto Harrassowitz, 1890), 466–525.

History of Pseudo-Sebeos, ed. by G. A. Abgaryan as *Patmutʻiwn Sebeosi* (Yerevan: Izdatelstvo Akademii Nauk Armyanskoi SSR, 1979); trans. by Robert W. Thomson as *The Armenian History Attributed to Sebeos* (Liverpool: Liverpool University Press, 1999).

History of Rabban Mar Saba, in *Acta martyrum et sanctorum II*, ed. Paul Bedjan (Paris: Otto Harrassowitz, 1891), 635–80.

History of Saba Pirgushnasp, in *Acta martyrum et sanctorum IV*, ed. Paul Bedjan (Paris: Otto Harrassowitz, 1894), 222–48.

History of Sabrisho, in *Histoire de Mar-Jabalaha, de trois autres patriarches, d'un prêtre et de deux laïques, Nestoriens*, ed. Paul Bedjan, (Paris: Otto Harrassowitz, 1895), 288–331.

History of Simeon, in *Patrologia Syriaca*, ed. M. Kmosko (Paris: Firmin-Didot, 1907), 778–960; in *The Martyrdom and the History of Blessed Simeon bar Ṣabbaʻe*, trans. Kyle Smith (Piscataway: Gorgias, 2014), 68–210.

History of Sultan Mahduk, in *Acta martyrum et sanctorum II*, ed. Paul Bedjan (Paris: Otto Harrassowitz, 1891), 1–39.

History of the Monastery of Sabrisho, in *Sources syriaques*, vol. 1, ed. and trans. Alphonse Mingana (Leipzig: Otto Harrassowitz, 1907), 171–267.

History of Yazdpaneh, in *Histoire de Mar-Jabalaha, de trois autres patriarches, d'un prêtre et de deux laïques, Nestoriens*, ed. Paul Bedjan (Paris: Otto Harrassowitz, 1895), 394–415.

Hōm Yašt, ed. and trans. by Judith Josephson as *The Pahlavi Translation Technique as Illustrated by Hōm Yašt* (Uppsala: Uppsala Universitet, 1997).

Husraw and the Youth, ed. and trans. by Davoud Monchi-Zadeh as "Xusrōv Kavātān ut Rētak," in *Monumentum Georg Morgenstierne II*, ed. Jacques Duchesne-Guillemin and Pierre Lecoq (Leiden: Brill, 1982), 47–92.

Ibn Miskawayh, *Tajārib al-umam*, ed. Abū al-Qāsim Imāmī (Tehran: Dār Surūsh, 1987).

Ishobokht, *Book of Judgments*, in *Syrische Rechtsbücher*, vol. 3, ed. and trans. Eduard Sachau (Berlin: Georg Reimer, 1914), 2–201.

Ishodad of Merv, *Commentary on the Old Testament*, ed. by Ceslas van den Eynde as *Commentaire d'Išoʻdad de Merv sur l'Ancient Testament*, vol. 1, *Genèse* (Leuven: L. Durbecq, 1950); trans. by van den Eynde as *Commentaire d'Išoʻdad de Merv sur l'Ancien Testament*, vol. 1, *Genèse* (Leuven: Imprimerie orientaliste, 1955).

Ishodenah of Basra, *Book of Chastity*, ed. and trans. by J. B. Chabot as *Le livre de la chasteté, composé par Jésusdenah évêque de Baçrah* (Rome: L'École française de Rome, 1896).

Ishoyahb III of Adiabene, *Correspondence*, ed. by Rubens Duval as *Išōʻyahb Patriarchae III: Liber Epistularum* (Leuven: Peeters, 1962).

———, *History of Ishosabran*, ed. by J. B. Chabot as "Histoire de Jésus-Sabran," *Nouvelles Archives des Missions Scientifiques et Littéraires* 7 (1897): 485–584.

John Malalas, *Chronographia*, ed. by L. Dindorf as *Ioannis Malalae Chronographia* (Bonn: Weber, 1831); trans. by Johannes Thurn and Mischa Meier as *Johannes Malalas: Weltchronik* (Stuttgart: Anton Hiersemann, 2009).

John of Ephesus, *Ecclesiastical History*, ed. by E. W. Brooks as *Iohannis Ephesini Historiae Ecclesiasticae pars tertia* (Leuven: Officina orientali et scientifica, 1935).
——, *Lives of the Eastern Saints*, ed. and trans. E. W. Brooks (Paris: Firmin-Didot, 1923), vol. 1.
John of Nikiu, *Chronicle*, trans. by R. H. Charles as *The Chronicle of John of Nikiu* (Oxford: Williams and Norgate, 1916).
John of Phenek, *Book of the Main Points*, in *Sources syriaques*, vol. 1, ed. and trans. Alphonse Mingana (Leipzig: Otto Harrassowitz, 1907), 1–204.
Jōišt ī Friyān, ed. and trans. by Matthias Weinreich as "Die Geschichte von *Jōišt ī Friyān*," *Altorientalische Forschungen* 19 (1992): 44–101.
Kerdir, *Inscription at the Ka'aba-ye Zardosht*, ed. and trans. by Philippe Gignoux as *Les quatre inscriptions du mage Kirdir: Textes et concordances* (Paris: Association pour l'avancement des études iraniennes, 1991).
Łazar P'arpec'i, *History of the Armenians*, ed. by G. Ter-Mkrtchean as *Patmut'iwn Hayoc'* (Tbilisi: Tparan Ōr. N. Aghaneani, 1904); trans. by Robert W. Thomson as *The History of Łazar P'arpec'i* (Atlanta: Scholars, 1991).
Letter of Tansar, ed. by Mojtaba Minovi as *Nāmah-e Tansar bih Jushnasf* (Tehran: Matba'ah-e Majlis, 1932); trans. by Mary Boyce as *The Letter of Tansar* (Rome: Istituto italiano per il medio ed estremo Oriente, 1968).
Martyrdom of Anastasios the Persian, ed. and trans. by Bernard Flusin as *Saint Anastase le Perse et l'histoire de la Palestine au début du VIIe siècle*, vol. 1 (Paris: Centre national de la recherche scientifique, 1992).
Martyrdom of Aqebshma, in *Acta martyrum et sanctorum II*, ed. Paul Bedjan (Paris Otto Harrassowitz, 1891), 351–96.
Martyrdom of Azad, in *Acta martyrum et sanctorum II*, ed. Paul Bedjan (Paris: Otto Harrassowitz, 1891), 248–54.
Martyrdom of Baboi, in *Acta martyrum et sanctorum II*, ed. Paul Bedjan (Paris: Otto Harrassowitz, 1891), 631–34.
Martyrdom of Badai the Priest, in *Acta martyrum et sanctorum IV*, ed. Paul Bedjan (Paris: Otto Harrassowitz, 1894), 163–65.
Martyrdom of Badma, in *Acta martyrum et sanctorum II*, ed. Paul Bedjan (Paris: Otto Harrassowitz, 1891), 347–51.
Martyrdom of Barbashmin, in *Acta martyrum et sanctorum II*, ed. Paul Bedjan (Paris: Otto Harrassowitz, 1891), 296–303.
Martyrdom of Barhadbeshabba, in *Acta martyrum et sanctorum II*, ed. Paul Bedjan (Paris: Otto Harrassowitz, 1891), 314–16.
Martyrdom of Bar Shebya, in *Acta martyrum et sanctorum II*, ed. Paul Bedjan (Paris: Otto Harrassowitz, 1891), 281–84.
Martyrdom of Bishop Abraham, in *Acta martyrum et sanctorum IV*, ed. Paul Bedjan (Paris: Otto Harrassowitz, 1894), 130–31.
Martyrdom of Dado, in *Acta martyrum et sanctorum IV*, ed. Paul Bedjan (Paris: Otto Harrassowitz, 1895), 218–21.
Martyrdom of Eustathius of Mtskheta, trans. by G. Dschawachoff as "Das Martyrium des heiligen Eustathius des Mzchetha aus dem georgischen übersetzt," *Sitzungsberichte des königlich preussischen Akademie der Wissenschaften zu Berlin* 34 (1901): 875–902.

Martyrdom of Gubralaha, in Acta martyrum et sanctorum IV, ed. Paul Bedjan (Paris: Otto Harrassowitz, 1895), 141–63.

Martyrdom of Hnanya the Worldly, in *Acta martyrum et sanctorum IV*, ed. Paul Bedjan (Paris: Otto Harrassowitz, 1894), 131–32.

Martyrdom of Jacob, in *Acta martyrum et sanctorum II*, ed. Paul Bedjan (Paris: Otto Harrassowitz, 1891), 307.

Martyrdom of Jacob the Notary, in *Acta martyrum et sanctorum IV*, ed. Paul Bedjan (Paris: Otto Harrassowitz, 1894), 189–200.

Martyrdom of Jacob the Priest and Azad the Deacon, in *Acta martyrum et sanctorum IV*, ed. Paul Bedjan (Paris: Otto Harrassowitz, 1894), 137–41.

Martyrdom of Jacob the Sliced, in *Acta martyrum et sanctorum II*, ed. Paul Bedjan (Paris: Otto Harrassowitz, 1891), 539–58.

Martyrdom of John the Bishop and Jacob the Priest, in *Acta martyrum et sanctorum IV*, ed. Paul Bedjan (Paris: Otto Harrassowitz, 1894), 128–30.

Martyrdom of Mar Abda, in *Acta martyrum et sanctorum IV*, ed. Paul Bedjan (Paris: Otto Harrassowitz, 1894), 250–53.

Martyrdom of Mihrshabur, in *Acta martyrum et sanctorum II*, ed. Paul Bedjan (Paris: Otto Harrassowitz, 1891), 535–39.

Martyrdom of Miles, in *Acta martyrum et sanctorum II*, ed. Paul Bedjan (Paris: Otto Harrassowitz, 1891), 260–75.

Martyrdom of Narsai, in Acta martyrum et sanctorum IV, ed. Paul Bedjan (Paris: Otto Harrassowitz, 1895), 170–80.

Martyrdom of Narsai and Joseph, in *Acta martyrum et sanctorum II*, ed. Paul Bedjan (Paris: Otto Harrassowitz, 1891), 284–86.

Martyrdom of 111 Men and Women, in *Acta martyrum et sanctorum II*, ed. Paul Bedjan (Paris: Otto Harrassowitz, 1891), 291–95.

Martyrdom of Peroz, in *Acta martyrum et sanctorum IV*, ed. Paul Bedjan (Paris: Otto Harrassowitz, 1894), 253–62.

Martyrdom of Pethion, Adurohrmazd, and Anahid, in *Acta martyrum et sanctorum II*, ed. Paul Bedjan (Paris: Otto Harrassowitz, 1891), 559–631; Sogdian version ed. and trans. by Nicholas Sims-Williams as *The Christian Sogdian Manuscript C2* (Berlin: Akademie Verlag, 1985), 31–68.

Martyrdom of Pusai, in *Acta martyrum et sanctorum II*, ed. Paul Bedjan (Paris: Otto Harrassowitz, 1891), 208–32.

Martyrdom of Tarbo, in *Acta martyrum et sanctorum II*, ed. Paul Bedjan (Paris: Otto Harrassowitz, 1891), 254–60.

Martyrdom of Teqla, in *Acta martyrum et sanctorum II*, ed. Paul Bedjan (Paris: Otto Harrassowitz, 1891), 308–13.

Martyrdom of the Captives, in *Acta martyrum et sanctorum II*, ed. Paul Bedjan (Paris: Otto Harrassowitz, 1891), 316–24.

Martyrdom of the Forty Martyrs, in *Acta martyrum et sanctorum II*, ed. Paul Bedjan (Paris: Otto Harrassowitz, 1891), 325–47.

Martyrdom of the Ten Martyrs of Beth Garmai, in *Acta martyrum et sanctorum IV*, ed. Paul Bedjan (Paris: Otto Harrassowitz, 1894), 184–88.

Martyrdom of Shahdost, in *Acta martyrum et sanctorum II,* ed. Paul Bedjan (Paris: Otto Harrassowitz, 1891), 276–81.

Martyrdom of Shapur, ed. and trans. by Geoffrey Herman as "The Passion of Shabur, Martyred in the 18th Year of Yazdgird, with a Fragment of the Life of Mar Aba Catholicos," *Journal of Semitic Studies* 58 (2013): 121–30.

Martyrdom of Shapur of Beit Niẓator, in *Acta martyrum et sanctorum II,* ed. Paul Bedjan (Paris: Otto Harrassowitz, 1851), 51–56.

Martyrdom of Shirin, ed. by Paul Devos as "Sainte Šīrīn, martyre sous Khusrau 1er Anōšarvān," *Analecta Bollandiana* 64 (1946): 87–131; trans. by Devos as "La jeune martyre perse sainte Širin," *Analecta Bollandiana* 112 (1994): 5–31.

Martyrdom of Simeon, in *Patrologia Syriaca,* ed. M. Kmosko (Paris: Firmin-Didot, 1907), 715–77; trans. by Kyle Smith as *The Martyrdom and the History of Blessed Simeon bar Ṣabba'e* (Piscataway: Gorgias 2014), 6–58.

Martyrdom of Yazdbozid, in *Vark' ew vkayabanut'iwnk' srbotc',* ed. Ł. Alishan (Venice: I Tparani Mkhit'areants', 1874), 124–30.

Martyrdom of Zebina and Companions, in *Acta martyrum et sanctorum II,* ed. Paul Bedjan (Paris: Otto Harrassowitz, 1851), 39–51.

Mēnōg ī Xrad, ed. by O. M. Chunakova as *Zoroastriiskie Teksti: Suzhdeniya Dukha Razuma (Dadestan-i Menog-i Khrad)—Sotvorenie Osnovi (Bundahishn) i Drugie Teksti* (Moscow: Vostochnaya Literatura, 1997), 28–78; trans. by Ahmad Tafazzoli as *Minu-ye Kherad* (Tehran: Intishārāt-e Tus, 1975).

Michael the Syrian, *Chronicle,* ed. and trans. by J. B. Chabot as *Chronique de Michel le Syrien,* 4 vols. (Paris: Académie des inscriptions et belles-lettres, 1910).

Movses Daskhurants'i, *History of the Albanians,* ed. by V. Arakelyan as *Patmut'iwn Ałuanits' Ashkharhi* (Yerevan: Izdatelstvo Akademii Nauk Armyanskoi SSR 1983); trans. by C. J. F. Dowsett as *The History of the Caucasian Albanians* (London: Oxford University Press, 1961).

al-Muqaddasī, *Aḥsan al-taqāsīm fī ma'rifat al-aqālīm,* trans. by Basil A. Collins as *Al Muqaddasi: The Best Divisions for Knowledge of the Regions* (Reading, England: Garnet, 1994).

Nērangestān, Fragard 1, ed. and trans. by Firoze M. Kotwal and Philip G. Kreyenbroek as *The Hērbedestān and the Nērangestān,* vol. 2, *Nērangestān, Fragard 1* (Paris: Association pour l'avancement des études iraniennes, 1995).

Nērangestān, Fragard 2, ed. and trans. by Firoze M. Kotwal and Philip G. Kreyenbroek as *The Hērbedestān and the Nērangestān,* vol. 3, *Nērangestān, Fragard 2* (Paris: Association pour l'avancement des études iraniennes, 2004).

Pahlavi Rivāyat Accompanying the Dādestān ī Dēnīg, ed. and trans. A. V. Williams (Copenhagen: Munksgaard, 1990).

Photios, *Bibliotheca,* ed. and trans by René Henry as *Bibliothèque* (Paris: Les belles lettres, 1959), vol. 1.

Pseudo-Joshua the Stylite, *Chronicle,* ed. and trans. by W. Wright as *The Chronicle of Joshua the Stylite* (Cambridge: Cambridge University Press, 1882); trans. by Frank R. Trombley and John W. Watt as *The Chronicle of Pseudo-Joshua the Stylite* (Liverpool: Liverpool University Press, 2000).

Pseudo-Zachariah, *Chronicle of Pseudo-Zachariah of Mytilene*, ed. by E. W. Brooks as *Historia ecclesiastica Zachariae Rhetori vulgo adscripta* (Paris: Typographeus reipublicae, 1921), vol. 2; trans. by Robert R. Phenix and Cornelia B. Horn as *The Chronicle of Pseudo-Zachariah Rhetor: Church and War in Late Antiquity* (Liverpool: Liverpool University Press, 2001).

Pursišnīhā, ed. and trans. by Kaikhusroo M. Jamaspasa and Helmut Humbach as *Pursišnīhā: A Zoroastrian Catechism* (Wiesbaden: Harrassowitz Verlag, 1971).

Sāwīrus b. al-Muqaffa', *History of the Patriarchs*, ed. and trans. by B. Evetts as *History of the Patriarchs of the Coptic Church of Alexandria*, vol. 2, *Peter I to Benjamin I (661)* (Paris: Firmin Didot, 1948).

Šāyast-nē-Šāyast, ed. and trans. by Jehangir C. Tavadia as *Šāyast-nē-Šāyast: A Pahlavi Text on Religious Customs* (Hamburg: Friederichsen, De Gruyter, 1930).

Simeon of Revardashir, *Ecclesiastical Judgments*, in *Syrische Rechtsbücher*, vol. 3, ed. and trans. Eduard Sachau (Berlin: Georg Reimer, 1914), 208–53.

Sīrat Ānūšīrwān, ed. by Abū al-Qāsim Imāmi as *Tajārib al-umam* (Tehran: Dār Surūsh, 1987), 188–209; trans. by Mario Grignaschi in "Quelques spécimens de la littérature sassanide conservés dans les bibliothèques d'Istanbul," *Journal Asiatique* 254 (1966): 1–142.

Speech for a Feast, ed. and trans. by Jehangir C. Tavadia as "Sur Saxvan: A Dinner Speech in Middle Persian," *Journal of the K. R. Cama Oriental Institute* 29 (1935): 1–99.

Srōš Yašt Hādōxt, ed. and trans. by Philip G. Kreyenbroek as *Sraoša in the Zoroastrian Tradition* (Leiden: Brill, 1985).

Strategius, *Capture of Jerusalem*, trans. by Gérard Garitte as *La prise de Jérusalem par les perses en 614* (Leuven: Secrétariat du Corpus SCO, 1960).

Supplementary Texts to the Šāyast-nē-Šāyast, ed. and trans. by Firoze M. P. Kotwal as *The Supplementary Texts to the Šāyest nē-Šāyest* (Copenhagen: Det Kongelige Videnskabernes Selskab, 1969).

Sūr ī Saxwan, ed. and trans. by Jehangir C. Tavadia as "Sur Saxvan: A Dinner Speech in Middle Persian," *Journal of the K.R. Cama Oriental Institute* 29 (1935): 1–99.

Synodicon Orientale, ed. and trans. by J. B. Chabot as *Synodicon Orientale, ou recueil de synodes nestoriens* (Paris: Imprimerie nationale, 1902).

al-Ṭabarī, *Ta'rikh al-rusul wa'l-mulūk*, ed. by M. De Goeje as *Annales quos scripsit Abu Djafar Mohammed Ibn Djarir at-Tabari*, series 1 (Leiden: Brill, 1964–65); trans. by C. E. Bosworth as *The History of al-Ṭabarī*, vol. 5, *The Sāsānids, the Byzantines, the Lakhmids, and Yemen* (Albany: State University of New York Press, 1999).

al-Tha'ālibī, *Ghurar akhbār mulūk al-Furs wa siyarihim*, ed. and trans. by H. Zotenberg as *Histoire des rois des perses* (Paris: Imprimerie nationale, 1900).

Theodore bar Koni, *Book of Scholia*, ed. by Addai Scher as *Theodorus bar Kōnī: Liber Scholiorum*, vol. 1 (Leuven: Peeters, 1960); trans. by Robert Hespel and René Draguet as *Théodore bar Koni: Livre des Scolies (Recension de Séert)*, vol. 1, *Memrè I–V* (Leuven: Peeters, 1981).

Theodoret of Cyrrhus, *Ecclesiastical History*, ed. by L. Parmentier and G. C. Hansen and trans. by Pierre Canivet as *Histoire ecclésiastique* (Paris: Cerf, 2009).

Theophanes Confessor, *Chronicle*, ed. by Carolus de Boor as *Theophanis Chronographia* (Leipzig: Teubner, 1883–85); trans. by Cyril Mango and Roger Scott as *The Chronicle of Theophanes the Confessor: Byzantine and Near Eastern History, AD 284–813* (Oxford: Oxford University Press, 1997).

Theophylact Simocatta, *History*, ed. by C. de Boor and Peter Wirth as *Theophylacti Simocattae Historiae* (Stuttgart: Teubner, 1972); trans. by Michael Whitby and Mary Whitby as *The History of Theophylact Simocatta* (Oxford: Clarendon, 1986).
Thomas of Marga, *Book of Governors*, ed. and trans. by E. A. Wallis Budge as *The Book of Governors: The Historia Monastica of Thomas Bishop of Marga*, A.D. 840, 2 vols. (London: K. Paul, Trench, Trübner, 1893).
Timothy, *Correspondence*, ed. and trans. by Oscar Braun as *Timothei Patriarchae I Epistulae* (Paris: Karolus de Luigi, 1915), vol. 2.
———, *Regulations for Ecclesiastical Judgments and Inheritances*, in *Syrische Rechtsbücher*, vol. 2, ed. and trans. Eduard Sachau (Berlin: Georg Reimer, 1908), 53–117.
Vaeθā Nask, ed. and trans. by Helmut Humbach and Kaikhusroo M. Jamaspasa as *Vaeθā Nask: An Apocryphal Text on Zoroastrian Problems* (Wiesbaden: Otto Harrassowitz, 1969).
Widēwdād, ed. by Hoshang Jamasp as *Vendidâd: Avesta Text with Pahlavi Translation and Commentary* (Bombay: Government Central Book Depôt, 1907); trans. by Mahnaz Moazami as *Wrestling with the Demons of the Pahlavi Widēwdād: Transcription, Translation, and Commentary* (Leiden: Brill, 2014).
Wizīdagīhā ī Zādspram, ed. and trans. by Philippe Gignoux and Ahmad Tafazzoli as *Anthologie de Zādspram: Édition critique du texte pehlevi traduit et commenté* (Paris: Association pour l'avancement des études iraniennes, 1993).
Wonders and Magnificence of Sistan, ed. and trans. by Bo Utas as "The Pahlavi Treatise Avdēh u sahikēh ī Sakistān or 'Wonders and Magnificence of Sistan,'" *Acta Antiqua Academiae Scientiarum Hungaricae* 28 (1980): 259–67.
Zand ī Wahman Yasn, ed. and trans. by Carlo G. Cereti as *The Zand ī Wahman Yasn: A Zoroastrian Apocalypse* (Rome: Istituto italiano per il medio ed estremo Oriente, 1995).

SECONDARY SOURCES

Abdi, Kamyar, "Archaeological Research in the Islamabad Plain, Central Western Zagros Mountains: Preliminary Results from the First Season, Summer 1998," *Iran* 37 (1999): 33–43.
Abramowski, Luise, "Der Bischof von Seleukia-Ktesiphon als Katholikos und Patriarch der Kirche des Ostens," in *Syrien im 1.–7. Jahrhundert nach Christus*, ed. Dmitrij Bumazhnov and Hans Reinhard Seeliger (Tübingen: Mohr Siebeck, 2011), 1–55.
Adams, Robert McC., *The Land behind Baghdad: A History of Settlement in the Diyala Plains* (Chicago: University of Chicago Press, 1965).
———, *Heartland of Cities: Surveys of Ancient Settlement and Land Use on the Central Floodplain of the Euphrates* (Chicago: University of Chicago Press, 1981).
Alizadeh, Karim, and Jason A. Ur, "Formation and Destruction of Pastoral and Irrigation Landscapes on the Mughan Steppe, North-western Iran," *Antiquity* 81 (2007): 148–60.
Altheim-Stiehl, Ruth, "Wurde Alexandreia im Juni 619 n. Chr. Durch die Perser erobert? Bemerkungen zur zeitlichen Bestimmung der sāsānidischen Besetzung Ägyptens unter Chosroes II Parwēz," *Tyche* 6 (1991): 3–16.
Amen Ali, Narmen Muhamad, "The 'Monastic Church' of Bāzyān in Iraqi Kurdistan," *Journal of the Canadian Society for Syriac Studies* 8 (2008): 74–84.

Ando, Clifford, "Die Riten der Anderen," *Mediterraneo Antico* 15 (2012): 31–50.
Andrade, Nathanaell, "Assyrians, Syrians and the Greek Language in the Late Hellenistic and Roman Imperial Periods," *Journal of Near Eastern Studies* 73 (2014): 299–317.
Arjava, Antti, *Women and Law in Late Antiquity* (Oxford: Clarendon, 1996).
Asmussen, Jes P., "Das Christentum in Iran und sein Verhältnis zum Zoroastrismus," *Studia Theologica* 16 (1962): 1–24.
———, "Zoroastriernes kritik af kristendomen," *Dansk teologisk tidsskrift* (1968): 161–77.
———, "Iranische neutestamentliche Zitate und Texte und ihre textkritische Bedeutung," *Altorientalische Forschungen* 2 (1975): 79–92.
———, "Christians in Iran," in *The Cambridge History of Iran*, vol. 3(2), *The Seleucid, Parthian and Sasanian Periods,* ed. Ehsan Yarshater (Cambridge: Cambridge University Press, 1983), 924–48.
———, "The Sogdian and Uighur Turkish Christian Literature in Central Asia before the Real Rise of Islam," in *Indological and Buddhist Studies: Volume in Honor of Prof. J. W. de Jong on His Sixtieth Birthday,* ed. L. A. Hercus, F. B. J. Kuiper, T. Rajapatirana, and E. R. Skrypczak (Delhi: Sri Satguru, 1984), 11–29.
Assmann, Jan, *Of God and Gods: Egypt, Israel, and the Rise of Monotheism* (Madison: University of Wisconsin Press, 2008).
Avni, Gideon, "The Persian Conquest of Jerusalem (614 C.E.)—Archaeological Assessment," *Bulletin of the American Schools of Oriental Research* 357 (2010): 35–48.
Azarnouche, Samra, *Husraw ī Kawādān ud Rēdag-ē: Khosrow fils de Kawād et un page* (Paris: Association pour l'avancement des études iraniennes, 2013). [Azarnouche 2013a]
———, "La terminologie normative de l'enseignement zoroastrien: Analyse lexicographique et sémantique de quatre termes pehlevis relatifs à l'apprentissage des textes sacrés," *Studia Iranica* 42 (2013): 163–94. [Azarnouche 2013b]
Azarnoush, Massoud, *The Sasanian Manor-House at Hājjiābād* (Florence: Le lettere, 1994).
———, "New Evidence on the Chronology of the 'Anahita Temple,'" *Iranica Antiqua* 44 (2009): 393–402.
Azarpay, Guitta, "The Role of Mithra in the Investiture and Triumph of Shapur II," *Iranica Antiqua* 17 (1982): 181–88.
Bachmann, W., *Kirchen und Moscheen in Armenien und Kurdistan* (Leipzig: J. C. Hinrichs, 1913).
Bagnall, Roger S., *Egypt in Late Antiquity* (Princeton: Princeton University Press, 1993).
Bailey, Harold Walter "Iranian Studies III," *Bulletin of the School of Oriental Studies* 7 (1934): 275–98.
———, *Zoroastrian Problems in the Ninth Century Books* (Oxford: Clarendon, 1943).
Banaji, Jairus, "Precious Metal Coinages and Monetary Expansion in Late Antiquity," in *Dal denarius al dinar: L'Oriente e la moneta romana,* ed. Federico De Romanis and Sara Sorda (Rome: Istituto italiano di numismatica, 2006), 265–303.
———, "Aristocracies, Peasants, and the Framing of the Early Middle Ages," *Journal of Agrarian Change* 9 (2009): 59–91.
Barnes, Timothy D., "Constantine and the Christians of Persia," *Journal of Roman Studies* 75 (1985): 126–36.
———, "The Persian Sack of Antioch in 253," *Zeitschrift für Papyrologie und Epigraphik* 169 (2009): 294–96.

Barrett, T. H., "Buddhism, Taoism and the Eighth-Century Chinese Term for Christianity," *Bulletin of the School of Oriental and African Studies* 65 (2002): 555–60.
Bartholomae, Christian, *Altiranisches Wörterbuch* (Strasbourg: K. J. Trübner, 1904).
Baum, Wilhelm, *Schirin: Christin—Königen—Liebesmythos* (Vienna: Verlag Kitab, 2003).
Baum, Wilhelm, and Dietmar W. Winkler, *The Church of the East: A Concise History* (London: Routledge, 2000).
Baumer, Christoph, *The Church of the East: An Illustrated History of Assyrian Christianity* (London: I. B. Tauris, 2006).
Baumstark, Anton, *Geschichte der syrischen Literatur* (Bonn: A. Marcus and E. Weber, 1922).
Bayly, C. A., *Rulers, Townsmen and Bazaars: North Indian Society in the Age of British Expansion, 1770–1870* (Cambridge: Cambrdige University Press, 1983).
Beaucamp, Joëlle, and Christelle Robin, "L'évêché nestorien de Mâšmâhîg dans l'archipel d'al-Baḥrayn (V^e–IXe siècle)," in *Dilmun: New Studies in the Archaeology and Early History of Bahrain*, ed. D. T. Potts (Berlin: Dietrich Reimer Verlag, 1983), 171–96.
Becker, Adam, "Anti-Judaism and Care for the Poor in Aphrahat's Demonstration 20," *Journal of Early Christian Studies* 10 (2002): 305–27.
———, "The Dynamic Reception of Theodore of Mopsuestia in the Sixth Century: Greek, Syriac, and Latin," in *Greek Literature in Late Antiquity: Dynamism, Didacticism, Classicism*, ed. Scott Fitzgerald Johnson (Aldershot: Ashgate, 2006), 29–47. [Becker 2006a]
———, *Fear of God and the Beginning of Wisdom: The School of Nisibis and Scholastic Culture in Late Antique Mesopotamia* (Philadelphia: University of Pennsylvania Press, 2006). [Becker 2006b]
———, "The Ancient Near East in the Late Antique Near East: Syriac Christian Appropriation of the Biblical East," in *Antiquity in Antiquity: Jewish and Christian Pasts in the Greco-Roman World*, ed. Gregg Gardner and Kevin Osterloh (Tübingen: Mohr Siebeck, 2008), 394–415.
———, "Martyrdom, Religious Difference, and 'Fear' as Religious Categories in the Sasanian Empire: The Case of the *Martyrdom of Gregory* and the *Martyrdom of Yazdpaneh*," *Journal of Late Antiquity* 2 (2009): 300–336.
———, "Political Theology and Religious Diversity in the Sasanian Empire," in *Jews, Christians and Zoroastrians: Religious Dynamics in a Sasanian Context*, ed. Geoffrey Herman (Piscataway: Gorgias, 2014), 7–25.
Bedrosian, Robert, "*Dayeakut'iwn* in Ancient Armenia," *Armenian Review* 37 (1984): 23–47.
Bell, Gertrude, *Churches and Monasteries of the Tûr 'Abdîn and Neighboring Districts* (Heidelberg: C. Winter's Universitätsbuchhandlung, 1913).
Benveniste, Émile, "Sur la terminologie iranienne du sacrifice," *Journal Asiatique* 252 (1964): 45–58. [Benveniste 1964a]
———, "Le vocabulaire chrétien dans les langues d'Asie Centrale," in *L'Oriente cristiano nella storia della civiltà*, ed. Vincenzo Arangio-Ruiz (Rome: Accademia Nazionale dei Lincei, 1964), 85–92. [Benveniste 1964b]
Berger, Peter L., and Thomas Luckmann, *The Social Construction of Reality: A Treatise in the Sociology of Knowledge* (London: Allen Lane, 1966).
Berghe, Louis vanden, *La découverte d'un château-fort du début de l'époque islamique à Pūskān (Iran): Survivance d'éléments architecturaux sassanides* (Ghent: Iranica antiqua supplementa, 1990).

Bettiolo, Paolo, "Contrasting Styles of Ecclesiastical Authority and Monastic Life in the Church of the East at the Beginning of the Seventh Century," in *Foundations of Power and Conflicts of Authority in Late-Antique Monasticism*, ed. Alberto Camplani and Giovanni Filoramo (Leuven: Peeters, 2007), 297–331.

Beyer, Klaus, *Die aramäischen Inschriften aus Assur, Hatra, und dem übrigen Ostmesopotamien* (Göttingen: Vanderhoek und Ruprecht, 1998).

Binder, Matthias, "Mart Christina: Eine Märtyrin am Ende des Sassanidenreiches," in *Geschichte, Theologie, Liturgie und Gegenwartslage der syrischen Kirchen*, ed. Dorothea Weltecke (Wiesbaden: Harrassowitz Verlag, 2012), 13–26.

———, *Asket und Eschaton: Das Endzeitbuch des Šubḥālmāran von Kirkuk* (Wiesbaden: Harrassowitz Verlag, 2013).

Bivar, A. D. H., "Glyptica Iranica," *Bulletin of the Asia Institute* 4 (1990): 191–99.

Blois, François de, "'Freemen' and 'Nobles' in Iranian and Semitic Languages," *Journal of the Royal Asia Society* (1985): 5–15.

———, "The Middle Persian Inscription from Constantinople: Sasanian or Post-Sasanian?," *Studia Iranica* 19 (1990): 208–18.

———, "Dualism in Iranian and Christian Traditions," *Journal of the Royal Asiatic Society* 10 (2000): 1–19.

———, "*Naṣrānī* and *ḥanīf*: Studies in the Religious Vocabulary of Christianity and of Islam," *Bulletin of the School of Oriental and African Studies* 65 (2002): 1–30.

———, "Pahr(ag)bed," in *Iranica selecta: Studies in Honour of Professor Wojciech Skalmowski*, ed. Alois van Tongerloo (Turnhout: Brepols, 2003), 37–40.

Blum, G., "Zur religionspolitischen Situation der persischen Kirche im 3. und 4. Jahrhundert," *Zeitschrift für Kirchengeschichte* 91 (1980): 11–32.

Bogolyubov, M. N., "Pekhleviiskaya Nadpis iz Konstantinopolya," *Palestinskii Sbornik* 23 (1971): 92–100.

Bonner, Michael, "Eastern Sources on the Roman and Persian War in the Near East, 540–545," in *Late Antiquity: Eastern Perspectives*, ed. Teresa Bernheimer and Adam Silverstein (London: Gibb Memorial Trust, 2012), 42–56.

Booth, Phil, *Crisis of Empire: Doctrine and Dissent at the End of Late Antiquity* (Berkeley: University of California Press, 2013).

Börm, Henning, "Der Perserkönig im Imperium Romanum: Chosroes I und der sasanidische Einfall in das Oströmische Reich 540 n. Chr.," *Chiron* 36 (2006): 299–328.

———, *Prokop und die Perser: Untersuchungen zu Den römisch-sasanidischen Kontakten in der ausgehenden Spätantike* (Stuttgart: Franz Steiner, 2007).

———, "'Es war allerdings nicht so, dass sie es im Sinne eines Tributes erhielten, wie viele moisten . . .': Anlässe und Function der persischen Geldforderungen an die Römer," *Historia* 57 (2008): 327–46.

———, "Herrscher und Eliten in der Spätantike," in *Commutatio et contentio: Studies in the Late Roman, Sasanian, and Early Islamic Near East in Memory of Zeev Rubin*, ed. Börm and Josef Wiesehöfer (Düsseldorf: Willem Verlag, 2010), 159–98.

Bosl, K., "Der 'Adelsheilige': Idealtypus und Wirchlichkeit, Gesellschaft, und Kultur im merovongischen Bayern des 7. und 8. Jahrhunderts," in *Speculum historical: Geschichte im Spiegel der von Geschichtsforschung und Geschichtsdeutung*, ed. Clemens Bauer, Letitia Boehm, and Max Müller (Freiberg: Albers, 1965), 167–87.

Bosworth, Edmund C., "Dīnavar," in *Encyclopaedia Iranica*, ed. Ehsan Yarshater vol. 7 (Costa Mesa: Mazda, 1996), 416–17.
Bowersock, G. W., *Martyrdom and Rome* (Cambridge: Cambridge University Press, 1995).
———, "Polytheism and Monotheism in Arabia and the Three Palestines," *Dumbarton Oaks Papers* 51 (1997): 1–10.
———, "Helena's Bridle, Ethiopian Christianity, and Syriac Apocalyptic," *Studia Patristica* 45 (2010): 211–20.
———, *Empires in Collision in Late Antiquity* (Waltham: Brandeis University Press, 2012).
Bowes, Kim, *Private Worship, Public Values, and Religious Change in Late Antiquity* (Cambridge: Cambridge University Press, 2008).
Boyarin, Daniel, "Hellenism in Jewish Babylonia," in *The Cambridge Companion to the Talmud and Rabbinic Literature*, ed. Charlotte Elisheva Fonrobert and Martin S. Jaffee (Cambridge: Cambridge University Press, 2007), 336–64.
Boyce, Mary, "The Parthian *gōsān* and Iranian Minstrel Tradition," *Journal of the Royal Asiatic Society* (1957): 10–45. [Boyce 1957a]
———, "Some Reflections on Zurvanism," *Bulletin of the School of Oriental and African Studies* 19 (1957): 304–16. [Boyce 1957b]
———, "Bībī Shahrbānū and the Lady of Pārs," *Bulletin of the School of Oriental and African Studies* 30 (1967): 30–44.
———, "Middle Persian Literature," in *Handbuch der Orientalistik, erste Abteilung IV*, vol. 2, Abschnitt, Lieferung 1: *Iranistik—Literatur*, ed. Bertold Spuler (Leiden: Brill, 1968) 31–66.
———, "Toleranz und Intoleranz im Zoroastrismus," *Saeculum* 21 (1970): 325–43.
———, "Iconoclasm among the Zoroastrians," in *Christianity, Judaism, and Other Greco-Roman Cults: Studies Presented to Morton Smith at Sixty*, ed. Jacob Neusner, vol. 4 (Leiden: Brill, 1975), 93–111. [Boyce 1975a]
———, "On the Zoroastrian Temple Cult of Fire," *Journal of the American Oriental Society* 95 (1975): 454–65. [Boyce 1975b]
———, *Zoroastrians: Their Religious Beliefs and Practices* (London: Routledge, 1979).
———, ed. and trans., *Textual Sources for the Study of Zoroastrianism* (Manchester: Manchester University Press, 1984).
———, *A History of Zoroastrianism*, vol. 3, *Zoroastrianism under Macedonian and Roman Rule* (Leiden: E. J. Brill, 1991) [Boyce 1991a]
———, "Pādyāb and Nērang: Two Pahlavi Terms Further Considered," *Bulletin of the School of Oriental and African Studies* 54 (1991): 281–91. [Boyce 1991b]
———, "On the Orthodoxy of Sasanian Zoroastrianism," *Bulletin of the School of Oriental and African Studies* 59 (1996): 11–28.
———, "Further on the Calendar of Zoroastrian Feasts," *Iran* 43 (2005): 1–33.
Boyce, Mary, and Firoze Kotwal, "Zoroastrian *bāj* and *drōn*—I," *Bulletin of the School of Oriental and African Studies* 34 (1971): 56–73.
Brakke, David, *Athanasius and the Politics of Asceticism* (Oxford: Oxford University Press, 1995).
Braun, Oscar, *Das Buch der Synhados nach einer Handschrift des Museo Borgiano* (Stuttgart: J. Rothsche Verlagshandlung, 1900).
Braund, David, *Georgia in Antiquity: A History of Colchis and Transcaucasian Iberia, 550 BC–AD 562* (Oxford: Oxford University Press, 1994).

Brock, Sebastian P., "A Martyr at the Sasanid Court under Vahran II: Candida," *Analecta Bollandiana* 96 (1978): 167–81.

———, "Christians in the Sasanian Empire: A Case of Divided Loyalties," in *Religion and National Identity*, ed. Stuart Mews (Oxford: Basil Blackwell, 1982), 1–19.

———, "The Christology of the Church of the East in the Synods of the Fifth to Early Seventh Centuries: Preliminary Considerations and Materials," in *Aksum-Thyateira: A Festschrift for Archbishop Methodios of Thyateira and Great Britain*, ed. George Dragas (London: Thyateira House, 1985), 125–42.

———, "Greek and Syriac in Late Antique Syria," in *Literacy and Power in the Ancient World*, ed. Alan K. Bowman and Greg Woolf (Cambridge: Cambridge University Press, 1994), 149–60.

———, "Bar Shabba / Mar Shabbay, First Bishop of Merv," in *Syrisches Christentum weltweit: Studien zur syrischen Kirchengeschichte*, ed. Martin Tamcke, Wolfgang Schwaigert, and Egbert Schlarb (Münster: Lit, 1995), 190–201.

———, "The 'Nestorian' Church: A Lamentable Misnomer," *Bulletin of the John Rylands University Library* 78 (1996): 23–35.

———, *The History of Mar Ma'in with a Guide to the Persian Martyr Acts* (Piscataway: Gorgias, 2008). [Brock 2008a]

———, "Regulations for an Association of Artisans from the Late Sasanian or Early Arab Period," in *Transformations of Late Antiquity: Essays for Peter Brown*, ed. Philip Rousseau and Emmanuel Papoutsakis (Aldershot: Ashgate, 2008), 51–62. [Brock 2008b]

———, "Saints in Syriac: A Little-Tapped Resource," *Journal of Early Christian Studies* 16 (2008): 181–96. [Brock 2008c]

———, "A West Syriac Life of Mar Shabbay (Bar Shabba), Bishop of Merv," in *Bibel, Byzanz und Christlicher Orient: Festschrift für Stephen Gerö zum 65. Geburtstag*, ed. D. Bumazhnov, E. Grypeou, T. B. Sailors, and A. Toepel (Leuven: Peeters, 2011), 259–79.

Brock, Sebastian P., and Susan Ashbrook Harvey, *Holy Women of the Syrian Orient* (Berkeley: University of California Press, 1987).

Brody, Robert, "Judaism in the Sasanian Empire: A Case Study in Coexistence," *Irano-Judaica* 2 (1990): 52–62.

Brown, Peter, "The Rise and Function of the Holy Man in Late Antiquity," *Journal of Roman Studies* 61 (1971): 80–101.

———, "The Saint as Exemplar in Late Antiquity," *Representations* 2 (1983): 1–25.

———, *Authority and the Sacred: Aspects of the Christianisation of the Roman World* (Cambridge: Cambridge University Press, 1995).

———, "The Rise and Function of the Holy Man in Late Antiquity, 1971–1997," *Journal of Early Christian Studies* 6 (1998): 353–76.

Brown, Wendy, *Regulating Aversion: Tolerance in the Age of Identity and Empire* (Princeton: Princeton University Press, 2008).

Bruns, Peter, "Von Adam und Eva bis Mohammed—Beobachtungen zur syrischen Chronik des Johannes bar Penkaye," *Oriens Christianus* 87 (2003): 47–64.

———, "Barsauma von Nisibis und die Aufhebung der Klerikerenthaltsamkeit im Gefolge der Synode von Beth-Lapat (484)," *Annuarium Historiae Conciliorum* 37 (2005): 1–42.

———, "Beobachtungen zu den Rechtsgrundlagen der Christenverfolgung im Sasanidenreich," *Römische Quartalschrift für christliche Altertumskunde und Kirchengeschichte* 103 (2008): 82–112.

———, "Das Martyrium des hl. Mar Qardagh (BHO 555/56)—Ein christlich-iranischer Ritter- und Bekehrungsroman," in *Volksglaube im antiken Christentum*, ed. Heike Grieser and Andrew Merkt (Darmstadt: Wissenschaftliche Buchgesellschaft, 2009), 187–202. [Bruns 2009a]

———, "Paul der Perser—Christ und Philosoph im spätantiken Sasanidenreich," *Römische Quartalschrift für christliche Altertumskunde und Kirchengeschichte* 104 (2009): 28–53. [Bruns 2009b]

———, "Schnittpunkte zwischen Christentum und Medizin im spätantiken Sasanidenreich," *Oriens Christianus* 93 (2009): 41–58. [Bruns 2009c]

———, "Antizoroastrische Polemik in den Syro-Persischen Märtyrerakten," in *Jews, Christians and Zoroastrians: Religious Dynamics in a Sasanian Context*, ed. Geoffrey Herman (Piscataway: Gorgias, 2014), 47–65.

Buc, Philippe, "Martyre et ritualite dans l'antiquité tardive: Horizons de l'écriture médiévale des rituels," *Annales: Histoire, Sciences Sociales* 52 (1997): 63–92.

Bulliet, Richard, *Cotton, Climate, and Camels in Early Islamic Iran: A Moment in World History* (New York: Columbia University Press, 2009).

Bunyatov, Ziya, *Azerbaidzhan v VII–IX vv.* (Baku: Akademiya Nauk Azerbaidzhanskoi SSR, 1965).

Cameron, Averil, "The Theotokos in Sixth-Century Constantinople: A City Finds Its Symbol," *Journal of Theological Studies* 29 (1978): 79–108.

———, "Images of Authority: Elites and Icons in Late Sixth-Century Byzantium," *Past and Present* 84 (1979): 3–35.

———, "The Jews in Seventh-Century Palestine," *Scripta Classica Israelica* 13 (1994): 75–93.

———, "On Defining the Holy Man," in *The Cult of Saints in Late Antiquity and the Early Middle Ages: Essays on the Contribution of Peter Brown*, ed. James Howard-Johnston and Paul Antony Hayward (Oxford: Oxford University Press, 1999), 27–43.

Camplani, Alberto, "The Revival of Persian Monasticism (Sixth to Seventh Centuries): Church Structures, Theological Academy, and Reformed Monks," in *Foundations of Power and Conflicts of Authority in Late-Antique Monasticism*, ed. Camplani and Giovanni Filoramo (Leuven: Peeters, 2007), 277–95.

Canepa, Matthew, *The Two Eyes of the Earth: Art and Ritual of Kingship between Rome and Sasanian Iran* (Berkeley: University of California Press, 2009).

———, "Technologies of Memory and Early Sasanian Iran: Achaemenid Sites in Sasanian Identity," *American Journal of Archaeology* 114 (2010): 563–96.

Cantera, Alberto, *Studien zur Pahlavi-Übersetzung des Avesta* (Wiesbaden: Harrassowitz Verlag, 2004).

———, "Legal Implications of Conversion in Zoroastrianism," in *Iranian Identity in the Course of History: Proceedings of the Conference Held in Rome, 21–24 September 2005*, ed. Carlo G. Cereti (Rome: Istituto italiano per l'Africa e l'Oriente, 2010), 53–66.

Carlsen, B. H., "The *čakar* Marriage Contract and the *čakar* Children's Status in the *Mātiyān i hazār Dātistān* and *Rivāyat i Ēmēt i Ašavahištān*," in *Middle Iranian Studies: Proceedings of the International Symposium Organized by the Katholieke Universiteit Leuven from the*

17th to the 20th of May 1982, ed. Wojciech Skalmowski and Alois van Tongerloo (Leuven: Peeters, 1984), 103–14.

Carter, R. A., "Christianity in the Gulf during the First Centuries of Islam," *Arabian Archaeology and Epigraphy* 19 (2008): 71–108.

Caseau, Béatrice, "ΠΟΛΕΜΕΙΝ ΛΙΘΟΙΣ: La désacralisation des espaces et des objets religieux païens durant l'antiquité tardive," in *Le sacré et son inscription dans l'espace à Byzance et en Occident: Études comparées*, ed. Michel Kaplan (Paris: Publications de la Sorbonne, 2001), 61–123. [Caseau 2001a]

———, "Sacred Landscapes," in *Interpreting Late Antiquity: Essays on the Postclassical World*, ed. G. W. Bowersock, Peter Brown, and Oleg Grabar (Cambridge, MA: Harvard University Press, 2001), 21–59. [Caseau 2001b]

Cassis, Marica, "Kokhe, Cradle of the Church of the East: An Archaeological and Comparative Study," *Journal of the Canadian Society for Syriac Studies* 2 (2002): 62–78.

Castelli, Elizabeth, *Martyrdom and Memory: Early Christian Culture Making* (New York: Columbia University Press, 2004).

Cereti, Carlo G., "On the Pahlavi Cursive Script and the Sasanian Avesta," *Studia Iranica* 37 (2008): 175–95.

———, "The Pahlavi Signatures on the Quilon Copper Plates (Tabula Quilonensis)," in *Exegesti monumenta: Festschrift in Honor of Nicholas Sims-Williams*, ed. François de Blois, Almut Hintze, and Werner Sundermann (Wiesbaden: Harrassowitz Verlag, 2009), 31–50.

———, "'Xiiaona- and Xyôn in Zoroastrian Texts," in *Coins, Art and Chronology*, vol. 2, *The First Millennium C.E. in the Indo-Iranian Borderlands*, ed. Michael Alram, Deborah Klimburg-Salter, Minoru Inaba, and Matthias Pfisterer (Vienna: Verlag der österreichischen Akademie der Wissenschaften, 2010), 59–72.

Cereti, Carlo G., Luca M. Olivieri, and Joseph Vazhuthanapally, "The Problem of the St. Thomas Crosses and Related Questions: Epigraphical Survey and Preliminary Research," *East and West* 52 (2002): 285–310.

Chaumont, M. L., "Études d'histoire parthe III: Les villes fondées par les Vologèse," *Syria* 51 (1974): 75–89.

———, "Recherches sur quelques villes helléniques de l'Iran occidental," *Iranica Antiqua* 17 (1982): 147–73.

———, *La christianisation de l'empire iranien: Des origines aux grandes persécutions du IVe siècle* (Leuven: Peeters, 1988).

Choksy, Jamsheed K., *Purity and Pollution in Zoroastrianism: Triumph over Evil* (Austin: University of Texas Press, 1989).

———, *Conflict and Cooperation: Zoroastrian Subalterns and Muslim Elites in Medieval Iranian Society* (New York: Columbia University Press, 1997).

———, *Evil, Good, and Gender: Facets of the Feminine in Zoroastrian Religious History* (New York: Peter Lang, 2002).

———, "Reassessing the Material Contexts of Ritual Fires in Ancient Iran," *Iranica Antiqua* 42 (2007): 229–69.

Christensen, Arthur, *Romanen om Bahrâm Tschôbîn: Et Rekonstruktionsforsøg* (Copenhagen: Tillge's Boghandel, 1907).

———, *Les Kayanides* (Copenhagen: Andr. Fred. Høst and Søn, 1931).

———, *L'Iran sous les Sassanides* (Copenhagen: E. Munksgaard, 1944).
Ciancaglini, Claudia, *Iranian Loanwords in Syriac* (Wiesbaden: Ludwig Reichert, 2008).
Colditz, Iris, "Hymnen an Šād-Ohrmezd: Ein Beitrag zur frühen Geschichte der Dīnāwarīya in Transoxanien," *Altorientalische Forschungen* 19 (1992): 322–41.
———, "'... werdet mit den Schriften vertraut': Schriftgelehrtheit, Mehrsprachigkeit und Bildungsvermittlung in manichäischen Gemeinden," in *Iran und Turfan: Beiträge Berliner Wissenschaftler, Werner Sundermann zum 60. Geburtstag gewidmet*, ed. Christiane Reck and Peter Zieme (Wiesbaden: Harrassowitz Verlag, 1995), 35–57.
———, *Zur Sozialterminologie der iranischen Manichäer: Eine semantische analyse im Vergleich zu den nichtmanichäischen iranischen Quellen* (Wiesbaden: Harrassowitz Verlag, 2000).
———, "Zur Adaption zoroastrischer Terminologie in Manis *Šāpuhragān*," in *Languages of Iran: Past and Present*, ed. Dieter Weber (Wiesbaden: Harrassowitz Verlag, 2005), 17–26.
Compareti, Matteo, "The Last Sasanians in China," *Eurasian Studies* 2 (2003): 197–213.
Corcoran, Simon, "Observations on the Sasanian Law-book in the Light of Roman Legal Writing," in *Law, Custom and Justice in Late Antiquity and the Early Middle Ages*, ed. Alice Rio (London: Centre for Hellenic Studies, 2011), 77–113.
Crone, Patricia, "Kavad's Heresy and Mazdak's Revolt," *Iran* 29 (1991): 21–42.
———, "Zoroastrian Communism," *Comparative Studies in Society and History* 36 (1994): 447–62.
———, "Buddhism as Ancient Iranian Paganism," in *Late Antiquity: Eastern Perspectives*, ed. Teresa Bernheimer and Adam Silverstein (Oxford: Gibb Memorial Trust, 2012), 25–41. [Crone 2012a]
———, *The Nativist Prophets of Early Islamic Iran: Rural Revolt and Local Zoroastrianism* (Cambridge: Cambridge University Press, 2012). [Crone 2012b]
Crone, Patricia, and Michael Cook, *Hagarism: The Making of the Islamic World* (Cambridge: Cambridge University Press, 1977).
Dagron, Gilbert, and Vincent Déroche, "Juifs et chrétiens dans l'Orient du VIIe siècle," *Travaux et Mémoires* 11 (1991): 17–273.
Dal Santo, Matthew, "The God-Protected Empire? Scepticism towards the Cult of Saints in Early Byzantium," in *An Age of Saints? Power, Conflict and Dissent in Early Medieval Christianity*, ed. Peter Sarris, Matthew Dal Santo, and Phil Booth (Leiden: Brill, 2011), 129–49.
Daryaee, Touraj, "Keyanid History or National History? The Nature of Sasanian Zoroastrian Historiography," *Iranian Studies* 28 (1995): 121–45.
———, "The Use of Religio-political Propaganda on Coins of Xusro II," *Journal of the American Numismatic Society* 7 (1997): 41–54.
———, "The Coinage of Queen Boran and Its Significance for Late Sasanian Imperial Ideology," *Bulletin of the Asia Institute* 13 (1999): 77–82. [Daryaee 1999a]
———, "Sources for the Economic History of Late Sasanian Fārs," in *Matériaux pour l'histoire économique du monde Iranien*, ed. Rika Gyselen and Maria Szuppe (Paris: Association pour l'avancement des études iraniennes, 1999), 131–48. [Daryaee 1999b]
———, "The Effect of the Arab Muslim Conquest on the Administrative Division of Sasanian Persis/Fars," *Iran* 31 (2003): 194–204. [Daryaee 2003a]

———, "The Persian Gulf Trade in Late Antiquity," *Journal of World History* 14 (2003): 1–16. [Daryaee 2003b]

———, "Ethnic and Territorial Boundaries in Late Antique and Early Medieval Persia (Third to Tenth Century)," in *Borders, Barriers, and Ethnogenesis: Frontiers in Late Antiquity and the Middle Ages,* ed. Florin Curta (Turnhout: Brepols, 2005), 123–37.

———, "The Construction of the Past in Late Antique Persia," *Historia: Zeitschrift für Alte Geschichte* 55 (2006): 493–503. [Daryaee 2006a]

———, "The Sasanians and Their Ancestors," in *Ancient and Middle Iranian Studies,* vol. 1 of *Proceedings of the 5th Conference of the Societas Iranologica Europaea,* ed. Antonio Panaino and Andrea Piras (Milan: Mimesis, 2006), 389–93. [Daryaee 2006b]

———, "Yazdgerd III's Last Year: Coinage and History of Sīstān at the End of Late Antiquity," *Iranistik* 5 (2006–7): 21–29.

———, "The Middle Persian Text *Sūr ī Saxwan* and the Late Sasanian Court," in *Des Indo-Grecs aux Sassanides: Données pour l'histoire et la géographie historique,* ed. Rika Gyselen (Bures-sur-Yvette: Groupe pour l'étude de la civilisation du Moyen-Orient, 2007), 65–72.

———, *Sasanian Persia: The Rise and Fall of an Empire* (London: I. B. Tauris, 2009).

———, "The Idea of Ērānšahr: Jewish, Christian, and Manichaean Views in Late Antiquity," in *Iranian Identity in the Course of History: Proceedings of the Conference Held in Rome, 21–24 September 2005,* ed. Carlo G. Cereti (Rome: Istituto italiano per l'Africa e l'Oriente, 2010), 91–108. [Daryaee 2010a]

———, "When the End Is Near: Barbarized Armies and Barracks Kings of Late Antique Iran," in *Ancient and Middle Iranian Studies: Proceedings of the Sixth European Conference of Iranian Studies,* ed. Maria Macuch, Dieter Weber, and Desmond Durkin-Meisterernst (Wiesbaden: Harrassowitz Verlag, 2010), 43–52. [Daryaee 2010b]

———, "Food, Purity and Pollution: Zoroastrian Views on the Eating Habits of Others," *Iranian Studies* 45 (2012): 229–42.

———, "Marriage, Property and Conversion among the Zoroastrians: From Late Sasanian to Islamic Iran," *Journal of Persianate Studies* 6 (2013): 91–100.

Dauphin, Claudine, *La Palestine byzantine: Peuplement et population* (Oxford: Archaeopress, 1998).

Debié, Muriel, "Record Keeping and Chronicle Writing in Antioch and Edessa," *Aram* 11–12 (1999–2000): 409–17.

———, "Jean Malalas et la tradition chronographique de langue syriaque," in *Recherches sur la chronique de Jean Malalas,* ed. Joëlle Beaucamp (Paris: Association des amis du Centre d'histoire et civilisation de Byzance, 2004), 147–64.

———, "L'héritage de la chronique d'Eusèbe dans l'historiographie syriaque," *Journal of the Canadian Society for Syriac Studies* 6 (2006): 18–29.

———, "Devenir chrétien dans l'Iran sassanide: La conversion à la lumière des récits hagiographiques," in *Le problème de la christianisation du monde antique,* ed. Hervé Inglebert (Paris: Picard, 2010), 329–58. [Debié 2010a]

———, "L'empire perse et ses marges," in *Histoire générale du christianisme,* vol. 1, *Des origines au XV*^{e} *siècle,* ed. Jean-Robert Armogathe, Pascal Montaubin, and Michael-Yves Perrin (Paris: Presses universitaires de France, 2010), 611–46. [Debié 2010b]

———, "Writing History as 'Histoires': The Biographical Dimension of East Syriac Historiography," in *Writing 'True Stories': Historians and Hagiographers in the Late Antique and*

Medieval Near East, ed. Arietta Papaconstantinou (Turnhout: Brepols, 2010), 43–75. [Debié 2010c]

———, "'Marcher dans leurs traces': Les discours de l'hagiographie et de l'histoire," in *L'hagiographie syriaque,* ed. André Binggeli (Paris: Geuthner, 2012), 9–48.

de Jong, Albert, *Traditions of the Magi: Zoroastrianism in Greek and Latin Literature* (Leiden: Brill, 1997).

———, "Purification *in absentia:* On the Development of Zoroastrian Ritual Practice," in *Transformations of the Inner Self in Religious Traditions,* ed. Jan Assmann and Guy G. Stroumsa (Leiden: Brill, 1999), 301–29.

———, "Animal Sacrifice in Ancient Zoroastrianism: A Ritual and Its Interpretations," in *Sacrifice in Religious Experience,* ed. A. I. Baumgarten (Leiden: Brill, 2002), 127–48.

———, "Zoroastrian Self-Definition in Contact with Other Faiths," *Irano-Judaica* 5 (2003): 16–26.

———, "Sub specie maiestatis: Reflections on Sasanian Court Rituals," in *Zoroastrian Rituals in Context,* ed. Michael Stausberg (Leiden: Brill, 2004), 345–65. [de Jong 2004a]

———, "Zoroastrian Religious Polemics and Their Contexts: Interconfessional Relations in the Sasanian Empire," in *Religious Polemics in Context,* ed. T. L. Hettema and A. van der Kooij (Assen: Royal van Gorcum, 2004), 48–63. [de Jong 2004b]

———, "The First Sin: Zoroastrian Ideas about the Time before Zarathustra," in *Genesis and Regeneration: Essays on Conceptions of Origins,* ed. Shaul Shaked (Jerusalem: Israel Academy of Sciences and Humanities, 2005), 192–209.

———, "One Nation under God? The Early Sasanians as Guardians and Destroyers of Holy Sites," in *Götterbilder, Gottesbilder, Weltbilder: Polytheismus und Monotheismus in der Welt der Antike,* vol. 1, ed. Reinhard Gregor Kratz and Herman Spieckermann (Tübingen: Mohr Siebeck, 2006), 223–38.

———, "The Culture of Writing and the Use of the Avesta in Sasanian Iran," in *Zaratnushtra entre l'Inde et l'Iran: Études indo-iraniennes et indo-européennes offertes à Jean Kellens,* ed. Éric Pirart and Xavier Tremblay (Wiesbaden: Ludwig Reichert Verlag, 2009), 27–41.

de Jong, Mayke, "To the Limits of Kinship: Anti-incest Legislation in the Early Medieval West (500–900)," in *From Sappho to de Sade: Moments in the History of Sexuality,* ed. Jan Bremmer (Routledge: London, 1989), 36–59.

Delly, Emmanuel-Karim, "La place du métropolite de Nisibe parmi les électeurs du patriarche," *L'Orient Syrien* 2 (1957): 389–94.

Déroche, Vincent, "Polémique anti-judaïque et emergence de l'Islam (7e–8e siècles)," *Revue des études byzantines* 57 (1999): 141–61.

Devos, Paul, "Le dossier hagiographique de S. Jacques l'Intercis," *Analecta Bollandiana* 71 (1953): 157–210.

———, "Abgar: Hagiographe perse méconnu (début du Ve siècle)," *Analecta Bollandiana* 83 (1965): 303–28.

———, "Les martyrs persans à travers leurs actes syriaques," in *Atti del convegno sul tema: La Persia e il mondo greco-romano,* ed. Angelo Monteverdi (Rome: Accademia Nazionale dei Lincei, 1966), 213–25.

———, "La jeune martyre perse sainte Širin," *Analecta Bollandiana* 112 (1994): 5–31.

Dickens, Mark, "Multilingual Christian Manuscripts from Turfan," *Journal of the Canadian Society for Syriac Studies* 9 (2009): 22–42.

———, "The Importance of the Psalter at Turfan," in *From the Oxus River to the Chinese Shores: Studies in East Syrian Christianity in China and Central Asia*, ed. Li Tang and Dietmar W. Winkler (Zurich: Lit Verlag, 2013), 357–80.

Dignas, Beate, and Engelbert Winters, *Rome and Persia in Late Antiquity: Neighbours and Rivals* (Cambridge: Cambridge University Press, 2007).

Douglas, Mary, *How Institutions Think* (Syracuse: Syracuse University Press, 1986).

Drake, H. A., *Constantine and the Bishops: The Politics of Intolerance* (Baltimore: Johns Hopkins University Press, 2000).

Drijvers, Han J. W., "The Image of Edessa in the Syriac Tradition," in *The Holy Face and the Paradox of Representation*, ed. Herbert L. Kessler and Gerhard Wolf (Bologna: Nuova Alfa Editoriale, 1998), 13–31.

Drijvers, Jan Willem, *Helena Augusta: The Mother of Constantine the Great and the Legend of Her Finding of the True Cross* (Leiden: Brill, 1992).

———, "Heraclius and the *Restitutio Crucis*: Notes on Symbolism and Ideology," in *The Reign of Heraclius (610–41): Crisis and Confrontation*, ed. Gerrit J. Reinink and Bernard H. Stolte (Leuven: Peeters, 2002), 175–90.

Drost-Abgarjan, Armenuhi, "Ein neuer Fund zur armenischen Version der Eusebios-Chronik," in *Julius Africanus und die christliche Weltchronistik*, ed. Martin Wallraff (Berlin: Walter de Gruyter, 2006), 255–62.

Elman, Yaakov, "Marriage and Marital Property in Rabbinic and Sasanian Law," in *Rabbinic Law in Its Roman and Near Eastern Context*, ed. Catherine Hezser (Tübingen: Mohr Siebeck, 2003), 227–76.

———, "The Other in the Mirror: Iranians and Jews View One Another," *Bulletin of the Asia Institute* 19 (2005): 15–25.

———, "The Other in the Mirror: Questions of Identity, Conversion, and Exogamy in the Fifth-Century Iranian Empire," *Bulletin of the Asia Institute* 20 (2006): 25–46.

———, "Middle Persian Culture and Babylonian Sages: Accommodation and Resistance in the Shaping of Rabbinic Legal Tradition," in *The Cambridge Companion to the Talmud and Rabbinic Literature*, ed. Charlotte Elisheva Fonrobert and Martin S. Jaffee (Cambridge: Cambridge University Press, 2007), 165–97.

———, "Toward an Intellectual History of Sasanian Law: An Intergenerational Dispute in *Hērbedestān* Nine and Its Rabbinic and Roman Parallels," in *The Talmud in Its Iranian Context*, ed. Carol Bakhos and M. Rahim Shayegan (Tübingen: Mohr Siebeck, 2010), 21–57.

Emmel, Stephen, "Shenoute of Atripe and the Christian Destruction of Temples in Egypt: Rhetoric and Reality," in *From Temple to Church: Destruction and Renewal of Local Cultic Topography in Late Antiquity*, ed. Johannes Hahn, Stephen Emmel, and Ulrich Gotter (Leiden: Brill, 2008), 161–201.

Erhart, Victoria, "The Development of Syriac Christian Canon Law in the Sasanian Empire," in *Law, Society, and Authority in Late Antiquity*, ed. Ralph W. Mathisen (Oxford: Oxford University Press, 2001), 115–29.

Espéronnier, M., "Al-Nuwayri: Les fêtes islamiques, persanes, chrétiennes et juives," *Arabica* 32 (1985): 80–101.

Fiey, J. M., "Encore 'Abdulmasīh de Sinğār," *Le Muséon* 77 (1964): 205–21. [Fiey 1964a]

———, "Vers la réhabilitation de l'*Histoire de Karka d'Bēṯ Slōḥ*," *Analecta Bollandiana* 82 (1964): 189–222. [Fiey 1964b]

———, *Assyrie chrétienne: Contribution à l'étude de l'histoire et de la géographie ecclésiastiques et monastiques du nord de l'Iraq*, vol. 1 (Beirut: Imprimerie Catholique, 1965).
———, "Îshô'denah, métropolite de Basra et son œuvre," *L'Orient Syrien* 11 (1966): 431–50.
———, "Les étapes de la prise de conscience de son identité patriarcale par l'Église syrienne orientale," *L'Orient Syrien* 12 (1967): 3–22. [Fiey 1967a]
———, "Topographie chrétienne des Mahozé," *L'Orient Syrien* 12 (1967): 397–420. [Fiey 1967b]
———, "Topography of al-Mada'in," *Sumer* 23 (1967): 3–38. [Fiey 1967c]
———, *Assyrie chrétienne: Contribution à l'étude de l'histoire et de la géographie ecclésiastiques et monastiques du nord de l'Iraq*, vol. 3, *Bét Garmaï, Bét Aramāyé et Maišān nestoriens* (Beirut: Dar El-Mashreq, 1968).
———, "Diocèses syriens-orientaux du Golfe Persique," in *Mémorial Mgr. Gabriel Khouri-Sarkis* (Leuven: Imprimerie orientaliste, 1969), 177–219. [Fiey 1969a]
———, "L'Elam, la première des métropoles ecclésiastiques syriennes orientales," *Melto* 5 (1969): 221–67. [Fiey 1969b]
———, "Išo'yaw le Grand: Vie du catholicos nestorien Išo'yaw III de Adiabène (580–659)," *Orientalia Christiana Periodica* 35 (1969): 305–33; 36 (1970): 5–46. [Fiey 1969–70]
———, *Jalons pour une histoire de l'Église en Iraq* (Leuven: Secrétariat du Corpus SCO, 1970). [Fiey 1970a]
———, "Les marcionites dans les textes historiques de l'Eglise de Perse," *Le Muséon* 83 (1970): 183–88. [Fiey 1970b]
———, "Médie chrétienne," *Parole de l'Orient* 1 (1970): 357–84. [Fiey 1970c]
———, "Les provinces sud-caspiennes des églises syriennes," *Parole de l'Orient* 2 (1971): 329–43.
———, "Ādarbāyğān chrétien," *Le Muséon* 86 (1973): 397–435. [Fiey 1973a]
———, "Chrétientés du Ḫorāsān et du Ségestān," *Le Muséon* 86 (1973): 75–104. [Fiey 1973b]
———, "Les residences d'été des rois perses d'après les actes syriaques des martyrs," *Parole de l'Orient* 20 (1995): 325–36.
Fisher, Greg, *Between Empires: Arabs, Romans, and Sasanians in Late Antiquity* (Oxford: Oxford University Press, 2011).
Flusin, Bernard, *Saint Anastase le Perse et l'histoire de la Palestine au début du VIIe siècle*, vol. 2 (Paris: Centre national de la recherche scientifique, 1992).
Fonrobert, Charlotte Elisheva, *Menstrual Purity: Rabbinic and Christian Reconstructions of Biblical Gender* (Stanford: Stanford University Press, 2000).
———, "The Didascalia Apostolorum," *Journal of Early Christian Studies* 9 (2001): 483–511.
Forrest, S. K. Mendoza, *Witches, Whores, and Sorcerers: The Concept of Evil in Early Iran* (Austin: University of Texas Press, 2011).
Foss, Clive, "The Persians in Asia Minor and the End of Antiquity," *English Historical Review* 90 (1975): 721–47.
———, "Syria in Transition, A.D. 550–750: An Archaeological Approach," *Dumbarton Oaks Papers* 51 (1997): 189–269.
———, "The *Sellarioi* and Other Officers of Persian Egypt," *Zeitschrift für Papyrologie und Epigraphik* 138 (2002): 169–72.
———, "The Persians and the Roman Near East (602–630 A.D.)," *Journal of the Royal Asiatic Society* 13 (2003): 149–70.

Fouracre, Paul, "Merovingian History and Merovingian Hagiography," *Past and Present* 127 (1990): 3-38.
Fowden, Elizabeth Key, *The Barbarian Plain: Saint Sergius between Rome and Iran* (Berkeley: University of California Press, 1999).
———, "Constantine and the Peoples of the Eastern Frontier," in *The Cambridge Companion to the Age of Constantine,* ed. Noel Lenski (Cambridge: Cambridge University Press, 2006), 377-98.
Fowden, Garth, *Empire to Commonwealth: Consequences of Monotheism in Late Antiquity* (Princeton: Princeton University Press, 1993).
Frankfurter, David, "Syncretism and the Holy Man in Late Antique Egypt," *Journal of Early Christian Studies* 11 (2003): 339-85.
Frend, W. H. C., *The Rise of the Monophysite Movement* (Cambridge: Cambridge University Press, 1972).
Frendo, David, "Constantine's Letter to Shapur II: Its Authenticity, Occasion, and Attendant Circumstances," *Bulletin of the Asia Institute* 15 (2001): 57-69.
———, "Religious Minorities and Religious Dissent in the Byzantine and Sasanian Empires (590-641): Sources for the Historical Background," *Bulletin of the Asia Institute* 22 (2008): 223-37.
Frye, Richard N., "Zurvanism Again," *Harvard Theological Review* 52 (1959): 63-73.
———, "The Persepolis Middle Persian Inscriptions from the Time of Shapur II," *Acta Orientalia* 30 (1966): 83-93.
———, "Minorities in the History of the Near East," in *A Green Leaf: Papers in Honour of Professor Jes P. Asmussen,* ed. W. Sundermann, J. Duchesne-Guillemin, and F. Vahman (Leiden: Brill, 1988), 461-71.
Gaddis, Michael, *There Is No Crime for Those Who Have Christ: Religious Violence in the Christian Roman Empire* (Berkeley: University of California Press, 2005).
Gafni, Isaiah, *Evrei Vavilonii v Talmudicheskuyu Epokhu* (Moscow: Mosti Kulturi, 2003).
Gagos, Troianos, and Peter van Minnen, *Settling a Dispute: Towards a Legal Anthropology of Late Antique Egypt* (Ann Arbor: University of Michigan Press, 1994).
Gaibov, V. A., and G. A. Koshelenko, "Khristianskie Arkheologicheskie Pamyatniki na Vostoke (Pervoe Tisyacheletie N.E.)," *Khristianskii Vostok* 4 (2006): 136-76.
Gall, Hubertus von, "Entwicklung und Gestalt des Thrones im vorislamischen Iran," *Archäologische Mitteilungen aus Iran* 4 (1971): 207-35.
———, "The Figural Capitals at Taq-e Bustan and the Question of the So-Called Investiture in Parthian and Sasanian Art," *Silk Road Art and Archaeology* 1 (1990): 100-122.
———, "Der große Reliefblock am sog. Partheranhang," in *Bisutun: Ausgrabungen und Forschungen in den Jahren 1963-1967,* ed. Wolfram Kleiss and Peter Calmeyer (Berlin: Gebr. Mann Verlag, 1996), 85-88.
Galletti, Mirella, "Reports on Kirkuk by Modern European Visitors," in *Karkūk, madīnat al-qawmīyāt al-muta'ākhīyah: Waqā'i' al-nadwah al-'ilmīyah allatī 'aqadahā Markz Karbalā' lil-Buḥūth wa-al-Dirāsāt fī Landan min 21-22 Tammūz, Yūliyū 2001* (London: Markaz Karbalā' lil-Buḥūth wa-al-Dirāsāt, 2002), 1-31.
Gariboldi, Andrea, "Social Conditions in Egypt under Sasanian Occupation (619-29 A.D.)," *La Parola del Passato* 64 (2009): 149-70.

Garnsey, Peter, "Religious Toleration in Classical Antiquity," *Persecution and Toleration*, ed. W. J. Sheils (Oxford: Blackwell, 1984), 1–29.

Garsoïan, Nina, "Le role de l'hiérarchie chrétienne dans les rapports diplomatiques entre Byzance et les Sassanides," *Revue des Études Arméniennes* 10 (1973–74): 119–38.

———, "Sur le titre *Protecteur des pauvres*," *Revue des études arméniennes* 15 (1981): 21–32.

———, "Secular Jurisdiction over the Armenian Church (Fourth–Seventh Centuries)," in *Okeanos: Essays Presented to Ihor Ševčenko on His Sixtieth Birthday by His Colleagues and Students*, ed. Cyril Mango and Omeljan Pritsak (Cambridge, MA: Harvard University Press, 1984), 220–50.

———, "The Early-Mediaeval Armenian City: An Alien Element," *Journal of the Ancient Near Eastern Society* 16–17 (1984–85): 67–83.

———, "The Two Voices of Armenian Medieval Historiography: The Iranian Index," *Studia Iranica* 25 (1996): 7–43.

———, "Les éléments iraniens dans l'Arménie paléochrétienne," in *Des Parthes au Califat: Quatre leçons sur la formation de l'identité arménienne*, ed. Garsoïan and Jean-Pierre Mahé (Paris: De Boccard, 1997), 9–37.

———, "La Perse: L'Église d'Orient," in *Les Églises d'Orient et d'Occident (432–610)*, vol. 3 of *Histoire du Christianisme des origines à nos jours*, ed. Jean-Marie Mayeur, Charles Pietri, Luce Pietri, André Vauchez, and Marc Venard (Paris: Desclée Fayard, 1998), 1103–24.

———, *L'église arménienne et le grand schisme de l'Orient* (Leuven: Peeters, 1999).

———, "L'interrègne arménien: Esquisse préliminaire," *Le Muséon* 122 (2009): 81–92. [Garsoïan 2009a]

———, "La politique arménienne des sassanides," in *Trésors d'Orient: Mélanges offerts à Rika Gyselen*, ed. Philippe Gignoux, Christelle Jullien, and Florence Jullien (Paris: Association pour l'avancement des études iraniennes, 2009), 67–79. [Garsoïan 2009b]

———, *Interregnum: Introduction to a Study on the Formation of Armenian Identity (ca 600–750)* (Leuven: Peeters, 2012).

Gaube, Heinz, *Die südpersische Provinz Arraǧān/Kūh-Gīlūyeh von der arabischen Eroberung bis zur Safavidenzeit* (Vienna: Verlag der österreichischen Akademie der Wissenschaften, 1973).

Geary, Patrick, "Saints, Scholars, and Society: The Elusive Goal," in *Living with the Dead in the Middle Ages* (Ithaca: Cornell University Press, 1994), 9–29.

Gero, Stephen, *Barsauma of Nisibis and Persian Christianity in the Fifth Century* (Leuven: Peeters, 1981). [Gero 1981a]

———, "'Die Kirche des Ostens': Zum Christentum in Persien in der Spätantike," *Ostkirchliche Studien* 30 (1981): 22–27. [Gero 1981b]

———, "The See of Peter in Babylon: Western Influences on the Ecclesiology of Early Persian Christianity," in *East of Byzantium: Syria and Armenia in the Formative Period*, ed. Nina Garsoïan, Thomas F. Matthews, and Robert W. Thomson (Washington DC: Dumbarton Oaks, 1982), 45–51.

———, "Die antiasketische Bewegung im persischen Christentum: Einfluss zoroastrischer Ethik?," in *III Symposium Syriacum 1980: Les contacts du monde syriaque aves les autres cultures*, ed. René Lavenant (Rome: Pontificium institutum orientalium studiorum, 1983), 187–91.

Ghodrat-Dizaji, Mehrdad, "Administrative Geography of the Early Sasanian Period: The Case of Ādurbādagān," *Iran* 45 (2007): 87-96.

———, "Ādurbādagān during the Late Sasanian Period: A Study in Administrative Geography," *Iran* 48 (2010): 69-80.

Gignoux, Philippe, *Glossaire des inscriptions pehlevies et parthes* (London: Lund Humphries, 1972).

———, "Problèmes d'interprétation historique et philologique de titres et noms propres sasanides," *Acta Antiqua Academiae Scientiarum Hungaricae* 24 (1976): 103-8.

———, "Problèmes de distinction et de priorité des sources," in *Prolegomena to the Sources on the History of Pre-Islamic Central Asia*, ed. Janos Harmatta (Budapest: Akadémiai Kiadó, 1979), 137-41.

———, "Sceaux chrétiens d'époque sasanide," *Iranica Antiqua* 15 (1980): 299-314.

———, "Die religiöse Administration in sasanidischer Zeit: Ein Überblick," in *Kunst, Kultur, und Geschichte der Achämenidenzeit und ihr Fortleben*, ed. Heidemarie Koch and David N. Mackenzie (Berlin: Reimer, 1983), 253-66.

———, "Church-State Relations in the Sasanian Period," in *Monarchies and Socio-religious Traditions in the Ancient Near East*, ed. H.I.H. Prince T. Mikasa (Wiesbaden: Harrassowitz Verlag, 1984), 72-80. [Gignoux 1984a]

———, "L'organisation administrative sasanide: Le cas du marzbān," *Jerusalem Studies in Arabic and Islam* 4 (1984): 1-29. [Gignoux 1984b]

———, "Pour une esquisse des fonctions religieuses sous les Sasanides," *Jerusalem Studies in Arabic and Islam* 7 (1986): 93-108.

———, *Les quatre inscriptions du mage Kirdīr* (Paris: Association pour l'avancement des études iraniennes, 1991).

———, "Dietary Laws in Pre-Islamic and Post-Sasanian Iran: A Comparative Study," *Jerusalem Studies in Arabic and Islam* 17 (1994): 16-42.

———, "Le traité syriaque anonyme sur les médications," in *Symposium Syriacum VII*, ed. René Lavenant (Rome: Pontificium institutum orientalium studiorum, 1998), 725-33.

———, "Sur quelques relations entre chrétiens et mazdéens d'après des sources syriaques," *Studia Iranica* 28 (1999): 83-94.

———, "Une typologie des miracles des saints et martyrs perses dans l'Iran sassanide," in *Miracle et Karāma: Hagiographies médiévales comparées*, ed. Denise Aigle (Turnhout: Brepols, 2000), 499-523.

———, "L'apport scientifique des chrétiens à l'Iran sassanide," *Journal Asiatique* 289 (2001): 217-36. [Gignoux 2001a]

———, *Man and Cosmos in Ancient Iran* (Rome: Istituto italiano per l'Africa e l'Oriente, 2001). [Gignoux 2001b]

———, "A propos de l'anthroponymie religieuse d'époque sassanide," in *Languages of Iran: Past and Present—Iranian Studies In Memoriam David Neil MacKenzie*, ed. Dieter Weber (Wiesbaden: Harrassowitz Verlag, 2005), 35-42.

———, "La démonisation d'Alexander le Grand d'après la littérature pehlevie," in *Iranian Languages and Texts from Iran and Turan*, ed. Maria Macuch (Wiesbaden: Harrassowitz Verlag, 2007), 87-97.

———, "Prices and Drachms in the Late Sasanian Period," in *The Sasanian Era,*: vol. 3 of *The Idea of Iran*, ed. Vesta Sarkhosh Curtis and Sarah Stewart (London: I. B. Tauris, 2008), 132–39.

———, "Réflexions sur l'hagiographie et le multilingualisme des chrétiens syro-orientaux," in *Monachismes d'Orient*, ed. Florence Jullien and Marie-Joseph Pierre (Turnhout: Brepols, 2011), 123–32.

Gignoux, Philippe, and Christelle Jullien, "L'onomastique iranienne dans les sources syriaques: Quand les chrétiens changent de nom (IVᵉ–VIIᵉ siècle)," *Parole de l'Orient* 31 (2006): 279–94.

Gignoux, Philippe, Christelle Jullien, and Florence Jullien, *Noms propres syriaques d'origine iranienne* (Vienna: Verlag der österreichischen Akademie der Wissenschaften, 2009).

Gil, Moshe, "King Qubādh and Mazdak," *Journal of Near Eastern Studies* 71 (2012): 75–90.

Gippert, Jost, *Iranica Armeno-Iberica: Studien zu den iranischen Lehnwörtern im Armenischen und Georgischen* (Vienna: Verlag der Akademie der Wissenschaften, 1993).

Gnoli, Gheradro, *Zoroaster's Time and Homeland: A Study on the Origins of Mazdeism and Related Problems* (Naples: Istituto universitario orientale, 1980).

———, *The Idea of Iran: An Essay on Its Origin* (Rome: Istituto italiano per il medio ed estremo Oriente, 1989).

———, *Iran als religiöser Begriff im Mazdaismus* (Opladen: Westdeutscher Verlag, 1993).

———, "Nuovi Studi sul Mazdakismo," in *La Persia e Bisanzio: Convegno internazionale, Roma 14–18 ottobre 2002*, ed. Antonio Carile, Lellia Cracco Ruggini, Gnoli, Giovanni Pugliese Carratelli, and Gianroberto Scarcia (Rome: Accademia Nazionale dei Lincei, 2004), 439–56.

Göbl, R., "Christliche Siegel der sāsānidischen Zeit: Ein erster Nachtrag," *Wiener Zeitschrift für die Kunde des Morgenlandes* 71 (1979): 53–62.

Gobrecht, Günter, "Das Artā Vīrāz Nāmak," *Zeitschrift der deutschen morgenländischen Gesellschaft* 117 (1967): 382–409.

Goodblatt, David, "The Poll Tax in Sasanian Babylonia: The Talmudic Evidence," *Journal of the Social and Economic History of the Orient* 22 (1979): 233–95.

Goody, Jack, *The Development of the Family and Marriage in Europe* (Cambridge: Cambridge University Press, 1983).

Graf, David F., "The Persian Royal Road System," *Achaemenid History* 7 (1994): 167–89.

Graus, František, *Volk, Herrscher, und Heiliger im Reich der Merovinger* (Prague: Nakladatelství Československé Akademie Věd, 1965).

Greatrex, Geoffrey, "Khusro II and the Christians of His Empire," *Journal of the Canadian Society for Syriac Studies* 3 (2003): 78–88.

———, "Khusro II and the Christians of the Roman Empire," *Studia Patristica* 39 (2006): 47–52.

———, "Le chronique de pseudo-Zacharie de Mytilène et l'historiographie syriaque au sixième siècle," in *L'historiographie syriaque*, ed. Muriel Debié (Paris: Geuthner, 2009), 33–55.

Greatrex, Geoffrey, and Samuel Lieu, *The Roman Eastern Frontier and the Persian Wars: Part II, AD 363–630* (London: Routledge, 2002).

Greenwood, Timothy, "A History of Armenia in the Seventh and Eighth Centuries" (DPhil diss., Oxford University, 2000).

———, "Sasanian Echoes and Apocalyptic Expectations: A Reevaluation of the Armenian History Attributed to Sebeos," *Le Muséon* 115 (2002): 323–97.

Grenet, Frantz, "Observations sur les titres de Kirdīr," *Studia Iranica* 19 (1990): 87–94.

———, "Regional Interaction in Central Asia and Northwest India in the Kidarite and Hephthalite Periods," in *Indo-Iranian Languages and Peoples*, ed. Nicholas Sims-Williams (Oxford: British Academy, 2002), 203–24.

Griffith, Sidney, "Asceticism in the Church of Syria: The Hermeneutics of Early Syrian Monasticism," in *Asceticism*, ed. Vincent Wimbush and Richard Valantasis (Oxford: Oxford University Press, 1995), 220–45.

Grignaschi, Mario, "Quelques spécimens de la littérature sassanide conservés dans les bibliothèques d'Istanbul," *Journal Asiatique* 254 (1966): 1–142.

Gropp, G., "Die Pahlavi-Inschrift auf dem Thomaskreuz in Madras," *Archäologische Mitteilungen aus Iran* 3 (1970): 267–71.

———, *Archäologische Forschungen in Khorasan, Iran* (Wiesbaden: Harrassowitz Verlag, 1995).

Gropp, G., and S. Nadjmabadi, "Bericht über eine Reise in West- und Südiran," *Archäologische Mitteilungen aus Iran* 3 (1970): 173–230.

Gruzinski, Serge, *La pensée métisse* (Paris: Fayard, 1999).

Guidi, Ignacio, "Ostsyrische Bischöfe und Bischofssitze im V., VI., und VII. Jahrhundert," *Zeitschrift der deutschen morgenländishcen Gesellschaft* 43 (1889): 388–414.

Gutas, Dimitri, *Greek Thought, Arabic Culture: The Graeco-Arabic Translation Movement in Baghdad and Early 'Abbāsid Society (2nd–4th / 8th–10th Centuries)* (London: Routledge, 1998).

Gyselen, Rika, "Les données de géographie administrative dans la *Šahrestānīhā-ī Ērānšahr*," *Studia Iranica* 17 (1988): 191–206.

———, *La géographie administrative de l'empire sassanide: Les témoignages sigillographiques* (Paris: Peeters, 1989).

———, *Arab-Sasanian Copper Coinage* (Vienna: Verlag der österreichischen Akademie der Wissenschaften, 2000).

———, "La désignation territoriale des quatre *spahbed* de l'empire sassanide d'après les sources primaires sigillographiques," *Studia Iranica* 30 (2001): 137–41. [Gyselen 2001a]

———, *The Four Generals of the Sasanian Empire: Some Sigillographic Evidence* (Rome: Istituto italiano per l'Africa e l'Oriente, 2001). [Gyselen 2001b]

———, "Lorsque l'archéologie rencontre la tradition littéraire: Les titres militaires des *spāhbed* de l'empire sassanide," *Comptes rendus de l'Académie des Inscriptions et Belle Lettres* (2002): 447–58.

———, "La reconquête de l'est iranien par l'empire sassanide au VIe siècle, d'après les sources 'iraniennes,'" *Arts Asiatiques* 58 (2003): 162–67.

———, "L'administration 'provinciale' du *naxwār* d'après les sources sigillographiques," *Studia Iranica* 33 (2004): 31–46.

———, "Les témoignages sigillographiques sur la présence chrétienne dans l'empire sassanide," in *Chrétiens en terre d'Iran*, vol. 1, *Implantation et acculturation*, ed. Gyselen (Paris: Association pour l'avancement des études iraniennes, 2006), 17–78.

———, *Sasanian Seals and Sealings in the A. Saeedi Collection* (Leuven: Peeters, 2007).

———, "The Great Families in the Sasanian Empire: Some Sigillographic Evidence," in *Current Research in Sasanian Archaeology, Art and History*, ed. Derek Kennet and Paul Luft (Oxford: Archaeopress, 2008), 107–13.

———, "Primary Sources and Historiography of the Sasanian Empire," *Studia Iranica* 38 (2009): 163–90.

Gyselen, Rika, and Hermann Gasche, "Suse et Ivān-e Kerkha, capitale provinciale d'Ērān-Xwarrah-Šāpūr," *Studia Iranica* 23 (1994): 19–35.

Haas, Christopher, "Mountain Constantines: The Christianization of Aksum and Iberia," *Journal of Late Antiquity* 1 (2008): 101–26.

Hage, Wolfgang, *Das orientalische Christentum* (Stuttgart: W. Kohlhammer, 2007).

Hainthaler, Theresia, "Der persische Disputator Simeon von Bet Aršam und seine antinestorianische Positionsbestimmung," in *Die Kirchen von Jerusalem und Antiochien nach 451 bis 600*, vol. 2, pt. 3 of *Jesus der Christus im Glauben der Kirche*, ed. Alois Grillmeier (Freiburg: Herder, 2002), 262–39.

———, "Thomas of Edessa, *Causa de Nativitate*: Some Considerations," *Parole de l'Orient* 31 (2006): 63–85.

Haldon, John, *Byzantium in the Seventh Century: The Transformation of a Culture* (Cambridge: Cambridge University Press, 1990).

———, "The Idea of the Town in the Byzantine Empire," in *The Idea and Ideal of the Town between Late Antiquity and the Early Middle Ages*, ed. G. P. Brogiolo and Bryan Ward-Perkins (Leiden: Brill, 1999), 1–24. [Haldon 1999a]

———, *Warfare, State and Society in the Byzantine World, 565–1204* (London: Routledge, 1999). [Haldon 1999b]

———, "The Resources of Late Antiquity," in *The New Cambridge History of Islam*, vol. 1, *The Formation of the Islamic World, Sixth to Eleventh Centuries*, ed. Chase Robinson (Cambridge: Cambridge University Press, 2010), 19–71.

Harrak, Amir, "Tales about Sennacherib: The Contribution of the Syriac Sources," in *The World of the Aramaeans III: Studies in Language and Literature in Honour of Paul-Eugène Dion*, ed. P. M. Michèle Daviau, John W. Wevers, and Michael Weigl (Sheffield: Sheffield Academic Press, 2001), 168–89.

———, "Trade Routes and the Christianization of the Near East," *Journal of the Canadian Society for Syriac Studies* 2 (2002): 46–61.

Harries, Jill, "Creating Legal Space: Settling Disputes in the Roman Empire," in *Rabbinic Law and Its Roman and Near Eastern Context*, ed. Catherine Hezser (Tübingen: Mohr Siebeck, 2003), 63–81.

Hartmann, Udo, "Wege des Wissens: Formen des Gedankenaustauschs und der kulturellen Beeinflussung zwischen dem spätantiken Rom und dem Sāsānidenreich," in *Getrennte Wege? Kommunikation, Raum und Wahrnehmung in der alten Welt*, ed. Robert Rollinger, Andreas Luther, and Josef Wiesehöfer (Berlin: Verlag Antike, 2007), 50–107.

Harvey, Susan Ashbrook, *Asceticism and Society in Crisis: John of Ephesus and the Lives of the Eastern Saints* (Berkeley: University of California Press, 1987).

Hauser, Stefan, "Chronologische und historisch-politische Untersuchungen zur östlichen Ġazīra in vorislamischer Zeit" (PhD diss., Freie Universität, Berlin, 1994).

———, "'Greek in Subject and Style, but a Little Distorted': Zum Verhältnis von Orient und Okzident in der Altertumswissenschaft," in *Posthumanistische Klassische Archäologie:*

Historizität und Wissenschaftlichkeit von Interessen und Methoden, ed. Stefan Altekamp, Mathia René Hofter, and Michael Krumme (Munich: Hirmer, 2001), 83–104. [Hauser 2001a]

———, "Not Out of Babylon? The Development of Ancient Near Eastern Studies in Germany and Its Current Significance," in *Proceedings of the XLV Rencontre Assyriologique Internationale*, ed. I. Tzvi Abusch, Carol Noyes, William Hallo, and Irene Winter (Bethesda: CDL Press, 2001), 211–37. [Hauser 2001b]

———, "Christliche Archäologie im Sasanidenreich: Grundlagen der Interpretation und Bestandsaufnahme der Evidenz," in *Inkulturation des Christentums im Sasanidenreich*, ed. Arafa Mustafa, Jürgen Tubach, and G. Sophia Vashalomidze (Wiesbaden: Reichert Verlag, 2007), 93–136. [Hauser 2007a]

———, "Vēh Ardashīr and the Identification of the Ruins at al-Madā'in," in *Facts and Artefacts: Art in the Islamic World*, ed. Annette Hagedorn and Avinoam Shalem (Leiden: Brill, 2007), 461–88. [Hauser 2007b]

———, "'Die Christen vermehrten sich in Persien und bauten Kirchen und Klöster': Eine Archäologie des Christentum im Sasanidenreich," in *Grenzgänge im östlichen Mittelmeerraum: Byzanz und die islamische Welt vom 9. bis 13. Jahrhundert*, ed. Ulrike Koenen and Martina Müller-Wiener (Wiesbaden: Reichert Verlag, 2008), 29–57.

Healey, John F., "The Christians of Qatar in the 7th Century A.D.," in *Studies in Honour of Clifford Edmund Bosworth*, vol. 1, ed. Ian Richard Netton (Leiden: Brill, 2000), 222–37.

Hendy, Michael, *Studies in the Byzantine Monetary Economy, c. 300–1450* (Cambridge: Cambridge University Press, 1985).

Herman, Geoffrey, "Ahasuerus, the Former Stable Master of Belshazzar, and the Wicked Alexander of Macedon: Two Parallels between the Babylonian Talmud and Persian Sources," *American Jewish Studies Review* 29 (2005): 283–97.

———, "'Bury My Coffin Deep!' Zoroastrian Exhumation in Jewish and Christian Sources," in *Tiferet Leyisrael: Jubilee Volume in Honor of Israel Francus*, ed. Joel Roth, Menahem Schmelzer, and Yaacov Francus (New York: Jewish Theological Seminary, 2010), 31–59.

———, *A Prince without a Kingdom: The Exilarch in the Sasanian Era* (Tübingen: Mohr Siebeck, 2012).

———, "The Passion of Shabur, Martyred in the 18th Year of Yazdgird, with a Fragment of the Life of Mar Aba Catholicos," *Journal of Semitic Studies* 58 (2013): 121–30.

———, "The Last Years of Yazdgird I," in *Jews, Christians and Zoroastrians: Religious Dynamics in a Sasanian Context*, ed. Herman (Piscataway: Gorgias, 2014), 67–90.

Hewsen, Robert, "Ecclesiastical Analysis of the Naxarar System: A Re-examination of Adontz's Chapter XII," in *From Byzantium to Iran: Armenian Studies in Honour of Nina G. Garsoïan*, ed. Jean-Pierre Mahé and Robert W. Thomson (Atlanta: Scholars, 1997), 97–149.

Higgins, M. J., "Chosroes II's Votive Offerings at Sergiopolis," *Byzantinische Zeitschrift* 48 (1955): 89–107.

Hintze, Almut, *Der Zamyād-Yašt: Edition, Übersetzung, Kommentar* (Wiesbaden: Dr. Ludwig Reichert Verlag, 1994).

Hjerrild, Bodil, *Studies in Zoroastrian Family Law: A Comparative Analysis* (Copenhagen: Museum Tusculanum Press, 2003).

———, "Succession and Kinship in the Late Sasanian Era," in *Ancient and Middle Iranian Studies*, vol. 1 of *Proceedings of the 5th Conference of the Societas Iranologica Europaea*, ed. Antonio Panaino and Andrea Piras (Milan: Mimesis, 2006), 479–84.

———, "Some Aspects of the Institution of *stūrīh*," in *Religious Texts in Iranian Languages: Symposium Held in Copenhagen, May 2002*, ed Fereydun Vahman and Claus V. Pedersen (Copenhagen: Det Kongelige Danske Videnskabernes Selskab, 2007), 165–74.

Hoffmann, Georg, *Auszüge aus syrischen Akten persischer Märtyrer* (Leipzig: F. A. Brockhaus, 1880).

Holmberg, Bo, "Berättelsen om Karka de-Bet-Selokh och martyrerna där," in *Svenskt Patristiskt Bibliotek*, vol. 2, *Martyrer och Helgon*, ed. Samuel Rubenson (Lund: Artos Bokförlag, 2000), 111–27.

Holum, Kenneth G., "Pulcheria's Crusade A.D. 421–22 and the Ideology of Imperial Victory," *Greek, Roman, and Byzantine Studies* 18 (1977): 153–72.

———, "Archaeological Evidence for the Fall of Byzantine Caesarea," *Bulletin of the American Schools of Oriental Research* 286 (1992): 73–85.

Hopkins, Keith, *Death and Renewal* (Cambridge: Cambridge University Press, 1983).

———, "Christian Number and Its Implications," *Journal of Early Christian Studies* 6 (1998): 185–226.

Horden, Peregrine, "The Earliest Hospitals in Byzantium, Western Europe, and Islam," *Journal of Interdisciplinary History* 35 (2005): 361–89.

Howard-Johnston, James, "The Siege of Constantinople in 626," in *Constantinople and Its Hinterland*, ed. Cyril Mango and Gilbert Dagron (Aldershot, 1995), 131–42. [Howard-Johnston 1995a]

———, "The Two Great Powers in Late Antiquity: A Comparison," in *The Byzantine and Early Islamic Near East*, vol. 3, *States, Resources, and Armies*, ed. Averil Cameron (Princeton: Darwin, 1995), 157–226. [Howard-Johnston 1995b]

———, "Pride and Fall: Khusro II and His Regime, 626–28," in *La Persia e Bisanzio: Convegno internazionale, Roma 14–18 ottobre 2002*, ed. Antonio Carile, Lellia Cracco Ruggini, Gherardo Gnoli, Giovanni Pugliese Carratelli, and Gianroberto Scarcia (Rome: Accademia Nazionale dei Lincei, 2004), 93–113.

———, "The Destruction of the Late Antique World Order," in *Current Research in Sasanian Archaeology, Art, and History*, ed. Derek Kennet and Paul Luft (Oxford: Archaeopress, 2008), 79–85. [Howard-Johnston 2008a]

———, "State and Society in Late Antique Iran," in *The Sasanian Era*, vol. 3 of *The Idea of Iran*, ed. Vesta Sarkhosh Curtis and Sarah Stewart (London: I. B. Tauris, 2008), 118–29. [Howard-Johnston 2008b]

———, "The Sasanians' Strategic Dilemma," in *Commutatio et contentio: Studies in the Late Roman, Sasanian, and Early Islamic Near East in Memory of Zeev Rubin*, ed. Henning Börm and Josef Wiesehöfer (Düsseldorf: Wellem Verlag, 2010), 37–70. [Howard-Johnston 2010a]

———, *Witnesses to a World Crisis: Historians and Histories of the Middle East in the Seventh Century* (Oxford: Oxford University Press, 2010). [Howard-Johnston 2010b]

Hübner, Sabine, "'Brother-Sister' Marriage in Roman Egypt: A Curiosity of Humankind or a Widespread Family Strategy?," *Journal of Roman Studies* 97 (2007): 21–49.

Hübner, Sabine R., and David M. Ratzan, "Fatherless Antiquity? Perspectives on Fatherlessness in the Ancient Mediterranean," in *Growing up Fatherless in Antiquity,* ed. Hübner and Ratzan (Cambridge: Cambridge University Press, 2009), 3–28.

Huff, Dietrich, "Ein christliches Felsgrab bei Istakhr," in *Archaeologia Iranica et Orientalis,* ed. L. De Meyer and E. Haerinck (Ghent: Peeters, 1989), 713–29.

———, "Beobachtungen zum Čahartaq und zur Topographie zum Girre," *Iranica Antiqua* 30 (1995): 71–92.

———, "Das 'Medische' Grabrelief von Deh Now," *Studia Iranica* 28 (1999): 7–40.

———, "Archaeological Evidence of Zoroastrian Funerary Practices," in *Zoroastrian Rituals in Context,* ed. Michael Stausberg (Leiden: Brill, 2004), 593–630.

———, "Formation and Ideology of the Sasanian State in the Context of Archaeological Evidence," in *The Sasanian Era* vol. 3 of *The Idea of Iran,* ed. Vesta Sarkhosh Curtis and Sarah Stewart (London: I. B. Tauris, 2008), 31–59.

Humfress, Caroline, "Law and Legal Practice in the Age of Justinian," in *The Cambridge Companion to the Age of Justinian,* ed. Michael Maas (Cambridge: Cambridge University Press, 2005), 161–84.

———, *Orthodoxy and the Courts in Late Antiquity* (Oxford: Oxford University Press, 2007).

———, "Bishops and Law Courts in Late Antiquity: How (Not) to Make Sense of the Legal Evidence," *Journal of Early Christian Studies* 19 (2011): 375–400.

———, "Thinking through Legal Pluralism: 'Forum Shopping' in the Later Roman Empire," in *Law and Empire: Ideas, Practices, Actors,* ed. Jeroen Duindam, Jill Harries, Caroline Humfress, and Nimrod Hurvitz (Leiden: Brill, 2014), 225–50.

Hunter, Erica C. D., "Aramaic-Speaking Communities of Sasanid Mesopotamia," *Aram* 7 (1995): 319–35.

———, "The Christian Matrix of al-Hira," in *Controverses chrétiens dans l'Iran sassanide,* ed. Christelle Jullien (Paris: Association pour l'avancement des études iraniennes, 2008), 41–56.

———, "The Persian Contribution to Christianity in China: Reflections in the Xi'an Fu Syriac Inscriptions," in *Hidden Treasures in Intercultural Encounters: Studies in East Syriac Christianity and Central Asia and China,* ed. Dietmar Winkler and Tang Li (Berlin: Lit, 2009), 71–86.

Hutter, Manfred, "Manichaeism in the Early Sasanian Empire," *Numen* 40 (1993): 2–15.

———, "Shirin, Nestorianer und Monophysiten: Königliche Kirchenpolitik im späten Sasanidenreich," in *Symposium Syriacum VII,* ed. René Lavenant (Rome: Pontificium institutum orientalium studiorum, 1998), 373–86.

———, "Manichaeism in Iran in the Fourth Century," in *Studia Manichaica IV: Internationaler Kongreß zum Manichäismus, Berlin 14.-18. Juli 1997,* ed. Ronald E. Emmerick, Werner Sundermann, and Peter Zieme (Berlin: Akademie Verlag, 2000), 308–17.

———, "Mār Aba and the Impact of Zoroastrianism on Christianity in the 6th Century," in *Religious Themes and Texts of Pre-Islamic Iran and Central Asia: Studies in Honor of Prof. Gherardo Gnoli on the Occasion of His 65th Birthday,* ed. Carlo Cereti, Mauro Maggi, and Elio Provasi (Wiesbaden: Harrassowitz Verlag, 2003), 167–73.

Huyse, Philip, "Kerdīr and the First Sasanians," in *Proceedings of the Third European Conference of Iranian Studies,* pt. 1, *Old and Middle Iranian Studies,* ed. Nicholas Sims-Williams (Wiesbaden: Harrassowitz Verlag, 1998), 109–20.

———, "La revendication de territoires achéménides par les Sassanides: Une réalité historique?," in *Iran: Questions et Connaissances, Actes du IVe congrès européen des études iraniennes*, vol. 1, ed. Huyse (Leuven: Peeters, 2002), 297-311.

———, "Late Sasanian Society between Orality and Literacy," in *The Sasanian Era*, vol. 3 of *The Idea of Iran*, ed. Vesta Sarkhosh Curtis and Sarah Stewart (London: I. B. Tauris, 2008), 140-55.

———, "Inscriptional Literature in Old and Middle Iranian Languages," in *The Literature of Pre-Islamic Iran: Companion Volume I to "A History of Persian Literature,"* ed. Ronald E. Emmerick and Maria Macuch (London: I. B. Tauris, 2009), 72 -115.

Ioan, Ovidiu, *Muslime und Araber bei Īšō'jahb III. (649-659)*, (Wiesbaden: Harrassowitz Verlag, 2009).

Inostrancev, K. A., "Sasanidskii Prazdnik Vesni," in *Sasanidskie Etudi* (St. Petersburg: Kirschbaum, 1909), 82-109.

Jacobs, Andrew, *Remains of the Jews: The Holy Land and Christian Empire in Late Antiquity* (Stanford: Stanford University Press, 2004).

Jany, János, "The Jurisprudence of the Sasanian Sages," *Journal Asiatique* 294 (2006): 291-323.

———, "Criminal Justice in Sasanian Persia," *Iranica Antiqua* 42 (2007): 347-86.

Jullien, Christelle, "Peines et supplices dans les *Actes des martyrs persans* et droit sassanide: Nouvelles prospections," *Studia Iranica* 33 (2004): 243-69.

———, "Kaškar 'la sublime' et sa singulière prééminence sur la siège patriarcal de Séleucie-Ctésiphon," in *Ancient and Middle Iranian Studies*, vol. 1 of *Proceedings of the 5th Conference of the Societas Iranologica Europaea*, ed. Antonio Panaino and Andrea Piras (Milan: Mimesis, 2006), 543-52.

———, "Martyrs en Perse dans l'hagiographie syro-orientale: Le tournant du IVe siècle," in *Juifs et chrétiens en Arabie aux Ve et VIe siècles: Regards croisés sur les sources*, ed. Joëlle Beaucamp, Francoise Briquel-Chatonnet, and Christian Julien Robin (Paris: Association des amis du Centre d'histoire et civilisation de Byzance, 2010), 279-90.

———, "Les chrétiens déportés dans l'empire sassanide sous Šābūr Ier," *Studia Iranica* 40 (2011): 288-93.

Jullien, Christelle, and Florence Jullien, "Les Actes de Mār Māri: Une figure apocryphe au service de l'unité communautaire," *Apocrypha* 10 (1999): 177-94.

———, "La Chronique d'Arbèles: Propositions pour la fin d'une controverse," *Oriens Christianus* 85 (2001): 41-83.

———, *Apôtres des confins: Processus missionaire chrétiens dans l'empire iranien* (Bures-sur-Yvette: Groupe pour l'etude de la civilisation du Moyen-Orient, 2002). [C. Jullien and F. Jullien 2002a]

———, "Aux frontières de l'iranité: 'Nāsrāyē' et 'Krīstyonē' des inscriptions du *mobad* Kirdir: Enquête littéraire et historique," *Numen* 69 (2002): 282-335. [C. Jullien and F. Jullien 2002b]

———, *Aux origines de l'Église de Perse: Les Actes de Mār Māri* (Leuven: Peeters, 2003).

———, "Du Ḥnana ou la benediction contestée," in *Sur les pas des Araméens chrétiens: Mélanges offerts à Alain Desreumaux*, ed. Françoise Briquel-Chatonnet and Muriel Debié (Paris: Geuther, 2010) 333-48.

Jullien, Florence, "Parcours à travers l'*Histoire d'Īšō'sabran*, martyr sous Khosrau II," in *Contributions à l'histoire et la géographie historique de l'empire sassanide*, ed. Rika

Gyselen (Bures-sur-Yvette: Groupe pour l'étude de la civilisation du Moyen-Orient, 2004), 171–83.

———, "Un exemple de relecture des origines dans l'Église syro-orientale: Théocrite et l'évêche de Šahrgard," in *Ancient and Middle Iranian Studies*, vol. 1 of *Proceedings of the 5th Conference of the Societas Iranologica Europaea*, ed. Antonio Panaino and Andrea Piras (Milan: Mimesis, 2006), 553–60.

———, "La chronique du Ḥūzistān: Une page d'histoire sassanide," in *Trésors d'Orient: Mélanges offerts à Rika Gyselen*, ed. Philippe Gignoux, Christelle Jullien, and Florence Jullien (Paris: Association pour l'avancement des études iraniennes, 2009), 159–86.

———, "La passion syriaque de Mār 'Abdā: Quelques relations entres chrétiens et mazdéens," in *Rabā l'almīn: Florilège offert à Philippe Gignoux*, ed. Rika Gyselen, Christelle Jullien, and Florence Jullien (Paris: Association pour l'avancement des études iraniennes, 2011), 195–205. [F. Jullien 2011a]

———, "Stratégies du monachisme missionaire chrétien en Iran," in *Itinéraires missionaires: Échanges et identités*, ed. Christelle Jullien (Paris: Association pour l'avancement des études iraniennes, 2011), 49–69. [F. Jullien 2011b]

———, "Une pratique religieuse en médiation culturelle entre chrétiens et mazdéens," *Orientalia Christiana Periodica* 79 (2013): 337–53.

———, "Édesse, un creuset de traditions sur les mages évangeliques," *Le Muséon* 127 (2014): 77–93.

al-Ka'bi, Nasir, "A New Repertoire of Crosses from the Ancient Site of Ḥīra, Iraq," *Journal of the Canadian Society for Syriac Studies* 14 (2014): 90–102.

Kaegi, Walter E., *Heraclius: Emperor of Byzantium* (Cambridge: Cambridge University Press, 2003).

———, "The Heraclians and Holy War," in *Byzantine War Ideology between Roman Imperial Concept and Christian Religion*, ed. Johannes Koder and I. Stouraitis (Vienna: Verlag der österreichischen Akademie der Wissenschaften, 2012), 17–26.

Kalmin, Richard, *Jewish Babylonia between Persia and Roman Palestine* (Oxford: Oxford University Press, 2006).

———, "The Adiabenian Royal Family in Rabbinic Literature of Late Antiquity," in *Tiferet Leyisrael: Jubilee Volume in Honor of Israel Francus*, ed. Joel Roth, Menahem Schmelzer, and Yaacov Francus (New York: Jewish Theological Seminary, 2010), 61–77.

Kanga, M., "Barsom," in *Encyclopaedia Iranica*, ed. Ehsan Yarshater, vol. 3 (London: Routledge and Kegan Paul, 1989), 825–27.

Kaufhold, Hubert, "Der Richter in den syrischen Rechtsquellen: Zum Einfluß islamischen Rechts auf die christlich-orientalische Rechtsliteratur," *Oriens Christianus* 68 (1984): 91–113.

Kawami, Trudy S., *The Monumental Art of the Parthian Period in Iran* (Leiden: E. J. Brill, 1987).

Kellens, Jean, "Considérations sur l'histoire de l'Avesta," *Journal Asiatique* 286 (1998): 451–519.

———, "Structure de l'espace-temps dans le mazdéisme ancien," in *The Past in the Past: Concepts of Past Reality in Ancient Near Eastern and Early Greek Thought*, ed. Hans M. Barstad and Pierre Briant (Oslo: Novus, 2009), 37–45.

Kelly, Christopher, *Ruling the Later Roman Empire* (Cambridge, MA: Harvard University Press, 2004).

Kennedy, Hugh, "From Shahristan to Medina," *Studia Islamica* 102-3 (2006): 5-34.
———, "The Survival of Iranianness," in *The Rise of Islam*, vol. 4 of *The Idea of Iran*, ed. Vesta Sarkhosh Curtis and Sarah Stewart (London: I. B. Tauris, 2009), 13-29.
———, "Great Estates and Elite Lifestyles in the Fertile Crescent from Byzantium and Sasanian Iran to Islam," in *Court Cultures in the Muslim World: Seventh to Nineteenth Centuries*, ed. Albrecht Fuess and Jan-Peter Hartung (London: Routledge, 2011), 54-79.
Kennet, Derek, "The Decline of Eastern Arabia in the Sasanian Period," *Arabian Archaeology and Epigraphy* 18 (2007): 86-122.
Kervran, Monique, "Transformations de la ville de Suse et de son économie de l'époque sasanide à l'époque abbaside," *Paléorient* 11 (1985): 91-100.
Kettenhofen, Erich, "Deportations II: In the Parthian and Sasanian Periods," in *Encyclopaedia Iranica*, ed. Ehsan Yarshater, vol. 7 (Costa Mesa: Mazda, 1996), 297-308.
Khan, Geoffrey, "Newly Discovered Arabic Documents from Early Abbasid Khurasan," in *From Al-Andalus to Khurasan: Documents from the Medieval Muslim World*, ed. Petra M. Sijpesteijn, Lennart Sundelin, Sofía Torallas Tovar, and Amelia Zomeño (Leiden: Brill, 2007), 201-15.
Kiperwasser, Reuven, and Dan D. Y. Shapira, "Irano-Talmudica I: The Three-Legged Ass and *Ridyā* in B. Ta'anith: Some Observations about Mythic Hydrology in the Babylonian Talmud and in Ancient Iran," *American Jewish Studies Review* 32 (2008): 101-16.
Kister, M. J., "Al-Ḥīra: Some Notes on Its Relations with Arabia," *Arabica* 15 (1968): 143-69.
Klein, Holger A., *Byzanz, der Westen und das 'wahre' Kreuz: Die Geschichte einer Reliquie und ihrer künstlerischen Fassung in Byzanz und im Abendland* (Wiesbaden: Reichert Verlag, 2004). [Klein 2004a]
———, "Constantine, Helena, and the Cult of the True Cross in Constantinople," in *Byzance et les reliques du Christ*, ed. Jannic Durand and Bernard Flusin (Paris: Association des amis du Centre d'histoire et civilization de Byzance, 2004), 31-59. [Klein 2004b]
Kleiss, W., "Alte Wege in West-Iran," *Archäologische Mitteilunger aus Iran* 10 (1977): 151-61.
Klingenschmitt, G., "Die Erbtochter im zoroastrischen Recht nach dem *Mādiyān ē hazār dādistān*," *Münchener Studien zur Sprachwissenschaft* 21 (1967): 59-70.
Knauth, Wolfgang, "Die sportlichen Qualifikationen der iranischen Fürsten," *Stadion* 2 (1976): 1-89.
Knust, Jennifer Wright, *Abandoned to Lust: Sexual Slander and Ancient Christianity* (New York: Columbia University Press, 2006).
Kolesnikov, Ali I., *Iran v Nachale VII Veka* (Moscow: Palestinskii Sbornik, 1970).
———, "O Termine 'Marzban' v Sasanidskom Irane," *Palestinskii Sbornik* 27 (1981): 49-56.
———, *Zavoevanie Irana Arabami: Iran pri 'Pravednikh' Khalifakh* (Moscow: Nauka, 1982).
———, *Denezhnoe Xozyaistvo v Irane v VII veke* (Moscow: Vostochnaya Literatura, 1998). [Kolesnikov 1998a]
———, "Khristianskaya Simbolika na Pozdnesasanidskoi i Arabo-Sasanidskoi Medi v Irane VII v N.E.," *Palestinskii Sbornik* 98 (1998): 196-205. [Kolesnikov 1998b]
———, "Kresti na Sasanidskikh Drakhmakh: Numizmaticheskie Svidetelsтva o Raspostrenenii Khristianstva v Irane v VI Veke," *Khristianskii Vostok* 4 (2002): 207-17.
Kominko, Maja, *The World of Kosmas: Illustrated Byzantine Codices of the Christian Topography* (Cambridge: Cambridge University Press, 2013).

König, Götz, *Geschlechtsmoral und Gleichgeschlechtlichkeit im Zoroastrismus* (Wiesbaden: Harrassowitz Verlag, 2010).
Koshelenko, G., A. Bader, and V. Gaibov, "The Beginnings of Christianity in Merv," *Iranica Antiqua* 30 (1995): 55–70.
Kottje, Raymund, *Studien zum Einfluss des alten Testaments auf Recht und Liturgie des frühen Mittelalters (6. bis 8. Jahrhundert)* (Bonn: Roehrscheid, 1965).
Kotwal, Firoze M., and James W. Boyd, *A Persian Offering, the Yasna: A Zoroastrian High Liturgy* (Paris: Association pour l'avancement des études iraniennes, 1991).
Kreiner, Jamie, *The Social Life of Hagiography in the Merovingian Kingdom* (Cambridge: Cambridge University Press, 2014).
Kreyenbroek, Philip G., *Sraoša in the Zoroastrian Tradition* (Leiden: Brill, 1985).
———, "The Zoroastrian Priesthood after the Fall of the Sasanian Empire," in *Transition Periods in Iranian History: Actes du Symposium de Fribourg-en-Brisgau (22–24 Mai 1985)*, ed. Philippe Gignoux (Leuven: Association pour l'avancement des études iraniennes, 1987), 151–66.
———, "Ritual and Rituals in the *Nērangestān*," in *Zoroastrian Rituals in Context*, ed. Michael Stausberg (Leiden: Brill, 2004), 317–31.
———, "Storytelling, History, and Communal Memory in Pre-Islamic Iran," in *Remembering the Past in Iranian Societies*, ed. Christine Allison and Kreyenbroek (Wiesbaden: Harrassowitz Verlag, 2013), 21–31.
Kristensen, Troels Myrup, "Embodied Images: Christian Response and Destruction in Late Antique Egypt," *Journal of Late Antiquity* 2 (2009): 224–50.
Kröger, Jens, *Sasanidischer Stuckdekor: Ein Beitrag zum Reliefdekor aus Stuck in sasanidischer und frühislamischer Zeit* (Mainz: P. von Zabern, 1982).
Krueger, Derek, *Writing and Holiness: The Practice of Authorship in the Early Christian East* (Philadelphia: University of Pennsylvania Press, 2004).
Krüger, Paul, "Die Regenbitten Aphrems des Syrers: Ihre Überlieferung unter besonderer Berücksichtigung des nestorianischen Officiums des Ninivetenfasten und ihre religionsgeschichtliche Bedeutung," *Oriens Christianus* 8 (1933): 13–61.
Labourt, Jérôme, *Le Christianisme dans l'empire perse sous la dynastie Sassanide (224–632)* (Paris: Librarie Victor Lecoffre, 1904).
Lamoreaux, John, "Episcopal Courts in Late Antiquity," *Journal of Early Christian Studies* 3 (1995): 143–67.
Lange, Christian, *Mia Energeia: Untersuchungen zur Einigungspolitik des Kaisers Heraclius und des Patriarchen Sergius von Constantinopel* (Tübingen: Mohr Siebeck, 2012).
Lankarany, Firouz-Thomas, *Daēnā im Avesta: Eine semantische Untersuchung* (Reinbek: Verlag für Orientalischen Fachpublikationen, 1985).
Lerner, Judith, *Christian Seals of the Sasanian Period* (Leiden: Brill, 1977).
Levine, Louis D., "Geographical Studies in the Neo-Assyrian Zagros: II," *Iran* 12 (1974): 99–124.
Lieu, Samuel N. C., "Captives, Refugees, and Exiles: A Study of Cross-Frontier Civilian Movements and Contacts between Rome and Persia from Valerian to Jovian," in *The Defence of the Roman and Byzantine East: Proceedings of a Colloquium Held at the University of Sheffield in April 1986*, ed. Philip Freeman and David Kennedy (Oxford: Archaeopress, 1986), 475–505.

———, *Manichaeism in the Later Roman Empire and Medieval China* (Tübingen: Mohr Siebeck, 1992).

———, "The Church of the East in Quanzhou," in *Medieval Christian and Manichaean Remains from Quanzhou (Zayton)*, ed. Lieu, Lance Eccles, Majella Franzmann, Iain Gardner, and Ken Perry (Turnhout: Brepols, 2012), 25–52.

———, "The 'Romanitas' of the Xi'an Inscription," in *From the Oxus River to the Chinese Shores: Studies in East Syrian Christianity in China and Central Asia*, ed. Li Tang and Dietmar W. Winkler (Zurich: Lit Verlag, 2013), 123–40.

Lifshitz, Felice, "Beyond Positivism and Genre: 'Hagiographical' Texts as Historical Narrative," *Viator* 25 (1994): 95–113.

Lincoln, Bruce, *Authority: Construction and Coercion* (Chicago: University of Chicago Press, 1994).

———, "Retiring Syncretism," *Historical Reflections / Réfléxions historiques* 27 (2001): 453–59.

———, "Češmag, the Lie, and the Logic of Zoroastrian Demonology," *Journal of the American Oriental Society* 129 (2009): 45–55.

———, "Human Unity and Diversity in Zoroastrian Mythology," *History of Religions* 50 (2010): 7–20.

———, *'Happiness for Mankind': Achaemenian Religion and the Imperial Project* (Leuven: Peeters, 2012).

Lopez, Ariel, *Shenoute of Atripe and the Uses of Poverty: Royal Patronage, Religious Conflict, and Monasticism in Late Antique Egypt* (Berkeley: University of California Press, 2013).

Lukonin, Vladimir, *Kultura Sasanidskovo Iran v III–V vv.: Ocherki po Istorii Kulturi* (Moscow: Nauka, 1969).

———, "Khram Anahiti v Kangavare," *Vestnik Drevnei Istorii* (1977): 105–11.

Luschey, Heinz, "Der Berg von Bisutun," in *Bisutun: Ausgrabungen und Forschungen in den Jahren 1963–1967*, ed. Wolfram Kleiss and Peter Calmeyer (Berlin: Gebr. Mann Verlag, 1996), 17–18. [Luschey 1996a]

———, "Die sasanidische Quadern in Bisutun," in *Bisutun: Ausgrabungen und Forschungen in den Jahren 1963–1967*, ed. Wolfram Kleiss and Peter Calmeyer (Berlin: Gebr. Mann Verlag, 1996), 91–92. [Luschey 1996b]

MacEvitt, Christopher, *The Crusades and the Christian World of the East: Rough Tolerance* (Philadelphia: University of Pennsylvania Press, 2008).

MacKenzie, David N., *A Concise Pahlavi Dictionary* (London: Oxford University Press, 1971).

———, "Gumēzišn," in *Encyclopaedia Iranica*, ed. Ehsan Yarshater, vol. 11 (New York: Bibliotheca Persica, 2002), 398–99.

MacMullen, Ramsay, "Judicial Savagery in the Roman Empire," *Chiron* 16 (1986): 147–66.

Macomber, William, "The Authority of the Catholicos Patriarch of Seleucia-Ctesiphon," *Orientalia Christiana Analecta* 181 (1968): 179–200.

Macuch, Maria, *Das Sasanidische Rechtsbuch "Mātakdān i Hazār Dātistān,"* pt. 2 (Wiesbaden: Harrassowitz Verlag, 1981).

———, "Die Zeitehe im sasanidischen Recht—ein Vorläufer der šī'itischen Mut'a-Ehe in Iran?," *Archaeologische Mitteilungen aus Iran* 18 (1985): 187–203.

———, "Die Erwähnung der Ordalzeremonie des Ādurbād i Māraspandān im Ardā Wīrāz Nāmag," *Archaeologische Mitteilungen aus Iran* 20 (1987): 319–22. [Macuch 1987a]

———, "Sasanidische Institutionen in frühislamischer Zeit," in *Transition Periods in Iranian History: Actes du Symposium de Fribourg-en-Brisgau (22–24 Mai 1985)*, ed. Philippe Gignoux (Leuven: Association pour l'avancement des études iraniennes, 1987), 177–79. [Macuch 1987b]

———, "Ein mittelpersischer *terminus technicus* im syrischen Rechtskodex des Īšōʿbōht und im sasanidischen Rechtsbuch," in *Studia Semitica necnon Iranica: Rudolpho Macuch septuagenario ab amicis et discipulis dedicata*, ed. Macuch (Wiesbaden: Harrassowitz Verlag, 1989), 149–16.

———, "Inzest im vorislamischen Iran," *Archaeologische Mitteilungen aus Iran* 24 (1991): 141–54.

———, *Rechtskasuistik und Gerichtspraxis zu Beginn des siebenten Jahrhunderts in Iran: Die Rechtssammlung des Farroḫmard i Wahrāmān* (Wiesbaden: Harrassowitz Verlag, 1993).

———, "Die sasanidische Stiftung 'für die Seele'—Vorbild für islamischen waqf?" in *Iranian and Indo-European Studies: Memorial Volume of Otakar Kilma*, ed. Petr Vavroušek (Prague: Enigma, 1994), 163–80.

———, "Herrschaftskonsolidierung und sasanidische Familienrecht: Zum Verhältnis von Kirche und Staat unter den Sasaniden," in *Iran und Turfan: Beiträge Berliner Wissenschaftler, Werner Sundermann zum 60. Geburtstag gewidmet*, ed. Christiane Reck and Peter Zieme (Wiesbaden: Harrassowitz Verlag, 1995), 149–67.

———, "The Use of Seals in Sasanian Jurisprudence," in *Sceaux d'Orient et leur emploi*, ed. Rika Gyselen (Bures-sur-Yvette: Groupe pour l'étude de la civilisation du Moyen-Orient, 1997), 79–87.

———, "Iranian Legal Terminology in the Babylonian Talmud in the Light of Sasanian Jurisprudence," *Irano-Judaica* 4 (1999): 91–101.

———, "The Talmudic Expression 'Servant of the Fire' in Light of Pahlavi Legal Sources," *Jerusalem Studies in Arabic and Islam* 26 (2002): 109–29.

———, "On the Treatment of Animals in Zoroastrian Law," in *Iranica selecta: Studies in Honour of Professor Wojciech Skalmowski*, ed. Alois van Tongerloo (Turnhout: Brepols, 2003), 167–90.

———, "Pious Foundations in Byzantine and Sasanian Law," in *La Persia e Bisanzio: Convegno internazionale, Roma 14–18 ottobre 2002*, ed. Antonio Carile, Lellia Cracco Ruggini, Gherardo Gnoli, Giovanni Pugliese Carratelli, and Gianroberto Scarcia (Rome: Accademia Nazionale dei Lincei, 2004), 181–96.

———, "The *Hērbedestān* as a Legal Source: A Section on the Inheritance of a Convert to Zoroastrianism," *Bulletin of the Asia Institute* 19 (2005): 91–102. [Macuch 2005a]

———, "Language and Law: Linguistic Peculiarities in Sasanian Jurisprudence," in *Languages of Iran: Past and Present—Iranian Studies In Memoriam David Neil Mackenzie*, ed. Dieter Weber (Wiesbaden: Harrassowitz Verlag, 2005), 95–108. [Macuch 2005b]

———, "The Function of Temporary Marriage in the Context of Sasanian Family Law," in *Ancient and Middle Iranian Studies*, vol. 1 of *Proceedings of the 5th Conference of the Societas Iranologica Europaea*, ed. Antonio Panaino and Andrea Piras (Milan: Mimesis, 2006), 585–97. [Macuch 2006a]

———, "Inheritance I: Sasanian Period," in *Encyclopedia Iranica*, ed. Ehsan Yarshater, vol. 13 (New York: Routledge and Kegan Paul, 2006), 125–31. [Macuch 2006b]

———, "An Iranian Legal Term in the Babylonian Talmud and in Sasanian Jurisprudence: Dastwar(īh)," *Irano-Judaica* 6 (2008): 126–38.

———, "Pahlavi Literature," in *The Literature of Pre-Islamic Iran: Companion Volume I to "A History of Persian Literature,"* ed. Ronald E. Emmerick and Macuch (London: I. B. Tauris, 2009), 116–96.

———, "Allusions to Sasanian Law in the Babylonian Talmud," in *The Talmud in Its Iranian Context*, ed. Carol Bakhos and M. Rahim Shayegan (Tübingen: Mohr Siebeck, 2010), 100–11. [Macuch 2010a]

———, "Incestuous Marriage in the Context of Sasanian Family Law," in *Ancient and Middle Iranian Studies: Proceedings of the Sixth European Conference of Iranian Studies*, ed. Macuch, Dieter Weber, and Desmond Durkin-Meisterernst (Wiesbaden: Harrassowitz Verlag, 2010), 133–48. [Macuch 2010b]

———, "Legal Constructions of Identity in the Sasanian Period," in *Iranian Identity in the Course of History: Proceedings of the Conference Held in Rome, 21–24 September 2005*, ed. Carlo G. Cereti (Rome: Istituto italiano per l'Africa e l'Oriente, 2010), 193–212. [Macuch 2010c]

Magness, Jodi, "Archaeological Evidence for the Sasanian Persian Invasion of Jerusalem," in *Shaping the Middle East: Jews, Christians, and Muslims in an Age of Transition, 400–800 C.E.*, ed. Kenneth Holum and Hayim Lapin (Bethesda: University Press of Maryland, 2011), 85–98.

Mahé, Jean-Pierre, "Die Bekehrung Transkaukasiens: Eine Historiographie mit doppeltem Boden," in *Die Christianisierung des Kaukasus*, ed. Werner Seibt (Vienna: Verlag der österreichischen Akademie der Wissenschaften, 2002), 107–24.

Malekandathil, Pius, *Maritime India: Trade, Religion and Polity in the Indian Ocean* (Delhi: Primus, 2010).

Mango, Cyril, "Deux études sur Byzance et la Perse sasanide," *Travaux et Mémoires* 9 (1985): 91–118.

———, "The Temple Mount, AD 614–38," in *Bayt al-Maqdis: 'Abd al-Malik's Jerusalem*, ed. Julian Raby and Jeremy Johns (Oxford: Oxford University Press, 1992), 1–16.

Mardirossian, Aram, *Le livre des canons arméniens (Kanonagirk' Hayocc) de Yovhannēs Awjnec'i: Église, droit, et société en Arménie du IVe au VIIIe siècle* (Leuven: Peeters, 2004).

Mariès, Louis, *Le De Deo d'Eznik de Kołb, connu sous le nom de "Contre les Sectes": Études de critique littéraire et textuelle* (Paris: Imprimerie orientale, 1924).

Markus, Robert, "How on Earth Could Places Become Holy? Origins of the Christian Idea of Holy Places," *Journal of Early Christian Studies* 2 (1994): 257–72.

Markwart, Joseph, *A Catalogue of the Provincial Capitals of Ērānšahr (Pahlavi Text, Version and Commentary)* (Rome: Pontificio istituto biblico, 1931).

Marlow, Louise, *Hierarchy and Egalitarianism in Islamic Thought* (Cambridge: Cambridge University Press, 1987).

Martin-Hisard, Bernadette, "Le 'Martyre d'Eustathe de Mcxeta': Aspects de la vie politique et religieuse en Ibérie à l'époque de Justinien," in *Eupsychia: Mélanges offerts à Hélène Ahrweiler*, vol. 2, ed. Michel Balard, Joëlle Beaucamp, Jean-Claude Cheynet, Catherine Jolivet-Lévy, Michel Kaplan, Martin-Hisard, Paule Pagès, Catherine Piganiol, and Jean-Pierre Sodini (Paris: Publications de la Sorbonne, 1998), 493–520.

———, "Controverses chrétiennes en terre géorgienne à l'époque sassanide dans la littérature géorgienne originale," in *Controverses chrétiens dans l'Iran sassanide*, ed. Christelle Jullien (Paris: Association pour l'advancement des études iraniennes, 2008), 171–90.

McDonough, Scott John, "Power by Negotiation: Institutional Reform in the Fifth Century Sasanian Empire" (PhD diss., University of California–Los Angeles, 2005).

———, "A Question of Faith? Persecution and Political Centralization in the Sasanian Empire of Yazdgard II (438–57 CE)," in *Violence in Late Antiquity: Perceptions and Practices*, ed. Hal A. Drake (Aldershot: Ashgate, 2006), 69–81.

———, "Bishops or Bureaucrats? Christian Clergy and the State in the Middle Sasanian Period," in *Current Research in Sasanian Archaeology, Art and History*, ed. Derek Kennet and Paul Luft (Oxford: Archaeopress, 2008), 87–92. [McDonough 2008a]

———, "A Second Constantine? The Sasanian King Yazdgard in Christian History and Historiography," *Journal of Late Antiquity* 1 (2008): 127–40. [McDonough 2008b]

———, "The Legs of the Throne: Kings, Elites, and Subjects in Sasanian Iran," in *The Roman Empire in Context: Historical and Comparative Perspectives*, ed. Johann P. Arnason and Kurt A. Raaflaub (Malden: Wiley, 2011), 290–321. [McDonough 2011a]

———, "Were the Sasanians Barbarians? Roman Writers on the 'Empire of the Persians,'" in *Romans, Barbarians, and the Transformation of the Roman World: Cultural Interaction and the Creation of Identity in Late Antiquity*, ed. Ralph Mathison and Danuta Shanzer (Farnham: Ashgate, 2011), 55–65. [McDonough 2011b]

Menasce, Jean de, "Autour d'un texte syriaque inédit sur la religion des Mages," *Bulletin of the School of Oriental and African Studies* 9 (1937–39): 587–601.

———, "Inscriptions pehlevies en écriture cursive," *Journal Asiatique* 244 (1956): 423–31.

———, "La conquête de l'Iranisme et la récupération des mages hellenisés,"*Annuaire de l'École Pratique des Hautes Études: Section des Sciences Religieuses* (1956–57): 3–12.

———, "Refléxions sur Zurvān," in *A Locust's Leg: Studies in Honour of S. H. Taqizadeh*, ed. W. B. Henning and Ehsan Yarshater (London: Percy Lund, 1962), 182–88.

———, "Le protecteur des pauvres dans l'Iran sassanide," in *Mélanges d'orientalisme offerts à Henri Massé* (Tehran: Imprimerie de l'université, 1963), 282–87.

———, "Some Pahlavi Words in the Original and in the Syriac Translation of Išōbōxt's Corpus juris," in *Études iraniennes* (Paris: Asssociation pour l'avancement des études iraniennes, 1985), 119–24.

Menze, Volker, *Justinian and the Making of the Syrian Orthodox Church* (Oxford: Oxford University Press, 2008).

Metzler, David, "Ziele und Formen königlicher Innenpolitik im vorislamischen Iran" (PhD diss., Universität Münster, 1977).

Meytarchiyan, M., *Pogrebalnie Obryadi Zoroastriitsev* (Moscow: Letnii Sad, 2001).

Millar, Fergus, *A Greek Roman Empire: Power and Belief under Theodosius II (408–450)* (Berkeley: University of Cailfornia Press, 2006).

Minov, Sergey, "Iranskie Motivi v 'Peshchere Sokrovishch' i Problemi Akkulturatsii Siriiskikh Khristian v Sasanidskoi Imperii," *Simvol: Zhurnal Khristianskoi Kulturi* (2012): 9–70.

———, "Regarder la montagne sacrée: Représentations du paradis dans la tradition chrétienne syrienne," in *Mondes clos: Cultures et jardins*, ed. Daniel Barbu, Philippe Borgeaud, Mélanie Lozat, and Youri Volokhine (Gollion: Infolio, 2013), 241–69.

Moazami, Mahnaz, "Ancient Iranian Civil Legislation: A Legal Section of the Pahlavi *Vidēvdād*," *Studia Iranica* 30 (2001): 199–224.
———, "Evil Animals in the Zoroastrian Religion," *History of Religions* 44 (2005): 300–317.
Mokhtarian, Jason Sion, "Rabbinic Depictions of the Achaemenid King Cyrus the Great," in *The Talmud in Its Iranian Context*, ed. Carol Bakhos and M. Rahim Shayegan (Tübingen: Mohr Siebeck, 2010), 112–39.
———, "Empire and Authority in Sasanian Babylonia: The Rabbis and King Shapur In Dialogue," *Jewish Studies Quarterly* 19 (2012): 148–80.
Molé, Marijan, "Le problème zurvanite," *Journal Asiatique* 247 (1959): 431–69.
———, "Le problème des sectes zoroastriennes dans les livres pehlevis," *Oriens* 13–14 (1960–61): 1–28.
Monneret de Villard, Ugo, *Le chiese della Mesopotamia* (Rome: Pontificium institutum orientalium studiorum, 1940).
Monnickendam, Yifat, "The Kiss and the Earnest: Early Roman Influences on Syriac Matrimonial Law," *Le Muséon* 125 (2012): 307–34.
Morony, Michael, "Religious Communities in Late Sasanian and Early Muslim Iraq,' *Journal of the Economic and Social History of the Orient* 17 (1974): 113–35.
———, "The Effects of the Muslim Conquest on the Persian Population of Iraq," *Iran* 14 (1976): 41–59.
———, "Landholding in Seventh-Century Iraq: Late Sasanian and Early Islamic Patterns," in *The Islamic Middle East, 700–1900: Studies in Economic and Social History*, ed. Abraham L. Udovitch (Princeton: Darwin, 1981), 135–75.
———, *Iraq after the Muslim Conquest* (Princeton: Princeton University Press, 1984).
———, "Land Use and Settlement Patterns in Late Sasanian and Early Islamic Iraq," in *The Byzantine and Early Islamic Near East*, vol. 2, *Land Use and Settlement Patterns*, ed. G. R. D. King and Averil Cameron (Princeton: Darwin, 1994), 221–29.
———, "The Late Sasanian Economic Impact on the Arabian Peninsula," *Nāme-ye Irān-e Bāstān* (2001–2): 25–37.
———, "Magic and Society in Late Sasanian Iraq," in *Prayer, Magic, and the Stars in the Ancient and Late Antique World*, ed. Scott Noegel and Joel Walker (University Park: Pennsylvania State University, 2003), 83–107.
———, "Population Transfers between Sasanian Iran and the Byzantine Empire," in *La Persia e Bisanzio: Convegno internazionale, Roma 14–18 ottobre 2002*, ed. Antonio Carile, Lellia Cracco Ruggini, Gherardo Gnoli, Giovanni Pugliese Carratelli, and Gianroberto Scarcia (Rome: Accademia dei Lincei, 2004), 161–79. [Morony 2004a]
———, "Social Elites in Iraq and Iran: After the Conquest," in *The Byzantine and Early Islamic Near East*, vol. 6, *Elites Old and New in the Byzantine and Early Islamic Near East*, ed. John Haldon and Lawrence I. Conrad (Princeton: Darwin, 2004), 275–84. [Morony 2004b]
———, "History and Identity in the Syrian Churches," in *Redefining Christian Identity: Cultural Interaction in the Middle East since the Rise of Islam*, ed. J. J. van Ginkel H. L. Murre-van den Berg, T. M. van Lint (Peeters: Leuven, 2005), 1–33.
Mosig-Walburg, Karin, "Zur Westpolitik Shāpūrs II," in *Iran: Questions et connaissances, Actes du IVe congrès européen des études iraniennes*, vol. 1, ed. Philippe Huyse (Leuven: Peeters, 2002), 329–47.

———, "Christenverfolgung und Römerkrieg: Zu Ursachen, Ausmaß und Zielrichtung der Christenverfolgung unter Šāpūr II.," *Iranistik* 7 (2005): 5-84.

———, "Die Christenverfolgung Shapurs II. vor dem Hintergrund des persisch-römischen Krieges," in *Inkulturation des Christentums im Sasanidenreich*, ed. Arafa Mustafa, Jürgen Tubach, and G. Sophia Vashalomidze (Wiesbaden: Reichert Verlag, 2007), 171-86.

———, "Deportationen römischer Christen in das Sasanidenreich durch Shapur I. und ihre Folgen—Eine Neubewertung," *Klio* 92 (2010): 117-56. [Mosig-Walburg 2010a]

———, "Königtum und Adel in der Regierungs Zeit Ardashirs II., Shapurs III., und Wahrams IV.," in *Commutatio et contentio: Studies in the Late Roman, Sasanian, and Early Islamic Near East in Memory of Zeev Rubin*, ed. Henning Börm and Josef Wiesehöfer (Düsseldorf: Wellem Verlag, 2010), 159-98. [Mosig-Walburg 2010b]

Moss, Candida, *Ancient Christian Martyrdom: Diverse Practices, Theologies, and Traditions* (New Haven: Yale University Press, 2012).

Movassat, Johanna D., *The Large Vault at Taq-i Bustan: A Study in Late Sasanian Royal Art* (Lewiston: Edwin Mellon, 2005).

Müller, C. D. G., "Die ältere Kirchenrechtsliteratur der Perserkirche," *Oriens Christianus* 59 (1975): 47-59.

Müller-Kessler, Christa, and Karlheinz Kessler, "Spätbabylonische Gottheiten in spätantiken mandäischen Texten," *Zeitschrift für Assyriologie* 89 (1999): 65-87.

Nau, François, "Étude historique sur la transmission de l'Avesta et sur l'époque probable de sa dernière rédaction," *Revue de l'histoire des religions* 95 (1927): 149-99.

Naymark, Alexander, "Sogdiana, Its Christians and Byzantium: A Study of Artistic and Cultural Connections in Late Antiquity and Early Middle Ages" (PhD diss., University of Indiana, Bloomington, 2001).

Neusner, Jacob, *From Shapur I to Shapur II*, vol. 3 of *A History of the Jews in Babylonia* (Leiden: E. J. Brill, 1968).

Nirenberg, David, *Communities of Violence: Persecution of Minorities in the Middle Ages* (Princeton: Princeton University Press, 1996).

Noble, Thomas F. X., "Secular Sanctity: Forging an Ethos for the Carolingian Nobility," in *Lay Intellectuals in the Carolingian World*, ed. Patrick Wormald and Janet Nelson (Cambridge: Cambridge University Press, 2007), 8-36.

Nöldeke, Theodore, *Geschichte der Perser und Araber zur Zeit der Sasaniden* (Leiden: Brill, 1879).

———, "Syrische Polemik gegen die persische Religion," *Festgruss an Rudolf von Roth zum Doktor-Jubiläum 24. August 1893 von seinen Freunden und Schülern* (Stuttgart: W. Kohlhammer, 1893), 34-38.

———, *Das iranische Nationalepos* (Berlin: De Gruyter, 1920).

Nováček, Karel, Narmin Ali Muhammad Amin, and Miroslav Melčák, "A Medieval City within Assyrian Walls: The Continuity of the Town of Arbīl in Northern Mesopotamia," *Iraq* 75 (2013): 1-42.

Nyberg, Henrik S., "Questions de cosmogonie et de cosmologie mazdéennes," *Journal Asiatique* 214 (1929): 193-310.

———, "Questions de cosmogonie et de cosmologie mazdéennes II: Analyse des données," *Journal Asiatique* 216 (1931): 1-134, 193-244.

———, *Irans Forntida Religioner* (Uppsala: Almkvist och Wiksell Boktryckeri, 1937).

Ohme, Heinz, *Kanon Ekklesiastikos: Die Bedeutung des altkirchlichen Kanonbegriffs* (Berlin: Walter de Gruyter, 1998).
Olajos, Thérèse, *Les sources de Théophylacte Simocatta historien* (Leiden: Brill, 1988).
Olster, David, *The Politics of Usurpation in the Seventh Century: Rhetoric and Revolution in Byzantium* (Amsterdam: Adolf M. Hakkert, 1993).
———, *Roman Defeat, Christian Response, and the Literary Construction of the Jew* (Philadelphia: University of Pennsylvania Press, 1994).
Orsatti, Paola, "Syro-Persian Formulas in Poetic Form in Baptismal Liturgy," in *Persian Origins: Early Judaeo-Persian and the Emergence of New Persian—Collected Papers of the Symposium, Göttingen 1999*, ed. Ludwig Paul (Wiesbaden: Harrassowitz Verlag, 2003), 147–76.
Overlaet, Bruno, "Čāle Ğār (Kāšān Area) and Votives, *favissae*, and Cave Deposits in Pre-Islamic and Islamic Traditions," *Archäologische Mitteilungen aus Iran und Turan* 43 (2011): 113–40.
———, "And Man Created God? Kings, Priests and Gods on Sasanian Investiture Reliefs," *Iranica Antiqua* 48 (2013) 313–54.
Panaino, Antonio, "La Chiesa di Persia e l'impero Sasanide: Conflitto e integrazione," in *Settimane di studio della Fondazione Centro italiano di studi sull'alto Medioevo 51: Cristianità d'Occidente e cristianità d'Oriente* (Spoleto: Fondazione Centro italiano di studi sull'alto Medioevo, 2004), 765–863.
———, "Women and Kingship: Some Remarks about the Enthronisation of Queen Boran and Her Sister Azarmigduxt," in *Ērān ud Anērān: Studien zu den Bzeihungen zwischen dem Sasanidenreich und der Mittelmeerwelt*, ed. Josef Wiesehöfer and Philip Huyse (Stuttgart: Franz Steiner, 2006), 221–40.
———, "The Pāzand Version of the Our Father," in *Inkulturation des Christentums im Sasanidenreich*, ed. Arafa Mustafa and Jürgen Tubach (Wiesbaden: Reichert, 2007), 73–90.
———, "The Zoroastrian Incestuous Unions and Christian Sources and Canonical Laws: Their (Distorted) Aetiology and Some of the Problems," in *Controverses chrétiens dans l'Iran sassanide*, ed. Christelle Jullien (Paris: Association pour l'avancement des etudes iraniennes, 2008), 69–87.
Partsch, J., "Neue Rechtsquellen der nestorianischen Kirche," *Zeitschrift der Savigny-Stiftung für Rechtsgeschichte* 30 (1909): 355–98.
Patlagean, Évelyne, "Ancienne hagiographie byzantine et histoire sociale," *Annales: Economies, Sociétés, Civilisations* 23 (1968): 106–26.
———, *Pauvreté économique et pauvreté sociale à Byzance, 4ᵉ–7ᵉ siècles* (Paris: Mouton, 1977).
Payne, Richard, "Persecuting Heresy in Early Islamic Iraq: The Catholicos Ishoyahb III and the Elites of Nisibis," in *The Power of Religion in Late Antiquity*, ed. Noel Lenski and Andrew Cain (Aldershot: Ashgate, 2009), 397–409.
———, "The Emergence of Martyrs' Shrines in Late Antique Iran: Conflict, Consensus, and Communal Institutions," in *An Age of Saints? Conflict and Dissent in the Cult of Saints (300–1000 AC)*, ed. Matthew dal Santo and Philip Booth (Leiden: Brill, 2011), 89–113. [Payne 2011a]
———, "Monks, Dinars, and Date Palms: Hagiographical Production and the Expansion of Monastic Institutions in the Early Islamic Persian Gulf," *Arabian Archaeology and Epigraphy* 22 (2011): 97–111. [Payne 2011b]

———, "Avoiding Ethnicity: Uses of the Past in Late Antique Northern Mesopotamia," in *Visions of Community in the Post-Roman World: The West, Byzantium, and the Islamic World, 300–1100*, ed. Walter Pohl, Clemens Gantner, and Richard Payne (Farnham: Ashgate, 2012), 205–21.

———, "Cosmology and the Expansion of the Iranian Empire, 502–628 CE," *Past and Present* 220 (2013): 3–33.

———, "The Reinvention of Iran: The Sasanian Empire and the Huns," in *The Cambridge Companion to the Age of Attila*, ed. Michael Maas (Cambridge: Cambridge University Press, 2014), 282–99.

———, "East Syrian Bishops, Elite Households, and Iranian Law after the Islamic Conquest," *Iranian Studies* 48 (2015): 5–32.

Peeters, Paul, "S. Eleutherios-Guhištazad," *Analecta Bollandiana* 29 (1910): 151–56.

———, "S. Démétrianus évêque d'Antioche?," *Analecta Bollandiana* 42 (1924): 288–314.

———, "Le 'Passionnaire d'Adiabène,'" *Analecta Bollandiana* 43 (1925): 261–304.

———, "Les ex-voto de Khosrau Aparwez à Sergiopolis," *Analecta Bollandiana* 65 (1947): 5–56.

———, *Orient et Byzance: Le tréfonds oriental de l'hagiographie byzantine* (Brussels: Société des Bollandistes, 1950).

———, "Observations sur la vie syriaque de Mar Aba, catholicos de l'Église perse (540–552)," in *Recherches d'histoire et de philologie orientales*, ed. Peeters, vol. 1 (Brussels: Société des Bollandistes, 1951), 117–63.

Perikhanian, Anahit, "Agnaticheskie Gruppi v Drevnem Irane," *Vestnik Drevnei Istorii* (1968): 28–53. [Perikhanian 1968a]

———, "Notes sur le lexique iranien at arménien," *Revue des études arméniennes* 5 (1968): 9–30. [Perikhanian 1968b]

———, "Ordalya i Klyatva v Sudoproizvodstve Doislamskovo Irana," *Peredneaziatskii Sbornik* 3 (1979): 182–92.

———, "Iranian Society and Law," in *The Cambridge History of Iran*, vol. 3(2), *The Seleucid, Parthian and Sasanian Periods*, ed. Ehsan Yarshater (Cambridge: Cambridge University, 1983), 627–80. [Perikhanian 1983a]

———, *Obshchestvo i Pravo Irana v Parfyanskii i Sasanidskii Periodi* (Moscow: Izdatelstvo Nauka, 1983). [Perikhanian 1983b]

Piccirillo, Michele, "The Province of Arabia during the Persian Invasion (613–629/630)," in *Shaping the Middle East: Jews, Christians, and Muslims in an Age of Transition, 400–800 CE*, ed. Kenneth Holum and Hayim Lapin (Bethesda: University Press of Maryland, 2011), 99–114.

Pierre, Marie-Joseph, "Thèmes de la controverse d'Aphraate avec les tendances judaïsantes de son Église," in *Controverse des chrétiens dans l'Iran sassanide*, ed. Christelle Jullien (Paris: Association pour l'avancement des études iraniennes, 2008), 115–28.

Pietruschka, Ute, "Topoi in der Schilderung nomadischen Lebens in der syrischen Literatur," in *Edessa in hellenistisch-römischer Zeit: Religion, Kultur, und Politik zwischen Ost und West*, ed. Lutz Greisiger, Claudia Rammelt, and Jürgen Tubach (Beirut: Ergon Verlag, 2009), 209–17.

Pigulevskaya, Nina, *Vizantiya i Iran na rubezhe VI i VII vekov* (Moscow: Izdatelstvo Akademii Nauk SSSR, 1946).

———, "Mar Aba I: K istorii kulturi VI veka," *Sovetskoe Vostokovedenie* 5 (1948): 73–84.

———, "Iuridicheskie Pamyatniki Epokhi Sasanidov (Pekhleviiskii Sbornik 'Matikan' i Siriiskii Sbornik Ishobokhta)," in *Pamyati Akademika Ignatiya Yulianovicha Krachkovskovo*, ed. I. A. Orbeli (Leningrad Izdatelstvo Leningradskovo Universiteta, 1958), 163–75. [Pigulevskaya 1958a]

———, "Zarozhdenie Feodalnikh Otnoshenii na Blizhnem Vostoke," *Uchenie Zapiski Instituta Vostokovedeniya* 16 (1958): 5–30. [Pigulevskaya 1958b]

———, "Mar Aba I: Une page de l'histoire de la civilisation au VIe siècle de l'ère nouvelle," in *Mélanges d'orientalisme offerts à Henri Massé* (Tehran: Imprimerie de l'université, 1963), 327–36. [Pigulevskaya 1963a]

———, *Les villes de l'état iranien aux époques parthe et sassanide: Contribution à l'histoire sociale de la Basse Antiquité* (Paris: Mouton, 1963). [Pigulevskaya 1963b]

———, *Arabi u Granits Vizantii i Irana v IV-VI vv.* (Moscow: Izdatelstvo Nauka, 1964).

———, *Kultura Siriitsev v Srednie Veka* (Moscow: Nauka, 1979).

———, *Siriiskaya Srednevekovaya Istoriografiya* (St. Petersburg: Rossiiskaya Akademiya Nauk, 2000).

Pinggéra, Karl, "Nestorius in der 'nestorianischen' Kirche: Streiflichter zum Selbstverständnis der Apostolischen Kirche des Ostens," in *"Prüft alles, und das Gute behaltet!": Zum Wechselspiel von Kirchen, Religionen und säkularer Welt*, ed. Friederike Schönemann and Thorsten Maaßen (Frankfurt: Lembeck, 2004), 190–213.

———, "Nestorianische Weltchronistik: Johannes Bar Penkaye und Elias von Nisibis," in *Julius Africanus und die christliche Weltchronistik*, ed. Martin Wallraff (Berlin: Walter de Gruyter, 2006), 263–83.

Potter, David, "Martyrdom as Spectacle," in *Theater and Society in the Classical World*, ed. R. Schoedel (Ann Arbor: University of Michigan Press, 1993), 53–88.

Pottier, Henri, *Le monnayage de la Syrie sous l'occupation Perse (610–630)* (Paris: Centre national de la recherche scientifique, 2004).

Pourshariati, Parvaneh, "Recently Discovered Seals of Wistaxm, Uncle of Husraw II?," *Studia Iranica* 35 (2006): 163–80.

———, *Decline and Fall of the Sasanian Empire: The Sasanian-Parthian Confederacy and the Arab Conquest of Iran* (London: I. B. Tauris, 2008).

———, "The Mihrāns and the Articulation of Islamic Dogma: A Preliminary Prosopographical Analysis," in *Trésors d'Orient: Mélanges offerts à Rika Gyselen*, ed. Philippe Gignoux, Christelle Jullien, and Florence Jullien (Paris: Association pour l'avancement des études iraniennes, 2009), 283–315.

———, "The *Akhbār al-ṭiwāl* of Abū Ḥanīfa Dīnawarī: A *Shuʿūbī* Treatise on Late Antique Iran," in *Sources for the History of Sasanian and Post-Sasanian Iran*, ed. Rika Gyselen (Bures-sur-Yvette: Groupe pour l'étude de la civilisation du Moyen-Orient, 2010), 201–39. [Pourshariati 2010a]

———, "The Parthians and the Production of the Canonical Shāhnāmas: Of Pahlavī, Pahlavānī and the Pahlav," in *Commutatio et contentio: Studies in the Late Roman, Sasanian, and Early Islamic Near East in Memory of Zeev Rubin*, ed. Henning Börm and Josef Wiesehöfer (Düsseldorf: Wellem Verlag, 2010), 347–92. [Pourshariati 2010b]

Pratsch, Thomas, *Der hagiographische Topos: Griechische Heiligenviten in mittelbyzantinischer Zeit* (Berlin: Walter de Gruyter, 2005).

Prinz, Friedrich, "Heiligenkult und Adelherrschaft im Spiegel Merowingischer Hagiographie," *Historische Zeitschrift* 204 (1967): 528–44.
Rapaport, Yossef, *Marriage, Money and Divorce in Medieval Islamic Society* (Cambridge: Cambridge University Press, 2005).
Rapp, Claudia, *Holy Bishops in Late Antiquity: The Nature of Christian Leadership in an Age of Transition* (Berkeley: University of California Press, 2005).
Rapp, Stephen H., Jr., "From *Bumberazi* to *Basileus*: Writing Cultural Synthesis and Dynastic Change in Medival Georgia (K'art'li)," in *Eastern Approaches to Byzantium: Papers from the Thirty-Third Spring Symposium of Byzantine Studies, University of Warwick, Coventry, March 1999*, ed. Antony Eastmond (Aldershot: Ashgate, 2001), 101–16.
——— , *Studies in Medieval Georgian Historiography: Early Texts and Eurasian Contexts* (Leuven: Peeters, 2003).
——— , "The Iranian Heritage of Georgia: Breathing New Life into the Pre-Bagratid Historiographical Tradition," *Iranica Antiqua* 44 (2009): 645–92.
Reade, Julian P., "Greco-Parthian Nineveh," *Iraq* 60 (1998): 65–83.
Reinink, Gerrit J., "'Edessa Grew Dim and Nisibis Shone Forth': The School of Nisibis at the Transition of the Sixth–Seventh Century," in *Centres of Learning: Learning and Location in Pre-modern Europe and the Near East*, ed. Jan Willem Drijvers and A. A. MacDonald (Leiden: Brill, 1995), 77–89.
——— , "Babai the Great's *Life of George* and the Propagation of Doctrine in the Late Sasanian Empire," in *Portraits of Spiritual Authority: Religious Power in Early Christianity, Byzantium, and the Christian Orient*, ed. Jan Willem Drijvers and John M. Watt (Leiden: Brill, 1999), 171–94.
——— , "Theology and Medicine in Jundishapur: Cultural Change in the Nestorian School Tradition," in *Learned Antiquity: Scholarship and Society in the Near East, the Greco-Roman World, and the Early Medieval West*, ed. Alasdair A. MacDonald, Michael W. Twomey, and Reinink (Leuven: Peeters, 2003), 163–74.
——— , "East Syrian Historiography in Response to the Rise of Islam: the Case of John bar Penkaye's *Ktaba D-Res Melle*," in *Redefining Christian Identity: Cultural Interaction in the Middle East since the Rise of Islam*, ed. J. J. van Ginkel, H. L. Murre-van den Berg, and T. M. van Lint (Leuven: Peeters, 2005), 77–89.
Rezania, Kianoosh, "Zurvan: Limitless Time or Timeless Time? The Question of Eternity and Time in Zoroastrianism," *Journal of the K. R. Cama Institute* 68 (2008): 48–71.
——— , *Die zoroastrische Zeitvorstellung: Eine Untersuchung über Zeit- und Ewigkeitsvorstellungen und die Frage des Zurvanismus* (Wiesbaden: Harrassowitz Verlag, 2010).
——— , "Mazdakism and the Canonisation of Pahlavi Translations of the Avestan Texts," in *The Transmission of the Avesta*, ed. Alberto Cantera (Wiesbaden: Harrassowitz Verlag, 2012), 479–94.
Ri, Andreas Su-Min, *Commentaire de la "Caverne des trésors": Étude sur l'histoire du texte et de ses sources* (Leuven: Peeters, 2000).
Richardson, Seth, "The First 'World Event': Sennacherib at Jerusalem," in *Sennacherib at the Gates of Jerusalem: Story, History and Historiography*, ed. Isaac Kalimi and Richardson (Leiden: Brill, 2014), 433–505.
Rist, Josef, "Die Verfolgung der Christen im spätantiken Sasanidenreich: Ursachen, Verlauf und Folgen," *Oriens Christianus* 80 (1996): 17–42.

———, "Geschichte und Geschichten: Die Christenverfolgungen in Edessa und ihr populäres Echo in den syrischen Märtyrerakten," in *Volksglaube im antiken Christentum*, ed. Heike Grieser and Andrew Merkt (Darmstadt: Wissenschaftliche Buchgesellschaft, 2009), 157–75.

Ritter, Nils C., "Altorientalische Ikonographie in neuem Gewand: Zur Darstellung Daniels in der Löwengrube auf einer Spätantiken Tonlampe aus Tell Feḥerīye," in *Fundstellen: Gesammelte Schriften zur Archäologie und Geschichte ad honorem Hartmut Kühne*, ed. Dominik Bonatz, Rainer M. Czichon, and F. J. Kreppner (Wiesbaden: Harrassowitz Verlag, 2008), 163–73.

Robinson, Chase, *Empire and Elites after the Muslim Conquest: The Transformation of Northern Mesopotamia* (Cambridge: Cambridge University Press, 2000).

———, "The Chronicle of Khūzistān: A Historiographical Reassessment," *Bulletin of the School of Oriental and African Studies* 67 (2004): 14–39.

Rothstein, Gustav, *Die Dynastie der Lakhmiden in al-Ḥīra: Ein Versuch zur arabisch-persischen Geschichte zur Zeit der Sasaniden* (Berlin: Reuther und Reichard, 1899).

Rubin, Zeev, "The Reforms of Khusro Anushirvan," in *The Byzantine and Early Islamic Near East*, vol. 3, *States, Resources, and Armies*, ed. Averil Cameron (Princeton: Darwin, 1995), 227–97.

———, "The Sassanid Monarchy," in *The Cambridge Ancient History*, vol. 14, *Late Antiquity: Empire and Successors, A.D. 425–600*, ed. Averil Cameron, Bryan Ward-Perkins, and Michael Whitby (Cambridge: Cambridge University Press, 2000), 638–61.

———, "Nobility, Monarchy and Legitimation under the Later Sasanians," in *The Byzantine and Early Islamic Near East*, vol. 6, *Elites Old and New in the Byzantine and Early Islamic Near East*, ed. John Haldon and Lawrence I. Conrad (Princeton: Darwin, 2004), 235–73.

———, "Ibn al-Muqaffaʿ and the Account of Sasanian History in the Arabic Codex Sprenger 30," *Jerusalem Studies in Arabic and Islam* 30 (2005): 52–93.

———, "Islamic Traditions on the Sāsānian Conquest of the Ḥimyarite Realm," *Der Islam* 84 (2007): 185–99.

———, "Ḥamza al-Iṣfahānī's Sources for Sasanian History," *Jerusalem Studies in Arabic and Islam* 35 (2008): 27–58. [Rubin 2008a]

———, "Al-Ṭabarī and the Age of the Sasanians," in *Al-Ṭabarī: A Medival Muslim Historian and His Work*, ed. Hugh Kennedy (Princeton: Darwin, 2008), 41–71. [Rubin 2008b]

Rücker, Adolf, *Die Canones des Simeon von Rêvârdašîr* (Leipzig: W. Drugulin, 1908).

Russell, James R., "Bad Day at Burzēn Mihr: Notes on an Armenian Legend of St. Bartholomew," *Bazmavep* 144 (1985): 255–67.

———, *Zoroastrianism in Armenia* (Cambridge, MA: Harvard University Press, 1987).

———, "Christianity i. In Pre-Islamic Persia: Literary Sources," in *Encylopaedia Iranica*, ed. Ehsan Yarshater vol. 5 (Costa Mesa: Mazda, 1992), 523–28.

———, "A Manichaean Apostolic Mission to Armenia?," in *Proceedings of the Third European Conference of Iranian Studies*, ed. Nicholas Sims-Williams (Wiesbaden: Reichert, 1999), 21–26.

Sachau, Eduard, "Von den rechtlichen Verhältnissen der Christen im Sasanidenreich," *Mitteilungen des Seminars für Orientalische Sprachen* 10 (1907): 69–95.

———, "Vom Christentum in der Persis," *Sitzungsberichte der königlichen preussischen Akademie der Wissenschaften—Sitzung der philosophisch-historischen Klasse* 39 (1916): 958–80.

Saeki, P. Y. *The Nestorian Monument in China* (London: Society for Promoting Christian Knowledge, 1916).

Sako, Louis, *Le rôle de la hiérarchie syriaque orientale dans les rapports diplomatiques entre la Perse et Byzance aux Ve–VIIe siècles* (Paris: Université de Paris IV, 1986).

Saller, Richard, *Patriarchy, Property, and Death in the Roman Family* (Cambridge: Cambridge University Press, 1994).

Salveson, Alison, "The Legacy of Babylon and Nineveh in Aramaic Sources," in *The Legacy of Mesopotamia*, ed. Stephanie Dalley (Oxford: Oxford University Press, 1998), 139–61.

Sänger, Patrick, "The Administration of Sasanian Egypt: New Masters and Byzantine Continuity," *Greek, Roman, and Byzantine Studies* 51 (2011): 653–65.

Sarris, Peter, *Empires of Faith: The Fall of Rome to the Rise of Islam, 500–700* (Oxford: Oxford University Press, 2011).

Satlow, Michael L., *Jewish Marriage in Antiquity* (Princeton: Princeton University, 2001).

Savant, Sarah, *The New Muslims of Post-Conquest Iran: Tradition, Memory, and Conversion* (Cambridge: Cambridge University Press, 2013).

Scarcia, Gianroberto, "Cosroe secondo, San Sergio e il Sade," *Studi sull'Oriente Cristiano* 4 (2000): 171–227.

———, "Sergio/Sorush in Firdusi?," in *Religious Themes and Texts of Pre-Islamic Iran and Central Asia: Studies in Honor of Professor Gherardo Gnoli*, ed. Carlo G. Cereti, Mauro Maggi, and Elio Provasi (Wiesbaden: Ludwig Reichert Verlag, 2003), 353–61.

Scheidel, Walter, "Emperors, Aristocrats, and the Grim Reaper: Toward a Demographic Profile of the Roman Élite," *The Classical Quarterly* 49 (1999): 254–81.

Schilling, Alexander Markus, *Die Anbetung der Magier und die Taufe der Sāsāniden: Zur Geistesgeschichte des iranischen Christentums in der Spätantike* (Leuven: Peeters, 2008). [Schilling 2008a]

———, "L'apôtre du Christ, la conversion du roi Ardašīr et celle de som vizir," in *Controverses chrétiens dans l'Iran sassanide*, ed. Christelle Jullien (Paris: Association pour avancement des études iraniennes, 2008), 89–111. [Schilling 2008b]

Schindel, Nikolaus, *Sylloge Nummorum Sasanidarum Paris-Berlin-Wien*, vol. 3, pt. 1 (Vienna: Verlag der österreichischen Akademie der Wissenschaften, 2004).

Schippmann, Klaus, *Die iranischen Feuerheiligtümer* (Berlin: Walter De Gruyter, 1971).

Schmidt, Andrea, *Kanon der Entschlafenen: Das Begräbnisrituale der Armenier, der altarmenische Bestattungsritus für die Laien* (Wiesbaden: Harrassowitz Verlag, 1994).

Schmidt, J. Heinrich, "L'expédition de Ctésiphon en 1931–1932," *Syria* 15 (1934): 1–23.

Schrier, Omert J., "Syriac Evidence for the Roman-Persian War of 421–422," *Greek, Roman, and Byzantine Studies* 33 (1992): 75–86.

Schwaigert, Wolfgang, "Aspects of the Persecution of Christians in the Sasanian Empire during the Reign of Shapur II (309–79)," *Harp* 2 (1988): 73–82.

———, "Das Christentum im Ḥūzistān im Rahmen der frühen Kirchengeschichte Persiens bis zur Synode von Seleukeia-Ktesiphon im Jahre 410" (PhD diss., Philipps-Universität Marburg, 1989).

———, "Miles und Papa: Der Kampf um den Primat," in *V Symposium Syriacum 1988*, ed. René Lavenant (Rome: Pontificium institutum orientalium studiorum, 1990), 393–402.

———, "Katholikos Isaak (399–410 n. Chr.) und seine Zeit: Ein Beitrag zur nestorianischen Patriarchengeschichte," in *Syrisches Christentum weltweit: Studien zur syrischen Kirchengeschichte*, ed. Martin Tamcke, Schwaigert, and Egbert Schlarb (Münster: Lit, 1995), 180–89.

Schwartz, Daniel, *Paideia and Cult: Christian Initiation in Theodore of Mopsuestia* (Washington DC: Center for Hellenic Studies, 2013).

Secunda, Shai, "Studying with a Magus/Like Giving a Tongue to a Wolf," *Bulletin of the Asia Institute* 19 (2005): 151–57.

———, "On the Age of Zoroastrian Authorities of the Zand," *Iranica Antiqua* 46 (2012): 317–49.

———, *The Iranian Talmud: Reading the Bavli in Its Sasanian Context* (Philadelphia: University of Pennsylvania Press, 2014).

Segal, J. B., *Edessa: 'The Blessed City'* (Oxford: Clarendon, 1970).

———, "The Arabs in Syriac Literature before the Rise of Islam," *Jerusalem Studies in Arabic and Islam* 4 (1984): 89–124.

Selb, Walter, *Orientalisches Kirchenrecht*, vol. 1 (Vienna: Verlag der österreichischen Akademie der Wissenschaften, 1981).

———, "Zur Christianisierung des Eherechts," in *Eherecht und Familiengut in Antike und Mittelalter*, ed. Dieter Simon (Munich: Oldenbourg, 1992), 1–14.

Selb, Walter, and Hubert Kaufhold, *Das syrisch-römische Rechtsbuch* (Vienna: Verlag der österreichischen Akademie der Wissenschaften, 2002).

Seleznyov, Nikolai, *Nestorii i Tserkov Vostoka* (Moscow: Put, 2005).

———, "Iraklii i Ishoyav II: Vostochnii Epizod v Istorii 'Ekumenicheskovo' Proyekta Vizantiiskovo Imperatora," *Simvol: Zhurnal Khristianskoi Kulturi* (2012): 280–300.

Semenov, Grigori L., *Studien zur sogdischen Kultur an der Seidenstrasse* (Wiesbaden Harrassowitz Verlag, 1996).

Shahbazi, Alireza Shapour, "On the *Xwadāy-Nāmag*," in *Papers in Honor of Professor Ehsan Yarshater* (Leiden: Brill, 1990), 208–29.

———, "The Parthian Origins of the House of Rustam," *Bulletin of the Asia Institute* 7 (1993): 155–63.

Shahid, Irfan, "The Last Sasanid-Byzantine Conflict in the Seventh Century: The Causes of Its Outbreak," in *La Persia e Bisanzio: Convegno internazionale, Roma 14–18 ottobre 2002*, ed. Antonio Carile, Lellia Cracco Ruggini, Gherardo Gnoli, Giovanni Pugliese Carratelli, and Gianroberto Scarcia (Rome: Accademia Nazionale dei Lincei, 2004), 223–44.

Shaked, Shaul, "Some Notes on Ahreman, the Evil Spirit, and His Creation," in Efraim E. Urbach, R.J. Werblowsky, and Chaim Werszubski (ed.), *Studies in Mysticism and Religion Presented to G. G. Scholem* (Jerusalem: Magnes Press, 1967): 227–54.

———, "Esoteric Trends in Zoroastrianism," *Proceedings of the Israel Academy of Sciences and Humanities* 3 (1969): 175–221.

———, "The Notions of *mēnōg* and *gētīg* in the Pahlavi Texts and Their Relation to Eschatology," *Acta Orientalia* 33 (1971): 59–107.

———, "Some Legal and Administrative Terms of the Sasanian Period," in *Monumentum H. S. Nyberg*, vol. 2 (Leiden: Brill, 1975), 213–25.

———, "Jewish and Christian Seals of the Sasanian Period," in *Studies in Memory of G. Wiet*, ed. Myriam Rosen Ayalon (Jerusalem: Hebrew University, 1977), 17–31.

———, "First Man, First King: Notes on Semitic-Iranian Syncretism and Iranian Mythological Transformations," in *Gilgul: Essays on Transformation, Revolution and Permanence in the History of Religions*, ed. Shaked, D. Shulman, and G. G. Stroumsa (Leiden: Brill, 1987), 238–56.

———, "Administrative Functions of Priests in the Sasanian Period," in *Old and Middle Iranian Studies*, pt. 1 of *Proceedings of the First European Conference of Iranian Studies*, ed. Gherardo Gnoli and Antonio Panaino (Rome: Istituto italiano per il medio ed estremo Oriente, 1990), 261–73.

———, "Aspekte von Noruz, dem iranischen Neujahrsfest," in *Das Fest und das Heilige: Religiöse Kontrapunkte zur Alltagswelt*, ed. Jan Assmann (Gütersloh: Gütersloher Verlagshaus Mohn, 1991), 88–102.

———, "The Myth of Zurvan: Cosmogony and Eschatology," in *Messiah and Christos: Studies in the Jewish Origins of Christianity Presented to David Flusser*, ed. Ithamar Gruenwald, Shaked, and Gedaliahu Stroumsa (Tübingen: J. C. B. Mohr, 1992), 219–40.

———, *Dualism in Transformation: Varieties of Religion in Sasanian Iran* (London: School of Oriental and African Studies, 1994).

———, "Quests and Visionary Journeys in Sasanian Iran," in *Transformations of the Inner Self in Ancient Religions*, ed. Jan Assmann and Guy G. Stroumsa (Leiden: Brill, 1999), 65–86.

———, "The Yasna Ritual in Pahlavi Literature," in *Zoroastrian Rituals in Context*, ed. Michael Stausberg (Leiden: Brill, 2004), 333–34.

———, "Religion in the Late Sasanian Period: Eran, Aneran, and Other Religious Designations," in *The Sasanian Era*, vol. 3 of *The Idea of Iran*, ed. Vesta Sarkhosh Curtis and Sarah Stewart (London: I. B. Tauris, 2008), 103–17.

———, "Human Identity and Classes of People in the Pahlavi Books," in *Iranian Identity in the Course of History: Proceedings of the Conference Held in Rome, 21–24 September 2005*, ed. Carlo G. Cereti (Rome: Istituto italiano per l'Africa e l'Oriente, 2010), 331–45. [Shaked 2010a]

———, "'No Talking during a Meal': Zoroastrian Themes in the Babylonian Talmud," in *The Talmud in Its Iranian Context*, ed. Carol Bakhos and M. Rahim Shayegan (Tübingen: Mohr Siebeck, 2010), 161–77. [Shaked 2010b]

Shaw, Brent, "Body/Power/Identity: Passions of the Martyrs," *Journal of Early Christian Studies* 4 (1996): 269–312.

Shayegan, M. Rahim, "Approaches to the Study of Sasanian History," in *Paitimāna: Essays in Iranian, Indo-European, and Indian Studies in Honor of Hans-Peter Schmidt*, ed. Siamak Adhami (Costa Mesa: Mazda, 2003), 363–84.

———, *Arsacids and Sasanisns: Political Ideology in Post-Hellenistic and Late Antique Persia* (Cambridge: Cambridge University Press, 2011).

———, *Aspects of History and Epic in Ancient Iran: From Gaumāta to Wahnām* (Washington DC: Center for Hellenic Studies, 2012).

Sheidel, Walter, "Emperors, Aristocrats, and the Grim Reaper: Toward a Demographic Profile of the Roman Élite," *Classical Quarterly* 49 (1999): 254–81.

Silk, Jonathan, "Putative Persian Perversities: Buddhist Condemnations of Zoroastrian Close-Kin Marriage in Context," *Bulletin of the School of Oriental and African Studies* 71 (2008): 433–64.

Simonsohn, Uriel, "Communal Boundaries Reconsidered: Jews and Christians Appealing to Muslim Authorities in the Medieval Near East," *Jewish Studies Quarterly* 14 (2007): 328–63.

———, "Seeking Justice among the 'Outsiders': Christian Recourse to Non-ecclesiastical Judicial Systems under Early Islam," *Church History and Religious Culture* 89 (2009): 191–216.

———, *A Common Justice: The Legal Allegiances of Christians and Jews under Early Islam* (Philadelphia: University of Pennsylvania Press, 2011).

Simpson, St John, "From Tekrit to the Jaghjagh: Sasanian Sites, Settlement Patterns and Material Culture in Northern Mesopotamia," in *Continuity and Change in Northern Mesopotamia from the Hellenistic to the Early Islamic Period*, ed. Karin Bartl and Stefan R. Hauser (Berlin: Dietrich Reimer Verlag, 1996), 87–126.

———, "Christians and Ninevah in Late Antiquity," *Iraq* 67 (2005): 285–94.

———, "Rams, Stags and Crosses from Sasanian Iraq: Elements of a Shared Visual Vocabul," in *Animals, Gods and Men from East to West: Papers on Archeology and History in Memory of Roberta Venco Ricciardi*, ed. Alessandra Peruzzetto, Francesca Dorna Metzger, and Lucinda Dirven (Oxford: Archaeopress, 2013), 103–17.

Simpson, St John, and Theya Molleson, "Old Bones Overturned: New Evidence for Funerary Practices from the Sasanian Empire," in *Regarding the Dead: Human Remairs in the British Museum*, ed. A. Fletcher, D. Antoine, and J. D. Hill (London: British Museum Press, 2014), 77–90.

Sims-Williams, Nicholas, *The Christian Sogdian Manuscript C2* (Berlin: Akademie Verlag, 1985).

———, "Christian Literature in Middle Iranian Languages," in *The Literature of Pre-Islamic Iran: Companion Volume I to "A History of Persian Literature,"* ed. Ronald E. Emmerick and Maria Macuch (London: I. B. Tauris, 2009), 266–87.

———, "Early New Persian in Syriac Script: Two Texts from Turfan," *Bulletin of the School of Oriental and African Studies* 74 (2011): 353–74.

Sivan, Hagith, "From Byzantine to Persian Jerusalem: Jewish Perspectives and Jewish-Christian Polemics," *Greek, Roman, and Byzantine Studies* 41 (2000): 277–306.

———, "Palestine between Byzantium and Persia (CE 614–19)," in *La Persia e Bisanzio: Convegno internazionale, Roma 14–18 ottobre 2002*, ed. Antonio Carile, Lellia Cracco Ruggini, Gherardo Gnoli, Giovanni Pugliese Carratelli, and Gianroberto Scarcia (Rome: Accademia Nazionale dei Lincei, 2004), 77–92.

———, *Palestine in Late Antiquity* (Oxford: Oxford University Press, 2008).

Sizgorich, Thomas, *Violence and Belief in Late Antiquity: Militant Devotion in Christianity and Islam* (Philadelphia: University of Pennsylvania Press, 2009).

Skjærvø, Prods Oktor, "Homosexuality i. In Zoroastrianism," in *Encyclopaedia Iranica*, ed. Ehsan Yarshater, vol. 12 (New York: Bibliotheca Persica, 2004), 440–41.

———, "The Avestan Yasna: Ritual and Myth," in *Religious Texts in Iranian Languages: Symposium Held in Copenhagen, May 2002*, ed. Fereydun Vahman and Claus V. Pedersen (Copenhagen: Det Kongelige Danske Videnskabernes Selskab, 2007), 57–84.

Smith, Kyle R., "The Persian Persecution: Martyrdom, Politics, and Religious Identity in Late Ancient Syriac Christianity" (PhD diss., Duke University, 2011).
Sotinel, Claire, "Les lieux de culte chrétiens et le sacré dans l'antiquité tardive," *Revue de l'histoire des religions* 222 (2005): 411–34.
Speck, Paul, "Die Predigt des Strategios," in *Varia IV: Beiträge zum Thema Byzantinische Feindseligkeit gegen die Juden im frühen siebten Jahrhundert nebst einer Untersuchung zu Anastasios dem Perser*, ed. Speck (Bonn: Dr. Rudolf Habelt, 1997), 37–129.
Stausberg, Michael, *Die Religion Zarathustras: Geschichte—Gegenwart—Rituale*, vol. 1 (Stuttgart: W. Kohlhammer, 2002).
———, "Hell in Zoroastrian History," *Numen* 56 (2009): 217–53.
Stavisky, Boris J., "The Fate of Buddhism in Middle Asia in the Light of Archeological Data," *Silk Road Art and Archeology* 3 (1993–94): 113–42.
Stern, Sacha, "Near Eastern Lunar Calendars in the Syriac Martyr Acts," *Le Muséon* 117 (2004): 447–72.
Steve, Marie-Joseph, *L'Île de Kharg: Une page de l'histoire du Golfe Persique et du monachisme oriental* (Neuchâtel: Civilisations du Proche-Orient, 2003).
Stewart, Charles, "Syncretism and Its Synonyms: Reflections on Cultural Mixture," *Diacritics* 29 (1999): 40–62.
Stoyanov, Yuri, *Defenders and Enemies of the True Cross: The Sasanian Conquest of Jerusalem in 614 and the Byzantine Ideology of Anti-Persian Warfare* (Vienna: Verlag der österreichischen Akademie der Wissenschaften, 2011).
Sundermann, Werner, "Commendatio pauperum: Eine Angabe der sassanidischen politisch-didaktischen Literatur zur gesellschaftlichen Struktur Irans," *Altorientalische Forschungen* 4 (1976): 167–94.
———, "Namen von Göttern, Dämonen und Menschen in iranischen Versionen des manichäischen Mythos," *Altorientalische Forschungen* 6 (1979): 95–134.
———, *Mitteliranische manichäische Texte kirchengeschichtlichen Inhalts* (Berlin: Akademie Verlag, 1981).
———, "Ein soghdisches Fragment der Mār Eugen-Legende," in *Splitter aus der Gegend von Turfan: Festschrift für Peter Zieme anläßlich seines 60. Geburtstags*, ed. Mehmet Ölmez and Simone-Christiane Raschmann (Istanbul: Şafak Matbaacılık, 2002), 309–31.
———, "Zoroastrian Motifs in Non-Zoroastrian Traditions," *Journal of the Royal Asiatic Society* 18 (2008): 155–65.
Swidler, Ann, *Talk of Love: How Culture Matters* (Chicago: University of Chicago Press, 2001).
Tafazzoli, Ahmad, *Sasanian Society* (New York: Bibliotheca Persica, 2000).
Tamcke, Martin, *Der Katholikos-Patriarch Sabrīšōʿ I. (596–604) und das Mönchtum* (Frankfurt: Peter Lang, 1988).
———, "Henanischoʿ I," in *Studien zur Semitistik und Arabistik: Festschrift für Hartmut Bobzin zum 60. Geburtstag*, ed. Otto Jastrow, Shabo Talay, and Herta Hafenrichter (Wiesbaden: Harrassowitz Verlag, 2008), 395–402.
Taqizadeh, S. H., "The Iranian Festivals Adopted by the Christians and Condemned by the Jews," *Bulletin of the School of Oriental and African Studies* 10 (1940): 632–53.
Taylor, David G. K., "Bilingualism and Diglossia in Late Antique Syria and Mesopotamia," in *Bilingualism in Ancient Society: Language, Contact and the Written Word*, ed. J. N. Adams, M. Janse, and S. Swain (Oxford: Oxford University Press, 2002), 298–331.

Thomson, Robert W., "The Formation of the Armenian Literary Tradition," in *East of Byzantium: Syria and Armenia in the Formative Period*, ed. Nina G. Garsoian, Thomas F. Mathews, and Thomson (Washington DC: Dumbarton Oaks, 1982), 135–50.

———, "The Writing of History: The Development of the Armenian and Georgian Traditions," in *Il Caucaso: Cerniera fra Culture dal Mediterraneo alla Persia* (Spoleto: Centro italiano di studi sull'alto Medioevo, 1996), 493–514.

———, "Armenian in the Fifth and Sixth Century," in *The Cambridge Ancient History*, vol. 14, *Late Antiquity: Empire and Successors, A.D. 425–600*, ed. Averil Cameron, Bryan Ward-Perkins, and Michael Whitby (Cambridge: Cambridge University Press, 2000), 638–61.

———, "Armenian Ideology and the Persians," in *La Persia e Bisanzio: Convegno internazionale, Roma 14–18 ottobre 2002*, ed. Antonio Carile, Lellia Cracco Ruggini, Gherardo Gnoli, Giovanni Pugliese Carratelli, and Gianroberto Scarcia (Rome: Accademia Nazionale dei Lincei, 2004), 373–89.

Toral-Niehoff, Isabel, "The 'Ibād of al-Ḥīra: An Arab Christian Community in Late Antique Iraq," in *The Qur'ān in Context: Historical and Literary Investigations into the Qur'ānic Milieu*, ed. Angelika Neuwirth, Nicolai Sinai, and Michael Marx (Leiden: Brill, 2010), 323–48.

———, *Al-Ḥīra: Eine arabische Kulturmetropole im spätantiken Kontext* (Leiden: Brill, 2014).

Toumanoff, Cyril, *Studies in Christian Caucasian History* (Washington DC: Georgetown University Press, 1963).

Tubach, Jürgen, "Der Apostel Thomas in China: Die Herkunft einer Tradition," *Zeitschrift für Kirchengeschichte* 108 (1997): 58–74.

———, "Abgrenzung und Selbstbehauptung in einer multikulturellen Umwelt: Die Christlichen Gemeinde von Merw, einer Metropole an der Seidenstraße, in der ausgehenden Sasanidenzeit," in *Symposium Syriacum VII*, ed. René Lavenant (Rome: Pontificium institutum orientalium studiorum, 1998), 409–19.

Tyler-Smith, Susan, "Calendars and Coronations: The Literary and Numismatic Evidence for the Accession of Khusrau II," *Byzantine and Modern Greek Studies* 28 (2004): 33–65.

van Bladel, Kevin, *The Arabic Hermes: From Pagan Sage to Prophet of Science* (Oxford: Oxford University Press, 2009).

———, "The Bactrian Background of the Barmakids," in *Islam and Tibet—Interactions along the Musk Routes*, ed. Anna Akasoy, Charles Burnett, and Ronit Yoeli-Tlalim (Farnham: Ashgate, 2011), 43–88.

Van Dam, Raymond, *Becoming Christian: The Conversion of Roman Cappadocia* (Philadelphia: University of Pennsylvania Press, 2003).

van Rompay, Lucas, "Eznik de Kołb et Théodore de Mopsueste: À propos d'une hypothèse de Louis Mariès," *Orientalia Lovaniensia Periodica* 15 (1984): 159–75.

———, "Impetuous Martyrs? The Situation of the Persian Christians in the Last Years of Yazdgard I (419–20)," in *Martyrium in Multidisciplinary Perspective: Memorial Louis Reekmans*, ed. M. Lamberigts and P. van Deun (Leuven: Peeters, 1995), 363–75.

van Unnik, Wilhelm, "The Significance of Moses' Law for the Church of Christ According to the Syriac Didascalia," in *Patristica—Gnostica—Liturgica*, vol. 3 of *Sparsa collecta: The Collected Essays of W. C. Van Unnik* (Leiden: E. J. Brill, 1983), 7–39.

van Uytfanghe, Marc, "L'hagiographie: Un 'genre' chrétien ou antique tardif?," *Analecta Bollandiana* 111 (1993): 135–88.

———, "L'hagiographie antique tardive: Une littérature populaire?," *Antiquité Tardive* 9 (2001): 201–18.

Vevaina, Yuhan Sohrab-Dinshaw, "Miscegenation, 'Mixture,' and 'Mixed Iron': The Hermeneutics, Historiography, and Cultural Poesis of the 'Four Ages' in Zoroastrianism," in *Revelation, Literature, and Community in Late Antiquity*, ed. Philippa Townsend and Moulie Vidas (Tübingen: Mohr Siebeck, 2011), 237–69.

Visotzky, Burton, "Anti-Christian Polemic in Leviticus Rabbah," *Proceedings of the American Academy for Jewish Research* 56 (1990): 83–100.

Vries, Wilhelm de, *Der Kirchenbegriff der von Rom getrennten Syrer* (Rome: Pontificium institutum orientalium studiorum, 1955).

Walker, Joel, "Against the Eternity of the Stars: Disputation and Christian Philosophy in Late Sasanian Mesopotamia," in *La Persia e Bisanzio: Convegno internazionale, Roma 14–18 ottobre 2002*, ed. Antonio Carile, Lellia Cracco Ruggini, Gherardo Gnoli, Giovanni Pugliese Carratelli, and Gianroberto Scarcia (Rome: Accademia Nazionale dei Lincei, 2004), 510–37.

———, *The Legend of Mar Qardagh: Narrative and Christian Heroism in Late Antique Iraq* (Berkeley: Univesity of California Press, 2006).

———, "The Legacy of Mesopotamia in Late Antique Iraq: The Christian Martyr Shrine at Melqi (Neo-Assyrian Milqia)," *Aram* 18–19 (2006–7): 483–508.

———, "A Saint and His Biographer in Late Antique Iraq: The *History of St. George of Izla* (d. 614) by Babai the Great," in *Writing 'True Stories': Historians and Hagiographers in the Late Antique and Medieval Near East*, ed. Arietta Papaconstantinou (Turnhout: Brepols, 2010), 31–41.

———, "From Nisibis to Xi'an: The Church of the East in Late Antique Eurasia," in *The Oxford Handbook of Late Antiquity*, ed. Scott Fitzgerald Johnson (Oxford: Oxford University Press, 2012), 994–1052.

Weber, Dieter, "The Vienna Collection of Pahlavi Papyri," in *Akten des 23. Internationalen Papyrologenkongresses*, ed. Bernhard Palme (Vienna: Verlag der österreichischen Akademie der Wissenschaften, 2007), 725–38.

———, *Berliner Pahlavi-Dokumente: Zeugnisse spätsassanidischer Brief- und Rechtskultur aus frühislamischer Zeit* (Wiesbaden: Harrassowitz Verlag, 2008).

———, "Ein Pahlavi-Fragment des Alexanderromans aus Ägypten?," in *Literarische Stoffe und ihre Gestaltung in mitteliranischer Zeit*, ed. Desmond Durkin-Meisterernst, Christine Reck, and Weber (Wiesbaden: Reichert, 2009), 307–18.

———, "Writing Exercises in Late Sasanian Times: A Contribution to the Culture of Writing Pahlavi," in *Ancient and Middle Iranian Studies: Proceedings of the 6th European Conference of Iranian Studies*, ed. Maria Macuch, Weber, and Desmund Durkin-Meisterernst (Wiesbaden: Harrassowitz Verlag, 2010), 255–63.

———, "Die persische Besetzung Ägyptens 619–29 n. Chr.," in *Ägypten und sein Umfeld in der Spätantike vom Regierungsantritt Diokletians 284/285 bis zur arabischen Eroberung des Vorderen Orients um 635–46*, ed. Frank Feder and Angelika Lohwasser (Wiesbaden: Harrassowitz Verlag, 2013), 221–46.

Weisberg, Dvora, "The Babylonian Talmud's Treatment of Levirate Marriage," *Annual of Rabbinic Judaism: Ancient, Medieval, and Modern* 3 (2000): 35–66.

Weisweiler, John, "Christianity and War: Ammianus on Power and Religion in Constantius' Persian War," in *The Power of Religion in Late Antiquity*, ed. Noel Lenski and Andrew Cain (Aldershot: Ashgate, 2009), 383–96.

Weitz, Lev E., "Syriac Christians in the Medieval Islamic World: Law, Family, and Society" (PhD diss., Princeton University, 2013).

Wheeler, Brandon, "Imagining the Sasanian Capture of Jerusalem: The 'Prophecy and Dream of Zerubbabel' and Antiochus Strategos' 'Capture of Jerusalem,'" *Orientalia Christiana Periodica* 57 (1991): 69–85.

Whitby, Mary, "A New Image for a New Age: George of Pisidia on the Emperor Heraclius," in *The Roman and Byzantine Army in the East*, ed. E. Dąbrowa (Kraków: Drukarnia Uniwersytetu Jagiellońskiego, 1994), 197–225.

Whitby, Michael, *The Emperor Maurice and His Historian: Theophylact Simocatta on Persian and Balkan Warfare* (Oxford: Clarendon, 1988).

Whitcomb, Donald, "Qasr-i Abu Nasr and the Gulf," in *Arabie orientale, Mésopotamie, et Iran méridional: De l'âge du fer au début de la période islamique*, ed. Rémy Boucharlat and Jean-François Salles (Paris: Recherche sur les civilisations, 1984), 331–37.

———, "Islamic Archaeology and the 'Land behind Baghdad,'" in *Settlement and Society: Essays Dedicated to Robert McCormick Adams*, ed. Elizabeth C. Stone (Los Angeles: Cotsen Institute of Archaeology, 2007), 255–59.

Wickham, Chris, *Framing the Early Middle Ages: Europe and the Mediterranean, 400–800* (Oxford: Oxford University Press, 2005).

———, "Bounding the City: Concepts of Urban-Rural Difference in the West in the Early Middle Ages," in *Città e Campagna nei secoli altomedievali: Spoleto 27 marzo–1 aprile 2008* (Spoleto: Fondazione Centro italiano di studi sull'alto Medioevo, 2009), 61–80.

Widengren, Geo, "Recherches sur le féodalisme iranien," *Orientalia Suecana* 5 (1956): 79–182.

———, *Die Religionen Irans* (Stuttgart: W. Kohlkammer, 1965).

———, *Der Feudalismus im alten Iran: Männerbund, Gefolgswesen, Feudalismus in der iranischen Gesellschaft im Hinblick auf die indogermanischen Verhältnisse* (Cologne: Westdeutscher Verlag, 1967). [Widengren 1967a]

———, "Zervanitische Texte aus dem 'Avesta' in der Pahlavi-Überlieferung: Eine Untersuchung zu Zātspram und Bundahišn," in *Festschrift für Wilhelm Eilers*, ed. Gernot Wiessner (Wiesbaden: Otto Harrassowitz, 1967), 278–87. [Widengren 1967b]

———, "The Nestorian Church in Sasanian and Post-Sasanian Iran," in *Incontro di religioni in Asia tra il III e il X d.C.*, ed. Lionello Lanciotti (Florence: L. S. Olschki, 1984), 1–30.

Wiesehöfer, Josef, "'Geteilte Loyalitäten': Religiöse Minderheiten des 3. und 4. Jahrhunderts n. Chr. im Spannungsfeld zwischen Rom und dem sasanidischen Iran," *Klio* 75 (1993): 362–82.

———, *Ancient Persia: From 550 BC to 650 AD* (London: I. B. Tauris, 1996).

———, "King, Court, and Royal Representation in the Sasanian Empire," in *The Court and Court Society in Ancient Mesopotamia*, ed. A. J. S. Spawforth (Cambridge: Cambridge University Press, 2007), 58–81. [Wiesehöfer 2007a]

———, "Narseh, Diokletian, Manichäer und Christen," in *Inkulturation des Christentums im Sasanidenreich,* ed. Arafa Mustafa, Jürgen Tubach, and G. Sophia Vashalomidze (Wiesbaden: Reichert Verlag, 2007), 161–69. [Wiesehöfer 2007b]

———, "The Late Sasanian Near East," in *The New Cambridge History of Islam,* vol. 1, *The Formation of the Islamic World, Sixth to Eleventh Centuries,* ed. Chase Robinson (Cambridge: Cambridge University Press, 2010), 98–152.

———, "Mehrfrontenkriege: Ostrom und das Sasanidenreich zu Beginn des 7. Jahrhunderts n. Chr.," in *Ägypten und sein Umfeld in der Spätantike vom Regierungsantritt Diokletians 284/285 bis zur arabischen Eroberung des Vorderen Orients um 635–46,* ed. Frank Feder and Angelika Lohwasser (Wiesbaden: Harrassowitz Verlag, 2013), 193–206.

Wiessner, Gernot, "Zu den Subskriptionslisten der ältesten christlichen Synoden in Iran," in *Festschrift für Wilhelm Eilers,* ed. Wiessner (Wiesbaden: Otto Harrassowitz, 1967), 288–98. [Wiessner 1967a]

———, *Zur Märtyrerüberlieferung aus der Christenverfolgung Schapurs II.* (Göttingen: Vandenhoeck und Ruprecht, 1967). [Wiessner 1967b]

———, "Zum Problem der zeitlichen und örtlichen Festlegung der erhaltenen syro-persischen Märtyrerakten: Das Pusai-Martyrium," in *Paul de Lagarde und die syrische Kirchengeschichte* (Göttingen: Lagarde Haus, 1968), 231–51.

———, "Zur Auseinandersetzung zwischen Christentum und Zoroastrismus in Iran," in supplement 1, *Zeitschrift der deutschen morgenländischen Gesellschaft* (1969): 411–17.

———, "Christlicher Heiligenkult im Umkreis eines sassanidischen Großkönigs," in *Festgabe deutscher Iranisten zur 2500 Jahrfeier Irans,* ed. Wilhelm Eilers (Stuttgart: Hochwacht Druck, 1971), 141–55.

———, "Die Behnām-Legende," in *Synkretismusforschung: Theorie und Praxis,* ed. Wiessner (Wiesbaden: Otto Harrassowitz, 1978), 119–33.

Wikander, Stig, "Tansarnāmeh och Mahābhārata," *Acta Orientalia* 30 (1966): 214–17.

Wilkinson, Charles, "Christian Remains from Nishapur," in *Forschungen zur Kunst Asiens: In Memoriam Kurt Erdmann,* ed. Oktay Aslanapa and Rudolf Naumann (Istanbul: Baha Matbaasi, 1969), 79–87.

Williams, A. V., "Zoroastrians and Christians in Sasanian Iran," *Bulletin of the John Rylands University Library of Manchester* 78 (1996): 37–53.

Wilmshurst, David, *The Martyred Church: A History of the Church of the East* (London: East and West, 2011).

Witakowski, Witold, *The Syriac Chronicle of Pseudo-Dionysius of Tel-Mahrē: A Study in the History of Historiography* (Uppsala: Uppsala Universitet, 1987).

———, "The Magi in Syriac Tradition," in *Malphono w-Raba d-Malphone: Studies in Honor of Sebastian P. Brock,* ed. George A. Kiraz (Piscataway: Gorgias, 2008); 809–43.

Wood, Ian, "Incest, Law, and the Bible in Sixth-Century Gaul," *Early Medieval Europe* 7 (1998): 291–304.

Wood, Philip, *'We Have No King but Christ': Christian Political Thought in Greater Syria on the Eve of the Arab Conquest (c. 400–585)* (Oxford: Oxford University Press, 2010).

———, "Collaborators and Dissidents: Christians in Sasanian Iraq in the Early Fifth Century CE," in *Late Antiquity: Eastern Perspectives,* ed. Teresa Bernheimer and Adam Silverstein (Oxford: Gibb Memorial Trust, 2012), 57–70.

———, *The Chronicle of Seert: Christian Historical Imagination in Late Antique Iraq* (Oxford: Oxford University Press, 2013).
———, "Hira and Her Saints," *Analecta Bollandiana* 132 (2014): 5–20.
Yarshater, Ehsan, "Were the Sasanians Heirs of the Achaemenids?," in *La Persia nel Medioevo*, ed. Enrico Cerulli (Rome: Accademia Nazionale dei Lincei, 1971), 517–31.
———, "The Iranian National History," In *The Cambridge History of Iran*, vol. 3(1), *The Seleucid, Parthian and Sasanian Periods*, ed. Yarshater (Cambridge: Cambridge University, 1983), 359–477.
Younansardaroud, Helen, "Die Legende von Mar Behnām," in *Syriaca: Zur Geschichte, Theologie, Liturgie und Gegenwartslage der syrischen Kirchen, 2. Deutsches Syrologen-Symposium, Juli 2000, Wittenberg*, ed. Martin Tamcke (Hamburg: Lit Verlag, 2002), 185–96.
Younansardaroud, Helen, and Mirko Novák, "Mar Behnam, Sohn des Sanherib von Nimrud: Tradition und Rezeption einer assyrischen Gestalt im iraqischen Christentum und die Frage nach den Fortleben der Assyrer," *Altorientalische Forschungen* 29 (2002): 166–94.
Zaehner, R. C., *Zurvanism: A Zoroastrian Dilemma* (Oxford: Clarendon, 1955).
Zakeri, Mohsen, *Sāsānid Soldiers in Early Muslim Society: The Origins of ʿAyyārān and Futuwwa* (Wiesbaden: Harrassowitz Verlag, 1995).
Zuckerman, Constantin, "Heraclius and the Return of the Holy Cross," *Travaux et Mémoires* 17 (2013): 197–218.

INDEX

Abarag, Zoroastrian scholar of the Sasanian era, 20, 70
Abda, early fifth-century East Syrian martyr and militant ascetic, 47–48
Abraham of Nethpar, seventh-century East Syrian monk, 143
Achaemenians, 59, 132, 140–41, 146, 159–60, 175
Adams, Robert McC., 159
Adiabene, 127–63
Adurbad, fourth-century mowbedān mowbed, 87
Adurfarrobag, early fifth-century Zoroastrian patron of a Christian church, 50
Adur Gushnasp, 59, 177
Adurohrmazd, mid fifth-century aristocratic convert to Christianity, 52, 60, 68, 72–74, 79, 83, 89–91
Agatangełos, fifth-century Armenian historian, 155–56
Agathias, sixth-century Roman historian, 152
agdēn, Middle Persian term for adherents of "bad religion," 25, 29–33, 35–37, 66, 69–70, 105, 122, 150
ahlamōg, Middle Persian term for "religious deviant" within Zoroastrian ranks, 34, 62
Ahreman, supreme malevolent deity in Zoroastrianism, 9, 23–24, 27–28, 30–31, 35, 76, 80–87, 89, 109–10
Airyana Vaējah, Avestan model for Ērānšahr, 8, 29

Ak-Tepe, 135
Albania, 14, 155–56
Alexander the Great, Macedonian king 356–323 B.C.E., 140–41, 156, 160
Alexandria, 96, 181–82, 186
āmārgar, Middle Persian term for "fiscal administrator," 96, 99, 120, 135, 145, 160
Amida, 171
Anahid, Zoroastrian deity, 59, 79
Anahid, mid fifth-century aristocratic convert to Christianity, 60, 68, 74–77, 79, 83–87, 89–91
Anastasios the Persian, early seventh-century aristocratic convert to Christianity, 192, 195–96
andarz, Zoroastrian literature of political advice, 9
anēr, "non-Iranian," Middle Persian term for non-Zoroastrians who could not claim membership among the *ēr,* 29–30, 66, 70, 150
anšahrīg, Middle Persian term for "slave," 73, 138
anti-Judaism, 183–84
Antioch, 64, 98, 141, 174
Anushzad, son of Husraw I, 125–26
apostasy (in Zoroastrianism), 48–56, 69, 93, 106, 192–96
apostolic traditions, 98, 144
Aqeblaha, fourth-century bishop of Karka d-Beit Slok, 138, 144
Aramaic language 11, 16, 136–37

Arbela (modern Arbil), 18, 34, 43, 52, 98, 102, 127–63, 170
archive, 154
archery, 151
Ardashir I, Sasanian king of kings 224–242 C.E., 6–7, 35, 153–56, 165, 189, 192, 199
Ardashir III, Sasanian king of kings 628–629 C.E., 197
Ardā Wirāz Nāmag, late Sasanian account of a journey into the afterlife, 86
Armenia, 9, 14–15, 46, 133, 164
Armenian Christianity, 14–15, 81–82, 91, 106, 117–18, 147
Armenian language, 16–17
artēštārānsālār, Middle Persian term for "military commander," 103
artisans, 41, 120–124, 159–160
asceticism, 19, 68, 96, 101, 102–3, 123, 162
ascetic militancy, 47–48
Assemani, Joseph, 18
Assmann, Jan, 82
Assyrians, 62, 127, 132, 140–42, 148–51, 158–59
Assyrian gods, 33, 158
astōdan, Middle Persian term for "ossuary," 31, 76
Athanasius of Antioch, West Syrian patriarch during the Iranian occupation, 186
Athens, 96
autonomy (of Christian communities), 14
authority (of East Syrian leaders), 14, 94–95, 100–103, 131–32
Avarayr, 142
Avars, 169
Avesta, 6–7, 62–63, 69–71, 73, 83–84, 91, 96, 105, 110, 118, 120, 125, 146, 152
ayvān, 11
Ayvan-e Kisra, 3–4, 180
āzād, Middle Persian term for "free men," middling aristocrats, 145–47, 201
Azerbaijian, 10, 59, 94, 99–100, 109, 149

Babai the Great, interim leader of the Church of the East 609–628 C.E., 186–87
Baboi, bishop of Seleucia-Ctesiphon (d. 484), 39
Babylonian Talmud, 15, 37, 81, 104–5, 112
Bactria, 10, 45, 109
Bagratunids, Armenian aristocratic dynasty, 168–70
baptism, 54, 70–71
Barbashmin, bishop of Seleucia-Ctesiphon in the 340s, 102

bnai ḥere, Syriac term for "free men," middling aristocrats in Mesopotamia, 136, 140–47, 150–51, 156–57, 201
Barsauma, bishop of Nisibis 460–491 C.E., 96–98
Bar Shabba, four-century bishop of Merv, 71
Bazyan, 10
bestiality, 109, 116
Bedjan, Paul, 17
Beit Arbaye, 134
Beit Aramaye, 96, 141
Beit Garmai, 127–63
Beit Lapat, also known as Jundishapur, 41–42, 49, 98, 101, 126
Beit Zabdai, 77
Bishapur, 65, 74
Bisutun, 59–61, 72, 75–77, 166
bnai qyama, Syriac term for "ascetics," 42–43, 96
bnai šebya, Syriac term for "captives," 66–67
Boran, Sasanian queen 630–631 C.E., 197
Book of Kings (*Xwadāy-nāmag*), historiographical account of the late Sasanian court, 21–22, 146–47, 152–57, 166–68, 188–91, 194, 200, 201
Booth, Phil, 177
Boyce, Mary, 25
Buddhism, 23, 33 109
Bundahišn, Middle Persian cosmogonical account, 79, 85
burial practices, 31–32

čagar marriage 110–11
captives, 64–72, 78, 91, 201
Capture of Jerusalem, early seventh-century account of the Iranian conquest of Jerusalem, 178
Cave of Treasures, sixth-century West Syrian compilation, 149
catholicos, bishop of Seleucia-Ctesiphon, 13, 64–65, 161
Chalcedon, 100
Chal Tarkhan, 138
Chang'an, 203
charity, 144, 162
Chinwad Bridge, 111
Christianization, 4–5, 9, 11–13, 66, 69, 165–66, 192–93
Chronicle of Arbela, medieval East Syrian compilation, 136
Chronicle of Khuzestan, late seventh-century East Syrian historiographical work, 149, 173, 179, 183
Chronicle of Pseudo-Joshua the Stylite, six-century Roman historiographical work, 171–72

Chronicle of Pseudo-Zachariah of Mytilene, late sixth-century West Syrian historiographical work, 171
Chronicle of Seert, tenth-century East Syrian historiographical work, 4, 166–67, 171, 173–74
church construction, 33–34, 44, 131, 144, 162, 166, 182–83, 192
Cities of Iran, Middle Persian account of urban foundations, 160–61, 163
Clovis, king of the Franks 481–509 C.E., 4
commensality, 117–22
consanguineous marriage, 106
Constantine, Roman emperor 306–337 C.E., 1, 4, 13, 39, 164, 170, 177–78, 183
Constantinople, 169, 181, 185
conversion (from Christianity to Zoroastrianism), 69
conversion (from Zoroastrianism to Christianity), 48–56, 69–70, 164–66, 189–96
cosmogony (Zoroastrian), 27–28, 78–87
Council of Chalcedon, 184
courts (Zoroastrian), 8, 14, 16, 104–5, 113
courts (episcopal), 15–16, 106–8
Cyrus, Achaemenian king ca. 559–530 B.C.E., 4, 98, 193

Darius I, Achaemenian king 550–486 B.C.E., 59
Darius III, Achaemenian king ca. 380–330 B.C.E., 140–41, 150, 154, 158, 160, 162
dād, Middle Persian term for "religious law," 32, 36
Dagron, Gilbert, 183
dahigān, Middle Persian term for "local aristocrat," 63, 145–47, 203
Damascus, 174
De Jong, Albert, 30
demography, 111
demon-worship (in Zoroastrian texts), 24, 35, 70
Dēnkard, 20, 29, 118
deportations, 11, 41, 64–66, 73, 137–38
destruction (of churches), 34
destruction (of fire temples), 46–48, 144, 170
destruction (of religious groups), 24–25
Al-Dīnawārī, Abbasid historiographer 828–896 C.E., 21, 167, 189–90
Dinawar Valley, 61, 76, 90
diplomacy, 13, 39, 190–91, 191
disputation, 187
doctrinal controversy (Christian), 184–88

Edessa, 81, 95, 161, 169, 172, 181–82
Elman, Yaakov, 15, 32

ecclesiastical factionalism, 97–98
Elias of Nisibis, eleventh-century East Syrian historiographer, 148
Ełishe, sixth-century Armenian historiographer, 146
Ephrem, fourth-century poet-theologian, 149
ēr, the "Iranians," a mythical historical ruling class in Iranian ideology, 8, 28–29, 30, 56, 66–67, 142, 150, 155
Ērānšahr, 6–7, 28, 66–67, 91, 202
Esarhaddon, Assyrian king 681–669 B.C.E., 140–41, 148, 158
eunuchs, 46
Eusebius of Caesarea, Roman Christian historiographer circa 260–340 C.E., 39, 132, 148–49, 163
Evagrius Scholasticus, sixth-century Roman ecclesiastical historian, 172
exilarch, head of the Jewish communities in the Iranian Empire, 15, 122, 184
Eznik of Kołb, fifth-century Armenian theologian, 81–82, 91

Fars, 6, 10–11, 61, 64, 66, 74, 94, 97, 105, 115, 137, 141–43, 180
feasting, 8–9, 117–22, 131, 151–52, 155, 202
Fereydun, mythical king in the Iranian historiographical tradition, 119, 149, 175
Firdawsī, author of the *Šāhnāme* 940–1020 C.E., 21, 190, 199–200
fire temples, 8, 9, 24, 28–35, 46–48, 59–60, 62, 144, 158
fosterage, 67–68, 103, 133
Frankia, 164
frašgird, eschatological restoration of the world to primordial perfection in Zoroastrianism, 28, 30

Gabriel of Basra, ninth-century East Syrian bishop, 123
Gabriel of Sinjar, West Syrian rival of the East Syrians at the court of Husraw II, 187, 195
Gafni, Isaiah, 15
Gariboldi, Andrea, 188
Garsoïan, Nina, 14–15, 46
Gayōmard, primordial first king in Iranian mythical historiography, 28, 191
George the Priest, early seventh-century aristocratic convert to Christianity and East Syrian monk, 193, 195–96
Ghassanids, Arab dynasty of Roman Syria, 172
gift-giving, 120–21, 172–73

Gōgušnasp, Zoroastrian scholar of the Sasanian era, 32, 36–37
Goody, Jack, 108
Gorgan, 10–11, 168, 169
gōsān, 147, 154
"Great Persecution," 18, 25, 38–44, 58, 136, 143
Greek language, 101, 132, 149
Greenwood, Timothy, 21, 152
Gregory, patriarch of the Church of the East 604–609 C.E., 186
Gregory the Commander, sixth-century aristocratic convert to Christianity, 51–52, 193
Gregory the Great, Roman pope 590–604 C.E., 164
guilds, 103, 123–24
gumēzišn, "state of mixture," age of cosmological struggle between good and evil deities and creations in Zoroastrianism, 9–10, 28
Gyselen, Rika, 17, 135

hagiography (Armenian), 26, 117–18, 133, 143, 147
hagiography (East Syrian), 17–19, 26–27, 37–56, 62, 66, 87–88, 117–18, 128–32, 139–44, 148–63
hagiography (Roman), 72, 78, 87–88, 118, 122
Haoma, Zoroastrian deity, 118
Hatra, 149
Hauser, Stefan, 10
Hazār Dādestān, early seventh-century compilation of Zoroastrian judicial cases, 20–21, 33, 51, 105, 112, 114
Hazza, 150–51, 160–61
Helena, mother of the Roman emperor Constantine, 177–78
Henanisho, late seventh-century patriarch of the Church of the East, 114, 116
Heraclius, Roman emperor 610–641 C.E., 166, 174–77, 182–84, 187–88, 197
hērbed, 69–71
Hērbedestān, Avestan treatise on Zoroastrian education with Middle Persian commentary of the Sasanian era, 51, 69–71
hērbedestān, schools of Zoroastrian religious specialists, 21–22, 63, 82, 97, 202
Hephthalites, 45, 52, 109, 133
Herat, 64, 160
Hijaz, 133
al-Ḥīra, 11, 133
hierarchical inclusion, 26–27, 35–38, 166, 200–201
historiography (Armenian), 21–22, 33, 153, 155–57, 164
historiography (early Islamic), 149, 167, 189

historiography (of the Iranian court), 21–22, 33, 119, 140, 144–62
historiography (West Syrian), 181, 185–88
History of the Albanians, tenth-century Armenian historiographical work, 155- 157
History of the Armenians, fifth-century Armenian historiographical work, 155–56
History of George the Priest, early seventh-century East Syrian hagiographical work, 187
History of Gregory the Commander, late sixth-century East Syrian hagiographical work, 119–22
History of Ishosabran, hagiographical work of Ishoyahb III, 52, 54
History of Karka d-Beit Slok, East Syrian hagiographical work circa 600 C.E., 45–46, 67, 127–63
History of Mar Aba, sixth-century East Syrian hagiographical work, 104, 106, 117–19, 122–23
History of Mar Mari, sixth-century East Syrian hagiographical work, 98, 195
History of Mar Qardagh, early seventh-century East Syrian hagiographical work, 78, 127–63, 169–70
History of Pseudo-Sebeos, late seventh-century Armenian historiographical work, 164, 183, 196
History of Rabban Mar Saba, early seventh-century East Syrian hagiographical work, 51, 54, 192, 194
History of Sabrisho, early seventh-century East Syrian hagiographical work, 192–93, 195–96
History of Simeon, fifth-century East Syrian hagiographical work, 18, 40–44, 109
History of Sultan Mahduk, late seventh-century East Syrian hagiographical work, 139
Hirbet Glal, 139, 159–62
ḥnana, 76, 170
holy men, 19, 63, 169, 173–74
holy places, 74–75, 90
Hōm Yašt, Avestan text with Middle Persian translation of the Sasanian era, 118
homosexuality, 109–10, 116
horsemanship, 3
Howard-Johnston, James, 145, 174
Huns, 13, 45, 133, 152, 155
Husraw I, Sasanian king of kings 525–579 C.E., 4, 25, 34, 41, 53, 93, 95, 121, 133, 145, 153–54, 169, 192, 193
Husraw II, Sasanian king of kings 590–628 C.E., 2–5, 25, 54, 59, 62, 134, 151, 164–98, 200
Husraw and the Youth, late Sasanian account of the court, 71

Iberia, 9, 14–15, 120, 135
idolatry, 24, 32–35, 48, 118, 122, 158
incestuous marriage, 108–17, 123–24
Indian Ocean, 10–11
inheritance, 108–17
institution (as sociological term), 16
intermarriage, 65
Iranian Highlands, 18
Isaac, late fourth-century bishop of Karka d-Beit Slok, 154
Isfahan, 136, 160
Ishobokht, late eighth-century bishop of Revardashir, 105, 111, 113–15
Ishodenah of Basra, ninth-century East Syrian bishop, 149–50
Ishosabran, early seventh-century aristocratic convert to Christianity, 52, 193, 196
Ishoyahb I, patriarch of the Church of the East 581–585 C.E., 173
Ishoyahb III, patriarch of the Church of the East 649–659 C.E., 42, 54, 102, 114–16, 123, 162
Israelites, 109–12
Istakhr, 31, 76, 137, 141, 144, 154

Jainism, 11
Jamshid, mythical king in the Iranian historiographical tradition, 86, 119
Jerusalem, 175–80, 182–84
Johannes Rusafoyo, West Syrian aristocrat from Edessa, 181
John the Almsgiver, Chalcedonian patriarch of Alexandria, 182, 186
John of Ephesus, sixth-century West Syrian historiographer, 186
John of Nikiu, seventh-century Egyptian historiographer, 164
John Philoponus, 132
Judaism, 3, 15, 37, 104–5, 112, 128, 131, 204
Jullien, Christelle, 196
jurisprudence (Armenian), 106
jurisprudence (East Syrian), 20, 103–17
jurisprudence (Zoroastrian), 20–21, 104–14
Justinian, Roman emperor 527–565 C.E., 183, 185, 186

Kalmin, Richard, 37
Kangavar, 59, 90
Karen, mythical Iranian hero, 146
Karenids, 145–46
Karka d-Beit Slok (modern Kirkuk), 18, 33, 34, 43, 52, 54, 62, 67, 127–63
Karka d-Ledan, 41–42, 65

Karka d-Maishan, 42
Kashkar, 43, 98
Kaufhold, Hubert, 20
Kawad I, Sasanian king of kings 488–531 C.E., 62, 96, 134, 152–54, 171, 185
Kayanian dynasty, 28–29, 146–47, 160, 173, 175, 189–91
Kay Husraw, mythical king in the Iranian tradition, 150
Kerdir, chief mowbed in the latter half of the third century, 23–25, 34, 56, 105
$k\bar{e}š$, Zoroastrian Middle Persian term for doctrine or sectarian group, 23–24, 36
Kharg, 11
Kidarites, 45
$kilīsyag$, Middle Persian term for "Christian," 69
$kirbag$, "good work," Middle Persian term for the actions through which Zoroastrians achieve ethical merit, 35–36, 57, 89
$kirrōgoed$, Middle Persian term for "master of the artisans," 103
Khurasan, 10, 45, 199
Khuzestan, 10–11, 18, 40–42, 62, 65, 66, 68, 90, 98, 101, 125–26, 135, 136, 160
$kolāh$, Iranian aristocratic headgear, 135, 203
Komitas, early seventh-century Armenian catholicos, 182
Kuh-e Rahmat, 31

labor, 138
Lakhmids, 133–34
Lashom, 107, 169
Łazar P'arpec'i, sixth-century Armenian historiographer, 146–47
Letter of Tansar, sixth-century account of the reign of Ardashir, 53, 153–54, 196
levirate marriage, 110, 112, 115–16
Levites, 109, 123
Life of Constantine, fourth-century work of Eusebius of Caesarea, 39
literacy, 71

Maccabean revolt, 40
MacEvitt, Christopher, 30
Magi, 154–65
magic bowls, 33
Mandylion of Edessa, 169, 172
Mamikoneans, Armenian aristocratic dynasty, 133–34, 147, 168
Mani, 24
Manichaeism, 23–24, 27, 34, 67, 73, 82, 131, 136, 142

Maishan, 138
Mango, Cyril, 197
Mar Aba, patriarch of the Church of the East 540–552 C.E., 20, 81–82, 88, 91, 93–126, 133, 139, 193
Mar Awgen, legendary East Syrian monastic founder, 88, 98
margarzān, "[offense] worth of death," Middle Persian term for category of sins, 50, 106
Maron, late fifth-century bishop of Karka d-Beit Slok, 132
marriage of bishops, 102
Martyrdom of Abda, fifth-century East Syrian hagiographical work, 47
Martyrdom of Aqebshma, fifth-century East Syrian hagiographical work, 38
Martyrdom of the Captives, fifth-century East Syrian hagiographical work, 66, 68
Martyrdom of Christina, early seventh-century hagiographical work of Babai, 52
Martyrdom of Eustathius of Mtskheta, late Sasanisn Georgian hagiographical work, 119–22
Martyrdom of Jacob the Notary, fifth-century East Syrian hagiographical work, 45
Martyrdom of Miles, late fourth- or early fifth-century East Syrian hagiographical work, 77, 98
Martyrdom of Pethion, Adurohrmazd, and Anahid, late fifth-/early sixth-century East Syrian hagiographical work, 60–92, 132, 145–46, 193, 201
Martyrdom of Peroz, fifth-century East Syrian hagiographical work, 34
Martyrdom of Pusai, early-fifth century East Syrian hagiographical work, 65–66
Martyrdom of Simeon, fifth-century East Syrian hagiographical work, 40–42, 109
Martyrdom of Shirin, sixth-century East Syrian hagiographical work surviving in Greek, 52, 54
Martyrdom of Yazdbozid, late Sasanian Armenian hagiographical work, 119–22
Maruta, early fifth-century bishop of Maipherqat, 13, 18
Mar Yonan, legendary East Syrian monastic founder, 88
marzbān, Middle Persian term for "frontier military commander," 137, 145, 151, 159, 195, 199
manuscripts (East Syrian), 17, 19–20
Masabadan, 68, 77
Maurice, Roman emperor 582–602 C.E., 164, 169, 175, 179, 182, 190

Mazdak, deviant Zoroastrian scholar of the sixth century, 34, 153–54
Media, 61, 64, 66
medicine, 68, 89, 96, 144
Melqi, 127–28, 143, 148
Mēnōg ī Xrad, late Sasanian work of Zoroastrian scholarship, 35–36, 50, 53
Merovingians, 140
Merv, 64, 71, 160, 199
Michael the Syrian, twelfth-century West Syrian historiographer, 188
Middle Persian language, 6, 16, 52, 62–63, 134, 152
Mihragan, 119–22, 131
Mihranids, Iranian aristocratic dynasty, 51–52, 120, 122, 125, 145–46, 189, 194
Mihrshapur, early fifth-century mowbed, 49
military service (of Christians), 51–52, 55
miracle, 3–4
Mirian III, king of Iberia 284–361 C.E., 9
Mithra, Zoroastrian deity, 59
mixture, 2, 9–10, 27, 63, 203
Modestos, patriarch of Jerusalem during the Iranian occupation, 182–84
Morony, Michael, 14
Mosig-Walburg, Karin, 39
mowbed, leading Zoroastrian ritual and judicial authorities, 8, 20–21, 23–26, 68, 73–74, 93–94, 99, 104–6, 118, 137
mowbedān mowbed, chief mowbed, 20, 87, 93, 99, 106
Mtskheta, 120
mythical history and mythical historiography (Zoroastrian), 6–8, 28–29, 140–42, 146–47
Mushel Mamikonean, 168

nakharar, Armenian term for "aristocrat," 15, 46, 146, 155–56, 168–70
Najran, 133
namosa, Syriac term for "law," 103
Naqsh-e Rustam, 23
Narsai, early fifth-century East Syrian martyr and militant ascetic, 47–48
nation, 14
naxwār, Middle Persian term for "regional military commander," 135, 137, 145, 151
nērang, Middle Persian term for "ritual power," 86, 89
Nestorian, 14
Nestorius, Roman dyophysite theologian 386–451 C.E., 187
Nicaea, 100
Nimrod, 140, 142, 148–50, 160–61, 163

INDEX 299

Nineveh, 10, 137, 140, 149 159–62
Nippur, 139
Nisibis, 40, 95–96, 133, 137–38, 149, 158–60
nobility, 136–62
Nowruz, 119–22, 131
al-Nu'man III, Lakhmid king ca. 583–602 C.E., 133
numismatics, 165, 202–203

Ohrmazd, supreme benevolent deity in Zoroastrianism, 9, 25, 27–28, 30, 52, 59, 79–86, 89–90, 109–10
Ohrmazd I, Sasanian king of kings 270–271 C.E., 23
Ohrmazd V, Sasanian king of kings 579–590 C.E., 166–71, 189
Ohrmazd-Ardashir, 42, 47
ordeal, 87–89
ōstāndār, Middle Persian term for "fiscal administrator," 99, 135

pādixšāy marriage, 110
papyri (Coptic), 188
papyri (Middle Persian), 181
Parthians, 6, 8, 35, 59, 73, 76, 136, 145, 147
Parthian language, 67
patriarch, title of bishop of Seleucia-Ctesiphon after the middle of the sixth century, 13, 95, 97–98
patriliny, 108–17, 124–25, 151–57, 194, 200–201
Paul the Persian, sixth-century East Syrian philosopher, 193
Peeters, Paul, 18, 132
Peroz I, Sasanian king of kings 459–484 C.E., 25
Peroz Shapur, 98
persecution, 25–27, 38–39, 44–45
Persepolis, 31
Persian Gulf, 10–11, 31
Persians, 137–38, 141–42, 145, 149–51, 156, 163
Pethion, mid fifth-century aristocratic convert to Christianity, 60, 68, 87–91
political theology, 4–5
pollution (Zoroastrian), 31–32
polo, 131, 151
polyandry, 109
Prat d-Maishan, 42
proselytism, 11, 46, 57
purity and purification (Zoroastrian) 31, 86
Pursišnīhā, early Islamic compilation of Zoroastrian scholarship, 36
Pusai, fourth-century East Syrian martyr, 65–66

Qara Tepe, 138
Qasr-e Shirin, 166
Quilon, 203

Rabban Mar Saba, fifth-century aristocratic convert to Christianity, 51
rad, Middle Persian term for "provincial judge," 68, 83, 89, 99, 106, 137
Rayy, 51, 65, 77
Richardson, Seth, 162
"rough tolerance," 30
Roman canons, 100
Roman law, 87, 107
Roman wars, 40–41, 45, 51, 64, 121–22, 133–34, 137, 151, 164–98
royal road, 59, 61
Rubin, Zeev, 21
Rusafa, 172
Rustam, mythical Iranian hero, 146

Sabrisho, patriarch of the Church of the East 596–604 C.E., 2–5, 107, 169, 173–74
Sachau, Eduard, 14, 20
sacrifice, 117–18
šahrab, 135
Samarqand, 160
Sar Mashad, 23
Schilling, Alexander, 189
scholarship (Zoroastrian), 25, 32, 35–37, 62–63, 69–70, 78–79
scribes, 45
secularization, 5, 14, 41–42
Selb, Walter, 14, 20
Seleucia-Ctesiphon, 2–5, 13, 18, 40–42, 59, 92, 93, 98–100, 109, 137, 160, 179–80, 187, 195–96
Seleucids, 132, 140–41, 158
Seleucus I Nikator, Seleucid king ca. 358–281 B.C.E., 140–41, 144, 158, 162
Sennacherib, Assyrian king 705–601 B.C.E., 140–42, 148–51, 162
Sergius, Christian saint, 172–74, 193
service aristocracy, 145
School of Nisibis, 95–96
Shahin, Iranian military commander under Husraw II, 174
Shahrabad, 159–60
Shahralanyozan, Iranian military commander under Husraw II, 181
Shahrgerd, 161
Shahrwaraz, Iranian military commander under Husraw II, 179, 197
Shaked, Shaul, 80–82, 86

Shapur I, Sasanian king of kings 241–270 C.E., 23, 41, 64
Shapur II, Sasanian king of kings 309–379 C.E., 13, 25, 38–44, 49, 59, 65–66, 127–28, 133, 138, 142, 159, 200
Shapur III, Sasanian king of kings 383–388 C.E., 59, 155
Shapur Braz, early fifth-century bishop of Karka d-Beit Slok, 144, 162
Shirin, aristocratic convert to Christianity (d. 559), 52, 54
Shirin, wife of Husraw II, 160, 172–73, 185, 187
shrines (of martyrs), 15–16, 75, 77, 102, 131–32, 172
sigillography, 17, 61, 134–36, 158–59
Simeon, early seventh-century bishop of Revardashir, 105, 113–15
Simeon, bishop of Seleucia-Ctesiphon (d. 344), 40–44, 202
Simeon of Beit Arsham, six-century West Syrian monk and polemicist, 185
Sinai, 127
Sīrat Ānušīrwān, autobiographical account of Husraw I preserved in the Abbasid historiographical work of Ibn Miskawayh, 34, 53
Sir Bani Yas, 11
Sistan, 73
slavery, 138
slaughter (in Zoroastrianism), 118
Smbat Bagratuni, 168–70
Smith, Kyle, 39
sodomy, 109
Sogdian language, 17, 62
Sophronius of Jerusalem, early seventh-century Roman theologian, 177
Sōšāns, Zoroastrian scholar of the Sasanian era, 20, 32, 36–37, 71–72
spāhbed, Middle Persian term for "military general," 134, 137, 145
Strategius, early seventh-century Roman ecclesiastical historian, 178
stūrīh, Middle Persian term for "substitute successorship," 105, 108–17, 125, 153
stucco, 10–12, 138
subordination, 24–27
Surenids, Iranian aristocratic dynasty, 125, 145–46
Sūr ī Saxwan, Middle Persian account of feasting, 119–20
Susa, 150
Synodicon Orientale, 19–20, 139
Synod of Aqaq (486 C.E.), 102
Synod of Babai (497 C.E.), 102
Synod of Joseph (554 C.E.), 102, 131–32
Synod of Isaac (410 C.E.), 10, 13, 25, 44, 99–100, 102, 173, 200
Synod of Ishoyahb I (585 C.E.), 119
Synod of Shahapivan (444 C.E.), 106
Syriac language, 16, 63, 101, 132
Syrians, 147

Al-Ṭabarī, Abbasid historiographer 839–923 C.E., 21, 167, 190
Takht-e Suleyman, 177
Taq-e Bustan, 59, 165–66, 180
taxation, 40–42, 145, 158–59, 168, 175, 181
Tell Dhahab, 180
temporary marriage, 15, 110, 153
Theocritus, legendary second-century bishop of Karka d-Beit Slok, 162
Theodora, wife of the Roman emperor Justinian, 186–87
Theodore of Mopsuestia, fourth-century Roman Christian theologian, 81–82, 96
Theophanes Confessor, ninth-century Byzantine historian, 177
Theodoret of Cyrrhus, ecclesiastical historian in Roman Syria ca. 393–457 C.E., 47
Theophylact Simocatta, early seventh-century Roman historian, 172
Timothy, patriarch of the Church of the East 780–823 C.E., 115
tolerance, 25–27
Trdat III, king of Armenia ca. 287–330, 4, 9
True Cross, 169–70, 175, 177–80, 190–91, 196
Turfan Oasis, 17–18, 62, 98
Turks, 36, 99, 133, 150, 155

urbanism, 158–62
uzdēs, middle Persian term for "idol," 33

Van Rompay, Lucas, 81
visions, 54, 172–73

Wahram, Zoroastrian deity, 80
Wahram I, Sasanian king of kings 271–274 C.E., 23
Wahram V, Sasanian king of kings 420–439 C.E., 25, 44–45, 49
Wahram Chobin, anti-Sasanian rebel and king of kings 590–591 C.E., 164–66, 172–73, 189–90
Walash II, Partheon king 128/29–47 C.E., 73
Walashfarr, 61–63, 67, 71, 73, 77, 90–92, 180
Walker, Joel, 128–31, 151
wāz, Middle Persian term for "Zoroastrian prayer before consuming food," 118, 120, 191

wet nurses, 51–52
Widengren, Geo, 192
Wiessner, Gernot, 18, 40, 43, 128, 192
Widēwdād, Avestan treatise with Middle Persian commentary of the Sasanian era, 32, 71
Wishtasp, mythical king and patron of Zoroaster in Iranian historiography, 29, 189
Weh-Ardashir, one of the constituent cities of Seleucia-Ctesiphon, known in Syriac as Kokhe, 3, 11, 34, 195–96
wehdēn, Middle Persian term for Zoroastrians, 29, 30, 32, 56, 66
Wonders and Magnificence of Sistan, Middle Persian work of mythical geography, 73, 163
wuzurg, Middle Persian term for the higher ranks of the aristocracy, 15, 145
wuzurg framādār, Middle Persian term for "chief administrative commander," 120, 134

xrafstar, animals part of the wicked creation of Ahreman in Zoroastrianism, 27, 75–77, 84–85
xwarrah, supernatural sanction of kingship in Iranian ideology, 15, 60, 65, 73, 83, 165, 188, 189
xwēdōdah, Middle Persian term for "incestuous marriage," 108–10

Yasna, primary Zoroastrian ritual, 8, 23, 28, 59, 76–78, 80, 83–87, 89–91, 118, 195
Yazdgird I, Sasanian king of kings 399–420 C.E., 13, 25, 43–44, 46–47, 49, 99
Yazdgird II, Sasanian king of kings 438–457 C.E., 25, 44–46, 49, 60, 117, 127, 143, 161
Yazdgird III, Sasanian king of kings 632–651 C.E., 197, 199–200
Yazdpanah, sixth-century aristocratic convert to Christianity, 193
Yazdin, mid fifth-century aristocratic convert to Christianity, 54, 60–61, 67–68, 71, 83
Yazdin, northern Mesopotamian Christian aristocrat in the service of Husraw II, 101, 134, 168, 179, 184, 186–87

Zab River, 159
zandīg, Middle Persian term for 'religious deviant,' someone who misinterprets the exegesis of the Avesta known as the Zand, 34
Zaradusht of Fasa, deviant Zoroastrian scholar of the third century, 153–54
Zoroaster, 6, 28, 87, 118, 146
Zurwan, Zoroastrian deity, 79–84
Zurwanism, 78–84

www.ingramcontent.com/pod-product-compliance
Lightning Source LLC
Chambersburg PA
CBHW030523230426
43665CB00010B/740